Monster Culture in
the 21st Century

Monster Culture in the 21st Century

A Reader

**EDITED BY MARINA LEVINA
AND DIEM-MY T. BUI**

B L O O M S B U R Y
LONDON • NEW DELHI • NEW YORK • SYDNEY

Bloomsbury Academic

An imprint of Bloomsbury Publishing Plc

175 Fifth Avenue   50 Bedford Square
New York   London WC1B 3DP
NY 10010 USA   UK

www.bloomsbury.com

First published 2013

Library of Congress Cataloging-in-Publication Data
Monster culture in the 21st century : a reader / edited by Marina Levina and Diem-My T. Bui.
pages cm
Includes index.
ISBN 978-1-4411-8797-0 (hardback) -- ISBN 978-1-4411-7839-8 (paperback) 1. Monsters in motion pictures. 2. Monsters on television. 3. United States–Social conditions–21st century. 4. United States–Civilization–21st century. I. Levina, Marina, 1975- II. Bui, Diem-My T.
PN1995.9.M6M635 2013
791.43'67'075–dc23
2012048383

ISBN: HB: 978-1-4411-8797-0
PB: 978-1-4411-7839-8
e-pdf: 978-1-4411-9326-1
e-pub: 978-1-4411-8537-2

Typeset by Fakenham Prepress Solutions, Fakenham, Norfolk NR21 8NN
Printed and bound in the United States of America

To Dmitry, Alia, and Paul – our favorite monsters

Contents

Figure list

About the contributors

Jeremy Biles holds a Ph.D. from the University of Chicago, and is the author of *Ecce Monstrum: Georges Bataille and the Sacrifice of Form* (Fordham University Press, 2007). He teaches courses on religion, philosophy, and art at the School of the Art Institute of Chicago. His work has appeared in such places as *Culture, Theory and Critique*, *Archaevs*, the *Journal for Cultural and Religious Theory*, the *Chicago Review*, and the *Journal of Religion*, as well as in edited volumes including *Religion and Material Culture: The Matter of Belief* (Routledge, 2009). He has contributed essays to exhibition catalogs for the Hyde Park Art Center, Chicago, where he has also done curatorial work.

Kyle William Bishop is a third-generation professor at Southern Utah University, where he teaches courses in American literature and culture, film studies, and fantasy literature. He has presented and published a variety of articles on popular culture and cinematic adaptation, including *Night of the Living Dead*, *Fight Club*, *Buffy the Vampire Slayer*, *Dawn of the Dead*, *The Birds*, and *Zombieland*. He received a Ph.D. in English from the University of Arizona in 2009, and his first book, *American Zombie Gothic: The Rise and Fall (and Rise) of the Walking Dead in Popular Culture*, is available from McFarland.

Mary K. Bloodsworth-Lugo, professor of comparative ethnic studies at Washington State University, has taught and published in the areas of race and ethnicity, gender and sexuality, post-9/11 discourse and cultural production, and contemporary continental political philosophy. In addition to numerous journal articles, Bloodsworth-Lugo is author of *In-Between Bodies: Sexual Difference, Race, and Sexuality* (2007). Joint books by Bloodsworth-Lugo and Lugo-Lugo include: *A New Kind of Containment: "The War on Terror," Race, and Sexuality*, editors (2009); *Animating Difference: Race, Gender, and Sexuality in Contemporary Films for Children*, also with C. Richard King (2010); and *Containing (Un)American Bodies: Race, Sexuality, and Post-9/11 Constructions of Citizenship* (2010).

Diem-My T. Bui is a visiting assistant professor in the Department of Communication at the University of Illinois at Chicago. Her research interests include transnational feminist media studies, critical cultural studies, ethnic studies, popular culture, and film. She focuses on cultural production, cultural memory, and embodiments of difference in racialized and sexualized representations of Asian Americans in popular culture. She is the author of essays on Vietnamese Americans and media, authoethnography, performativity, and war discourse published in journals and edited collections.

Peter Odell Campbell is a Ph.D. candidate in the Department of Communication and a Graduate College INTERSECT Fellow in "Cultures of Law in Global Contexts" at the University of Illinois, Urbana-Champaign. Peter is completing a dissertation on judicial arguments concerning race and sexuality in U.S. constitutional law, and he teaches courses in argumentation, public policy communication, sexuality and public culture, and gender and women's studies. Peter's work has appeared in the *Quarterly Journal of Speech*.

Michael S. Drake is lecturer in Sociology at the University of Hull, U.K. He is author of *Problematics of Military Power: Government, Discipline and the Subject of Violence* (Cass Routledge, 2001) and *Political Sociology for a Globalizing World* (Polity, 2010). He has also published on the war dead and the body politic, on the representation and contention of social identity, and on power and resistance. Work on literature includes a contribution to the forthcoming (2013) *Imaginative Methodologies: The Poetic Imagination in the Social Sciences* (eds Drake, Jacobsen, Keohane, and Petersen).

Megan Foley is an assistant professor of Communication at Mississippi State University. She received her Ph.D. in Rhetoric and Public Advocacy from the University of Iowa in 2008. Her work interrogates the articulation among speech, violence, and justice in both classical rhetorical theory and contemporary political controversies. Her essays have appeared or are forthcoming in the *Quarterly Journal of Speech, Communication & Critical/Cultural Studies, Rhetoric & Public Affairs, Philosophy & Rhetoric, Symplokē,* and the *Journal of Communication Studies.*

Ryan Gillespie is an assistant lecturer, Ph.D. candidate, and Annenberg Fellow in the Annenberg School for Communication and Journalism at the University of Southern California. His main area of study is value theory (especially ethics and religion) and argumentation, with related interests in critical-cultural approaches to economics, (global) public sphere studies, and rhetoric. Recent work can be found in the *International Journal of Communication, Communication, Culture & Critique*, the *Journal of Cultural Economy*, and *Philosophy & Rhetoric*.

Florian Grandena is Assistant Professor in the Department of Communication of the University of Ottawa, where he teaches courses on history of film, queer cinema, and vampire films. He is the author of *Showing the World to the World: Political Fictions in French Cinema of the 1990s and Early 2000s* (2008). Together with Cristina Johnston (University of Stirling), he co-edited two collections entitled *Cinematic Queerness: Representation of Homosexualities in Contemporary Francophone Features Films* and *New Queer Images: Representations of Homosexualities in Contemporary Francophone Visual Cultures* (2011). His current research focuses on French gay cinema, particularly the films of Olivier Ducastel and Jacques Martineau on which he is preparing a book.

Carolyn Harford is Dean of the Faculty of Humanities and Associate Professor in the Department of African Languages and Literature at the University of Swaziland. Prior to this appointment, she was Executive Dean of the Faculty of Arts, and Chair of the Department of English and Communication, at Midlands State University in Gweru, Zimbabwe. Other appointments have included the Department of Linguistics at the University of Zimbabwe and a two-year Fulbright Scholar award in the Department of African Languages and Literature at the same university, following a tenured appointment at Michigan State University. Her longstanding research and teaching in the area of structural linguistics as applied to African languages have been extended to research interests in the parallel areas of literature, mythology, and psychoanalysis, with the goal of gaining a better understanding of the relationship between structure in language and structure in narrative.

Roy Osamu Kamada is currently an associate professor in the Writing, Literature, and Publishing Department at Emerson College in Boston, MA. He received his Ph.D. in English literature from the University of California, Davis. He has taught literature and creative writing at Emerson College, the University of Virginia, the University of California, Davis, and for the Kearny St. Workshop. His work has appeared in *The Diasporic Imagination: Identifying Asian--American Representations in America* and *Ecological Poetry: A Critical Introduction*. His book, *Postcolonial Romanticisms: Landscape and the Possibilities of Inheritance*, appeared in 2010. He is currently working on a project tentatively titled *Uncanny Cosmopolitanisms: Haunting, Disjuncture and The Postcolonial*.

Marina Levina is an assistant professor of Communication at the University of Memphis. Her research focuses on critical cultural studies of science, technology, and medicine, visual culture, and media studies. Recent publications include an article on affective future and imagination of health information technologies in *Fibreculture Journal*; a book chapter on cyberfeminism and Health 2.0 discourse in *Cyberfeminism 2.0* (Radhika Gajjala and Yeon Ju Oh (eds), Peter Lang, 2012), and a chapter on cultural narratives of blood in *Braaaiiinnnsss!: From Academics to Zombies* (Robert Smith (ed.), University of Ottawa Press, 2011). She is the first editor of *Everyday Life in Post-Global Network*, with Grant Kien (Peter Lang, 2010). Currently she is working on a manuscript titled *Pandemics in the Media* (to be published by Peter Lang Press).

Susana Loza is an assistant professor of media culture at Hampshire College. Her research and teaching interests encompass science fiction and horror; digital media and cybercolonialism; the politics of online fandom; and power, privilege, and cultural appropriation. Her recent publications include "Vampires, Queers, and Other Monsters: Against the Homonormativity of *True Blood*," in *Fanpires: Audience Consumption of the Modern Vampire* (New Academia Press, 2011) and "Sampling (Hetero)sexuality: Diva-ness and Discipline in Electronic Dance Music" in *Electronica, Dance, and Club Music* (Ashgate, 2012). She is currently working on a project entitled *Post-Racial Performativities: Race, Sex, and Popular Culture in 21st Century America*.

Carmen R. Lugo-Lugo, associate professor of comparative ethnic studies at Washington State University, engages in research on Empire, "the War on Terror," and popular culture. In addition to numerous articles, with Mary K. Bloodsworth-Lugo, on the United States-led "War on Terror," she has published articles on the representation of Latinos and other minoritized groups within U.S. popular culture. Joint books by Bloodsworth-Lugo and Lugo-Lugo include: *A New Kind of Containment: "The War on Terror," Race, and Sexuality*, editors (2009); *Animating Difference: Race, Gender, and Sexuality in Contemporary Films for Children*, also with C. Richard King (2010); and *Containing (Un)American Bodies: Race, Sexuality, and Post-9/11 Constructions of Citizenship* (2010).

Jeffrey W. Mantz is an assistant professor of anthropology at George Mason University. He has active research projects in the Caribbean and the eastern Congo, with interests in political economy, religion, spiritual and supernatural beliefs, knowledge economies, and globalization. In addition to courses on political economy, myth, and magic, he also teaches a popular course called Zombies, a cross-cultural exploration in the folkloric beliefs and social anxieties that have reanimated so many undead; that work has been featured on NPR and in several documentaries. His recent publications include articles on beliefs in the Caribbean spiritual practice of Obeah (in *Anthropology and Humanism*), and articles on the trade in conflict minerals and digital technology (in *Social Anthropology* and the edited collection, *Inclusion and Exclusion in the Global Arena*, (ed.) Max Kirsch, Routledge).

Cynthia J. Miller is a cultural anthropologist, specializing in popular culture and visual media. She is the editor of *Too Bold for the Box Office: The Mockumentary From Big Screen to Small* (2012), and co-editor of: *Cadets, Rangers, and Junior Space Men: Televised "Rocketman" Series of the 1950s and Their Fans* (with A. Bowdoin Van Riper, 2012), *Undead in the West: Vampires, Zombies, Mummies and Ghosts on the Cinematic Frontier* (with A. Bowdoin Van Riper, 2012), and *Steaming into a Victorian Future: A Steampunk Anthology* (with Julie Anne Taddeo, 2012). Cynthia also serves on the editorial board of the *Encyclopedia of Women and Popular Culture*, and is series editor for Scarecrow Press's *Film and History* series.

Enrica Picarelli is the recipient of the "Michael Ballhaus" fellowship for postdoctoral research at Leuphana University (Lüneburg). She completed her Ph.D. in Cultural and Postcolonial Studies of the Anglophone World at "L'Orientale" University of Naples, where her dissertation addressed the reverberations of the post-9/11 culture of fear in American science fiction series. Her current research focuses on the televisual promotion of American shows, combining an interest in media theory and textual analysis with a focus on the affective economy of promotion. Picarelli has published articles and essays on *Battlestar Galactica*, *Mad Men* and *Lost*, and blogs at http://spaceofattraction.wordpress.com.

Amit S. Rai is senior lecturer in New Media and Communication in the School of Business and Management at Queen Mary, University of London. His study of new media in India, entitled *Untimely Bollywood: Globalization and India's New Media Assemblage*, was published by Duke University Press in May of 2009. His blog on the history of media assemblages and the politics of perception can be found at http://mediaecologiesresonate.wordpress.com.

Rosalind Sibielski received a Ph.D. in American Culture Studies from Bowling Green State University, where she is currently an instructor in the Department of Theatre and Film. Her research interests include representations of girlhood in popular media and media discourses surrounding feminism. She has had essays published in *Literature and Psychology*, *The Projector*, and *Feminist Media Studies*, and is currently working on a cultural history of media representations of girls in the U.S.

Jaroslav Švelch is a lecturer and Ph.D. candidate at Charles University in Prague, currently on a research internship at Microsoft Research New England, where he is examining humor in simulated spaces. In 2007–8 he was a Fulbright visiting researcher at MIT's Comparative Media Studies department. While his background is in media studies and linguistics, his research interests include the social history of video games, video games and ethics, and online language management.

A. Bowdoin Van Riper is a historian whose work focuses on the cultural dimensions of science and technology and depictions of history on film. The most recent of his eight books are *A Biographical Encyclopedia of Scientists and Inventors in American Film and TV since 1930* (2011) and two collections of essays co-edited with Cynthia J. Miller: *1950s "Rocketman" TV Series and their Fans: Cadets, Rangers, and Junior Space Men* and *Undead in the West: Vampires, Mummies, Zombies, and Ghosts on the Cinematic Frontier* (both 2012). He is the founding editor of the "Science Fiction Television" book series, and is currently at work, with Cynthia Miller, on the edited collection *Undead in the West II: They Just Keep Coming*.

Sherryl Vint is professor of Science Fiction Media Studies at the University of California, Riverside. She is the author of *Bodies of Tomorrow*, *Animal Alterity*, and *The Wire*; co-author of *The Routledge Concise History of Science Fiction*; and co-editor of the *The Routledge Companion to Science Fiction*, *Fifty Key Figures in Science Fiction*, and *Beyond Cyberpunk*. She co-edits the journals *Science Fiction Studies*, *Science Fiction Film and Television*, and *Humanimalia*.

Michele White is an associate professor in the Department of Communication at Tulane University. Duke University Press published her *Buy it now: Lessons from eBay* (2012). Recent articles on abjection and wedding cultures include: "Dirty brides and internet settings: The affective pleasures and troubles with trash the dress photography sessions," *South Atlantic Quarterly* 110, no. 3 (2011), and "Engaged with eBay: How heterosexual unions and traditional gender roles are rendered by the site and members," *Feminist Media Studies* 11, no. 3 (2011).

Acknowledgments

The editors would like to thank Katie Gallof at Continuum Press for early interest and unwavering support for this project. We want to offer a special thanks to Kent Ono for providing invaluable early critique of the project and Craig Robertson for helping to think through the title and early marketing strategies. We are grateful to the communication departments at the University of Memphis and the University of Illinois at Chicago for their support of "monster studies" courses, which served as an inspiration for this volume.

The original call for papers attracted an overwhelming number of excellent submissions, far more than we could include. We want to thank everyone who expressed early interest in this project—you have shown us the importance of monsters at the turn of the twenty-first century and we hope that you will enjoy the final product.

This book would not be possible without the dedication and hard work of all contributing authors. We thank them for trusting us with their ideas and words and we are excited to showcase their excellent essays.

Finally, we want to thank our partners, Dmitry and Paul, for their love, support, and the embrace of our monstrous selves.

Introduction:

Toward a comprehensive monster theory in the 21st century

Marina Levina and Diem-My T. Bui

In her famous book, *Our Vampires, Ourselves*, Nina Auerbach writes that each age embraces the vampire it needs.[1] This statement speaks to the essential role that monster narratives play in culture. They offer a space where society can safely represent and address anxieties of its time. In the past decade, our rapidly changing world faced terrorism, global epidemics, economic and social strife, new communication technologies, immigration, and climate change, to name a few. These fears and tensions reflect an ever more interconnected global environment where increased mobility of people, technologies, and disease have produced great social, political, and economic uncertainty. It is safe to say that, over the past decade, we have been terrorized by change. The speeding up of cultures, technologies, and environments—what Paul Virilio[2] refers to as a defining organizational concept for the contemporary world—has also led to a surge in narratives about vampires, zombies, werewolves, ghosts, cyborgs, aliens, and other monstrous bodies. Popular films and television shows, such as *True Blood*, *Twilight*, *28 Days/Weeks Later*, *Paranormal Activity*, *District 9*, *Battlestar Galactica*, *Avatar*, and other multiple monstrous iterations have allowed us to deal with the profound acceleration in changing symbolic, economic, and technological systems.

This collection of essays explores monstrous culture at the advent of the twenty-first century. As a whole, it argues that monstrous narratives of the past decade have become omnipresent specifically because they represent collective social anxieties over resisting and embracing change in the twenty-first century. They can be read as a response to a rapidly changing cultural, social, political, economic, and moral landscape. Therefore, we argue, monstrosity has transcended its status as a metaphor and has indeed become a necessary condition of our existence in the twenty-first century. In this we agree with Hardt and Negri (2004), who write "the new world of monsters is where humanity has to grasp its future."[3] The collection, as a whole, represents the way in which monstrous culture has become a lived experience of the past decade and a glimpse of the possibilities for the future. As we use the twenty-first century as a conceit to discuss the nature of global territories, identities, and technologies, we are also mindful of how monstrosity serves as a discourse and as a representation of change itself. And while monsters always tapped into anxieties over a changing world, they have never been as popular, or as needed, as in the past decade. Therefore, in this collection, we theorize monstrosity as a condition of the twenty-first century. The essays in this collection examine how monstrosity has been used to manage terror threats, global capitalism crises, new forms of warfare, rapid growth of new media, digital technologies, networks, and biotechnologies, territorial tensions between nation-states and the global empire, profound shifts in "post-racial" and "post-gender" identifications, and the increasing ambiguity and queering of sexual desires.

In the processes, we engage with three theoretical approaches to the study of monstrosity and horror: psychoanalytical, representational, and ontological.

Psychoanalytical approach to monsters

Horror film analysis takes root in the psychoanalytical approach and particularly in Freud's concept of the uncanny. As Linda Badley explains, "Freud defined horror in terms of the irrational 'gut level' fear, the uncanny, inspired by certain images and experiences in which the subject recognizes a repressed memory from childhood or an undiscovered aspect of the self."[4] Therefore, the power of horror lies in its ability to evoke a recollection of something that was once familiar and has since become repressed. Sigmund Freud connects the uncanny to something that is frightening, and much of his essay is spent on the articulation of the connection between the frightening and the familiar. He writes, "the uncanny is that class of the frightening which leads back to what is known of old and long familiar. … This uncanny is in reality nothing new or alien, but something which is familiar and old-established in the mind and which has become alienated from it only through the process of repression."[5] The fear thus lies not in the unknown, but rather in something previously known and in which the repressed is made suddenly recognizable. Thus, the feeling of the uncanny occurs when either "infantile complexes" or "primitive beliefs" are revived through the encounter with monsters. Sue Case uses the connection between the uncanny and the familiar as an explanation of proximity pervading the vampire lore.[6] She argues that in vampire film closeness to the monster is interpreted as horror because the uncanny feeling is often a result of suddenly finding oneself once more connected to something that was once lost. In fact, the uncanny is a kind of haunting proximity. The psychoanalytical approach thus perceives the monster as that which used to be a part of the self and needed to be cast away in order for the self to become unified or, at least, functional. Thus an encounter with the monster reminds the self of what it has lost.

The monster as an allusion to a loss also relates to Julia Kristeva's notion of the abject.[7] Following Lacan, Kristeva argues that the abject is situated in the Real—or a state of nature before we enter culture—or the Symbolic, through acquisition of language. In the Real, there is no separation of the self from its surroundings—in the womb, blood and guts are inseparable from the body. There is no separation, or even knowledge, of the self. As the child is born, she acquires the ability to separate herself from others and look upon herself as a separate individual as she enters the Symbolic. This transition is psychologically traumatic as an individual longs for the Real, and, at the same time, is terrified by the loss of the self that the Real implies.[8] The abject is that which must be cast away when we enter the Symbolic and that which reminds us of the Real. Kristeva writes "refuse and corpses *show me* what I permanently thrust aside in order to live. These body fluids, this defilement, this shit are what life withstands, hardly and with difficulty, on the part of death. There, I am at the border of my condition as a living being. My body extricates itself, as being alive, from that border. Such wastes drop so that I might live, until, from loss to loss, nothing remains in me and my entire body falls beyond the limit."[9] While Kristeva talks about blood, body fluids, and cadavers as the most potent abject reminders of the Real, others argue that monsters are frightening precisely because they are the abject—they are categorically incomplete and exist at the border between the Symbolic and the Real.[10] Therefore they are the abject—something that must be cast away in order for life to continue[11]. Moreover, Kristeva argues that the Real (and the abject) is the realm of the feminine or the maternal, while the Symbolic is associated with patriarchy and paternal order. Therefore the feminine must be destroyed or cast away in order for the paternal order to flourish. Barbara Creed extends this analysis to the portrayal of monstrous-feminine in horror films. She argues that the monstrous-feminine constructs the maternal or feminine figure as the abject that must be destroyed for the protagonist to enter the Symbolic realm. Theorization of the abject lies in the recognition of the borderline quality of the monster and in our desire to embrace and expel it at the same time. In the present analysis of monsters it is important to acknowledge that our anxieties are representational of the uncanny and the abject ways in which our collective social psyche deals with the monstrous changes of the twenty-first century. Chapters in this book address the multitude of ways in which the uncanny and the abject have been utilized and altered by twenty-first-century monsters.

Representational approach to monsters

A representational approach to the study of monsters focuses on the processes of repression outlined above as a cultural and social phenomenon. Robin Wood, in his influential work that combined psychoanalysis with a representational approach to horror films, connected the social with the psychological by suggesting that horror films, and specifically the monsters of horror films, represent our collective nightmares and that their visual embodiment on the movie screen empowers us to cope with our subconscious fears.[12] Wood argued that culture and society dictates that which we must repress. Calling this a "surplus repression," he argued that it is not necessary for an existence of civilization, but rather is shaped by the demands of a capitalist patriarchal society. Surplus repression, therefore, makes us monogamous, heterosexual, and bourgeois. Thus, for Wood, repression is closely linked to the concept of the Other, not as external to our culture, but rather as representational of those characteristics that we repress in order to fit into the cultural normative regime. The true Otherness is then a repressed unfamiliar familiar, or the uncanny.

Wood argues that monsters represent the return of the repressed, or our repressed collective cultural desires, anxieties, and nightmares made vivid on the movie screen. He writes, "it is the horror film that responds in the most clear-cut and direct way, because central to it is the actual dramatization of the dual concept of the repressed/the Other, in the figure of the Monster. One might say that the true subject of the horror genre is the struggle for recognition of all that our civilization represses or oppresses, its re-emergence dramatized, as in our nightmares, as an object of horror, a matter for terror, and the happy ending (when it exists) typically signifying the restoration of repression."[13] The idea that monsters represent particular social and historical conditions and their cultural anxieties is also echoed by

David Skal, who argues that the history of monster films is first and foremost a history of the culture that produced these monster images.[14]

The representational approach has often focused on a taxonomy of monsters in order to study the portrayal and representation of Otherness. Too often, though, the representational study of monsters relied on psychological universals and pre-established categories of identity to classify monstrous representations as either "good" or "bad." As Robin Wood argued, this methodological approach "offers us no more than a beginning from which one might proceed to interpret specific horror films in detail as well as to explore further the genre's social significance and the insights it offers into our culture. I shall add here simply that these notions of repression and the Other afford us not merely a means of access but a rudimentary categorization of horror films in social/political terms, distinguishing the progressive from the reactionary, the criterion being the way in which the monster is presented and defined."[15]

However, in the twenty-first century, representational studies have begun to concern themselves with the ways in which monstrosity, as any processes of identification, is a fluid category concerned with representation and ambiguity of change.[16] Inspired by global cultural, social, political, and economic shifts, which as we have argued above emphasized change in the twenty-first century, these studies examine the ways in which monsters produce and represent these changes. They address what Judith Halberstam called "the technology of monstrous,"[17] to argue that monsters, much like any technology, produce meaning that is beyond any one category of identification. This affords important insights into the production of meaning through representations of monstrosity. Therefore, what is at stake in the representational analysis of monster images is the definition of humanness, or, rather, a discursive production of subjectivity. As Michel Foucault argued, "What makes a human monster a monster is not just its exceptionality relative to the species form; it is the disturbance it brings to juridical regularities. ... The human monster combines the impossible and the forbidden."[18] This analysis draws our attention to the various technologies of power that produce historically contingent identities. Halberstam writes, "monstrosity (and the fear it gives rise to) is historically conditioned rather than a psychological universal. ... Monsters not only reveal certain material conditions of the production of horror, but they also make strange the categories of beauty, humanity, and identity that we cling to. ... If we measure one skin job against the other, we can read transitions between various signifying systems of identity."[19] Through the representational approach, chapters in this collection study the cultural and social discourses, not to classify monsters in pre-defined categories, but rather to illuminate discursive formations through which twenty-first-century texts shape bodies and subjectivities—both human and non-human.

Ontological approach to monsters

In May 2010 J. Craig Venter of Venter Laboratories—a biotechnology company—created a synthetic organism. This self-reproducing bacterium had no ancestors: its genome was artificially and digitally created. The achievement was lauded as the defining moment in the history of biology and *The Economist* published an article titled *And Man Made Life*. The article compared Venter's creation to a Frankenstein's monster—a life form beforehand thought to be impossible. This example exemplifies how life in the twenty-first century constructs monstrosity not just as a representational category, but also as ontology—a way of being, or a way of becoming.[20] From ontological threats of terrorism, globalization, and technological developments to the creation and reproduction of new forms of life itself, the twenty-first century introduces a refashioned monstrous milieu implicated in the construction of a necessarily monstrous future. As Jacques Derrida argues:

> A monster is also that which appears for the first time and, consequently, is not yet recognized. A monster is a species for which we do not yet have a name, which does not mean that the species is abnormal, namely, the composition or hybridization of already known species. Simply, it shows itself [elle se montre]—that is what the word monster means—it shows itself in something that is not yet shown and that therefore looks like a hallucination, it strikes the eye, it frightens precisely because no anticipation had prepared one to identify this figure. ... But as soon as one perceives a monster in a monster, one begins to domesticate it, one begins, because of the "as such"—it is a monster as monster—to compare it to the norms, to analyze it, consequently to master whatever could be terrifying in this figure of the monster. ... *[T]he future is necessarily monstrous: the figure of the future, that is, that which can only be surprising, that for which we are not prepared, you see, is heralded by species of monsters.* A future that would not be monstrous would not be a future; it would already be a predictable, calculable, and programmable tomorrow. All experience open to the future is prepared or prepares itself to welcome the monstrous arrivant, to welcome it, that is, to accord hospitality to that which is absolutely foreign or strange, but also, one must add, to try to domesticate it, that is, to make it part of the household and have it assume the habits, to make us assume new habits. This is the movement of culture.[21] [emphasis added]

Derrida argues here that monstrosity is that which is not recognized, and that the cultural process of recognition renders the monster known and therefore no longer a monster. Therefore, according to Derrida, the future—because it is not known and not recognizable—is necessarily monstrous. As Amit Rai argues, "the monstrosity of the future is audible in the infinite movement of time constantly and insistently announcing our own mortality. This same monstrous future—that is, the monstrosity of an inevitable yet unpredictable death—brings with it the possibility of transcending the monstrous body: time is the currency of the body."[22] Hence the monstrous future heralds the inevitability and unpredictability of death, or, it could be argued, of change as necessarily monstrous and eventually deadly: an affect/effect of a way of being or becoming. Much as ontological change only exists in the future tense, we need to explore monstrosity as an always future-situated event, or an imaginary space.

Monstrosity is an imaginary order prior to the Symbolic where the Ego creates a relationship between the self and its reflected image.[23] The way of culture, as Derrida describes it, is to recognize monstrosity as an image. In order to welcome monstrosity, we must draw a relationship between it and the self. We must see our ontologies reflected in the figure of the monster. But on the other hand, monstrosity as an imaginary also offers a possibility of monstrosity as a destabilizing change to the known regimes of truth. Precisely because monstrosity can never be, because it must exist in the future outside of the realm of the possible, it offers ways of becoming that are not known, not domesticated, and not appropriated by the existing discourses of power. As such, an ontological approach to monsters draws on Donna Haraway's essay *The Promises of Monsters*, in which she explicates the subversive potential of monstrosity, or inappropriate/d others, "to be inappropriate/d is not to fit in the taxon, to be dislocated from the available maps specifying kinds of actors and kinds of narratives, not to be originally fixed by difference. ... Diffraction does not produce "the same" displaced, as reflection and refraction do. Diffraction is a mapping of interference, not of replication, reflection, or reproduction. A diffraction pattern does not map where differences appear, but rather maps where the effects of difference appear."[24] The patterns of diffraction when applied to monstrosity create the topology of the imaginary. The chapters in this book engage with monstrosity as ways of becoming that illustrate the possibilities and the pitfalls of change as a primary ontology of the twenty-first century. In the first chapter of the book, Amit Rai expands on his previous important work on the topic to consider the ontological monstrosity as an event. He offers an analysis of monstrosity as an ontology rooted in duration, intensity, and the virtual. He argues that these elements should be important methodological points of analysis of monstrosity as an event and as a process.

The essays in this book engage with the theoretical approaches listed above; however, they also further those approaches by considering their implications to the study of monstrosity in the twenty-first century. The collection is divided into three sections, titled *Monstrous identities*, *Monstrous technologies*, and *Monstrous territories.* This thematic division was inspired by the plethora of ways in which monstrosity has been evoked, represented, and expressed in the twenty-first century.

Monstrous identities

Essays in this first section will look at representations of hybridity and post-humanness, identity politics and monstrosity in a "post-racial" and "post-gender" world, and monstrous subversion or reinforcement of "queer" sexualities. We continuously manage a multiplicity of desires and identities— and often we are unable to distinguish the monster within. In his essay, Florian Grandena argues that the films based on Stephanie Meyer's Twilight novels offer a complex relation to post-modernity where the authoritative vampire is contrasted with a docile and abject female body. Borrowing from Gilles Deleuze and Félix Guattari's concept of the rhizome and Foucault's Panopticon, Grandena asserts that the vampires in Meyer's stories are a panoptic regime and are characteristic of present-day monitoring through new media and surveillance technology. The reactionary past, coupled with a hypermodern present, depict an ambiguous post-modernity. In resisting a reading of the twenty-first century as a post-racial time, Susana Loza explores how the contemporary alien in the films *District 9* and *Avatar* serves as a figure for white guilt fantasies and fears. The films draw upon colonial history and nostalgia to present racialized performances of minstrelsy and masquerade.

The following two essays, by Kyle Bishop and Megan Foley, examine the monstrosities of humans. Post-human representations indicate a breaching of the imaginary border between humans and monsters. Bishop examines the value of the monster in *The Walking Dead* to indicate the threat of monstrous humans. Considered in the political and social context of a post-9/11 world, the human survivors of the zombie apocalypse in this graphic novel series parallel the real dangers of our responses to terrorist threats and immigration. Foley argues that the audience reception of the film *Monster*, about Aileen Wuornos, the first female serial killer to be executed in the U.S., reveals viewers' anxieties about monstrous mobility and domesticity. Applying a Lacanian analysis of the mirror to the monstrous human, viewers are invited to understand Wournos through a mask that allows for an idealized image of female domesticity.

The final two essays in this section examine identities in assertions of a post-racial and post-gender world. Peter Campbell offers an analysis of HBO's *True Blood* series that considers the intersectionality of race and sexuality as a queer political text that references the challenge of intersectional politics in the U.S. historically. Campbell argues that the vampires in this television show are what he terms post-racially queer, in which, despite their "multiple-axis" politics of identity, they stop short of addressing political intersections of race and sexuality. At the center of Rosalind Sibielski's essay are representational conventions used in gender lycanthropy. She argues that recent werewolf narratives essentialize gender differences by suggesting that even monstrosity operates within the rules of biological determinism. Twenty-first-century werewolf narratives reproduce gendered cultural norms, rather than offering a radical departure from them.

Monstrous technologies

Essays in this section argue that we are surrounded in the twenty-first century by technologies that, much like the monsters we create, seem to have achieved agency of their own.[25] We fight network wars against faceless ghosts and bioengineered post-human entities. We produce cloned bodies and embody monstrosity in virtual environments. We share evidence of our own monstrosity through social media. In other words, we embrace and resist the multitude of ways in which technology permeates, constructs, but also challenges subjectivities, bodies, and identities in the twenty-first century. In other words, technology is no longer a simple facilitator of monstrosity, à la *Videodrome* or *Poltergeist*, but rather it is an actor and an active monstrous embodiment of the global culture. In her essay, Sherryl Vint effectively ties together a psychoanalytical and ontological approach to theorize the emergence of abject post-human figures. She argues that the abject post-human is a necessary category with which to think about life in the twenty-first century, or in a "future without a future." Post-humanity allows us to conceptualize the role of technology in the twenty-first century, and the next two essays do just that. In his essay, Jeremy Biles uses Cylons—the post-human, post-robotic entities on *Battlestar Galactica*—as a starting point to examine the tension between technophobia and technophilia. Using George Bataille's work on eroticism,[26] he theorizes "the telepathology of the everyday life" in the global network society—an erotic and pathological dream of network and communication systems that embraces the tension between life and death in the twenty-first century. Roy Kamada argues for consideration of postmodern monstrosity as an articulation of global citizenship. Looking at David Mitchell's *Cloud Atlas* (2004) and Kazuo Ishiguro's *Never Let Me Go* (2005) he considers the post-human bodies of clones as discursive formations of contemporary flexible citizenship in the global society. The final three chapters in the section study how monstrosity is discursively and literally produced through technologies. Jeffrey Mantz warns us of the darker side of global technology. Using multiple meanings of zombification, he examines the often-monstrous consequences that mining for minerals essential to the production of digital technology has had in the Congo. Jaroslav Švelch's chapter illuminates the processes of monstrosity in video games. He argues that video games invite an engagement with monstrosity, not as a supernatural and unknown, but rather as a quantifiable and manageable identity reflective of control society.[27] Finally, Michele White examines the slew of Internet representations of zombie brides. Particularly focusing on the production of whiteness in these images, she argues that these representations have much to say about the role of social media in the twenty-first century as a place to explore numerous forms of identities and subjectivities.

Monstrous territories

Essays in this section argue that popular representations of monstrosity in the twenty-first century reflect anxieties and fears over physical, economic, and political boundaries in the globalized world.[28] The essays look at representations of monstrosities and terror threats post-9/11; exploration and exploitation of physical and fantastical national boundaries; and monstrous crises in modernity and globalization. Together they contend that we occupy unfamiliar, often frightening, sometimes promising monstrous territories that evoke stories of terror and hope. Much in the way that monstrous texts of the 1970s and 1980s often took place in enclosed, family-occupied spaces to reflect the unintended consequences of the dissolution of a traditional patriarchal family structure,[29] so do monstrous texts in the twenty-first century address the fears of open, unbounded spaces occupied by zombies, ghosts, and other unseen and unyielding enemies. The first three essays in this section look at the nature of threat and violence in the world post-9/11. In his essay, Michael Drake argues that zombification can help to understand how neo-nationalist constructions function in the age of globalization. Zombies reflect the destructiveness of contemporary national community as it tries to find its identity and place in the global society. Mary Bloodworth-Lugo and Carmen Lugo-Lugo further that point by looking at the rhetoric of the enemy in post-9/11 films. They argue that increasingly the monster is no longer a marginal entity hidden out of sight, but rather functions within the society—and within our collective psyche. In her essay, Enrica Piracelli continues the meditation on the nature of threat post-9/11. Looking at the popular TV series *Lost*, she finds "monstrosity at the heart of lives lived without guarantees." She argues that this incorporeal monstrosity is part of a current cultural landscape of uncertainty and apprehension. The final three essays in the section locate monstrosity at the center of changing cultural, economic, and interpersonal territories. Cynthia Miller and A. Bowdoin Van Riper look at the increasing presence of the undead in *American Western* genre films as a convergence of moral panics attacking the heartland of the United States. They argue that the undead in the twenty-first century's West challenge the myths of freedom and strength that shaped American modernity. Ryan Gillespie looks at the global financial crisis of 2008 as an elaborate story about wizards and monsters that shape the mythical character of global capital. Again, the uncertain nature of global territories becomes important, as he argues that monster and supernatural tropes tried, and failed, to exorcise uncertainty from current financial systems. Finally, and on a more optimistic note, Carolyn Harford looks at the popular novel and movie series *Twilight* as a reflection of changing identities in global societies. She argues that *Twilight* reflects the growing acceptance, and perhaps even an appeal, of cross-cultural and cross-ethnic relationships in the twenty-first century.

Together these excellent essays argue that there is much at stake in monstrosity as an abject terror, a cultural representation, and a way of being and becoming. As editors we would like our readers to consider these arguments as starting points on the often terrifying road to our monstrous future. Welcome to the twenty-first century and its glorious promise of monsters!

Notes

1 Nina Auerbach, *Our Vampires, Ourselves* (Chicago: University of Chicago Press, 1995).

2 Paul Virilio, *Speed and Politics: an Essay on Dromology* (New York: Columbia University Press, 1986).

3 Michael Hardt and Antonio Negri, *Multitude: War and Democracy in the Age of Empire* (New York: Penguin Press, 2004), 196.

4 Ibid., 11.

5 Sigmund Freud, "The Uncanny," in *The Standard Edition of the Complete Psychological Works of Sigmund Freud. Volume XVII (1917–1919)*, trans.

James Strachey, Anna Freud, Alix Strachey, and Alan Tyson (London: Hogarth Press, 1971) 220, 241.

6 Sue Ellen Case, "Tracking the Vampire," in *The Horror Reader*, (ed.) Ken Gelder (New York: Routledge, 2000).

7 Julia Kristeva and Leon S. Roudiez, *Powers of Horror: an Essay on Abjection* (New York: Columbia University Press, 1982).

8 Jacques Lacan, *The Four Fundamental Concepts of Psychoanalysis* (New York: W. W. Norton and Company, 1998)

9 Ibid., 3.

10 Vera Dika, "From Dracula—with love," *The Dread of Difference*, (ed.) Barry Keith Grant (Austin: University of Texas Press, 1996).

11 Ibid.

12 Robin Wood, "The American Nightmare: Horror in the 70's," in *Hollywood from Vietnam to Reagan* (New York: Columbia University Press, 1986).

13 Ibid., 75.

14 David J. Skal, *The Monster Show: a Cultural History of Horror* (New York: W. W. Norton and Company, 1993).

15 Wood, "American Nightmare," 77.

16 For more on representational study of monstrosity see Jeffrey Jerome Cohen, *Monster Theory: Reading Culture* (1996); Stephen T. Asma, *On Monsters: an Unnatural History of Our Worst Fears* (2009); Elaine Graham, *Representations of the Post/Human: Monsters, Aliens, and Others in Popular Culture* (2002).

17 Judith Halberstam, *Skin Shows: Gothic Horror and the Technology of Monsters* (Durham: Duke University Press, 1995).

18 Michel Foucault, *Abnormal: Lectures at the Collège de France, 1974–1975*, (ed.) Valerio Marchetti, Antonella Salomoni, and Arnold I. Davidson. English Series trans. Graham Burchell (New York: Picador, 2003).

19 Halberstam, *Skin Shows*, 6.

20 Gilles Deleuze and Félix Guattari, *A Thousand Plateaus: Capitalism and Schizophrenia* (Minneapolis: University of Minnesota Press, 1987).

21 Jacques Derrida and Elisabeth Weber, *Points …: Interviews, 1974–1994* (Stanford: Stanford University Press, 1995).

22 Amit Rai, "The Future Is a Monster," *Camera Obscura* 21 (2006): 61.

23 Lacan, *Four Fundamental Concepts*.

24 Donna Haraway, "The Promises of Monsters: a Regenerative Politics for Inappropriate/d Others," in *Cultural Studies*, ed. Lawrence Grossberg, Cary Nelson, and Paula Treichler (New York: Routledge, 1992), 300.

25 For further readings on technology in the twenty-first century see Manuel Castells, *The Rise of the Network Society* (2000); Alexander R. Galloway and Eugene Thacker, *The Exploit: a Theory of Networks* (2007); Tiziana Terranova, *Network Culture: Politics for the Information Age* (2004); and Mark Hansen, *Bodies in Code: Interfaces with New Media* (2005).

26 Georges Bataille, *Erotism: Death and Sensuality* (San Francisco: City Lights Books, 1962).

27 Gilles Deleuze, *Negotiations, 1972–1990* (New York: Columbia University Press, 1995).

28 For more on globalization in the twenty-first century see Saskia Sassen, *Territory, Authority, Rights: from Medieval to Global Assemblages* (2006); David Harvey, *Spaces of Global Capitalism* (2006); Eric Cazdyn and Imre Szeman, *After Globalization* (2011); and Jenny Edkins, *Sovereign Lives: Power in Global Politics* (2004).

29 Wood, "American Nightmare."

1

Ontology and monstrosity

Amit S. Rai

In the classic spoof of wartime futurity *Starship Troopers*, the monsters have a brain in the form of a huge slug with a vagina dentata mouth that sucks the brains out of humans. It has its minions, its probe heads, and its war machine. It plays with the classic representation of a monster-as-Other. Not unlike colonial-fascist administrators of a prior iteration of this cinematic discourse on monsters, wannabe citizen-soldiers capture the slug-become-brain and turn it into an object of human knowledge in the laboratory. It feels fear, says the sentient soldier, dressed like a Nazi SS officer. Through this satire what emerges is a powerful critique of militarism, fascism, nativism, imperialism, masculinism, and class, and suddenly, but with a duration that is not of the moment, the alien Other cliché itself becomes a little uncanny, a little monstrous. What is the nature, essence, being of this process of becoming monstrous? My argument in this chapter is that monstrosity and ontology are tied to the lived experience of duration, which is always a qualitative multiplicity, a "suddenly" that has no measure, and a relation that exceeds its terms. In what follows, I pose as a conjunction the problem of monstrosity and ontology: With what method, and through what pedagogy of becoming, could this problem of monstrous ontology make a difference?

Clearly, this question has little to do with ontology understood as the soliloquy of a timeless Being. Monstrosity problematizes becoming, understood as the changeless process of change itself.

Monsters have been within me and my ecologies for so long, as an immigrant child learning English in Flushing, New York, in my filmic dreams co-evolving with the pirated Hindi and Bengali VHS library spawned by my mother's VCR, in the desiring conjunctions of friends and lovers, in the improvised fairytales between father and daughter at bedtime. But when does the monster—a discrete figure—become a vector of mutation across a material, embodied field of force? Is monstrosity an event, or related more importantly to that which exceeds the event, the pure potentiality of the event? Monstrosity promises a reorganization of force, habit, and the body, but this promise of a line of flight is always submerged under various products or static entities: the slug-brain, the colonial monster, technology, difference. These become critical questions when attention becomes practical intuition, and the monster is decomposed into its composite fluxes, its lines of force, its rhythms of contraction and expansion, and thus through radical political practice the monster diagrams revolutionary becomings in duration itself.

I consider monstrosity a certain type of event in relations of force, an event of counter-actualization. What is important about monstrosity—that is, what is *problematic* about it from the point of view of radical political practice—is my central concern in this chapter. From the legacy of decolonization, through feminist and queer organizing for justice and equality, to the autonomist lines of flight that are re-occupying the people's commons today, the question of the monstrous in the desires for freedom should not be limited by this or that politics, but affirmed from the vantage of becoming itself. I argue that this problematizing of monstrosity can only happen through the careful yet *ad hoc* construction of a pragmatic method of potentializing capacities and returning to what Henri Bergson and, differently, Gilles Deleuze call the virtual.[1] Deleuze spoke of a life containing "only virtuals, or events, and singularities. What we call virtual is not something that lacks reality but something that is engaged in a process of actualization following the plane that gives it its particular reality. The immanent event is actualized in a state of things and of the lived that make it happen. The plane of immanence is itself actualized in an object and a subject to which it attributes itself. But however inseparable an object and a subject may be from their actualization, the plane of immanence is itself virtual, so long as the events that populate it are virtualities."[2]

In what sense is duration a method of counter-actualizing the monstrous event toward the virtual, monstrosity as that which exceeds the actualization of events? In other words, the practical notion of the virtual considers the question of monstrous ontology in terms of potentialities enfolding capacities and tendencies in a time-slip of the indeterminate future meeting a pure past, all at once. This method, as Deleuze notes in *Bergsonism*, is one of the most well-developed in the history of philosophy, and we do well to return to it with care and attention. The monstrosity imbuing ontology is an excellent pedagogical device with which to pose precisely the question of the virtual in life.[3] What experimental forms of thought, art, politics, and pedagogy would express this method and remain untimely in relation to the event of mutation itself? Thought revitalized by the body far from equilibrium:

a super-abstract inventionism. As I hope to show through a consideration of David Cronenberg's cinematic experimentations, what is at stake in the conjunction of monstrosity and ontology always is in fact a monstrous wager or impossible risk: can a continuous multiplicity of matter-becoming-lively, in which capacities, tendencies, and practices move far from equilibrium, help pose the problem of the construction of revolutionary Interzones?

To situate this argument I will contrast two figures of thought: the monster as punctum in space and time, and a thoroughgoing ontology of monstrosity rooted in processes, duration, intensity, and the virtual. Let's further clarify this framework through an example. In *Philosophy and the Adventure of the Virtual: Bergson and the Time of Life*, Keith Ansell-Pearson pursues the Bergsonian method of qualitative difference through an analysis of what he sees to be the central difference between Henri Bergson's notion of creative evolution and Alain Badiou's theory of the event. While, for the latter, the event "has no relation to duration, it is a punctuation in the order of being and time (if it can be given a temporality it is only of a retroactive kind)."[4] for Bergson the repetitions (refrains) that constitute lived duration are generative of difference in itself, a qualitative, self-varying, and distributed difference of correlated processes. Bergson calls us to attend to a method which thinks a "duration 'in which each form flows out of previous forms, while adding to them something new, and is explained by them as much as it explains them …'."[5] In this example, Ansell-Pearson works from the actual (a punctuation in the order of being and time) toward the virtual and its durations (difference in itself or qualitative difference). From a pedagogical point of view, the adventure of counteractualization follows a practice of intuiting differences in kind: which duration, which intensity combine with which material flow to produce which kinds of capacities? Deleuze's notion of the virtual is pedagogi-cally practical in that it intuits differences in kind, decomposes a multiplicity into its resonant fluxes and material processes, and in that decomposition of embedded timescales, parameters of intensive variation, tendencies toward change, and capacities to sense and be affected discovers a lesson for thought: follow the movements, move with the material processes behind the spatialized product, into the past and toward the future simultaneously.

This nondialectical difference between on the one hand what I will call a process ontology of monstrosity and on the other what might be termed the punctum of the monster has everything to do with the nature of difference and becoming. Is the monster a discourse, is it a metaphor, analogy for something else, i.e. capitalism, patriarchy, imperialism, or racism? Is the monster a representation that slides across the surface of discourse, something in the nature of a stain or *trompe l'oeil* [trick of the eye]? It will come as no surprise that representational analyses have dominated the thought of monstrosity in contemporary Western criticism. There are several reasons for this, but perhaps chief among them is the very fact that the monster has become a mechanism of producing cultural, artistic, even academic value in the neoliberal market. And so the fixation on the punctum of the monster (the monster as state enemy—i.e. the monster as terrorist—as much as the monster as conceptual abyss, as a figure of abjection and exception—Homo Sacer, difference) in fact in differently positioned critiques ends up taking the monstrosity out of the monster, and after some buffing with this or that discourse is presented as the Other *du jour*. This returns me to my initial example of *Starship Troopers*: the experience of apprehending a monster-Other, for instance in a film, and the experience of becoming-monstrous through an event that exceeds its actualization (in a film or in life) should be understood as two different methods of becoming. The first seeks to spatialize the monster in this or that figuration, this or that Other, quantifying its effects, and so rooting becoming in identity, habit, representation, and the similar or analogical, while the second form of monstrosity challenges all these habits of mind and body by posing the problem of monstrosity from the point of view of time, embodiment, and intensity. From the perspective of the second method of becoming, it is clear that we don't need more monsters, we need to intensify our monstrosities. In the face of the clichéd monster, we take up a collective cry of the autonomy of becoming: Monstrosity to the nth degree.

What, then, if monstrosity comes to re-enchant the world, as Prigogine and Stengers suggest of temporality, in dissipative structures?[6] Their work shows that irreversible processes are, in time, folded in the impersonal duration of the world, and yet this difference in itself is productive of difference, and so open to processes of conjunction and refunctioning through the coupling and decoupling of material processes, resulting in a state of affairs in which intensifications, accelerations, slownesses, passages, feedbacks, and viscosities are produced by the repetition and clinamen[7] of fluxes. Is this too hopelessly abstract or romantic? What would a non-romanticized image of monstrosity entail, or is the monstrous irreducibly theatrical? A re-enchantment of monstrosity proliferates its ontological effects because in such a method monstrosity-events involve the open explication and affective expression of intensive difference in the world. Experience David Cronenberg's cinema: No nostalgia in becoming monster! (I will return to Cronenberg's cinema later.) In other words, and conversely, in what sense is monstrosity an effect of a kind of experimentation or creation within intensive multiplicities, an experiment in resonance pushed to its immanent nth degree? Or is monstrosity merely the cultural trace of a bodily intuition, the method of which must begin and end with duration? Following Bergson, Deleuze, and Ansell-Pearson, by duration I understand that moving whole, that non-coinciding resonant unity that gives to perception blocs of sensation, and gives to becoming its internal variations; durations qualify the fluxes of life; in the durations of monstrosity potential conjunctions become active, contagious, promiscuous. This chapter explores this other, neglected aspect of monstrosity through an engagement with art, politics, and pedagogy.

What happens when the monster becomes simply a signpost, but a remarkable one of immanent processes of becoming? Recall what Michael Hardt says of the remarkable in Spinoza:

> Being is singular not only in that it is unique and absolutely infinite, but, more important, in that it is *remarkable*. This is the impossible opening of the *Ethics*. Singular being as substance is not "distinct from" or "different from" any thing outside itself; if it were, we would have to conceive it partly through another thing, and thus it would not be substance. ... The distinction of being rises from within. *Causa sui* means that being is both infinite and definite: Being is remarkable. The first task of the real distinction, then, is to define being as singular, to recognize its difference without reference to, or dependence on, any other thing. The real nonnumerical distinction defines the singularity of being, in that being is absolutely infinite and indivisible at the same time that it is distinct and determinate. Singularity, in Deleuze, has nothing to do with individuality or particularity. It is, rather, the correlate of efficient causality and internal difference: The singular is remarkable because it is different in itself.[8]

Let us consider carefully this passage. A monistic pantheism: If being is singular, and yet its immanent, nonnumerical difference refers to no other, nor is dependent on any other thing, being is purely potential (absolutely infinite and indivisible) at the same time that it is fully actualized (distinct and determinate). If we can link the Deleuzian concept of singularity to monstrosity through the "anomalous individuation" of the remarkable (following Alberto Toscano and Michael Hardt), we could begin to consider the emergence of the monster in terms of its capacity or power to potentialize (re-enchant) duration, force, and the event across the timespaces of communication, biology, perception, technology, and thought itself.[9] Keep in mind here that, in a Deleuzian ontology, there is no assumption of a pre-existing unity, but rather a focus on the specific processes constituting individuals or "singularities." In such an ontology, every aspect of reality evidences difference, "and there is nothing 'behind' such difference; difference is not grounded in anything else. Deleuze does not mean to refer, however, to differences of degree, by which he means distinctions among items that are considered identical or in any sense the same. Instead, he means the particularity or 'singularity' of each individual thing, moment, perception or conception."[10] For Deleuze, such difference is internal or immanent to a thing or event, implicit in the processes of that particular. In Deleuze's conception, singularity helps us to get at the qualitative differences among things, and this is the primary philosophical fact. Indeed, rather than theorizing how singularities might be grouped, it is more important to explore the specific and unique development or "becoming" of each singularity. "The genealogy of an individual lies not in generality or commonality, but in a process of individuation determined by actual and specific differences, multitudinous influences and chance interactions."[11] The practice of monstrosity, then, would be a kind of probe head for this anomalous morphogenesis, for the emergence of new forms, for a new theory and practice of singular multiplicities.

We could pose the above ellipsis into virtual ontology by returning to our topic anew: what is monstrosity an example of? We could say that monstrosity is an example of the anomalous in a process of becoming, keeping in mind that the anomalous haunts every material-virtual assemblage as its line of flight. In other words, we could ask if there are gradients of monstrosity? Are their forms of monstrosity that are fundamentally affirmative, and other forms that are fundamentally reactive? Is the cruelty of transvaluation (beyond good and evil: thresholds of becoming) what cuts across this gradient? My argument here, following the work of Bergson, Deleuze, and Guattari, Massumi, Parisi, Clough and others is that as neoliberal affect machines such as neuromarketing organize capacities around consumption, value/debt, and security, monstrosity emerges spontaneously as the unspoken wager of radical practices seeking new forms of intervention in the world and in the virtual. We can turn to two of Cronenberg's earlier films, *Videodrome* (1983) and *The Fly* (1986), in which we experience, through a reconstruction of entire ecologies of monstrosity, variable becoming animal, itself a becoming intense, a becoming through the gradual emergence of capacities once separated from what they could do, and now finding psychotic yet potentializing conjunctions, the body becomes carnivorous technology. Taking the becoming monstrous of the body toward chaos, Cronenberg stages suicidal deterritorializations of bodily and psychic form in scenes of visceral pain and desire, and an infinite cruelty. In *Videodrome*, Cronenberg delves into the gradients of monstrosity, grimly attending the gothic rituals and "viral" media accompanying the becoming reactive of monstrosity. In the refrains and contagions of his paranoid vision of machinic assemblages, an illumination of potentiality (capacities and tendencies are both real and potential at once) limns his scenes.

This is discernible, we should point out, in the context of pedagogy, study, and the classroom. Generally, people confuse the idea of the wager of monstrosity in pedagogy as a transference in the psychoanalytic sense, or as a transgression of sexual norms, or as the pursuit of a genealogy of monstrous representations in discourses of power, etc. It involves at different levels and scales the production of the monster as punctum. But the pursuit of monstrosity as virtual ontology would be transversal to the family, the state, or the subject; indeed, in addition to all the non-human becomings that Deleuze and Guattari liberated from the banality of the dialectic, we affirm the following movements: becoming-hacker, becoming-jugaad (trick, con, practical joke), becoming-assemblage, becoming-indiscernible.

Franco Berardi writes beautifully of Felix Guattari's[12] method of sidestepping, or transversalizing the refrains of everyday life. He argues that singularity—which is closely allied with the experience of the monstrous—does not presuppose any sense, nor does it discover any sense through its experience in the world—for instance the sense of the monster as an Other. Rather, sense unfolds as creation, as a connecting or conjunctive desire, as the "delirium that illuminates the event." For Berardi, Guattari's schizoanalysis wants to make a certain "lightness" possible, "dissolving obsessions and rigid refrains" through experimental techniques aimed at "displacing the focus of attention, through the proliferation of points from which semiotic flows, flows of worlds, can emanate."[13]

Cronenberg explores this singularization in the session, and in the assemblage potentializing it, in the film *A Dangerous Method* (2011).[14] The becoming woman of Sabina is this recorrelation between her intensive life (durations, expressivity, guilt, passion) and her identitarian memory-narrative. Cronenberg shows conjunctive series or habitual refrains counteractualizing an ecology of sense and sensation passing through critical thresholds of monstrosity: A passionate conjunction of refrains. Through the course of his career Cronenberg has created refrains of thought (transmutation, incorporation, nonlinearity between body and mind, the ontology of violence) and experience—e.g. the sounds of a transforming body: the handgun in the stomach-vagina in *Videodrome* is not entirely a visual image. In fact the event of morphogenesis (the brain growing a new limb, as the false prophet O'Blivion puts it), its visual actualization is prepared for by the elastic durations of a "three-dimensional" sound image, which is itself an assemblage of Cronenberg's repertoire of sound refrains: activated flesh against squishy flesh, scratching, lips smacking, deep breathing, swallowing, undulating organ-synths. This ominous sound image is doubled by, captured by a face (devoid of humanity, as Cronenberg says of Warhol's faces and his screen test films), and grimly, even voyeuristically the spectator is drawn into the secret poetry of a violently malignant growth. Differently, Cronenberg speaks of another doubling of sound and image in experimental filmmaking when he discusses Andy Warhol's botching of sound throughout his own films; in this meditation on Warhol, he marks a particularly experimental practice of (de)conjoining sound to image to modulate attention. These creative refrains involving the movements of sound, image, body have affirmed a subtle illumination of all that which exceeds the event.

What would a virtuosity of the refrain do in the world as we live it? It would produce events as virtualities and monstrosities, radically democratic and multiplicious events-as-critical thresholds. Paolo Virno notes of virtuosity:

> It is obvious that these two characteristics are inter-related: virtuosos need the presence of an audience precisely because they are not producing an end product, an object which will circulate through the world once the activity has ceased. Lacking a specific extrinsic product, the virtuoso has to rely on witnesses ... Implicitly resuming Aristotle's idea, Hannah Arendt compares the performing artists, the virtuosos, to those who are engaged in political action. She writes: "The performing arts [...] have indeed a strong affinity with politics. Performing artists-dancers, play-actors, musicians, and the like—need an audience to show their virtuosity, just as acting men need the presence of others before whom they can appear; both need a publicly organized space for their 'work,' and both depend upon others for the performance itself" ... One could say that every political action is *virtuosic*. Every political action, in fact, shares with virtuosity a sense of contingency, the absence of a "finished product," the immediate and unavoidable presence of others. ... all virtuosity is intrinsically political.[15]

I find Virno's notion of the refrain (borrowed from Guattari), in its focus on contingency, risk, relevant durations, and radical democratic practice a key component of what today we can affirm as a strategic conjunction between politics and monstrosity. Virno also shows us that virtuosity in its experiments with emergence breaks down the culture–nature binary. This is because a monstrous emergence is that for which we have no name (no cultural code), and simultaneously an emergent form (a contravention of majoritarian forms). The virtuosic performance is a provocation of monstrosity, as a gambit in morphogenesis requiring in some real way a new language, a becoming minor of language. What is the power of the monstrous? Where does it get this power? Jacques Derrida, who in his early work associated the future as such with a certain monstrosity (cf. Derrida's preface to *Of Grammatology*), said in an interview:

> A monster may be obviously a composite figure of heterogenous organisms that are grafted onto each other. This graft, this hybridization,

this composition that puts heterogeneous bodies together may be called a monster. This in fact happens in certain kinds of writing. At that moment, monstrosity may reveal or make one aware of what the norm is and when this norm has a history—which is the case with discursive norms, philosophical norms, socio-cultural norms, they have a history—any appearance of monstrosity in this domain allows an analysis of the history of the norms. But to do that, one must conduct not only a theoretical analysis, one must produce what in fact looks like a discursive monster so that the analysis will be a practical effect, so that people will be forced to become aware of the history of normality. But a monster is not just that, it is not just this chimerical figure in some way that grafts one animal onto another, one living being onto another. A monster is always alive, let us not forget. Monsters are living beings. This monster is also that which appears for the first time, and consequently, is not yet recognized. A monster is a species for which we do not yet have a name, which does not mean that the species is abnormal, namely, the composition or hybridization of already known species. Simply, it shows itself—that is what the word monster means—it shows itself in something that is not yet shown and that therefore looks like a hallucination, it strikes the eye, it frightens precisely because no anticipation had prepared one to identify this figure. ... But as soon as one perceives a monster in a monster, one begins to domesticate it, one begins, because of the "as such"—it is a monster as monster—to compare it to the norms to analyze it, consequently to master whatever could be terrifying in this figure of the monster. And the movement of accustoming oneself, but also of legitimation and, consequently, of normalization, has already begun. However monstrous events or texts may be, from the moment they enter into culture, the movement of acculturation, precisely, of domestication, of normalization has already begun. ... This is the movement of culture. Texts and discourses that provoke at the outset reactions of rejection, that are denounced precisely as anomalies or monstrosities are often texts that, before being in turn appropriated, assimilated, acculturated, transform the nature of the field of reception, transform the nature of social and cultural experience, historical experience. All history has shown that each time an event has been produced, for example in philosophy or in poetry, it took the form of the unacceptable, or even of the intolerable, of the incomprehensible, that is, of a certain monstrosity.[16]

There are some key tools for the method of ontogenesis in Derrida's words. Indeed, any radical pedagogy that risks the wager of monstrosity must communicate through an expressive method of becoming. Consider some of

Deleuze's levers. The first is a question of duration: monstrosity is a moment of awakening to the norm; the norm is historicized in the monstrous. But what is it about the processes of duration that remains central to the "life" of the monstrous? Isn't it simply in the fact that these processes are nothing other than the ingression of the world into the refrains of an actual entity? The second domain that Derrida opens is one of force. What is the force of the monster? From whence does it derive this force? For Derrida at least part of the aggression of the monster, its specific departure from the image of thought as Happy Soul, is in a Hegelian–Lacanian misrecognition, absence of recognition, or even failure of cognition. Finally, Derrida opens thought toward the event. However, this event that Derrida points to bears closer resemblance to the "punctum" of the monster that I charted above with the help of Ansell-Pearson. For Derrida (and others before and after him such as Bachelard and Badiou), the monster is like a suspension in time, monstrosity is the absolute Abyss.

But Derrida and this tradition of monster criticism takes the remarkable nature of the monster and turns it into external difference, they spatialize difference: the monster is appropriated by culture because its difference is externalized outside of both culture and nature, it is pure excess. It is then first and foremost representation, metaphor, and identity, which in its essential ambivalence none the less does not exceed dialectical thought. The intolerable and the incomprehensible are the badges of honor in this discourse of the monstrous, objectified, victimized Other.

I want to pragmatically experiment with Derrida's monstrous event and Gilles Deleuze's notion of a continuous, vital, virtual-actual circuit of becoming. My argument is that Deleuze takes us beyond the human into an unforeseen, mind-independent "interzone," as Burroughs has it, a zone of proximity, indiscernibility, miscegenation, and re/action (explored cinematically by Cronenberg). In *A Thousand Plateaus*, Deleuze and Guattari explain the genesis of such a zone through the material example of sound and song, bringing us again back to Cronenberg's experimentations in sound. In "Postulates of Linguistic" they describe procedures for placing the voice in variation such as "circular breathing techniques and zones of resonance in which several voices seem to issue from the same mouth." They go on to emphasize the significance of music across genres and distinctions in which secret languages emerge; characteristic of secret languages, "slangs, jargons, professional languages, nursery rhymes, merchants' cries," is to stand out less for their lexical inventions or rhetorical figures than for the way in which "they effect continuous variations of the common elements of language." Secret languages are "chromatic languages, close to a musical notation. A secret language does not merely have a hidden cipher or code still operating by constants and forming a subsystem; *it places the public language's system of variables in a state of variation.*"[17]

These "zones of indiscernibility" traverse the virtual and actual circuits of the multiplicities constituting an assemblage; this is why the process of attending to Cronenberg's sound-images counteractualizes sound itself in a secret language of variation itself. In such aesthetics of monstrosity, there is a specific method of moving thought and practice toward and into an interzone of becoming, the smooth plane of monstrosity itself. This method can be taught through pedagogical frameworks that take the frame itself as a plane of becoming. One key moment, event, or resonance of such an experimental pedagogy is the collective "decision" to risk the wager of monstrosity.

This is what Cronenberg (who also made *Naked Lunch*) successfully does in both *A History of Violence* (2005) and *A Dangerous Method* (2011): as I noted earlier, in the latter he creates an interzone between analyst and analysand that becomes a potentialized timespace of intensive becoming, an affirmation of monstrosity as an expression of freedom, a pragmatic yet abstract experimentation with bodies, affects, desire, and technology; in *A History of Violence*, a man is confronted with the residual effects of a violent past, but his monstrosity lies in the fact that his body has continued an affective resonance with that violence (i.e. he reconnects to his highly complex bodily capacity for physical violence), and it is that burst of a body re-enchanted by its own virtual monstrosity in a moment of life-threatening violence that catalyzes various becomings in the interzone of the fracturing family. We can say that, throughout his work, Cronenberg has bodied forth monstrous assemblages populating infinitely spongy interzones affirming becoming itself.

If monstrosity is a method of singularizing intensive multiplicities out of a population, as Deleuze writes, this line of flight emerges from a specific ecology's affective conditions, its relations of force, sense, duration. An ecology of mind-becoming-sensation. It is within this ecology of force and sensation that monstrosity does that thing it does. It does not represent an abyss in time, but is rather a fully historical, immanent process that is ontologically continuous with its own ecologies but transversal to its refrains, both abstract and empirical. We experience an affirmation of this transversal in the lush generativity of Cronenberg's oeuvre. In the cinematic explorations of contagions from vampires and zombies (*Rabid* [Rage; 1977]) to experiments in abstract morphogenesis (*Videodrome, eXistenz, The Fly, Naked Lunch*), in his new histories of the secrets of iniquity (*Eastern Promises, History of Violence*), each becoming has its uniqueness, its singularly exhilarating and irreversible events. Could we not say then that the hold of the monster in contemporary culture continues a simple but very old, because pragmatic, intuition: monsters catalyze the imagination of "a world in which the conjunction 'and' dethrones the interiority of the verb 'is'," as Brian Massumi once put it. In the sense of an experiment in intuitive imagining relations external to their terms, monstrosity and counter-actualization are closely allied methods.

My (whose?) imagination is drawn today to movements of solidarity across molar differences encouraging and giving sustenance to molecular revolutions, circuits of radical care and friendship, practices of hacktivism and information tactics, slow foods, D.I.Y., the practices of digital archivists, artists, and filmmakers in Mumbai (Ranjit Kandalgaonkar, the work on cinema and media at KRVI and CMCS, TISS), anonymous-uk,[18] re-occupying ecologies, and MUTE, Hi8us, and Furtherfield,[19] styles of media activism in London. The proliferation of sites, surfaces, and perceptions of value has produced zones of indetermination in which quasi-causal lines of flight hack transversally and pragmatically toward a new plane of consistency, a new assemblage, a monstrous imagination. Isn't this finally one sense of Donna Haraway's crucial essay, "The Promises of Monsters"—that monsters promise a return to intensive materialism, power-capacity, and to untimely history? This promise is affirmed in practices of creating a machinic conjunction, a feedbacked "and."

The question would then turn on how to make an affirmation of becoming in monstrosity, its becoming revolution, woman, minor, indiscernible. Not surprisingly the question returns us to a practice of politics commensurate to revolutionary becoming. Marx gives a historical sense of this affirmation as revolutionary practice. In contrast to eighteenth-century bourgeois revolutions, in which dramatic effects for a short time sweep up the current of events and the central actors in a mystical "ecstasy of the day,"

> ... proletarian revolutions, like those of the nineteenth century, constantly criticize themselves, constantly interrupt themselves in their own course, return to the apparently accomplished, in order to begin anew; they deride with cruel thoroughness the half-measures, weaknesses, and paltriness of their first attempts, seem to throw down their opponents only so the latter may draw new strength from the earth and rise before them again more gigantic than ever, recoil constantly from the indefinite colossalness of their own goals – until a situation is created which makes all turning back impossible, and the conditions themselves call out: *Hic Rhodus, hic salta!*[20]

Marx warns us of those refrains of seemingly revolutionary, but in fact reactionary enthusiasm in which "ecstasy is the order of the day." Materialist revolutions, on the other hand, molecularize people's enthusiasm (or desires), creating common concepts (concepts that are common to at least two multi-plicities) that grasp the real articulations of relations external to their terms, and the embedded timescales of their ecologies. Even when Cronenberg is at his most didactically cautionary or painfully paranoid, at stake always is a monstrous wager: can a continuous multiplicity of matter-becoming-lively, in which capacities, tendencies, and practices move far from equilibrium, help pose the problem of the construction of revolutionary interzones? Massumi writes of a supermolecular revolution that is not analogous to Marx's conception of proletarian revolution or Cronenberg's surreal interzone, but is continuous with their counteractualizations, an affirmation of becoming and materialism. "Becoming is an equilibrium-seeking system at a crisis point where it suddenly perceives a deterministic constraint, becomes 'sensitive' to it, and is catapulted into a highly unstable supermolecular state enveloping a bifurcating future."[21] *Hic Rhodus, hic salta!* (Here is Rhodes, jump here!)[22] Marx and Massumi both point us toward the durations of monstrosity-revolution: to move a revolutionary assemblage toward a critical threshold requires recursive practices of self-criticism and self-creation, an interruptive politics constantly relaunching itself on the basis of a radically republican materialism,[23] but one that equally well helps us to construct our own smooth spaces of conjunction and indiscernibility (visibility is still a trap, but for reasons of habituated sensation not representation). Paolo Virno continues that materialism in his articulation of the multitude, to whom monstrous becomings are endemic through the post-Fordist present because of the technologization of the general intellect (e.g. in the Internet, mobile phones, Facebook, user-generated content). For Virno, the post-Ford multitude has advanced the collapse of political representation: "not as an anarchic gesture, but as a means of calmly and realistically searching for new political forms." The non-representative democracy of the multitude which is based on the *general intellect* is not interstitial or marginal, but it is rather "the concrete appropriation and re-articulation of the knowledge/power unity which has congealed within the administrative modern machine of the States."[24] Non-representative democracy based upon the general intellect potentialized through a multitude in search of monstrous forms of radical democracy, forms that unfold the untimely in our own habits of friendship, care, technology, and consumption. This non-representative radical democracy is based on the wager of monstrosity, that is a continuous multiplicity of matter-becoming-lively, in which capacities, tendencies and practices move far from equilibrium, pragmatically fabricating revolutionary interzones.

How can monstrosity as a method of experimenting with forms and processes of material assemblages become a well-posed problem? This is what certain art practices (e.g. Cronenberg's oeuvre), or radical affective networks (Radio Alice—see below; Nanopolitics[25]) help us to do: create zones of indiscernibility, contact zones of miscegenation and dehabituation, and smooth spaces of a stochastic resonance. Only when monstrosity is enlivened through a method of intuition, which is nothing other than a thoroughgoing but abductive pragmatism, does the logic of conjunction come into force. That is, monstrosity is problematic in so far as it clarifies the distribution of singularities in its diagramming of the problem of becoming in the historically specific domain in question—through its method of creating resonances, proximities, conjunctions, we intuit the distribution of the singular and the ordinary, the composition of forces pushed far from equilibrium, the habits of perception estranged, and the activation of potentialities of becoming. Experimental aesthetic practices conjoin with radical democratic creations of the multitude in historically specific revolutionary becomings: this is the non-contradictory logic of monstrosity.

Monstrosity begins in the middle, with the intuition of the infinite giddiness of the event, the adventure of eternal objects and their external relations of "diversity and pattern." Whitehead writes, "The doctrine of organism is the attempt to describe the world as a process of generation of individual actual entities, each with its own absolute self-attainment. This concrete finality of the individual is nothing else than a decision referent beyond itself. The 'perpetual perishing' of individual absoluteness is thus foredoomed. But the 'perishing' of absoluteness is the attainment of 'objective immortality'."[26] Thus, monstrosity brings us to the abstract essence of ecologies as that critical threshold traversing and transforming their powers to affect and be affected. Monstrosity is "a passage of Life that traverses both the livable and the lived," as Deleuze suggested.[27] Monstrosity is a universal revolutionary becoming, not in the sense of a classic Enlightenment grand narrative but in the ontological processes of a thousand Radio Alices: Franco Berardi sings of the Altraverso zine in Bologna, in which the new "offset machine gave us the possibility of composing the page in a much freer way than the old typographic printing machine"; how the Dadaist technique of the collage, taking characters from the newspapers, cutting out pictures, mixing and sticking them to the page and then photographing and printing it all became an experiment in political agitation; and then how this collective mutated to launch Radio Alice in February 1976, "a group of young proletarian poets: autonomes desirants, creativi trasversali, younger brothers of the students with neckties of 1968." Pursuing a creative transversality, they were not reading so much Marx and Lenin, but William Burroughs and Roland Barthes, producing the music for new refrains: Collective happiness is subversion, subversion is collective happiness! "When Radio Alice started broadcasting in February 1976 a dozen anarcho-operaists, post-hippy and proto-punks met in a top-floor flat on the roof of the old city of Bologna, and emitted ambiguous signals. The excitation was growing ... *Il comunismo è libero e felice dieci cento mille radio alice.* [Communism is free and happy: ten hundred thousand Radio Alices] ... Thanks to the radios, thanks to the autonomous zines spreading all over, a large scale process of mass irony was launched ... We saw it as a suspension of the kingdom of necessity and were convinced that power has power as far as those who have no power take power seriously."[28]

A superabstract inventionism, the imagination of "and," experiments in mass irony, a preindividual yet strategic resonance: this is a pedagogy of giving thanks! These can be concepts in the pantheism of a certain Marxist vitalism, or become active practices. This line of flight—which could also be called a vagabond monotheism[29]—traversing Cronenberg's aesthetics, the radical multitudes, practices of "recommoning" autonomia, and a thousand radio Alices—is in fact a monstrous materialism.

Notes

1 Henri Bergson, *Matter and memory* (New York: Zone, 1988); Gilles Deleuze, *Pure immanence: essays on a life*, trans. A. Boyman (New York: Zone, 2001).

2 Deleuze, *Pure immanence*, 30–1.

3 Gilles Deleuze, *Essays critical and clinical* (London: Verso, 1998), 13.

4 Keith Ansell-Pearson, *Philosophy and the adventure of the virtual: Bergson and the time of life* (London: Routledge, 2001), 71. Badiou writes in *Theory of the Subject* (London: Continuum, 2009; 22): "There are others, like Deleuze, who posit the Multiple, which is never more than a semblance since positing the multiple amounts to presupposing the One as substance and excluding the Two from it. The ontology of the multiple is a veiled metaphysics. Its mainspring comes from Spinoza: first, affirmative substance, then the multiple that unfolds itself in the latter without ever becoming equal to it, and whose unifying nature one can pretend to have bracketed. This is only a feint. In the case of Spinoza, who is truly great, the spectre of the Two passes through the attributes, thought and extension. But in accordance with the beginning, this apparition must be rescinded: '[A]n absolutely infinite being is necessarily defined [...] as an entity which consists of infinite attributes.' The fact that human beings have access to the true only by the adequate connection of the idea and the thing, ultimately of the soul and the body, and can think Substance only in the double attributive infinity of extension and thought, attests exclusively to their limitation: this Two is an impairment of the multiple. The presupposed One only has the effect of the integral. Infinite multiplicity, the infinity of infinites. It is at this price that the Cartesian problematic of the subject can be made to

disappear—something for which Althusser so strongly credited Spinoza. For me, this 'process without a subject' of the multiple is the pinnacle of the One."

5 Ansell-Pearson, *Philosophy and the adventure of the virtual*, 71.

6 Isabelle Stengers, *Power and invention: situating science* (Minneapolis and London: University of Minnesota Press, 1997); I. Prigogine and Isabelle Stengers. *Order out of chaos: man's new dialogue with nature* (London: Heinemann, 1984; Boulder, CO: New Science Library, distributed by Random House).

7 Manuel De Landa, *A thousand years of nonlinear history* (New York: Zone Books, 1997).

8 Michael Hardt, *Gilles Deleuze: an apprenticeship in philosophy* (London: UCL Press, 1993), 93.

9 Alberto Toscano, *The theatre of production: philosophy and individuation between Kant and Deleuze* (Basingstoke: Palgrave Macmillan, 2006); Hardt, *Gilles Deleuze*.

10 Adrian Parr, *The Deleuze dictionary*, rev. edn (Edinburgh: Edinburgh University Press, 2010), 75.

11 Ibid.

12 Felix Guattari developed this notion of transversality from Ginette Michaud, a medical student and participant in the La Borde experiments. See François Dosse,. 2010. *Gilles Deleuze & Felix Guattari: intersecting lives* (New York and Chichester: Columbia University Press, 2010). Guattari's practice of transversality brought together Sartrean existentialism, militant Marxism, and a critique of Lacanian psychoanalysis, and pushed toward a materialism of conjunctions and refrains.

13 Franco Berardi, Giuseppina Mecchia, and Charles J. Stivale, *Felix Guattari: thought, friendship, and visionary cartography* (Basingstoke: Palgrave Macmillan, 2008), 114.

14 "Suffering from hysteria, Sabina Spielrein is hospitalized under the care of Dr. Carl Jung who has begun using Dr. Sigmund Freud's talking cure with some of his patients. Spielrain's psychological problems are deeply rooted in her childhood and violent father. She is highly intelligent however and hopes to be a doctor, eventually becoming a psychiatrist in her own right. The married Jung and Spielrein eventually become lovers. Jung and Freud develop an almost father–son relationship with Freud seeing the young Jung as his likely successor as the standard-bearer of his beliefs. A deep rift develops between them when Jung diverges from Freud's belief that while psychoanalysis can reveal the cause of psychological problems it cannot cure the patient" (Plot Summary for *A Dangerous Method*, http://www.imdb.com/title/tt1571222/ (accessed September 9, 2012)).

15 Paolo Virno, *A grammar of the multitude: for an analysis of contemporary forms of life* (Los Angeles Semiotext(e), 2004), 53–4. Virno quotes from Hannah Arendt, Between Past and Future, (New York: Viking Press, 1954), 154.

16 Jacques Derrida, *Points … : Interviews, 1974–1994* (Stanford: Stanford University Press, 1995), 385–7.

17 Gilles Deleuze, and Felix Guattari, 1987. *A thousand plateaus: capitalism and schizophrenia*, trans. B. Massumi (Minneapolis: University of Minnesota Press, 1987), 97.

18 http://www.anonymousuk.com

19 http://www.furtherfield.org

20 Karl Marx, *The 18th Brumaire of Louis Bonaparte*, (ed.) M. Harris (Moscow: Progress Publishers,1852 [1999]).

21 Brian Massumi, *A user's guide to Capitalism and schizophreni : deviations from Deleuze and Guattari* (Cambridge, MA and London: MIT, 1992), 95.

22 In Aesop's fable, "a boastful athlete brags that he once achieved a stupendous long jump in competition on the island of Rhodes. A bystander challenges him to dispense with the reports of the witnesses and simply repeat his accomplishment on the spot: 'Here is Rhodes, jump here!'" ("Hic Rhodes, Hic Salta,") http://en.wiktionary.org/wiki/hic_Rhodus, hic_salta/

23 Antonio Negri and Timothy S. Murphy, *Subversive Spinoza: (un)contemporary variations* (Manchester: Manchester University Press, 2004), 32.

24 Virno, *A grammar of the multitude*, 44.

25 http://www.culturalstudiesassociation.org/lateral/issue1/nanopolitics.html

26 Alfred North Whitehead, *Process and reality: an essay in cosmology*, (eds) D. R. Griffin and D. W. Sherburne; corrected edn (New York: Free Press, 1979), 60.

27 Deleuze, *Essays critical and clinical*, 1.

28 Franco Berardi,. 2009. *Precarious Rhapsody: Semiocapitalism and the pathologies of the post-alpha generation*, trans. E. E. Arianna Bove, Michael Goddard, Giuseppina Mecchia, Antonella Schintu, and Steve Wright (London: Minor Compositions, 2009), 20–1.

29 Deleuze and Guattari, *A thousand plateaus*, 383.

PART ONE

Monstrous identities

2

Heading toward the past:

The *Twilight* vampire figure as surveillance metaphor

Florian Grandena

To Bénédicte, who will never be like Bella...

In her *Celluloid Vampires: Life after Death in the Modern World*,[1] Stacey Abbott ponders about the relationship between modernity and one of the first cinematic monsters, Dracula: "Dracula represents how the modern world's desire for progress in science, business, and technology, sows the seeds to its own destruction, not in favor of the primitive but in favor of modernity itself."[2] Following her discussion of Bram Stoker's foundational *Dracula* as well as some classic vampire films such as Tod Browning's eponymous production,[3] as well as F. W. Murnau's *Nosferatu*,[4] Abbott's argument underlines that the vampire figure actually embodies the experience of modernity: indeed, Count Dracula relocates to London, the urban and buzzing modern space *par excellence* and, as he faces rational and professional methods of vampire hunting "to coordinate and compartimentalize the vampire hunters' investigation, as well as the vampire itself," the undead Transylvanian aristocrat succeeds in avoiding "categorization, just as he defies nineteenth-century concepts of time, gravity, and physics."[5]

Despite the relevance of Abbott's main line of argument in relation to feature films such as George Romero's *Martin*,[6] the *Blade* triptych,[7] as well as the recent vampiric blockbuster *Daybreakers*,[8] the most successful vampire films of the new millennium, *Twilight*,[9] *New Moon*,[10] and *Eclipse*[11] may seem at first resistant to Abbott's take on cinematic vampires. If, as Abbott states by drawing from authors such as Marshall Berman, modernity is based on destruction and rebirth and does suggest "a cycle of recreation, each fleeting moment replaced by the next,"[12] one can wonder about the meaning(s) of Stephenie Meyer's conservative and nostalgic undeads: the take on both sexuality and the place of the female character in a male-dominated world is undeniably conservative and symptomatic of Meyer's religious beliefs (she is a Mormon). However, it is interesting to note that the "liberal moral panic" that accompanied the films' critical reception prevented film critics from addressing in depth the particular nature of the *Twilight* cycle's God-believer, vegetarian undeads, a critical gap that we will attempt to fill in in the following pages.

The three films[13] based on Stephanie Meyer's chaste teenage novels have indeed been perceived as ideologically backward by many an academic and film critic, the vast majority of whom focused on Bella's virginity[14] and her unsatisfied sexual longings for her no-sex-before-marriage beau, Edward Cullens.[15] For example, Manohla Dargis points at Stephanie Meyer's retrograde suggestion "that there actually is something worse than death, especially for teenagers: sex,"[16] whereas Christine Seifert stresses that "the *Twilight* series has created a surprisingly new sub-genre of teen romance: it's abstinence porn, sensational, erotic, and titillating."[17] Marche[18] underlines that the *Twilight* saga contributes to the creation of a safe space for young females: "vampire fiction for young women is the equivalent of lesbian porn for men; both create an atmosphere of sexual abandon that is nonthreatening."[19] In contrast, Alison Happel and Jennifer Esposito[20] regret the sexualization of violence in the first opus, whereas film critic Jean-Marc Lalanne interestingly interprets the lack of sexual activity less as the effect of a "puritanical pro-abstinence manifesto" than a symptom of *Twilight*'s main pattern: *interruption* (interruption of the narrative justified by a sequel; interruption of the vampiric story to the benefit of the teenage love story; interruption of sexual fondling at the "right" time). Lalanne concludes: "the film plays with fire, it does not keep its promises but keeps promising more, having fun with the mechanism of desire itself. And what the film makes come true may be a young maiden's dream: never-ending indulgence into foreplay,"[21] a point[22] also made by Yabroff: "it's not the vampire's passion that is sexy, but its self-control."[23]

Only a small minority of reviewers have, however, attempted to discuss the *Twilight* vampire figure. In a virulent article condemning the progressive normalization of cinematic vampires,[24] Charles Brooker provocatively mentions the first opus's "disgraceful necro-bestiality theme" and concludes with an unequivocal "*Twilight*? Pisslight, more like."[25] Dargis is another rare film reviewer to ponder about the cinematic portrayal of Meyer's vampires: "the problem ... is that a vampire who doesn't ravish young girls or at least scarily nuzzle their flesh isn't much of a vampire or much of an interesting character ..."[26] What are, then, the meaning(s) and the originality of the *Twilight* vampires? What is, from Stacey Abbott's perspective (our main focus here), their participation into post-modernity?[27]

As I will argue throughout the following pages, *Twilight*, *Eclipse*, and *New Moon* entertain a relation to post-modernity that is contradictory and several-fold. The narrative of the *Twilight* saga is partly based on the structuring and sought-after absence (and repression) of mostly female sexuality, consequently creating a division between characters along specific lines: the eroticization of the female body vs. male erotophobia; female submissiveness and abjection vs. male agency/hyper-modern surveillance. The repression of sexuality and vampirism being here the two sides of the same coin, the two will be discussed concomitantly; attention will be first given to the conservative domestication of the *Twilight* vampires. More subversive, however, is the vampire's role in the constant control and monitoring of the female body, represented as a threat to social and sexual order: the *Twilight* conservative vampire (something of an oxymoron) constitutes and enacts rhizomatic surveillance networks and warfare-like practices, resulting, on the one hand, in a "docilization" and an intense abjection of the desiring female body and, on the other hand, an ambiguous, if not monstrous, post-modernity.

The *Twilight* film saga is told from its wide-eyed heroine's perspective, the 17-year-old Bella Swan, and relies heavily on polarized and dichotomized representations. The saga deals with three communities that co-habit in Forks, Washington: that of humans (which is not aware of the existence of the other two), that of vampires, and that of werewolves. Focus is mostly on the human heroine's love dilemma: as a gothic character (a "divided [product] of both reason and desire"),[28] the young Bella entertains exacerbated feelings for the classy vampire Edward, and later for her beefy werewolf friend, Jacob Black.[29] Some screen time is also given to her two contenders' rivalry (the Cullens' and the Blacks' relationship is one of ancestral animosity) and eventual reluctant collaboration: first chased by the "tracker" James,[30] a particularly ferocious vampire eventually killed by Edward towards the end of *Twilight*, Bella is then pursued by James's vindictive companion (*Eclipse*), an exceptionally fast and strong vampire named Victoria.[31] The unlikely Cullens–Blacks alliance helps Edward defeat Victoria in *New Moon*, and Bella eventually chooses Edward over Jacob.

The three films are indeed superficially dualistic as, from the first opus, several clear-cut dichotomies are activated, such dyads being symptomatic of the saga's conflicting themes: nature vs. culture, the former being mostly represented by sexual urges and the latter by erotophobia (conventionally defined as fear/disgust of sex or negative attitudes about sex) and self-improvement via sexual abstinence. Oppositions are prosaically conveyed through the characters' names, physical characteristics, and wardrobe: Bella Swan's name and surname, for example, convey a sense of classical European romanticism and conventional purity, and simplistically contrast with those of her good friend and contender, Jacob Black. The latter, one of the Native American shapeshifters, is by far the most sensuous beings of the whole saga (his impressive muscular torso being obsessively objectified by a lingering camera); he is also partly characterized by his high body temperature (as well as, rather awkwardly, his canine smell), whereas Edward and the other Cullens, also known as the Cold Ones, sport a streamlined and desensualizing wardrobe. In addition, the Blacks and the Cullens belong to opposite social classes. As an ethnic minority, the Blacks are repetitively identified with a disadvantaged, popular class, whereas the Cullens are represented through an accumulation of middle-class signifiers related to social and material success: expensive cars, tasteful clothes, and an impressive residence. Finally, the Cullens are repeatedly shown at school and in their tasteful homes, whereas Jacob and the other members of the Black clan are identified with nature, animality, and physical performance.

Oppositions between characters are often determined by their respective sensuality and potential sexuality, and also structure the overall saga's narrative. For example, a crucial distinction is made between different types of vampire through an uninspired opposition between good and evil and their respective alignment with, on the one hand, abstinence (addressed through a vegetarianism metaphor) and, on the other hand, sexuality (with which a parallel with human blood consumption is made). The Cullen family are vegetarians, that is, they are "virtuous" vampires who refuse to hunt humans to quench their thirst for blood and opt for animals instead: "good" vampires. In contrast, the three vampires Victoria, James, and Laurent[32] are "bad" vampires who embrace their murderous impulses instead of fighting them off. The respective goodness and badness of the Cullens and their carnivorous counterparts is inscribed in their very physique and fashion: indeed, the Cullens all seem to have been taken out of the glossy covers of trendy magazines. Their airbrushed appearance, however, does not exude sexuality, the latter being "neutralized" by their streamlined—if not sterilized—image. In contrast, Victoria, James, and Laurent's ooze sensuality and sex appeal, which are indicative of their potential danger. The first encounter between the God-believing Cullens and their carnivorous counterparts is a telling example of the Good/abstinence vs. Evil/sexuality conflict taking place throughout the whole saga: while Edward and his family are nicely dressed for a rather impressive cricket game, Victoria, James, and Laurent show much confidence as well as a little bit of skin: the three characters are objectified as sexual beings, their sensuous walk and their youthful, sexy dress sense underlined by a wide shot filmed in slow motion. The hyper-masculine Laurent shows off rather impressive abdominal muscles, whereas James's denim outfit à la James Dean and Victoria's furry shawl-like top suggest sensuousness and tactile pleasure.[33] In comparison, Bella is characterized by her gender-neutral sense of dressing and her general physical clumsiness (as opposed to the vampires' exceptional dexterity and speed and the werewolves' uncanny physical strength).

Taming vampires

The desexualization of Meyer's good vampires goes hand in hand with their own de-queering and their chaste heterosexualization. Since the first literary and cinematic days of Western vampires (and by extension many other monsters), homoerotic innuendos have been almost unavoidable[34] and the undeads' queer quality (that is, in the Butlerian sense, their potential subversion of conventional identity/sexual categories and politics) has been equally present. Throughout *Twilight*, *Eclipse*, and *New Moon* the good vampires are, however, presented as normalized, domesticated beings: some of the cinematic vampires' non-human characteristics (such as shapeshifting powers) and queer quality, commonly found in many a vampire films, are here reduced to a timid subtext.[35] However, rather surprisingly and ironically, the *Twilight* good vampires embody traditional family values and illustrate the conservative belief according to which, as queer activist Michael Warner states, "heterosexual desire, dating, marriage, reproduction, childrearing, and home life are not only valuable to themselves, but the bedrock on which every value in the world rests."[36]

Once gothic figures thriving on transgression, the vampires in the *Twilight* saga now attempt to forbid the very possibility of boundary-crossing or, in other words, abjection (Julia Kristeva defines abjection as something that disturbs and perturbs "an identity, a system, an order, what does not respect limits, places, rules").[37] Here, the vampires are polite, gregarious, and family-oriented, and work hard at controlling their own sexual/predatory impulses. They also manifest a varying degree of self-acceptance and self-hatred (or, from a Kristevian perspective, self-abjection). Their experience of vampirism is a problematic one: the *Twilight* vampires often equal their own undeadness with solitude and are very aware and wary of the danger that their vampiric nature represents to humans. Hence the vampires' never-ending quest for self-improvement, that is their desired permanent transcendence of their fundamental thirst for human blood (in other words, of their monstrosity).

Meyer's undeads do possess the fundamental characteristics of traditional vampires (undead creatures with a contagious bite who feed on human blood)[38] but their ambivalence toward their own vampirism translates into the reconfiguration of the vampiric body and functions. In contrast with the vast majority of cinematic portrayals of vampires (ranging from Hammer Horror productions of the 1950s and 1960s to more recent feature films such as *Daybreakers*, as well as the HBO series *True Blood*), the *Twilight* vampires are, as previously mentioned, deprived of their traditional manifestation of the vampiric phallus (retractable fangs), which is here crucially transferred to their quasi-reptilian, fixating gaze. Also, sunlight, which, in the 1960s, "began to replace the increasingly problematic cross as authorized antivampire weapon,"[39] is no longer synonymous with destruction, whereas, in many a vampire film, it remains the main threat to vampires' survival: for example, in *Near Dark*[40] as well as John Carpenter's awkward western-inflected *Vampires*,[41] the incompatibility between sunlight and vampirism result in the sudden conflagration and explosion of the vampiric body. In the *Twilight* saga, sunlight does not affect Edward's well-being but, on the contrary, graphically conveys the vampire's otherworldly attractiveness and superiority: under the sun, Edward glitters and shimmers like a piece of jewelry, direct sunlight revealing the vampire's inner saint-like quality. Consequently, coffins, the morbid lightproof receptacle essential for any traditional vampire's good-day's sleep, are obsolete and the draughty Gothic castle inhabited by a solitary fanged aristocrat is replaced by an elegantly decorated, large-windowed residence that houses the whole Cullen coven. Garlic and mirrors are as unproblematic as sunlight, and religious symbols have no effect on Meyer's vampiric creatures as the latter are, rather intriguingly, for once unwelcome manifestations of the Devil,[42] God-believers.[43] In sum, the Cullens embody a different species of vampires, the good and virtuous vampires with a conscience (as opposed to sexualized vampires as well as to ethnic, shirtless shapeshifters).

Twilight's human and vampiric protagonists embody conflicting attitudes toward sexual instincts and longings, a fact that, as previously mentioned, was underlined by the vast majority of film reviewers: Bella—"irrevocably" as she states—falls in love with the attractive Edward, whose name and British physique evoke an exotic and subtle charm slightly at odds with North American canons of virile, hegemonic masculinity. Quickly surrendering to the handsome vampire's magnetic charm, Bella quickly loses the control of her own emotions and surrenders to Edward, who is adamant about keeping the burgeoning relationship safe (that is, sexless).

Sexual intercourse seems to represent the ultimate test to the vampire's self-restraint: for Edward, sexuality before marriage is aligned with potential danger and death; it is thus "natural" that chastity becomes the *sine qua non* for Bella and Edward's (safe) relationship. Bella is indeed abjected by Edward at his reaction of virtual disgust when, in an early scene, Edward is deeply disturbed by Bella's seductive smell—the potential trigger of the vampire's murderous instincts—and runs away from the stunned girl at the first opportunity. In sum, Edward appears as a normalized and normalizing figure whose most salient vampiric features are smoothed over (from Fredric Jameson's post-modern perspective, Edward and his safe undead counterparts can be described as simulacra[44] of vampires): throughout the saga, Edward's monstrous otherness is virtually eradicated and passed on to Bella, an eroticized girl who threatens to disrupt the social and sexual order within the polite community of Forks.

Such a normalization of the vampire is enhanced by the fact that the vampire family unit in Meyer's saga is utterly desirable and attractive to Bella. It provides her with solace and protection, something that she does not seem able to find in her own fragmented biological family: "through divorce, the family unit is irreparably fractured and as such the deconstructed family is coded as dangerous not only within the Mormon faith but also within the *Twilight* narrative …"[45] The Cullens go to lengths to perform their human-ness and opt for patriarchal gender role attribution. In the case of Edward, however, pretending to be a real human being means aping human males by reaffirming a stereotypical, that is hegemonic, masculinity: "Edward represents a condition that I term supernatural masculinity in drag … He mimics the human male with his clothing, protector role, self-control and rationality despite being a vampire with heightened abilities. He is a vampire in human clothing, a supernatural macho-man in drag."[46]

Taming the maiden

The vampire's performance of hegemonic masculinity and his domestication go hand in hand with Edward's reiterated desire for control of both one's inner nature and seemingly undesirable or even frightening female emotions and sexuality. More precisely, Edward, together with the Cullen coven, embodies hyper-modern surveillance, conventionally defined as "a collection and processing of personal data, whether identifiable or not, for the purposes of influencing or managing those whose data have been garnered."[47] Crucially, the object of Edward's relentless control and observation is Bella's desiring body. As the target of Edward's coercion and power, this young body is successfully tamed and made docile, the docile body being one that "may be subjected, used, transformed and improved."[48] This also partly means that the signification of the body is changing from the supposed source of (sensual) authenticity to a malleable material transformed by reiterated male acts of volition.

The taming of the maiden through surveillance is mostly enacted by Edward: his ambiguous corporeality and un-deadness, by connecting a reactionary past with a discipline/surveillance-inclined hyper-modern present, allows the vampire to impose sets of—as Bella herself states—"ancient" or "old school" regulatory precepts to which the young girl, however, unhesitatingly subjects herself to. Edward's physical ubiquity does suggest a parallel with ever-present new media and surveillance technologies.[49] As predators, the *Twilight* vampires possess exceptionally sharp senses and superior physical abilities, characterized by inhuman speed and strength. Such faculties allow the Cold Ones to survey and monitor their territory as well as develop warfare-like strategies to enact both their own members' control and their protection (mostly Bella's). Thanks to his mind-reading gift doubled with his uncanny speed, Edward embodies the ubiquity of hyper-modern surveillance technology such as CCTV, and such an obsession for surveillance takes several forms throughout the saga: it can be of a military/disciplinary nature as well as have psychological abusive (if not perverse) undertones, but is always at the service of an obsessive male desire for social order through the control of female sexuality.

In the *Twilight* saga, the desire for order and control takes the form of complex, non-linear networks of surveillance or, more precisely, rhizomatic assemblages of surveillance and observation viewpoints. Gilles Deleuze and Félix Guattari have defined a rhizome as being partly characterized by multiplicity as well as principles of connection and heterogeneity: a rhizome has no beginning, nor end, it is always in the middle, the intermezzo, and "any point of a rhizome can be—and must be—connected with any other."[50] For the authors, rhizomes do not follow hierarchical subordination or classification; rather, a rhizome has no center, it can affect or influence any other, regardless of the actual position of the rhizome in question. It is characterized by diversity and multiplicity. Animals in their pack forms, such as rats, Deleuze and Guattari add, can be rhizomes. So can their burrows, "in their functions of shelter, supply, motion, avoidance and break-out."[51]

The *Twilight* vampires can indeed be read as rhizomatic metaphors; they constitute an efficient and omniscient system of surveillance in which heterogeneous elements are constantly connected to each other. Although the Cullens are depicted as a traditional, heterosexual family with a seemingly dominant member (Carlisle, the "father"), there is no hierarchy as such within the surveillance network as enacted by the vampires. Multiplicity, one of the basic characteristics of rhizomes, is illustrated by the multiple surveillance points enacted by a single character. For example, in *Twilight*, Bella quickly realizes that Edward's many idiosyncrasies (changing mood and eye color, hypersensitivity to specific smells, aloofness and frequent absences, to name a few) are actual manifestations of his vampirism. Following a conversation in the forest between Edward and his human sweetheart, Bella confronts Edward, who eventually "comes out" as a vampire. In order to graphically show the young girl his physical power and the potential danger that he represents to humans (one must not forget the vampire's self-loathing), the vampire literally performs his predatory nature by enacting some of his vampiric tricks: using both his strength and unnatural speed, Edward repeatedly jumps from rocks to trees and from trees to rocks, swirling around Bella, whose glance is unable to catch or follow Edward's eerie fast motion. Thus, by eluding human observation, the vampire can multiply possibilities of surveillance and observation viewpoints: he can read minds from a distance and simultaneously adopt different surveillance points thanks to his high-speed displacement.

When enhanced by danger, Bella's seemingly uncontrollable emotions triggers Edward's own surveillance instinct from a distance. In *Twilight*, the young girl finds herself surrounded by bad, harassing boys. Edward, whose powers are reminiscent of object-detection systems such as radar, is quick to emerge from the depth of the night to rescue his endangered sweetheart: having heard from a distance the thoughts of the aggressors, Edward is able to sense imminent danger (the latter has obvious sexual undertones, as the vampire hints at by suggesting the very nature of the boys' intention—another nod at sexuality as a dangerous and sleazy activity). In *New Moon*, during a speeding motorcycle scene in which a depressed Bella plays with her own physical safety, Edward's face flashes several times to her like a pop-up window, suggesting that, not unlike technological devices destined to street surveillance and direct individual communication, Edward is invisible, omnipresent, and unavoidable all at once.

Although the *Twilight* vampires do not possess any shapeshifting powers, they none the less have other supernatural gifts, some of which can be read as metaphors for science and warfare technology. The juvenile-looking Jane,[52] a feared member of the Italy-based Volturi coven (an unintentionally amusing clan of red-eyed vampires with British accents), has the ability to provoke strong, paralysing pains from a distance just by staring at her chosen target. Jane's powers are, on the one hand, symptomatic of direct-energy/electroshock weapons such as stun guns (and, by extension, projectile-free weaponry such as bacteriological warfare); on the other hand, the seemingly gratuitous physical ordeal endured by Jane's various victims is debatably reminiscent of the attempted trivialization and normalization of the post-9/11 pro-torture discourse in both America and Great Britain. For the merciless Jane, the vampiric end justifies the inhuman means.

Edward's "sister," Alice[53] is a clairvoyant: an enhancement of the premonitions that she used to experience as a human, her gift allows the vampire Alice to predict events that derive from a concrete decision/action. Thus, Alice's gift represents rational probability/deduction-based scientific reasoning and gives her an agency that other female characters are deprived of. Indeed, Alice is goal-and action-oriented, an efficient Cold One whose predictions usually lead to minute planning and strategy building. As a telepath, Edward can conveniently read minds from a distance, a hint at remote espionage and surveillance technologies such as listening devices and the interception of electronically messages. Rather mysteriously, Bella is immune to Edward's powers (as well as Jane's); as virtual radar, Edward cannot read, nor control, the girl's mind; this partly justifies the vampire's decision—and his seemingly unquestioned right—to intensify his unflagging scrutiny of Bella.

Deleuze and Guattari's concept of the rhizome becomes particularly relevant as the military and disciplinary metaphor reaches its peak in *Eclipse*. The saga's third opus illustrates the establishment of complex, non-linear surveillance points, each vampire and shapeshifter embodying a rhizome constantly connected with any other by exchanging specific data with each other (thus illustrating another essential characteristic of the rhizome: interconnectedness). *Eclipse* offers much screen time to the Cullens' and the Blacks' quasi-military preparation for the trilogy's main face-off. Victoria is setting up an army of new-born vampires, renowned for their exceptional energy and mercilessness, in order to defy the Cullens and eventually avenge her partner's death by killing Bella. This triggers off a whole series of (re)actions on behalf of the vampires and the werewolves. Alice succeeds in foreseeing Victoria's plan, which allows the Cullens and the Blacks to create their own resistance group. Jasper,[54] one of the Cullens, worked as a new-born trainer in the past and can now transmit his knowledge. By gathering information from a distance without being seen by those she is observing, Alice acts as a strategist and fulfills tasks similar to these of remote spying devices and technologies, such as spy radars. Edward's telepathic prowess is also put to good use during the fight against Victoria's enraged new-borns; Edward coordinates the efforts of both the werewolves and the Cullens by scanning the new-borns' minds from a distance and verbally transmitting their thoughts. A vampire in the intermezzo, he acts as a liaison officer, a transmitter, and a translator all at once, whereas the pack of werewolves and the remaining Cullens are foot soldiers. In sum, the vampiric body acts as the extension of advanced warfare technology, the latter being at the service of the virginal body's control and protection.

Deleuze and Guattari's rhizome aims at challenging ideas of hierarchical categorizations, and although, as previously shown, the Cullens themselves can be interpreted as rhizomatic elements of a surveillance network, one can none the less argue that Edward's physical omnipresence and unfaltering surveillance gaze is related to the central precept of the Panopticon, which relies heavily, on the one hand, on a predominant, hierarchical viewpoint and, on the other hand, on behavioral normalization and disciplinary observation originating from suspicion and social/personal control made possible by an ever-present regulatory look:

> ... no need for weapons, physical violence or material constraints. Just a look. A look that observes and that we, by feeling its weight on us, will end up internalizing to the point of self-observation; this way everybody will enact such a surveillance against and on themselves.[55]

In Meyer's saga, such an unflinching surveillance discreetly imposes itself against individuals' will. Edward's scrutiny of female behavior sometimes acquires abusive undertones. The vampire sometimes enters Bella's bedroom at night, without the young girl's consent or knowledge, in order to observe her in sleep, subjecting her to his piercing gaze; the discretion of the Panopticon system (either as "an actual architecture expressed in stone and cement" or "as an ideal, a metaphor and a set of practices")[56] is here central, and resistance to Edward's gaze is not possible: "the more stringent and rigorous the panoptic regime, the more it generates active resistance, whereas the more soft and subtle the panoptic strategies, the more it produces the desired docile bodies."[57] Such an omnipresence/invisibility duality, together with unwanted and obsessive attention (or, in other words, stalking) suggest Bella's objectification and progressive "docilization"; this is all the more problematic as Bella, when finally made aware of Edward's surveillance, obediently accepts the vampire's unsolicited nocturnal visits in her most vulnerable state and her most private environment.

A monstrous post-modernity?

In sum, *Twilight*, *Eclipse*, and *New Moon* almost obsessively promote sexual chastity through a good/safe/chaste/male vs. bad/dangerous/sexual/female dichotomy. Bella is indeed simultaneously defined as the saga's desiring subject and a physically awkward teenager, a conflation that results in the "natural" necessity to look after the heroine and the subsequent intervention of her dominating boyfriend. Sexuality is is here constantly equated with danger,[58] and, given Bella's reiterated sexual and physical inappropriateness, rescue can only come in the form of the young girl's antithesis: exceptionally strong male vampires who constitute efficient, rhizomatic assemblages of surveillance, which, from Stacey Abbott's perspective—my main guide in this brief journey through the cold territory of Cullenland—encapsulate the characteristics of ubiquitous new media and advanced surveillance technologies. Dedicated to the constant monitoring of the desiring female body, such surveillance eventually takes a military and disciplinary form during the physical confrontation between good/chaste and bad/sexualized vampires in *New Moon*; it also acquires abusive and manipulative undertones as Bella's nocturnal privacy is repeatedly submitted to Edward's powerful surveillance gaze.

A critical reading of the *Twilight* vampire figure as a metaphor for hyper-modern surveillance can problematize our understanding of both Jamesonian post-modernity and the place of the female character within Meyer's saga. Not unlike many pre-1960s vampires,[59] the Cullens and particularly Edward entertain an ambivalent relation to the present and the past: they embody and enact the contemporary culture of (self)surveillance by nostalgically reconnecting with the past as well as maintaining social and familial order. The *Twilight* vampire is indeed torn between two different temporalities: the early, modern twentieth century—during which Edward was born, and whose values and social practices he almost desperately clings to—and the early twenty-first century. Not unlike the two-faced god Janus, the vampire figure is torn between opposite temporalities: he looks at both the past and the future simultaneously, but unlike the ancient roman divinity—the god of beginnings and transitions—the vampire figure strives for fixity and determinism through the control of the desiring heroine. By embodying hyper-modern surveillance and constantly and consistently monitoring the heroine, Edward succeeds in altering the young girl's behavior and consequently remaining connected with a conservative and idealized past, one where, from the vampire's perspective, female obedience and subordination were *de rigueur*. Both conservative in his values and forward in his actions, the vampire embodies an ambiguous, if not monstrous, post-modernity: contrasting with Jameson's post-modern theory,[60] the post-modernity of the *Twilight* saga suggests less a schizophrenic experience of time than a "reversal" of the modern progress-based experience. The latter relies, as mentioned in the introduction, on one fleeting moment being replaced by the next. In the context of Meyer's trilogy, however, such progress paradoxically consists in Edward's almost desperate attempt to re-root himself in a bygone era. In sum, instead of moving forward, the vapid vampire attempts to head towards the past.

The main beneficiary of the rhizomatic networks of surveillance is Edward, the normalized vampire (or rather, the simulacrum of a vampire) who has eyes—literally—only for his human sweetheart, who is repeatedly abjected by her beloved undead. Bella is depicted as the saga's real monster who, as a desiring but desexualized female subject, is always about to cross boundaries,[61] sexuality being a no-go zone for any self-respecting vampire. Neverendingly contained in her role of the inadequate and therefore dangerous protagonist, the heroine shifts from the status of the wide-eyed, teenage girl in search of eternal love to the tamed and infantilized object of vampiric desire: Bella lacks rationality and agency,[62] whereas male characters, vampires and humans alike (Bella's father is the local sheriff), represent authority and wisdom.

Such passivity does not turn Bella into a sexual object but, rather, into the ideal target of Edward's unflinching surveillance gaze. In her seminal essay "Visual Pleasure and Narrative Cinema," Laura Mulvey argues that, in a mostly androcentric world, "pleasure in looking has been split between active/male and passive/female. The determining male gaze projects its fantasy onto the female figure, accordingly."[63] However, the *Twilight* female protagonist is less defined by her *to-be-looked-at-ness*[64] than her *to-be-spied-on-ness*: constantly de-eroticized by her controlling vampiric boyfriend but also de-feminized by a gender-neutral wardrobe, Bella is not quite a sexual being objectified by the male gaze, but a dehumanized, Orwellian individual dominated by her death drive and pinned down by a quasi-mechanical, hyper-modern gaze. Although central to the narrative, Bella is a non-character, omnipresent and invisible at the same time, an empty shell of an agency-less woman whose vacuity can only be compensated for by an all-dominant, ever-present male lover.

In the saga's fourth installment, *Breaking Dawn, Part I*, Edward and Bella tie the knot and quickly become expecting parents. Bella's pregnancy, however, proves to be horrendously difficult as the exceptionally strong fetus threatens to crush the mother from the inside, indicating that, as the saga's authentic monster, the young woman is mostly defined in terms of her repro-ductive functions as well as being abjectly aligned with mothering.[65] But this is another story. Or is it?

Notes

1 Stacey Abbott (Austin: University of Texas Press, 2007).

2 Ibid., 40.

3 1931.

4 1923.

5 Abbott, 17.

6 1973.

7 The triptych is made up of *Blade* (David S. Goyer, 1998), *Blade II* (Guillermo del Toro, 2002), and *Blade Trinity* (David S. Goyer, 2004).

8 Michael and Peter Spierig, 2009.

9 Catherine Harwicke, 2008.

10 Chris Weitz, 2009.

11 David Slade, 2010.

12 Abbott, 5–6.

13 *Breaking Dawn, Part 1* (Bill Condon, 2011) is not included in my film corpus as the saga's fourth opus focuses much less on the vampiric figure as surveillance metaphor than on the extreme abjection of the female character via her monstrous maternity.

14 Interpreted by Kristin Stewart.

15 Interpreted by Robert Pattinson.

16 Manohla Dargis, "The Love That Dare Not Bare Its Fangs," *The New York Times*, November 20, 2008, http://movies.nytimes.com/2008/11/21/movies/21twil.html (accessed June 1, 2011).

17 Christine Seifert, "Bite Me (or Don't)," *Bitch*, 42 (2009): 23.

18 Other reviewers expressed their doubts regarding the overall artistic quality of the films: "I can't comment on the acting because I didn't catch Pattinson, Stewart and Lautner doing any … You can almost hear the young cast thinking 'is that acting? It looks hard'" (Peter Travers, "*New Moon*," *Rolling Stone*, November 19, 2009, http://www.rollingstone.com/movies/reviews/new-moon-20091119 (accessed June 1, 2011)). See also Sarah O'Hara: "… if you buy into the central romance, you'll laugh, you'll cry, you'll swoon. Otherwise, the lingering glances, lip-chewing and regular de-shirting may cause uncontrollable giggles" (Helen O'Hara, "*Twilight: New Moon*," *Empire*, http://www.empireonline.com/reviews/reviewcomplete.asp?FID=135861 (accessed June 1, 2011)).

19 Stephen Marche, "What's *Really* Going on With all These Vampires," *Esquire*, October 13, 2009, http://www.esquire.com/features/thousand-words-on-culture/vampires-gay-men-1109 (accessed June 1, 2011).

20 Alison Harpel and Jennifer Esposito, "Vampires. Vixens and Feminists: An Analysis of *Twilight*," *Educational Studies*, 46 (2010): 529–31.

21 Jean-Marc Lalanne, "*Twilight* chapitre 2: la tentation," *Les Inrockuptibles*, November 16, 2009, http://www.lesinrocks.com/cine/cinema-article/t/41528/date/2009-11-16/article/twilight-chapitre-2-la-tentation (accessed June 3, 2011).

22 See also Melissa Rosenberg (screenwriter of both *Twilight* and *New Moon*) in Vognar, "*Twilight, True Blood* Take Opposing Approaches to Vampire Sex":

"... anticipating the act is more tantalizing than actually seeing it, and more erotic" (Chris Vognar, "*Twilight, True Blood* Take Opposing Approaches to Vampire Sex," *Dallas News*, November 23, 2009, http://www.dallasnews.com/entertainment/columnists/chris-vognar/20091121-Twilight-True-2790.ece (accessed June 6, 2011)).

23 Jennie Yabroff, "A Bit Long in the Tooth," *Newsweek*. December 5, 2008, http://www.thedailybeast.com/newsweek/2008/12/05/a-bit-long-in-the-tooth.html (accessed June 3, 2011).

24 "Early vampires were stiff and aloof, with a cold sexual intent which was, at the very least, slightly creepy. Now they've got bloody feelings. They're lonely and tortured and all messed up inside. They spend more time staring at their shoes than killing people" (Charles Brooker, "*Twilight*'s Sulky Vampires are Less Frightening than a Knitted Cushion," *Guardian*, July 12, 2010, http://www.guardian.co.uk/commentisfree/2010/jul/12/charlie-booker-twilights-unscary-monsters (accessed June 1, 2011).

25 Brooker, "*Twilight*'s Sulky Vampires."

26 Manohla Dargis, 2009. "Abstinence Makes the Heart Go … Oh, You Know," *The New York Times*. November 19, 2009, http://movies.nytimes.com/2009/11/20/movies/20twilightnewmoon.html (accessed June 1, 2011).

27 A controversial term/concept notoriously difficult to pinpoint, post-modernity (also known as the post-modern condition) can first be bluntly, if not tautologically, defined as the period of time after modernity. For example, for French intellectual Jean-François Lyotard, post-modernity refers, among other things, to "incredulity towards metanarratives," such as Marxism ("Answering the Question: What is Post-Modernism?" in *The Post-Modern Reader*, (ed.) Charles Jencks (London: Wiley, 2011), 39), whereas Elizabeth Deeds Ermarth identifies the reformulation of time (termed "rhythmic time," which she opposes to "historical temporality") as a central characteristic of the post-modern (*Sequel To History: Post-Modernism and The Crisis of Representational Time* (Princeton: Princeton University Press, 1992)). My use of the term "post-modernity" in this chapter follows Fredric Jameson's definition. According to the latter, modernity is made up of five salient characteristics: a blurring between high and low culture; the advent of new technologies symptomatic of a new world order; "a new depthlessness, which finds its prolongation both in contemporary 'theory' and in a whole new culture of the image or the simulacrum" (Fredric Jameson, *Post-modernism or the Cultural Logic of Late Capitalism* (Durham: Duke University Press, 1991), 6); affectlessness that, together with depthlessness, is counterbalanced by schizophrenic-like moments of intense emotions termed "intensities" (ibid. This aspect of post-modernity together with the blurring of high and low culture has little relevance in the *Twilight* narrative and therefore will not be discussed); and crucially a weakening of historicity that, not unlike the experience of a schizophrenic, results in "a series of pure and unrelated presents in time" (Jameson, 27). More precisely, post-modernity relies on a questioning of totalizing truths of modernity, but as these are not replaced, individuals are left with the obsolete referent of such truths and their contemplation of the latter. Such a radical

challenge to subjects' perception of objects echoes, according to Jameson, schizophrenia. This by no means is an exhaustive list of definitions.

28 Fred Botting, *Gothic* (London and New York: Routledge, 1996), 12.

29 Interpreted by Taylor Lautner.

30 Interpreted by Cam Gigandet.

31 Interpreted by Rachelle Lefevre in *Twilight* and *Eclipse* and Bryce Dallas Howard in *New Moon*.

32 Interpreted by Edi Gathegi.

33 Geographical locations also allow other dichotomies (South vs. North, light vs. darkness, heat vs. cold, city vs. countryside) to emerge and permeate the narrative: originally from Phoenix, Arizona (the sunniest city in the country and the fifth largest, with almost 1.6 million inhabitants), Bella decides to settle in the small town of Forks, Washington (the rainiest location in the USA), where her father resides.

34 See for example Harry M. Benshoff's *Monsters in the Closet: Homosexuality and the Horror Film* (Manchester and New York: Manchester University Press, 1997) and "The Monster and the Homosexual," in *Queer Cinema: the Film Reader*, (ed.) Harry Benshoff and Sean Griffin (New York and London: Routledge, 2004), 63–74; as well as George E. Haggerty, *Queer Gothic* (Urbana and Chicago: University of Illinois Press, 2006), 185–99.

35 One can detect, in *Twilight*, some same-sex innuendo in the representation of the Native young men who never miss an opportunity to take their tops off and collectively show off their muscular torsos: "It really is incredible how often these boys are to be glimpsed shirtless, and Jacob has stomach muscles so developed he looks like he could pick a pencil using the crevice between his abs … a real macho gym bunny" (Peter Bradshaw, "The *Twilight* Saga: *New Moon*," *Guardian*, November 19, 2009, http://www. guardian.co.uk/film/2009/nov/19/twilight-saga-new-moon-review (accessed June 1, 2011)).

36 Michael Warner, *The Trouble with Normal: Sex, Politics, and the Ethics of Queer Life* (Cambridge: Harvard University Press, 2000), 47.

37 Julia Kristeva, *Pouvoirs de l'horreur: essai sur l'abjection* (Paris: Editions du Seuil, 1980).

38 Jean Marigny, *La Fascination des vampires* (Paris: Klincksieck, 2009).

39 Nina Auerbach, *Our Vampires, Ourselves* (Chicago and London: University of Chicago Press, 1995), 177.

40 Kathryn Bigelow, 1987.

41 1998.

42 In Bram Stoker's *Dracula*, Van Helsing sees the vampire as an agent of the Devil.

43 In the novel, Bella is first surprised to notice the presence of a large cross during her first visit at the Cullens'.

44 A simulacrum is conventionally understood as synonymous of copy or mimesis. In the post-modern context, it is also conceptualized as a copy of a copy that no longer bears a resemblance to an original model. Fredric Jameson uses photorealism to discuss post-modern simulacra.

45 Kirsten Stevens, "Meet the Cullens: Family, Romance and Female Agency in *Buffy the Vampire Slayer* and *Twilight*," *Slayage* 8, no. 1[29] (2010), http://slayageonline.com/essays/slayage29/Stevens.htm (accessed June 3, 2011).

46 Pramod Nayar, "How to Domesticate a Vampire: Gender, Blood Relations and Sexuality in Stephenie Meyer's *Twilight*," *Nebula* 7, no. 3 (2010), 62.

47 David Lyon, *Theorizing Surveillance: the Panopticon and Beyond* (Abingdon: Willan Publishing, 2006), 2.

48 Michel Foucault, *Surveiller et punir* (Paris: Éditions Gallimard, 1998), 160.

49 This echoes directly the centrality of new technologies in post-modernity as underlined by Fredric Jameson. See Jameson's definition of post-modernity in the Introduction.

50 Gilles Deleuze and Félix Guattari, *Mille Plateaux: Capitalisme et schizophrénie* (Paris: Les Éditions de Minuit, 1980), 13.

51 Ibid.

52 Interpreted by Dakota Fanning.

53 Interpreted by Ashley Greene.

54 Interpreted by Jackson Rathbone.

55 Michel Foucault, 1994. "L'œil du pouvoir" in *Dits et écrits*, ed. Daniel Defert and François Ewald (Paris: Gallimard, 1994), 198.

56 Lyon, *Theorizing Surveillance: the Panopticon and Beyond*, 5.

57 Ibid., 4.

58 There are explicit references to rape in *Eclipse*: one of Edward's "sisters," Rosalie, was gang-raped and left for dead until Carlisle brought her to un-life by turning her into a vampire. However, Rosalie's never-ending life is now stamped with self-hatred: "I will always be this: frozen, never moving forward. That's what I miss the most: possibilities."

59 Abbott, 61–72.

60 See note 27.

61 Barbara Creed, *The Monstrous Feminine: Film, Feminism, Psychoanalysis* (London: Routledge, 2011), 11.

62 Bella's lack of agency is indeed bewildering, partly because she motivates one of her female friends to ask a boy out: "take control, you are a strong independent woman."

63 Laura Mulvey, *Visual and Other Pleasures* (Basingstoke and New York: Palgrave, 2009), 19.

64 "In their traditional exhibitionist role women are simultaneously looked at and displayed, with their appearance coded for strong visual and erotic impact so that they can be said to connote *to-be-at-looked-at-ness*" (Ibid.).

65 Creed, 83.

3

Playing alien in post-racial times

Susana Loza

In his essay "Monster Culture: Seven Theses," Jeffrey Jerome Cohen contends that the "monster is born only at [a] metaphoric crossroads, as an embodiment of a certain cultural moment—of a time, a feeling, a place."[1] Monstrous bodies are pure culture, constructs and projections that exist only to be read.[2] However, to say that monsters are "social constructs is not solely to say that they are constructed *by* their social contexts. It is, at the same time, to say that they are constructive *of* their social contexts: that they both *produce* and *reproduce* social discourse and practice."[3] In twenty-first-century America, monsters are more ubiquitous than ever. Aliens, vampires, zombies, werewolves, cyborgs, and ghosts haunt TV, cable, and the silver screen. What do these monstrous bodies, bodies birthed in the aftermath of apartheid and the civil rights movement, tell us about dread and desire of the racial Other? Utilizing an interdisciplinary amalgam of media studies, cultural studies, critical race theory, and post-colonial theory, this chapter will investigate how *District 9* (Blomkamp, 2009)[4] and *Avatar* (Cameron, 2009)[5] employ the figure of the alien to express and manage white fears of invasion, contamination, segregation, miscegenation, and conquest. In both films, the white Self overcomes racial guilt and xenophobia by becoming the alien Other (*Avatar's* Jake Sully trades his disabled white body for a sleek blue Na'vi model and *District 9's* Wikus van der Merwe painfully transforms into an alien after being accidentally dosed with a mysterious black alien substance). While playing alien may be new, racial masquerade is not. As countless scholars remind us,[6] white settlers and conquerors have long used racial drag as a way to simultaneously build and buttress the ever-shifting parameters of whiteness and Western identity. Although *District 9* is ostensibly an allegory about South African apartheid, the film has much to say to Americans, who have their own ignominious history of racial separatism and subjugation, a history that is often sanitized (which might explain why reparations for slavery have never been—and will likely never be—paid).[7] And *Avatar*, which has been derisively dubbed "Dances with Smurfs,"[8] and "Pocahontas in Space,"[9] clearly taps into America's imperialist nostalgia for the noble savages and squaw princesses that we vanquished. So what does the popularity of *District 9* and *Avatar* tell us about the place of race in post-racial America and post-apartheid South Africa? What do the transformations of the protagonists from human to alien convey about the boundaries of contemporary whiteness and colonial consciousness? Do these narratives unsettle the imperial logic of whiteness or reify it? These are the questions I investigate in this chapter. I first consider the pivotal role that minstrelsy and masquerade play in *Avatar* and *District 9* and how these racialized performances reveal that race remains a central concern in both post-racial America and post-apartheid South Africa. This is followed by a discussion about how these films simultaneously embody the fantasies and fears of settlers and concludes by contemplating what playing alien reveals about racism and imperialism today.

Playing Indian on Pandora

Spectacles do all sorts of political work in every society but are especially useful in settler societies because they continue to redirect emotions, histories, and possibilities away from the means of societal and historical production—Indigenous dispossession, disenfranchisement, and containment.

Audra Simpson, "Settlement's Secret"

Set in 2154, *Avatar* tells the story of Jake Sully (Sam Worthington), a white paraplegic ex-Marine, hired by a Halliburton-like corporation to gather intelligence on the Na'vi, the 10-foot-tall, blue-skinned, humanoid residents of Pandora, a lush moon rich in flora, fauna, and an extremely valuable mineral called "unobtainium." For this mission, Sully has been provided with a genetically engineered Na'vi body, or avatar, that his human mind pilots from the safe confines of the RDA Corporation's lab. The alien tribe that he is charged with infiltrating is a "childish pastiche of the 'ethnic',"[10] an "amalgam of noble savage cliché[s]."[11] Their lithe nearly naked blue bodies are clad in vaguely Amerindian loincloths[12] and decorated with Maori tattoos[13] and Maasai-style necklaces and beaded jewelry.[14] Their long, dark hair is adorned with feathers and either worn in mohawks or dreadlocked. On his first foray into the iridescent jungles of Pandora, Sully finds himself stranded overnight and is reluctantly rescued by Neytiri (Zoë Saldaña), the brave and beautiful daughter of a Na'vi chief. After receiving a sign from the Na'vi deity Eywa (Pandora's "Mother of Life") that Sully is a special soul, Neytiri takes him to Hometree, the sacred massive tree that her clan, the Omaticaya, call home. Thus begins Sully's journey from human grunt to alien leader. Neytiri teaches Sully the ways of the Omaticaya: what to eat and drink, how to speak and behave, and how to use his tail to connect and communicate with the animals of Pandora. While she resents her brash pupil at first, she comes to love Sully for his indomitable spirit. And even though she has already been promised to an Omaticayan warrior, Neytiri mates with Sully. Their bliss is cut short by a devastating military incursion using intelligence garnered by Sully. When the Omaticaya learn of Sully's betrayal he is cast out, but his exile is brief. He soon returns riding Toruk, a fearsome flying creature which had only been tamed four times in Pandoran history. Sully rallies the Omaticaya and convinces the other Na'vi clans to go to war against the Sky People (read: humans). The Na'vi are joined in battle by all the sentient beings of Pandora thanks to the networked consciousness of Eywa. The film ends with the Sky People defeated and departing Pandora. In the last scene, Sully uses the Tree of Souls' neural network to upload his human consciousness to his Na'vi avatar.

Despite its futuristic setting and ridiculous amalgamation of every ethnic "Indian and African sacred-cow cliché imaginable,"[15] *Avatar* is clearly a moral re-evaluation of American colonization.[16] It "imaginatively revisits the crime scene of white America's foundational act of genocide, in which entire native tribes and civilizations were wiped out by European immigrants to the American continent."[17] Like its cinematic predecessors[18]—*Dances with Wolves* (Costner, 1990),[19] *The Last of the Mohicans* (Mann, 1992),[20] and *Pocahontas* (Gabriel and Goldberg, 1995)[21]—*Avatar* evokes "sympathetic regret and retro-spective outrage"[22] for the original inhabitants of the Americas. Ironically, the film does so by narrating the experiences of a white male settler-explorer who has, in the words of Marianna Torgovnick, "gone primitive."[23] *Avatar* should thus be seen as an exceedingly popular and lucrative example of playing Indian[24]: "one of the most subtly entrenched, most profound and significant of American performances."[25] Throughout American history, Indian disguise has allowed white settlers "to cross the boundaries of law and civilization while simultaneously reaffirming the existence and necessity of those bound-aries."[26] Playing Indian has allowed European Americans to articulate their "widespread ambivalence about modernity as well as anxieties about the terrible violence marking the nation's origins."[27] This is precisely the narrative that Sully re-enacts in *Avatar;* the only difference is that instead of going native he goes Na'vi. Playing alien absolves Sully of his guilt over his role in the Sky People's genocide of the indigenous population. It allows him to become their white savior.[28] And since *Avatar* is told from Sully's perspective and he provides the "white audiences' point of identification, [the film] also symbolically purges white America of its responsibility for the terrible plights of Native Americans, past and present."[29] The inclusion of Neytiri is an obvious nod to the Pocahontas story, a mainstream American myth that explains to White settlers their right to be here and helps them deal with any lingering guilt about their role in the displacement of the Native inhabitants.[30] This symbolic expiation of settler sins prompted one film critic to designate *Avatar* as "the corniest movie ever made about the white man's need to lose his identity and assuage racial, political, sexual and historical guilt."[31]

In a heavily circulated blog post entitled "When Will White People Stop Making Movies Like *Avatar?*", *io9* editor-in-chief Annalee Newitz pondered the problematic role that swapping racial sides plays in white guilt fantasies:

> To purge their overwhelming sense of guilt, they switch sides, become "race traitors," and fight against their old comrades. But then they go beyond assimilation and become leaders of the people they once oppressed. This is the essence of the white guilt fantasy, laid bare. It's not just a wish to be absolved of the crimes whites have committed against people of color; it's not just a wish to join the side of moral justice in battle. It's a wish to lead people of color from the inside rather than from the (oppressive, white) outside.[32]

It's a wish not to just replicate the alien Others but to replace them. *Avatar* unwittingly reveals that the "living performance of 'playing Indian' by non-Indian peoples [still] depends upon the physical and psychological removal, even the death of real Indians."[33] Sully's deadly and dispossessory desires are most evident when he rallies the Na'vi before the final battle. His speech to them blatantly rehearses the rhetoric of American settler independence: "And we will show the Sky people that they can't take whatever they want! And that this is our land!"[34] Sully declares his independence and stakes a claim to the land. The logic that underpins this claim is manifestly settler colonial.[35] One could argue that psychoanalytically, but also ideologically, Sully is suffering from a colonial condition that Josefa Loshitzky brilliantly terms "native envy."[36] This is not surprising when one recalls that the conceptual core of the Avatar project, designed by the RDA Corporation but executed by anthropologist Dr. Grace Augustine (Sigourney Weaver) and her scientific team, is premised on mimicry, on literally cloning the native.[37]

Avatar rewrites the history of colonization, but it does so from the perspective of the settler. Like playing Indian, becoming alien is premised on a fantasy of appropriation. In *Avatar*, this means the young male hero gets the native princess and the white Western scientist gets access to indigenous ways and wisdom.[38] The film thus remains a fantasy tailored for white subjects "living with a heavy dose of liberal guilt. And it is one that, ultimately, marginalizes indigenous peoples and affirms white supremacy."[39] In the end, *Avatar* teaches us that "the only choice the aborigines have is to be saved by the human beings or be destroyed by them. In other words, they can choose either to be the victim of imperialist reality, or to play their allotted role in the white man's fantasy."[40] Either way, quips conservative pundit David Brooks, the natives are "going to be supporting actors in our journey to self-admiration."[41]

District 9 and the horrors of (becoming) the black Other

Images of "others" do not circulate because of their truthfulness but because they reflect the concerns of the image-producers and-consumers. Some images owe their currency precisely to their distortion of reality, as if they were magical formulae, or talismans in the pathologization of difference.

Jan Nederveen Pieterse, *White on Black: Images of Africa and Blacks in Western Popular Culture*

District 9 begins its story in 2010. It has been almost 30 years since the extraterrestrial refugees shipwrecked their spacecraft over Johannesburg, South Africa. Since their arrival, the aliens have been segregated from the city's human population and consigned to District 9, a barbed-wired enclave brimming with violence, squalor, and crime. White and black South Africans have grown fed up with living so close to the alien refugees, which they pejoratively call "prawns" because of their disgusting resemblance to Parktown Prawns, the huge crickets that infest large parts of Johannesburg. The South African government has contracted with Multinational United (MNU), a shady private security and defense firm, to relocate the aliens to District 10, a concentration camp-like tent city far from the nation's capital. Wikus van der Merwe (Sharlto Copley), a "nebbishy bureaucrat in MNU's Department of Alien Affairs who looks and acts like an Afrikaner version of Michael Scott,"[42] has been placed in charge of the relocation. While serving an eviction notice to an alien given the human name of Christopher Johnson (Jason Cope), and searching his shack for contraband, Wikus stumbles upon a small cylinder filled with alien fuel. He accidentally sprays himself with the black oily substance and thus begins his excruciating metamorphosis from human to alien. When the MNU learns that Wikus's DNA has begun to mutate, they realize that he may be the biological key they need to unlock the powerful alien weaponry that they have been secretly amassing since the aliens landed. Wikus is taken to the MNU's lab, "an underground bunker-cum-biotech facility where a latter-day Dr. Mengele heads an alien dissection-cum-weapons-development program."[43] Wikus is tortured, forced to fire alien weaponry at prawns, and eventually prepared for vivisection. He breaks free and flees to the only place that will accept him: District 9. As the hours pass, Wikus becomes increasingly insectoid. Repulsed, he tries to chop off the black claw that has replaced his hand, but fails. Desperate to reverse his body's transformation, Wikus convinces Christopher to break into the MNU lab to recover the fuel cylinder that will allow the alien to return to his ship to manufacture an antidote before departing Earth. At the lab, Christopher sees the burnt and brutalized bodies of his fellow aliens. He decides that he cannot spare the extra fuel to heal Wikus but needs it to return to his planet for reinforcements. Wikus is furious; he betrays Christopher, leading to their arrest, but then decides to sacrifice himself in hopes that the alien will return in three years and heal him as he promised to do. Wikus provides cover for Christopher, allowing the injured alien to make it back to the stalled ship and escape Earth. Aliens, humans, and Wikus watch in awe as the spacecraft departs. In the last scene of the film, we see that Wikus has become fully alien and is now a permanent resident of District 9.

In his review of *District 9*, Chris Lee observes: "It's impossible not to correlate the aliens' predicament with recent South African history ... [g]iven the film's real-life setting amid Soweto's teeming townships and its segregationist signage."[44] The analogy between the ghettoization of the prawns and the racial discrimination endured by black South Africans under apartheid is quite explicit.[45] The extraterrestrials are assigned human names by the government[46]; they are forced to exist under a "dehumanizing system of surveillance, interrogation, and police brutality"[47]; and this segregation and containment is "perpetuated under the guise of maintaining order and working for the greater good."[48] The film also analogizes what Neill Blomkamp, *District 9*'s white South African writer-director, terms "black on black xenophobia"[49]: specifically, the bloody pogroms of 2009, in which South Africans targeted Zimbabwean, Mozambican, Malawian, and Nigerian migrants seeking to escape war and poverty.[50] In the year prior to the release of *District 9*, black South Africans were charged with murder, rape, and looting "directed at the bodies and belongings of non-South Africans."[51] The survivors of these atrocities were "herded into insanitary, shelter-less camps,"[52] very similar to the grimy ghetto of District 9. The similarity between aliens and migrants is further accentuated through statements made by residents of Johannesburg (which are inserted in the film as interviews to uncover how South Africans truly feel about the foreigners in their midst).[53] The statements are deeply nativistic (the prawns have no understanding of ownership, they steal our wives, the government spends too much money on them but "at least they keep them separate from us")[54] and are drawn from authentic interviews, conducted by Blomkamp while shooting the short film Alive in Joburg (Blomkamp, 2005)[55] that inspired District 9. For that project, Blomkamp solicited black South Africans for their opinions on Zimbabwean and Nigerian refugees.[56] The film also references—and some commentators argue revives[57]—fiercely racist stereotypes about Africans, particularly in its xenophobic depiction of the aliens that reside alongside the aliens: the Nigerians. Led by a sadistic, cannibalistic, partially paralyzed warlord named Obesandjo (Eugene Khumbanyiwa), the Nigerians are cold-blooded thugs who make their living by exploiting the prawns.[58] They sell the aliens overpriced tins of cat food (to which the aliens have become addicted), operate an interspecies prostitution ring, and traffic in alien weaponry.[59] This begs the question, do the racist and xenophobic portrayals in District 9 prove that South Africans are still ensnared in the settler logic of apartheid; or does it demonstrate what they must overcome for racial reconciliation to be possible?

Unsurprisingly, critical opinion remains divided on the subject. Some see Wikus's transformation as a hopeful parable about the nation's reckoning with its racist past: it "evokes the trauma of awakening consciousness and the even more difficult journey toward change and redemption."[60] Others argue that, while District 9 "critiques xenophobia, it ultimately also perpetuates it."[61] But while reviewers acknowledge that the film's damaging portraits of the Nigerians resurrect that tired and tragic figure of colonialist fiction, the African savage, they do not seem to appreciate how Wikus's metamorphosis reworks an equally "politically retrograde trope of imperial romance: the (European) white man 'gone native'."[62] Could it be possible that Wikus's transformation is less radical than it seems and that those Nigerians are more resistant than they appear? Let us consider how Wikus became alien and why the Nigerians remain so.

For Wikus, becoming a black alien is a torturous process filled with pain, fear, disgust, and humiliation. He vomits black bile, sheds teeth and fingernails, weathers weeping wounds on his chest and back, rips hunks of flesh from his body, and craves cat food.[63] His metamorphosis into a humanoid crustacean costs him his job, wife, voice, and dignity.[64] And the process is irreversible. Against his will, Wikus is plunged into the "disenfranchised, vulnerable, impoverished misery of the alien shantytown."[65] MNU and the media make matters worse by reporting that Wikus's transformation has been caused by "prolonged sexual activity" with aliens (his exposure to alien DNA is thus likened to the contraction of a venereal disease).[66] In assuming the prawn's dark carapace, Wikus becomes a sort of interstellar minstrel. But this is a monstrous form of minstrelsy in which the white subject can never cross back. Wikus is trapped in the degraded and threatening body of the black Other. He ruefully learns that one of the purposes of the minstrel's mask is "designating another, politically weaker, less socially acceptable, people as the receptacle for one's own self-disgust, for one's own infantile rebellions, for one's own fears of, and retreats from, reality."[67] Although Wikus's harrowing metamorphosis evokes the pain, sadness, and confusion of confronting the apartheid legacy,[68] the fact that he cannot overcome his racial melancholia is troubling. Indeed, Wikus never stops mourning his human life with his wife or wishing to be "cured" of his alienness.[69] It is therefore difficult to imagine a more nightmarish or less progressive story about becoming alien.[70] But Wikus is not the only alien in *District 9*, nor is he the only misunderstood minstrel. To fully grasp the limitations and radical potentialities of racial simulation,[71] one must consider how the Nigerians perform their blackness for the South African citizens of Johannesburg.

First, let us acknowledge that the racist and xenophobic depictions of the Nigerians in *District 9* obviously correspond with the reprehensible colonial images of Africans ceaselessly churned out by Hollywood. The last decade alone saw the release of *Blood Diamond* (Zwick, 2006),[72] *The Constant Gardener* (Meirelles, 2005),[73] *Hotel Rwanda* (George, 2004),[74] *The Last King of Scotland* (MacDonald, 2006),[75] *Shooting Dogs* (Caton-Jones, 2005),[76] and *Tears of the Sun* (Fuqua, 2003).[77] In "'You Are Not Welcome Here': Post-Apartheid Negrophobia & Real Aliens in Blomkamp's *District 9*," Henriette Gunkel and Christian König propose that instead of fixating on these deplorable depictions we concentrate on how the Nigerian migrants position themselves as outsiders within the South African nation.[78] Gunkel and König suggest that focusing on the process of becoming alien, instead of being alien, opens up …

… the possibility of reading the behavior of the Nigerians as defying assimilation into a society that rejects them. As such, the Nigerians are working against occupying a "profitable and valuable/useful" position within society. They even resist the core morality of contemporary South African society—a morality that seems quite similar to that of the apartheid regime and to which Wikus as well as other decolonized South Africans ... still refer positively—by having sex with aliens and, on top of that, commercial sex. The Nigerians in the film follow their own interests and do not take up a subordinate role in relation to the aliens (although they are able to adapt) and where necessary they work against them.[79]

For the Nigerians, becoming alien means not just assuming the dehumanizing, distorting black mask imposed on Africans and colonized subjects, but flaunting it.[80] In "Of Blackface and Paranoid Knowledge: Richard Wright, Jacques Lacan, and the Ambivalence of Black Minstrelsy," Mikko Tuhkanen postulates that the mask, when "actively deployed, can also denote the racially marked subject's becoming inaccessible to the culture otherwise bent on determining him or her."[81] In other words, "when the oppressed assume categories of degradation in the name of resistance, stand inside them as a place of combat, the categories assumed are invested with novel, resistant, redirected and redirecting significance."[82] By cannily mimicking the savage stereotypes of colonialism,[83] by fomenting disorder and destruction, the Nigerians render themselves inaccessible to the repression and regulation of the South African state.[84] Our unwillingness to recognize this resistance as a legitimate response to oppression reveals our inability to distinguish between what the aliens "are" and what they have become as a result of the conflict with their human hosts.[85] The ferociously stereotypical and deeply essentialist Nigerians of *District 9* unmask the radical potential of minstrelsy and becoming-alien, but they also underline its very real ideological limits. For, as Esther Godfrey reminds us in "'To Be Real': Drag, Minstrelsy and Identity in the New Millennium," true racial liberation demands a "commitment to the subversion of essentialized identities—something we have yet to see fulfilled in this new millennium of race and gender anxieties."[86]

Settler nightmare or settler fantasy?

One could say then, as a general rule, that white misunderstanding, misrepresentation, evasion, and self-deception on matters related to race are among the most pervasive mental phenomena of the past few hundred years, a cognitive and moral economy psychically required for conquest, colonization, and enslavement. And these phenomena are in no way accidental, but prescribed by the terms of the Racial Contract, which requires a certain schedule of structured blindnesses and opacities in order to establish and maintain the white polity.

Charles Mills, *The Racial Contract*

In "*District 9* and *Avatar*: Science Fiction and Settler Colonialism," Lorenzo Veracini submits that it does not matter whether these films are "left- or right-wing," politically progressive or racially regressive, white savior stories or tales of indigenous rebellion, but rather that they reenact "specifically South African and American foundational settler colonial narratives."[87] Both films are about the forcible resettlement of aliens by humans and what happens when aliens refuse to comply with human desires. Both films recount the transformation of a white male human protagonist into an alien. Both narratives climax at the moment when the boundary between human Self and alien Other dissolves. However, as Veracini poetically observes, these are "quite different moments: while the shift is degrading and unwanted in *District 9*, change is regenerative and sought in *Avatar*. Consequently, one movie is about a reality that turns into a nightmare, and the other about a dream that turns into reality."[88] While this is certainly true, I would like to complicate matters by suggesting that *Avatar* can also be read as a settler nightmare and *District 9* can be interpreted as a dream, albeit a dark one. In what remains of this essay, I discuss how these texts embody the racial fears, and the fantasies, of contemporary white subjects.

District 9 is the dark fantasy of pure racial difference that European and American settlers have nurtured since they began colonizing, killing, and displacing the original inhabitants of the territories that they claim as their own. In *District 9*, the aliens represent the Africans that the Dutch had to dispatch and subjugate. By making the aliens look like prawns, Blomkamp implies that black Africans were/are a subhuman species. Intentionally or not, Blomkamp reproduces the biological racism of his ancestors who depicted Africans as vermin beings to justify their conquest and reduce them into things and thus "prepare them for annihilation using weapons befitting 'problem animals'."[89] Blomkamp also displays the cultural racism of the post-apartheid era by representing the aliens as shiftless violent degenerates that live amid filth, spend their time picking through trash, piss and vomit in public, and shamelessly sacrifice their principles for their next cat food fix.[90] *District 9* also enacts the self-serving white fantasy that blacks are just as racist by having Nigerians exploit the prawns instead of Afrikaners. But it is Wikus's horrific transformation from human to alien that most starkly reveals *District 9*'s apartheid approach to race. First, the fact that it only takes a few precious drops of black alien fluid to turn Wikus into a prawn gives credence to one of the most stubborn white supremacist delusions of all: that black blood is a pollutant and miscegenation is fatal. Second, the idea that Wikus must metamorphose into an alien to sympathize with the Other's suffering reinforces the idea that racism is natural, that achieving racial awareness is excruciatingly painful, and that avoiding those alien Others might be the best course of action. Finally, Wikus's yearning to just "go back" to how it was before is not just about recovering his human body. It is a deeper desire. He aches to return to a time and a place when aliens and humans were safely ensconced in their own spheres. He yearns for the era before Contact, before all the messy mixing, before the need for guilt or redemption. *District 9* is the dark fantasy of the settler to return to the time when the boundaries between the white Self and the racial Other were not so frighteningly permeable.

As my earlier discussion of *Avatar* emphasized, the film is steeped in imperialist nostalgia, and egregiously exemplifies the white savior fantasy. Not only does the transformation of the human protagonist, Jake Sully, into an alien give him access to indigenous ways, it earns him the love of the native princess and the worshipful respect of her tribe.[91] By having the colonial-settler assimilate a native identity at its conclusion, *Avatar* "symptomatically displaces their actual expropriation of power and wealth from the natives."[92] However, the fact that native peoples around the world from Bolivia to China to Palestine have embraced the film and used it to mobilize political support, a phenomenon that media studies scholar Henry Jenkins dubbed Avatar Activism,[93] should give settlers pause. But *Avatar* does more than invite the "imagination of indigenous resistance leading to definitive anticolonial victory"[94]; the hybrid nature of Pandora's natives opens up a space for indigenous peoples to apprehend how their struggles intertwine and how they can collectively resist erasure.[95] Ironically, it is *Avatar's* racist amalgamation of stereotypical tribal features in the Na'vi that "makes the film conducive to local interpretations and modifications of struggle on the ground, [allowing] the Na'vi [to] act as a mirror of desire, reflecting for different dispossessed groups their own local resistance and connecting it with other similar acts of resistance in different parts of the globe."[96] Lastly, let us not forget that *Avatar* is a narrative in which the (human) race traitor does not just "go native," he actually becomes an indigenous alien. This is a settler nightmare of the highest order. But perhaps the most terrifying aspect of *Avatar* for settler Selves is the conclusion of the major battle scene in which Neytiri "uses a wooden spear to skewer the hyper-masculine white male military commander, Colonel Quaritch (Stephen Lang), who epitomizes the arrogant, racist aggression of the mining corporation invading her planet."[97]

According to historian Paul Spickard, classical colonialism "involves several acts of domination: military intervention; political transfer of sovereignty, economic domination; and ultimately cultural domination." Those were all true in the cases of slavery, of Native American removal and genocide,[98] and European imperialism. He also suggests that the colonial period of American history is not yet over; it continues to be (re)written: the same could be said of European imperialism. This is what *District 9* and *Avatar* unmask: that we are not living in a post-racial and post-apartheid age. We have not transcended race. We are still trapped in the coils of colonial logic, still bound by its blindnesses and opacities. Five hundred years later, we are still re-enacting settler myths. The only difference is that we have displaced our desire and dread of the native onto the alien. Aliens are now the reluctant repositories of our dark fantasies of racial revenge and pure segregation.

Notes

1 Jeffrey Jerome Cohen, "Monster Culture (Seven Theses)," in *Monster Theory: Reading Culture*, (ed.) Jeffrey Jerome Cohen (Minneapolis: University of Minnesota Press, 1996), 4.

2 Ibid.

3 Joshua David Bellin, *Framing Monsters: Fantasy Film and Social Alienation* (Carbondale: Southern Illinois University Press, 2005), 9.

4 *District 9*, directed by Neill Blomkamp (2009; Culver City, CA: Tri-Star Pictures/Sony Pictures Home Entertainment, 2009), DVD.

5 *Avatar*, directed by James Cameron (2009; Beverly Hills: Twentieth Century Fox/Twentieth Century Fox Home Entertainment, 2010), DVD.

6 On the constitutive role that minstrelsy plays in maintaining racial hegemony, among others see S. Elizabeth Bird, ed., *Dressing in Feathers: The Construction of the Indian in American Popular Culture* (Boulder, CO: Westview Press, 1996); Ward Churchill, *Indians Are Us?: Culture and Genocide in Native North America* (Monroe, ME: Common Courage Press, 1994); Rosemary J. Coombe, *The Cultural Life of Intellectual Properties: Authorship, Appropriation and the Law* (Durham: Duke University Press, 1998); Philip Joseph Deloria, *Playing Indian* (New Haven: Yale University Press, 1998); Shari M. Huhndorf, *Going Native: Indians in the American Cultural Imagination* (Ithaca: Cornell University Press, 2001); Kimberly J. Lau, *New Age Capitalism: Making Money East of Eden* (Philadelphia: University of Pennsylvania Press, 2000); Eric Lott, *Love and Theft: Blackface Minstrelsy and Working Class Culture* (New York: Oxford University Press, 1993); Carter Jones Meyer and Diana Royer, eds, *Selling the Indian: Commercializing & Appropriating American Indian Cultures* (Tucson: University of Arizona Press, 2001); Jan Nederveen Pieterse, *White on Black: Images of Africa and Blacks in Western Popular Culture* (New Haven: Yale University Press, 1992); David Roediger, *The Wages of Whiteness: Race and the Making of the American Working Class* (New York: Verso, 2007); Michael Rogin, *Blackface, White Noise: Jewish Immigrants in the Hollywood Melting Pot* (Berkeley: University of California Press, 1998); Deborah Root, *Cannibal Culture: Art, Appropriation, & the Commodification* (Boulder, CO: Westview Press, 1996); and Marianna Torgovnick, *Gone Primitive: Savage Intellects, Modern Lives* (Chicago: University of Chicago Press, 1990).

7 See Taunya Lovell Banks, "Exploring White Resistance to Racial Reconciliation in the United States," *Rutgers Law Review* 55, no. 4 (2003): 903–64.

8 *South Park*, Episode 194 ("Dances with Smurfs"), first broadcast on November 11, 2009 on Comedy Central, directed and written by Trey Parker. Many commentators and scholars have sardonically noted the striking similarities between *Avatar* and *Dances with Wolves* (Costner, 1990). See, for example, Julio Cammarota, "Blindsided by the *Avatar*: White Saviors and Allies out of Hollywood and in Education," *Review of Education, Pedagogy, and Cultural Studies* 33, no. 3 (2011): 242–59; Carl Kozlowski, "'Dances with Wolves' in Space," *The Pasadena Weekly* (December 17, 2009), http://www.pasadenaweekly.com/cms/story/detail/dances_with_wolves_in_space/8179/; and Aaron Sutherland, "Dances with Wolves in Space: Aliens and Alienation in James Cameron's *Avatar*," M.A. Thesis, University of Saskatchewan, 2010. Cammarota has even opined that "*Avatar* parallels *Dances With Wolves* so much so that one might consider the screenplay a twenty-first century version" (247).

9 "'Avatar' = 'Pocahontas' in Space," *The Huffington Post* (March 18, 2010), http://www.huffingtonpost.com/2010/01/04/avatar-pocahontas-in-spac_n_410538.html. On the parallels between Pocahontas and *Avatar*, see Orin Starn, "Here Come the Anthros (Again): The Strange Marriage of Anthropology and Native America," *Cultural Anthropology* 26, no. 2 (2011): 179–204, and "*Avatar* and Pocahontas Side-by-Side" (January 24, 2010), http://www.youtube.com/watch?v=uGOCodaM4UM

10 Will Heaven, "James Cameron's *Avatar* Is a Stylish Film Marred by Its Racist Subtext," *The Telegraph* (December 22, 2009), http://blogs.telegraph.co.uk/news/willheaven/100020488/james-camerons-avatar-is-a-stylish-film-marred-by-its-racist-subtext/.

11 Eric Repphun, "Cinema as Exorcism (Four): *Avatar* as European Orientalist Fantasy," *The Dunedin School* (December 24, 2009), http://dunedinschool.wordpress.com/2009/12/24/cinema-as-exorcism-four-avatar-as-european-orientalist-fantasy/.

12 Ibid.

13 Ibid.

14 Heaven, "James Cameron's *Avatar*."

15 John Nolte, "Cameron's 'Avatar' Is a Big, Dull, America-Hating, PC Revenge Fantasy [Review]," *Andrew Breitbart Presents Big Hollywood* (December 11, 2009). http://bighollywood.breitbart.com/jjmnolte/2009/12/11/review-camerons-avatar-is-a-big-dull-america-hating-pc-revenge-fantasy/. As one online critic notes, by "blending all of these cultures into one, the film is guilty of doing exactly what it thinks it is condemning" (Repphun, "Cinema as Exorcism: *Avatar*"). In plundering all these cultures to create the Na'vi, Cameron demonstrates that indigenous particularity and cultural integrity do not matter to Euro-Americans. "What matters is that [these cultures] aren't European and thus are an open resource to plunder when trying to define Europe over and against what it is not. This is Orientalism par excellence"(ibid.). It is also a brilliant example of the primitivism that Marianna Torgovnick diagnosed in *Gone Primitive: Savage Intellects, Modern Lives*. Specifically, Cameron's grab-bag approach to Na'vi culture reveals that Euro-Americans see the "primitive as an inexact expressive w/hole – often with little correspondence to any specific or documented societies" (*Gone Primitive*, 20). In the end, "the West's fascination with the primitive has to do with its own crises of identity, with its own need to clearly demarcate subject and object, even while flirting with other ways of experiencing the universe" (ibid., 157).

16 Lisa Wade, "On *Avatar*," *Sociological Images* (December 28, 2009), http:// thesocietypages.org/socimages/2009/12/28/on-avatar-the-movie-spoiler-alert/

17 Annalee Newitz, "When Will White People Stop Making Movies Like *Avatar*?", *io9* (April 7, 2010), http://io9.com/5422666/when-will-white-people-stop-making-movies-like-avatar. Director James Cameron openly admits that *Avatar* rehearses "the violent struggles that took place in the past in North America" (as quoted in Jessica Lee, "Avatar Activism," *The Indypendent* (May 1, 2010), http://www.indypendent.org/2010/04/26/avatar-activism/).

18 The clichéd and formulaic nature of *Avatar* and its cinematic predecessors is cleverly lampooned in the remix video *A.V.A.T.A.R. [Anglos Valiantly Aiding Tragic Awe-inspiring Races]* (September 15, 2010), http://www.youtube.com/ watch?v=gWSiztP2Rp0. "With the aim of pointing to how *Avatar* simply regurgitated a strong history of white, Western self-congratulation," writes Lisa Wade, "Craig Saddlemire and Ryan Conrad re-mixed the movie with other similar movies, including *Blind Side*, *Dancing with Wolves*, *Blood Diamond*, *The Last Samurai*, Out of Africa, *Stargate*, and *Indiana Jones and the Temple of Doom*. They go through several features of these narratives: awe at the 'native' land/animals/people, the decision that they are helpless and doomed without White, Western intervention, the designation of a White savior who devotes him or herself to their rescue, native self-subordination, and more" ("Avatar as a Tired Colonialist Trope," *Sociological Images* (June 30, 2011), http://thesocietypages.org/socimages/2011/06/30/ avatar-as-a-tired-trope/).

19 *Dances with Wolves*, directed by Kevin Costner (1990; Los Angeles: Orion Pictures/MGM Video and DVD, 2011), DVD.

20 *The Last of the Mohicans*, directed by Michael Mann (1992; Los Angeles: Morgan Creek Productions/Fox Home Entertainment, 2007), DVD.

21 *Pocahontas*, directed by Mike Gabriel and Erik Goldberg (1995; Burbank: Walt Disney Pictures/Walt Disney Video, 2000), DVD.

22 Daniel Francis, as quoted in S. Elizabeth Bird, "Not My Fantasy: The Persistence of Indian Imagery in Dr. Quinn, Medicine Woman," in S. Elizabeth Bird, (ed.), *Dressing in Feathers*, 258.

23 In *Primitive Passions: Men, Women, and the Quest for Ecstasy* (New York: Alfred A. Knopf, 1997), Marianna Torgovnick suggests that Western fascination with the primitive reflects a "utopian desire to go back and recover irreducible features of the psyche, body, land, and community—to reinhabit core experiences" (5).

24 On the persistence and profitability of Playing Indian, see Lisa Aldred, "Plastic Shamans and Astroturf Sundances: New Age Commercialization of Native American Spirituality," *American Indian Quarterly* 24, no. 3 (Summer 2000): 329–52; Robert F. Berkhofer, *The White Man's Indian: Images of the American Indian, from Columbus to the Present* (New York: Vintage Books, 1979); Bird, *Dressing in Feathers*; Jason Edward Black, "The 'Mascotting' of Native America: Construction, Commodity, and Assimilation," *The American Indian Quarterly* 26, no. 4 (2004): 605–22; Ward Churchill, *Fantasies of the Master Race: Literature, Cinema, and the Colonization of American Indians* (San Francisco: City Lights Books, 1998); Deloria, *Playing Indian*; Karen M. Gagne, "Falling in Love with Indians: The Metaphysics of Becoming America," *CR: The New Centennial Review* 3, no. 3 (2004): 205–33; Rayna Green, "The Tribe Called Wannabee: Playing Indian in America and Europe," *Folklore* 99, no. 1 (1988): 30–55; Huhndorf, *Going Native*; Winona LaDuke, *Recovering the Sacred: The Power of Naming and Claiming*, (Cambridge, MA: South End Press, 2005); Meyer and Royer, *Selling the Indian*; Root, *Cannibal Culture*; Kathryn W. Shanley, "The Indians America Loves to Love and Read: American Indian Identity and Cultural Appropriation," *American Indian Quarterly* 21, no. 4 (1997): 675–702; Andrea Smith, "Spiritual Appropriation as Sexual Violence," *Wicazo Sa Review* 20, no. 1 (2005): 97–111; Rennard Strickland, *Tonto's Revenge: Reflections on American Indian Culture and Policy* (Albuquerque: University of New Mexico Press, 1997); and Laurie Anne Whitt, "Cultural Imperialism and the Marketing of Native America," *American Indian Culture & Research Journal* 19, no. 3 (1995): 1–31.

25 Green, "The Tribe Called Wannabee," 48.

26 Deloria, *Playing Indian*, 26.

27 Huhndorf, *Going Native*, 2.

28 For discussions of *Avatar*'s white savior complex, see Cammarota, "Blindsided by the *Avatar*"; David Brooks, "The Messiah Complex," *The New York Times* (January 7, 2010), http://www.nytimes.com/2010/01/08/opinion/08brooks.html?scp=1&sq=David%20Brooks%20%20avatar&st=cse; Brian Godawa, "Science and Faith at the Movies: 'Avatar'," *The BioLogos Foundation* (April 15, 2011), http://biologos.org/uploads/static-content/science_and_faith_movies_3.pdf; Heaven, "James Cameron's *Avatar*"; Daniel Heath Justice, "James Cameron's *Avatar*: Missed Opportunities," *First Peoples: New Directions in Indigenous Studies* (January 20, 2010), http://www.firstpeoplesnewdirections.org/blog/?p=169; Newitz, "When Will White People Stop"; Val D. Phillips, "A Science Fiction Masterpiece for Liberals: Fantasies of the Master Race Goes to Pandora," *As The Teaching Drum Turns* (December 26, 2009), http://astheteachingdrumturns.blogspot.com/2009/12/fantasies-of-master-race-goes-to.html; Repphun, "Cinema as Exorcism: *Avatar*"; Starn, "Here Come The Anthros (Again)"; Armond White, "Blue in the Face: James Cameron Delivers Dumb Escapism with His Expensive Special Effects in 'Avatar'," *New York Press* (December 15, 2009), http://www.nypress.com/article-20710-blue-in-the-face.html; and Slavoj Žižek, "Return of the Natives: Beneath the Idealism and Political Correctness of

Avatar Lie Brutal Racist Undertones," *The New Statesman* (March 4, 2010). http://www.newstatesman.com/film/2010/03/avatar-reality-love-couple-sex

29 Huhndorf, *Going Native*, 4–5.

30 S. Elizabeth Bird, "Introduction: Constructing the Indian, 1830s-1990s," in Bird, *Dressing in Feathers*, 2.

31 White, "Blue in the Face."

32 Newitz, "When Will White People Stop."

33 Green, "The Tribe Called Wannabee," 31.

34 Lorenzo Veracini, "*District 9* and *Avatar*: Science Fiction and Settler Colonialism," *Journal of Intercultural Studies* 32, no. 4 (2011), 362.

35 Ibid.

36 Josefa Loshitzky, "Popular Cinema as Popular Resistance: *Avatar* in the Palestinian (Imagi)Nation," *Third Text* 26, no. 2 (2012), 160.

37 Ibid.

38 John Rieder, "Race and Revenge Fantasies in *Avatar*, *District 9* and *Inglourious Basterds*," *Science Fiction Film and Television* 4, no. 1 (2011), 48.

39 Wade, "On *Avatar*."

40 Žižek, "Return of the Natives."

41 Brooks, "The Messiah Complex."

42 Daniel Engber, "They Came from the Boardroom: The Dull, Anti-Corporate Politics of *District 9*," *Slate* (August 13, 2009), http://www.slate.com/articles/arts/movies/2009/08/they_came_from_the_boardroom.html/

43 John Marx, "Alien Rule," Safundi 11, no. 1–2 (2010), 165.

44 Chris Lee, "Alien Nation," *Los Angeles Times*, August 8, 2009, 8. According to the film's writer-director Neill Blomkamp, an Afrikaner who grew up in South Africa during apartheid, this was absolutely intentional: "It all had a huge impact on me; the white government and the paramilitary police; the oppressive, iron-fisted military environment. Blacks, for the most part, were kept separate from whites. And where there was overlap, there were very clearly delineated hierarchies of where people were allowed to go. Those ideas wound up in every pixel in District 9" (as quoted in ibid., 8).

45 On the allegorical use of race in *District 9*, see Adrienne Maree Brown, "Alien Apartheid? A Race-Aware Viewing Guide for *District 9*," *Colorlines* (August 16, 2009), http://colorlines.com/archives/2009/08/is_peter_jackson_an_antizionis.html; Jayna Brown, "On Becoming Alien: *District 9*," *Bully Bloggers* (September 19, 2009), http://bullybloggers.wordpress.com/2009/09/19/on-becoming-alien-%E2%80%93-district/; Bao-Yun Chun, "Analyses of Blomkamp's *District 9* & Abrams' *Star Trek*," *Gathering Forces* (September 22, 2009), http://gatheringforces.org/2009/09/22/analyses-of-blomkamps-district-9-abrams-star-trek/; David Cox, "*District 9* Warns Us of a Dangerous Future," *Guardian* (September 7, 2009), http://www.guardian.co.uk/film/filmblog/2009/sep/07/district-9-immigration-climate-change; Scott Foundas, "Alien Invasion as Apartheid Metaphor? It Works in *District*

9," *SF Weekly* (August 12, 2009), http://www.sfweekly.com/2009-08-12/
film/alien-invasion-as-apartheid-metaphor-it-works-in-district-9/; Christopher
Garland, "Urban, Rural, or Someplace Else?: The Slums of the Global South
in Contemporary Film," *Many Cinemas* 1 (2011), http://www.manycinemas.
org/mc01garland.html; Gerald Gaylard, "*District 9* and the Parktown
Prawns," *Safundi* 11, no. 1–2 (2010): 167–9; Ralph Goodman, "The Allegory
of *District 9*," *Safundi* 11, no. 1–2 (2010): 170–2; Lucy Valerie Graham,
"Amakwerekwere and Other Aliens: *District 9* and Hospitality" *Safundi* 11,
no. 1–2 (2010): 161–4; Stefan Helgesson, "*District 9*: The Global South as
Science Fiction" *Safundi* 11, no. 1–2 (2010): 172–4; Chris Lee, "Alien Nation";
Marx, "Alien Rule"; Will Menaker, "Alien Apartheid (*District 9* Review),"
The Huffington Post (August 21, 2009), http://www.huffingtonpost.com/
will-menaker/idistrict-9i_b_265030.html; Annalee Newitz, "Your Oppression
Will Be Simulated in 'District 9' [Review]," *io9* (August 13, 2009), http://io9.
com/5337133/your-oppression-will-be-simulated-in-district-9; Eric Repphun,
"Cinema as Exorcism (Two): *District 9* as Postcolonial Science Fiction,"
The Dunedin School (August 19, 2009), http://dunedinschool.wordpress.
com/2009/08/19/cinema-as-exorcism-two-district-9-as-postcolonial-science-
fiction/; Sukdev Sandhu, "*District 9* [Review]," *Daily Telegraph* (September 3,
2009), http://www.telegraph.co.uk/culture/film/filmreviews/6133078/District-
9-review.html; Gemma Sieff, "Rainbow Alienation [*District 9* Review]," n+1
(August 30, 2009), http://www.nplusonemag.com/rainbow-alienation; Daniel
Smith-Rowsey, "From Santa Mira to South Africa: Updating the Invasion
Narrative for the 21st Century," *JGCinema: Cinema and Globalization*, http://
jgcinema.com/single.php?sl=invasion-body-snatchers-dossier-horror; Michael
Valdez Moses, "The Strange Ride of Wikus Van De Merwe," *Safundi* 11,
no. 1–2 (2010): 156–60; Jonah Weiner, "What Does *District 9* Have to Say
About Apartheid?" *Slate* (August 18, 2009), http://www.slate.com/content/
slate/blogs/browbeat/2009/08/18/what_does_district_9_have_to_say_about_
apartheid.html; and Teresa Wiltz, "Entering *District 9*," *The Root* (August 14,
2009), http://www.theroot.com/views/entering-district-9/

46 Repphun, "Cinema as Exorcism: *District 9*."

47 Garland, "Urban, Rural, or Someplace Else."

48 Repphun, "Cinema as Exorcism: *District 9*."

49 Neill Blomkamp, as quoted in Lee, "Alien Nation," 8.

50 Brown, "On Becoming Alien."

51 Garland, "Urban, Rural, or Someplace Else."

52 Cox, "*District 9* Warns."

53 Henriette Gunkel and Christian König, "'You Are Not Welcome Here':
Post-Apartheid Negrophobia & Real Aliens in Blomkamp's *District
9*," *darkmatter* 7 (February 7, 2010), http://www.darkmatter101.org/
site/2010/02/07/you-are-not-welcome-here/

54 Ibid.

55 *Alive in Joburg* can be viewed online at http://video.google.com/videoplay?
docid=-1185812222812358837/

56 Greg Bourke, "Bare Life's Bare Essentials: When All You've Got Is Hope – the State of Exception in *The Road*, *District 9* and *Blindness*," *Law, Culture and the Humanities* (February 13, 2012), 12.

57 On the racist portrayal of Nigerians in *District 9*, see Bourke, "Bare Life's Bare Essentials"; Graham, "Amakwerekwere and Other Aliens"; Tolu Olorunda, "District 9," *The Daily Voice* (September 4, 2009), http://thedailyvoice.com/voice/2009/09/district-9-hollywood-and-the-c-002243.php; David Smith, "*District 9* Labelled Xenophobic by Nigerians," *Guardian* (September 2, 2009), http://www.guardian.co.uk/film/2009/sep/02/district-9-labelled-xenophobic-nigerians; Smith-Rowsey, "From Santa Mira to South Africa"; Nicole Stamp, "*District 9* Is Racist [Alternate Perspective]," *Racialicious* (August 18, 2009), http://www.racialicious.com/2009/08/18/district-9-is-racist-alternate-perspective; and Valdez Moses, "The Strange Ride of Wikus."

58 Valdez Moses, "The Strange Ride of Wikus," 158.

59 Ibid.

60 Goodman, "The Allegory of *District 9*," 171.

61 Graham, "Amakwerekwere and Other Aliens," 162.

62 Valdez Moses, "The Strange Ride of Wikus," 158.

63 Ibid., 158–9.

64 Rieder, "Race and Revenge Fantasies," 49.

65 Ibid.

66 Valdez Moses, "The Strange Ride of Wikus," 159.

67 Ralph Ellison, as quoted in Barry Shank, "Bliss, or Blackface Sentiment," *Boundary 2* 30, no. 2 (2003): 57.

68 Gillian Straker, "Unsettling Whiteness," *Psychoanalysis, Culture & Society* 16, no. 1 (2011): 13.

69 Gunkel and König, "'You Are Not Welcome Here.'"

70 Valdez Moses, "The Strange Ride of Wikus," 158–9.

71 Unfortunately, as Susan Gubar reluctantly confesses in the conclusion of *Racechanges: White Skin, Black Face in American Culture* (Oxford: Oxford University Press, 2000), "the anarchic potential of racechange" has historically resulted in the "subordination, muting, or obliteration of the Other" (244).

72 *Blood Diamond*, directed by Edward Zwick (2006; Burbank: Warner Brother Studios/Warner Home Studio, 2007), DVD.

73 *The Constant Gardener*, directed by Fernando Meirelles (2005; Burbank: Universal Studios/Universal Studios Home Entertainment, 2006), DVD.

74 *Hotel Rwanda*, directed by Terry George (2004; Santa Monica: Lions Gates Films/MGM Video and DVD, 2005), DVD.

75 *The Last King of Scotland*, directed by Kevin MacDonald (2006; Los Angeles: Fox Searchlight Pictures/Twentieth Century Fox Home Entertainment, 2007), DVD.

76 Released as *Shooting Dogs,* the DVD was distributed as *Beyond the Gates,* directed by Michael Caton-Jones (2005; Beverly Hills: Twentieth Century Fox/ Twentieth Century Fox Home Entertainment, 2007), DVD.

77 *Tears of the Sun,* directed by Antoine Fuqua, (2003; New York: Sony Pictures/ Sony Pictures Home Entertainment, 2003), DVD.

78 Gunkel and König, "'You Are Not Welcome Here'."

79 Ibid.

80 Mikko Tuhkanen, "Of Blackface and Paranoid Knowledge: Richard Wright, Jacques Lacan, and the Ambivalence of Black Minstrelsy," *Diacritics* 31, no. 2 (2001), 17.

81 Ibid.

82 David Theo Goldberg, as quoted in Tuhkanen, "Of Blackface and Paranoid Knowledge," 12.

83 On the subversive uses of colonial mimicry, see Homi K. Bhabha, "Of Mimicry and Man: The Ambivalence of Colonial Discourse," in *The Location of Culture* (New York: Routledge, 1994): 121–31.

84 Gunkel and König, "'You Are Not Welcome Here'."

85 Ibid.

86 Esther Godfrey, "'To Be Real': Drag, Minstrelsy and Identity in the New Millennium," *genders,* 41 (2005), http://www.genders.org/g41/g41_godfrey. html/

87 Veracini, "*District 9* and *Avatar,*" 356.

88 Ibid., 357.

89 Clapperton Chakanetsa Mavhunga, "Vermin Beings: On Pestiferous Animals and Human Game," *Social Text* 29, 1 (2011), 154.

90 Valdez Moses, "The Strange Ride of Wikus," 159.

91 Rieder, "Race and Revenge Fantasies," 48.

92 Ibid.

93 Henry Jenkins, as quoted in Mark Deuze, "Survival of the Mediated," *Journal of Cultural Science* 3, no. 2 (2010), 6–7. The most well-known example is perhaps that of the Kayapo Indians of Brazil, who enlisted Cameron in their fight to stop the construction of the Belo Monte Dam (Alexei Barrionuevo, "Tribes of Amazon Find an Ally out of Avatar," *The New York Times* (April 11, 2010), http://www.nytimes.com/2010/04/11/world/ americas/11brazil.html). Cameron produced a documentary on the dam and its destructive consequences for the Kayapo, entitled "A Message From Pandora." Sigourney Weaver, who plays anthropologist Dr. Grace Augustine in *Avatar,* is the narrator. The short film is included as bonus material in the Director's Cut of *Avatar.* Although Cameron's partnership with the Kayapo delayed the dam's construction, it has since resumed (Gabriel Elizondo, "Dam It: Brazil's Belo Monte Stirs Controversy," *Al Jazeera* (January 20, 2012), http://www.aljazeera.com/indepth/features/2012/01/2012120153667 64400.html). For more on Avatar Activism, see Joni Adamson, "Indigenous

Literatures, Multinaturalism, and *Avatar:* The Emergence of Indigenous Cosmopolitics," *American Literary History* 24, no. 1 (2012): 143–62; "Avatar in the Amazon," Public Radio International (February 2, 2010), http://www.pri.org/arts-entertainment/movies/avatar-in-the-amazon1863.html; Stephen Corry, "'*Avatar* Is Real' Say Tribal People," *Survival* (January 25, 2010), http://www.survivalinternational.org/news/5466; James Clifford, "Response to Orin Starn: 'Here Come the Anthros (Again): The Strange Marriage of Anthropology and Native America'," *Cultural Anthropology* 26, no. 2 (2011): 218–24; "Head of State Fights for Environment: Evo Morales 'Identifies' with Avatar Film," *Buenos Aires Herald* (January 12, 2010), http://www.buenosairesherald.com/article/22287/evo-morales-identifies-withavatar-film; Lee, "Avatar Activism"; Loshitzky, "Popular Cinema as Popular Resistance"; and Tom Philips, "Hollywood and the Jungle: Director Joins Real-Life Avatar Battle in the Amazon Forest," *Observer*, April 18, 2010.

94 Ibid.

95 Loshitzky, "Popular Cinema as Popular Resistance," 162.

96 Ibid.

97 Rieder, "Race and Revenge Fantasies," 41.

98 Paul Spickard, *Almost All Aliens: Immigration, Race, and Colonialism in American History and Identity* (New York: Routledge, 2007), 24.

4

Battling monsters and becoming monstrous:

Human devolution in *The Walking Dead*

Kyle W. Bishop

During the twentieth century, most serious explorations of the zombie invasion narrative—that is, those tales following the generic formula established by George A. Romero with *Night of the Living Dead* (1968)—based their thematic essence on one key premise: the monsters represent humanity.[1] Now in a new century, one defined by social insecurities resulting from the September 11th terrorist attacks and cultural anxieties arising from natural disasters and global pandemics, the zombie is once again being called upon by filmmakers, novelists, comic book makers, and video game programmers alike to exorcise our collective fears and doubts. In both cases, zombie narratives address not only the expected monstrous behavior of the hordes of the walking dead, but also the monstrous acts committed by the few humans struggling to survive in a dangerous post-apocalyptic world. Yet, whereas the zombie tales of the previous century primarily limited monstrous human behavior to characters clearly coded as antagonists—such as the biker gang of *Dawn of the Dead* (1978) or the megalomaniac Captain Rhodes (Joseph Pilato) from *Day of the Dead* (1985)—a number of narratives that make up the modern-day "zombie renaissance"—such as Romero's *Survival of the Dead* (2009) and Robert Kirkman's sprawling and intricately developed comic book series *The Walking Dead* (2003–)—present the otherwise sympathetic *protagonists* as monstrous creatures. In other words, some recent zombie narratives have flipped the original allegory: humans are truly monstrous.

Although hints of this rhetorical inversion appeared in the very first zombie films, only a handful of the most recent zombie narratives have so aggressively asked audiences to question the definition of *monster*.[2] Following in the hallowed footsteps of *Frankenstein* (1818), in which Mary Shelley reveals the real villain of her novel to be the vain and single-minded Victor, some modern zombie tales demonstrate the otherwise heroic human characters to be the monstrous beings that should really be feared. Upon closer consideration, this change in attitude toward once delineated Manichean dichotomies comes as no surprise. Thanks to a perceived shift in U.S. foreign policy and military practices following 9/11, one that advocated invasions of autonomous nations and the unrestrained use of "enhanced interrogation techniques" such as waterboarding to keep everyone "safe," the most important allegorical function of zombie narratives may now belong to the human protagonists instead of the metaphorically pregnant zombies. The most overt example of this kind of criticism, Kirkman's *The Walking Dead* comic series,[3] sheds a harsh light upon the potential devolution of humanity—that we have become chaotic creatures of selfishness, violence, and unchecked aggression who do more damage to ourselves and the world around us than any reanimated corpse ever could. In Kirkman's paradigm, zombies are less important than the stories told around them, and such tales do important cultural work by providing audiences with ethical guideposts and a sober warning against atavistic barbarism.

Of course, contemporary zombie invasion narratives still feature hordes of reanimated corpses against which the humans must struggle to survive; the monsters are the primary draw of the subgenre, after all. However, as Friedrich Nietzsche memorably writes in *Beyond Good and Evil*, "Whoever battles with monsters had better see that it does not turn him into a monster,"[4] and this axiom has become the new standard for a number of post-9/11 zombie narratives. The so-called heroes of survival fiction must make difficult choices to ensure their continued existence, decisions that often mean protecting themselves and their allies at all cost. *The Walking Dead* epitomizes this potential "monstrozation" of humanity by featuring protagonists who combat both zombies and other humans with equal degrees of brutality. Kirkman's popular series follows the (mis)adventures of a motley group of people who struggle against zombies, other humans, and even each other to survive an ongoing global apocalypse. At the beginning of the series, the former deputy sheriff Rick Grimes heroically upheld the values of a civilized society. However, over the course of the series, Rick, along with his fellow protagonists, has been forced to make increasingly difficult decisions, and what is "right" has become supplanted by what is "necessary." Whether the United States has truly experienced a similar ideological shift is open to debate; however, the overt devolution demonstrated by *The Walking Dead*'s traumatized heroes can nonetheless be read as an indictment of the arguably aggressive stance American politics and foreign policy have taken since 9/11—one in which efforts to make the world safe may in fact be replicating the very atrocities committed by the perceived enemy—and, perhaps more importantly, a condemnation of the populace that so complacently allowed such changes to occur in the first place.

Traditionally speaking, monster narratives in general, and zombie stories in particular, operate on clearly delineated parameters: monsters are monstrous and humans are humane. According to Kevin Alexander Boon, what makes a monster decidedly monstrous is its difference from the human, its unnaturalness.[5] Zombies in particular are monstrous, Boon explains, because they act "in direct opposition to the living."[6] As "walking dead," Romero-style zombies flagrantly defy the established boundaries of living and dead, confronting audiences with dangerous bodies that challenge the natural order of things. As Jeffrey Jerome Cohen argues, such liminality is essential because monsters work as "disturbing hybrids whose externally incoherent bodies resist attempts to include them in any systematic structuration."[7] Monsters are thus "othered" due to their resistance of easy classification, and as such they more easily function as manifestations of frightening difference. In the past, hybrid creations such as vampires, werewolves, or aliens were used to represent Jews, homosexuals, Communists, and virtually all forms of the non-White, non-heteronormative Other. The value of the monster thus lies in its role as a cultural *monstrum*, a metaphorical figure that "reveals" and "warns" of something else, something larger than itself.[8] Ironically, by using markedly coded differences from humans, monsters function as revealing and didactic critics of the very humanity from which they ostensibly appear to be distanced.

But what about monstrous humans? The human antagonists in zombie fiction have almost always been sources of physical threat and violence as well, starting with the voodoo "puppet masters" in the earliest films, most notably Bela Lugosi's sinister "Murder" Legendre in Victor Halperin's *White Zombie* (1932). In the Romero tradition, human villains continue to be a substantial threat to beleaguered protagonists—a threat *in addition* to the zombies. *Dawn of the Dead*, to offer one of the most celebrated examples, pits Romero's four human survivors against not only an unstoppable horde of hungry zombies, but also racist SWAT members, undisciplined country militia, and a marauding biker gang. In the post-apocalyptic wasteland ravaged by the walking dead, everyone who isn't an ally—be they zombie or human—represents a very real threat. Because zombies are essentially slow moving, uncoordinated, and brain dead, they actually pose little danger for the careful human survivor, especially when encountered in small numbers; human antagonists, on the other hand, are far more insidious. Scott Kenemore enumerates the main differences between zombies and their feckless prey: "Humans—unlike composed, unflappable, focused zombies—fight with one another. They are jealous. They are manipulative. They care about things like other people not having sex with their wives."[9] Humans think, humans have emotions, and humans can plot against one another. In Romero's *Day of the Dead*, the most dangerous threat isn't a zombie at all but rather the insane sadomasochist Captain Rhodes, who sees everyone other than his military brothers as decidedly expendable. Romero's *Land of the Dead* (2005) takes the antagonistic shift even further, subordinating the role of the zombies to that of Kaufman (Dennis Hopper), the crazed captain of industry who has set himself up as a violently oppressive "king" in his palatial Fiddler's Green apartment complex. Throughout the tradition, then, zombie narratives have regularly shown villainous humans to be potentially monstrous.

In recent years, however, the human *protagonists* have taken on increasingly monstrous qualities as well, some of them horrifyingly so. What makes these "monstrous humans"[10] particularly disturbing and important are their decided *lack* of liminal difference and their being coded as those to whom the audience should relate. Romero's *Survival of the Dead*, for example, builds its narrative almost exclusively around unlikable, sociopathic main characters. The movie opens with a shot of Sarge Nicotine Crockett (Alan Van Sprang) in close-up, as he explains in impassive voiceover how the zombie apocalypse came about. This establishing presentation, along with Sprang's top billing in the credits, implies his role as the lead figure of the film, the protagonist with whom audience members are supposed to identify. Unfortunately, Crockett quickly proves to be a criminal and AWOL vigilante, the leader of a gang of self-described "lousy people" who routinely use their outward appearance as soldiers to take advantage of others. They kill humans and zombies with equal remorselessness, and they are motivated more by money than survival. Tomboy (Athena Karkanis), the gang's only female member and lone voice of sympathetic reason, sees the truth: "All the wrong people are dying. Seems like all we got left are assholes."[11] The film's ostensible hero Crockett acts with increasing villainy throughout the film, and none of the other characters he (and, by extension, the audience) encounters are much better—pretty much *all* the humans in *Survival of the Dead* act monstrously, regardless of their status as antagonists or protagonists.

Many zombie narratives appearing in the wake of 9/11 use allegory to address not only general fears of a post-apocalyptic future, but also the new cultural fears and anxieties associated with the threat of terrorism. Danny Boyle's *28 Days Later* (2002), for example, graphically depicts the after-effects of mass death and destruction, and *Land of the Dead* recreates the xenophobic paranoia people feel in the face of potential terrorists and illegal immigrants by using both zombies and disgruntled human survivors as their proxies. Narratives such as *Survival of the Dead* and Kirkman's *The Walking Dead*, however, demonstrate a new symbolic manifestation, one that reflects not cultural fears about what terrorists *might* do, but rather what the "good guys" *can* do against potential or suspected terrorists. In other words, that which we should most fear is not the monstrous Other but our monstrous *selves*. I believe this new kind of zombie story should be read as a direct reflection of the United States' dramatic actions taken in the wake of the 9/11 terrorist attacks. Instead of passively waiting for Al-Qaeda operatives to attack a second time, the Bush Administration chose to take the fight to them by invading both Afghanistan and Iraq (the latter on rather specious intelligence). In addition, military policies were allegedly altered to limit the rights of the suspected terrorists being held at the controversial *Guantanamo Bay* detention camp and to authorize the use of waterboarding and other problematic interrogation methods. Each of these changes to existing U.S. policy and practice—changes that could be perceived as a more offensive, aggressive position than in the past—were promoted as protecting the American public from future terror plots, and they were readily and unques-tioningly embraced by a frightened and paranoid public.

Such a perceived shift in political and military ideology, one implicitly endorsed by politicians and citizens alike, has since been manifested in key post-9/11 zombie narratives. The resultant attitude, one that casts the protag-onists of zombie stories in the problematic role of monstrous aggressors, is best illustrated in Kirkman's ongoing comic book series about Rick Grimes's efforts to keep himself, his family, and those around him alive through a zombie apocalypse—at all costs. In his introduction to the first trade collection of *The Walking Dead*, Kirkman argues that "good zombie movies show us how messed up we are,"[12] and it doesn't take long before readers of his epic realize he is actually talking about his "good guys" just as much as the zombies or even the human antagonists. Furthermore, Kirkman openly articulates the key purpose of his ongoing zombie comic: "I want to explore how people deal with extreme situations and how these events CHANGE them."[13] From the onset, then, Kirkman promises readers that Rick, his tragic hero and central protagonist, is going to *change*, and likely not in a good way: "[W]hen you look back on this book you won't even recognize [Rick]."[14] All the characters in *The Walking Dead* change over the course of the narrative, but none as dramatically as the one-time noble deputy. Because Kirkman's narrative question is "What happens to our humanity when we do inhumane things?",[15] Rick's slow, tragic loss of humanity develops into the most important subject of the story, one that mirrors the moral and ethical decline of a fearful U.S. population desperately seeking an Other they may scapegoat and blame.

From the beginning of Kirkman's long-arc narrative, The Walking Dead engages with the barbaric transformations that befall its protagonists, especially those in positions of authority. In the first volume, Days Gone Bye, Rick and his fellow police officer Shane almost immediately develop an uncharacteristically antagonistic stance toward one another. They argue heatedly about leaving the perceived safety of Atlanta, and Shane ends up punching Rick in the face. A traumatized Lori, Rick's protective wife, astutely points out: "It's never going to be the same again. We're never going to be normal. ... Just look at us."[16] Shane's increasingly erratic and dangerous behavior towards Rick comes to a crisis when he actually points a rifle at his former best friend, but, before he can act, Rick's son Carl shoots Shane through the neck, killing him instantly. After Shane's burial, Rick expresses his shock at what has happened and his fears concerning what it might mean for the rest of the survivors: "This shit we're in is not to be taken lightly. If it can change a man like Shane so drastically, we're in deeper shit that we thought."[17] The unexplained zombie apocalypse has clearly rewritten all of society's rules; as Kenemore observes: "For humans to survive ... they must become killers."[18] To keep the beleaguered masses safe, then, even the "good guys" are forced to kill, both zombies and humans alike.

Other characters soon follow Carl's lead and become killers of living people. Two of the more shocking examples take place after the survivors have taken refuge in a largely abandoned prison. A misguidedly romantic Chris botches the suicide pact he has with Tyreese's daughter Julie, and when Tyreese finds his daughter dead, he loses all reason. In his rage, he chokes the life out of the penitent Chris, and then he waits for the boy to return as a zombie so he can kill him again.[19] Days later, Tyreese confesses to Rick what really happened:

> [Chris] was trying to commit suicide with [Julie] and as far as I'm concerned I just finished the job! And I enjoyed it. After all these months and the hell we've been through—it's almost the only thing I've enjoyed.
> I turned into an animal on him—I mutilated him over and over—I ripped him apart and watched him come back for more! ...
> I killed for the right reasons. I murdered him, yes—but it was justified.[20]

As far as readers know, Tyreese has been a normal, law-abiding citizen, but his fear for his own safety and desire for revenge color his perspectives on violence and murder. Despite his admittedly inhuman actions, Tyreese tries to rationalize his behavior by explaining it in terms of justice, and Rick's own devolution from deputy sheriff to cold-blooded killer begins when he finds himself in a similar situation. After the former inmate Thomas murders two young girls and attacks Andrea with a knife, Rick, desperate to protect his flock, violently beats Thomas to a pulp with his bare hands. As the survivors argue about what to do with Thomas, Tyreese points out their new society lacks the rules necessary to keep order. Rick dictates his old-world philosophy: "You kill? You die."[21] Rick wants to maintain the legal system he had upheld in his former life, yet he orders Thomas's "lawful" execution with little thought of a trial, a decision that presciently mirrors actions by the Obama Administration to execute dangerous U.S. nationals such as Anwar al-Awlaki without due process.[22]

As Rick faces increasingly difficult circumstances, his journey from rational human being to monstrous killer only accelerates. Although Thomas has been safely "put down," Dexter leads an armed rebellion against Rick. Fortunately for the beleaguered survivors, Dexter leaves the doors to the armory—and the zombie-infested A-Block—wide open, and a desperate and chaotic battle against the walking dead interrupts the humans' standoff. As the extermination comes to a close, Rick coldly shoots Dexter in the head and tries to pass it off as an accident. Although Tyreese, who saw everything, thinks Rick ultimately did the right thing for the safety of the group, he points out how Rick's actions "kinda throws the whole 'you kill, you die' thing out the window."[23] Tyreese accuses Rick of having developed a bloodlust, thinking the former police officer now actually enjoys violence, but Rick insists, "Everything I did—*everything*—I did for the good of this group. ... That's what makes me right."[24] Reluctantly, Rick realizes the old ways are gone, and the new society needs a new rule: "You kill—you live."[25] Rather than attempting to rebuild society, then, Rick sees the need for the survivors to become something far more savage. As could be said of the post-9/11 Bush Administration's creation of the Patriot Act and its increasingly aggressive military actions overseas, Rick claims the old laws won't protect them, but self-defensive action and violence will.[26]

Rick embraces his protective barbarism further when he realizes Martinez, the man who had helped Rick and the others escape from Woodbury, is actually a spy working for the sinister Governor. After Martinez disappears, Rick takes Glen's RV by himself and violently runs the traitor down. Blinded at the thought of the Governor and his men finding the prison sanctuary, Rick chokes Martinez to death. Later, when he confesses the slaying to Lori, Rick says:

Killing him made me realize something—made me notice how much I've changed. I used to be a trained police officer—my job was to uphold the law. Now I feel more like a lawless savage—an animal. I killed a man today and I don't even care. …

I'd kill every single one of the people here if I thought it'd keep you safe. I know these people—I care for these people—but I know I'm capable of making that sacrifice. …

Does that make me evil?[27]

Rick clearly recognizes his frightening transformation, but, like Tyreese, he sees such drastic behavior as justified—he must protect his people by any means necessary. The otherwise peaceful and contrite Hershel is more willing to face what Rick must rationalize: "The good Lord's put us in a world where we gotta sin to survive."[28] As supporters of post-9/11 practice and policy might also say in defense of aggressive government action, terms such as *evil* and *sin* must be redefined in a world ruled by zombies (i.e. threatened by terrorists), and "survival" takes precedence over such antiquated ideas as "law and order" and "due process." Hershel, like many U.S. citizens, is a God-fearing man who none the less agrees to a monstrous course of action if it means keeping himself and his family safe.

Rick's atavistic behavior becomes most problematic when his actions shockingly come to resemble those of the zombies themselves. When a trio of savage highwaymen threatens to rape Carl, one of the assailants restrains Rick in a tight bear hug. With no gun or knife at his command, Rick resorts to his most primal and natural weapons: his teeth. In a series of unexpectedly violent panels, readers see Rick tear into his captor's neck, biting and rending the flesh as he viciously rips out the man's throat.[29] The one-time agent of law and justice then descends upon Carl's attacker with a knife, tearing the man apart like an animal. When it's all over, Rick wonders out loud if he's even human any more, but asserts he's still willing to do *anything* to protect his son.[30] Kenemore sees this transformation primarily as a good thing, a necessity for survival: "Kirkman's humans—however ineluctably—come to the realization that to survive a zombie apocalypse, they must *become like zombies themselves*."[31] Kenemore is partially correct, for, in this example particularly, Rick does become a zombie—a mindless animal that uses its teeth to bite and savage its prey. However, unlike a zombie, Rick does more than just follow his instincts for survival. Much like a battle-weary soldier for whom the concept of "murder" has grown hazy in a psychologically exhausting war zone, Rick is starting to indulge in unnecessary barbarism, starting to *enjoy* the violence, just as Tyreese feared. Rather than using the zombie monster as a metaphor for human violence, then, Kirkman is baldly presenting the human as directly and unequivocally monstrous, a devolution that becomes more overt and shocking as *The Walking Dead*'s narrative progresses.

After Dale is captured and partially eaten by a roving gang of human cannibals, Rick and his inner circle become their most monstrous, going beyond the necessity of survival and self-preservation and wallowing in atavistic violence. Rick confidently confronts the six rogues and impassively orders Andrea to shoot the ear from one and the index finger from another. Despite the ringleader's promise that they'll go away and leave Rick's group alone, Dale's friends are clearly more interested in exacting revenge than in simply keeping themselves "safe." In fact, their designs even transcend social justice—they see execution as too good for the cannibals. Mercifully, Kirkman spares reader most of the details of the resulting torture, but such horrors are indicated by an arresting two-page image of Rick's impassionate and haggard stare, as well as a series of eight vertical panels depicting splattered blood, gory weapons, and a spitted campfire.[32] Only later, as Rick speaks aloud to himself over Dale's fresh grave, does he allow himself to reflect on the gravity of what he has done: "What we've done to survive … sometimes I feel like we're no better than the dead ones. I can't stop thinking about what we did to the hunters. I know it's justifiable … but I see them when I close my eyes. … Doing what we did, to living people … after taking their weapons. … It haunts me."[33] Monsters such as zombies kill as part of their natural drive and instinct; Kirkman's monstrous humans, on the other hand, *chose* to perform their brutal acts. Rick has crossed a line, and he realizes he will forever run the risk of confusing justified self-defense with unnecessary sadism.

Because most of Rick's violence takes place outside of the panels, readers are allowed to maintain a sympathetic connection with him, however tenacious; the erstwhile lawyer Michonne's graphically depicted violence, on the other hand, alienates her from the audience. After being captured by the Governor, Michonne is repeatedly raped and abused, both physically and psychologically. He breaks her in every sense of the word, and after she is rescued by Rick and Martinez, her thoughts are on revenge, not escape. She confronts the Governor in his apartment, and over the course of *nine* vividly illustrated pages, she has her unrestrained way with him, drilling holes in his shoulder with a power drill, pulling out his fingernails, amputating his right arm, plucking out his left eye, and violating him in even worse ways.[34] Her savage behavior, in a perceptible parallel to the Abu Ghraib prison scandal of 2004, goes far beyond that feebly justified by Rick—Michonne's "justice" escalates to brutal cruelty and vengeful torture. Rick's excuse for his monstrous behavior, according to Brendan Riley, is that "even savage actions are acceptable in order to protect the group, but that savagery must be tempered by necessity, and the living must recognize it as 'bad'."[35] Michonne has no necessity behind her heinous crimes; she had been rescued and could have quietly escaped. Instead, her revenge transcends justifiable retaliation or lawful punishment—she even enjoys herself. By allowing the audience to see all the gruesome details of Michonne's vengeance, Kirkman viscerally condemns vengeful behavior, such as the waterboarding of accused terrorists that was sanctioned by the Bush Administration.

Although Kirkman may appear to approve tacitly of Rick's more justified behavior, he ultimately condemns that form of unchecked violence and aggression as well. Rick and his companions devolve so much over the course of their struggles that, by Volume 13: *Too Far Gone*, they can hardly reintegrate into a civilized social structure (as the title indicates). Although Rick is given the logical assignment of constable by Douglas, the former politician who leads a fortified survivalist camp just outside Washington D.C., Rick cannot quell his atavistic "fight or flight" impulses. One of his first acts as "keeper of the peace" is to violate the community's weapons ban, as he and Glen sneak into the armory to outfit themselves with firearms. Later, Rick loses all restraint when he breaks into the abusive Pete's home without anything resembling a warrant, assaulting the man without provocation, and throwing him through a plate glass window before threatening to kill him. Rick's actions are so violent and at odds with one-time "civilized" social codes that even Michonne recognizes he's out of control.[36] Racked with guilt and tormented by his fears, the priest Gabriel approaches Douglas secretly to warn him about Rick and his group: "These people who were with me are *not* good people. They've done things … horrible things … unspeakable things. They simply don't belong here."[37] Gabriel articulates Kirkman's warning about unchecked aggression and violence: Rick has been driven too far to the edge ever to be a compatible member of civilized society again. Do the complicit citizens of the United States face the same fate? Has the population's enthusiastic approval of aggressively violent policies toward suspected terrorists and their supporters turned honest, God-fearing, and law-abiding people into monstrous protagonists in their own right?

As *The Walking Dead* remains an incomplete and ongoing narrative, it's hard to speculate what Kirkman's ultimate resolution to these questions may be. Can one use monstrous means to accomplish noble outcomes? Is preemptive violence justified? Is it a matter of need, or simply of degree? Rick tries to explain the slaughter of the cannibals by telling Carl, "I do things … a lot of bad things, to help you and all the other people in our group … That's the world we live in now … but Carl, you need to never forget … when we do these things and we're good people … they're still bad things. … You can never lose sight of that. If these things start becoming easy that's when it's all over. That's when we become bad people."[38] The problem with Rick's impassioned speech isn't that he's wrong—it's that it *has* become easy for him. After Rick's brutal assault and murder of Carl's attacker, a stunned Abraham soberly tells Rick, "You don't just come back from something like that. ... You don't rip a man apart—hold his insides in your hand—you can't go back to being dear old dad after that. You're never the same. Not after what you did."[39] Abraham, the confessed murderer, is the only protagonist in *The Walking Dead* who sees things for what they really are. As much as Rick might tell himself and those around him that his violence is justified, such actions irrevocably change him, pushing him ever further away from his origins as an upholder of the peace. Perhaps Abraham speaks directly for Kirkman here, articulating the thesis of the series—it's already too late; the United States and its citizenry cannot go back to the way things were before they chose to become monstrous.

The Walking Dead demonstrates an increased level of violence and monstrosity on the part of the human protagonists, but should we really be surprised by this development in the subgenre? After all, a dangerous, barbaric protagonist stood at the center of the very first zombie invasion narrative, *Night of the Living Dead*. In his desperate efforts to protect himself from a countryside full of zombies, Ben (Duane Jones) not only slaps the hysterical Barbra (Judith O'Dea) into submission, but he also beats and shoots Harry (Karl Hardman) when the man disagrees with Ben's plans. The potential for human monstrosity, it appears, has always existed—but something *has* changed. These new stories manifest the world's increased tolerance for interpersonal violence, potentially unethical political policies, and a "kill before they kill us" attitude. In a chilling reflection of post-9/11 U.S. military and political actions, such vicious protagonists are direct analogs not only for contemporary national leaders, but also for a complicit and bloodthirsty citizenry. As with Rick's rag-tag group of calloused survivors, the monstrous actions of the U.S. have transformed its people as well—into the very thing they were initially fighting against. For Kirkman, the zombies aren't metaphors for human failings; they are the catalyst that reveals the monstrous potential that has been exposed within us all. It's no longer the terror of what *might* happen to humanity under such incredible circumstances but rather the realization of the horror our world has *already* become that really scares us.

Notes

1 Peter Dendle, *The Zombie Movie Encyclopedia* (Jefferson, NC: McFarland, 2001), 12.

2 In addition to the "serious" zombie narratives that present the human protagonists as monstrous—which is the focus of this essay—many zombie comedies, such as Andrew Currie's *Fido* (2006) and Matthew Kohnen's *Wasting Away* (2007), offer a similar inversion. These "zombedies" ask audiences to consider the zombies in sympathetic terms, pitted against cruel and menacing human antagonists, but such texts are beyond the scope of this investigation.

3 Although the AMC television series *The Walking Dead* (2010–) is headed in the same dark direction as its antecedent source material, I have limited this essay to an investigation of Kirkman's comic series alone.

4 Friedrich Nietzsche, *Beyond Good and Evil*, trans. Marianne Cowan (Chicago: Gateway, 1955), 85.

5 Kevin Alexander Boon, "Ontological Anxiety Made Flesh: The Zombie in Literature, Film and Culture," in *Monsters and the Monstrous: Myths and Metaphors of Enduring Evil*, ed. Niall Scott (Amsterdam: Rodophi, 2007), 33–43.

6 Ibid., 34.

7 Jeffrey Jerome Cohen, "Monster Culture (Seven Theses)," in *Monster Theory: Reading Culture*, (ed.) Jeffrey Jerome Cohen (Minneapolis: University of Minnesota Press, 1996), 3–25.

8 Ibid., 4.

9 Scott Kenemore, "Rick Grimes: A Zombie Among Men," in *Triumph of The Walking Dead: Robert Kirkman's Zombie Epic on Page and Screen*, (ed.) James Lowder (Dallas: Benbella Books, 2011), 185–99.

10 At the 33rd International Conference on the Fantastic in the Arts, China Mieville argued that humans, by definition, cannot be "monsters" but only described as "monstrous" ("Special Panel: The Monstrous," moderator: F. Brett Cox, March 22, 2012), thus my attempts to delineate the difference between a liminal Other acting according to its violent nature and a human being making horrifying and destructive choices.

11 George A. Romero, dir., *Survival of the Dead* (Blank of the Dead Productions, 2009).

12 Robert Kirkman, *Days Gone Bye*, The Walking Dead 1 (Orange, CA: Image Comics, 2004).

13 Ibid.

14 Ibid.

15 Brendan Riley, "Zombie People," in Lowder, *Triumph of The Walking Dead*, 81–97.

16 Kirkman, *Days Gone Bye*.

17 Robert Kirkman, *Miles Behind Us*, The Walking Dead 2 (Orange, CA: Image Comics, 2004).

18 Kenemore, 193.

19 Robert Kirkman, *Safety Behind Bars*, The Walking Dead 3 (Berkeley: Image Comics, 2005).

20 Robert Kirkman, *The Heart's Desire*, The Walking Dead 4 (Berkeley: Image Comics, 2005).

21 Kirkman, *Safety Behind Bars*.

22 On September 30, 2011, U.S.-born Anwar al-Awlaki was killed in a drone strike in Yemen on the direct orders of President Obama ("Islamist Cleric Anwar al-Awlaki Killed in Yemen," *News: Middle East*, BBC, September 30, 2011, http://www.bbc.co.uk/news/world-middle-east-15121879). Critics of the military action claim that, since al-Awlaki was still a U.S. citizen, he should have been tried in a court rather than being killed without due process and outside of an active war zone (see Jijo Jacob, "Anwar Al-Awlaki: Critics Say Killing Breaches Norms, Sets Wrong Precedent," *US, International Business Times*, October 3, 2011, http://www.ibtimes.com/articles/223724/20111003/anwar-al-awlaki-critics-say-killing-breaches-norms-sets-wrong-precedent-al-qaida-yemen-drone.htm).

23 Kirkman, *The Heart's Desire*.

24 Ibid.

25 Ibid.

26 This totalitarian approach to safety and order is made more explicit in the AMC television adaptation of *The Walking Dead*, when Rick's rule is cynically designated a "Ricktatorship" (Ernest R. Dickerson, dir., "Beside the Dying Fire," *The Walking Dead*, AMC, March 18, 2012).

27 Robert Kirkman, *This Sorrowful Life*, The Walking Dead 6 (Berkeley: Image Comics, 2007).

28 Kirkman, *The Heart's Desire*.

29 Robert Kirkman, *What We Become*, The Walking Dead 10 (Berkeley: Image Comics, 2009).

30 Ibid.

31 Kenemore, 187.

32 Robert Kirkman, *Fear the Hunters*, The Walking Dead 11 (Berkeley: Image Comics, 2009).

33 Ibid.

34 Kirkman, *This Sorrowful Life*.

35 Riley, 96.

36 Robert Kirkman, *Too Far Gone*, The Walking Dead 13 (Berkeley: Image Comics, 2010).

37 Ibid.

38 Robert Kirkman, *Life Among Them*, The Walking Dead 12 (Berkeley: Image Comics, 2010).

39 Kirkman, *What We Become*.

5

The *Monster* in the mirror:

Reflecting and deflecting the mobility of gendered violence onscreen

Megan Foley

Representations of gender have historically hinged on a division between private and public space. However, in an age characterized by accelerating mobility, the spatial divisions that structure traditional gender norms have begun to disintegrate. Destabilizing the boundaries of domestic space, that mobility appears monstrous. *Monster*, the 2003 Hollywood motion picture, presents a particularly vivid symptom of these popular fears about mobility and domesticity, depicting the circulation of "domestic violence" beyond the domestic sphere.

The film—which won critical and popular acclaim—presents a biographical portrait of Aileen Wuornos, the first convicted female serial killer in the United States. The film and its popular reception vacillate between, on the one hand, portraying Wuornos as a victim of child abuse, prostitution, and rape, and on the other, portraying her as a monstrous, inhuman murderess. Although the text of the film had the potential to complicate traditional gendered boundaries structured by feminized domestic space, the film's uptake ultimately resecured those gendered spatial divisions by protecting the popular investment in an idealized vision of the American family.

Initially, discussions about Aileen Wuornos as a predatory "highway hooker" in the mainstream American media crystallized popular anxieties about mobility, violence, and the intimate interior space of American family life. According to media reports, Wuornos exemplified monstrous femininity because, unlike other female murderers, she killed serially: randomly, repeatedly, rapaciously, and outside her own home. This aggressive, mobile, public, and strange form of violence challenged the public's imagination of women's violence as defensive, contained, private, and familiar.

Yet ultimately, critical and popular reception of the film disavowed these gendered cultural anxieties about monstrous mobility by focusing instead on actress Charlize Theron, whose media-hyped backstory as a victim of family violence came to stand in for proper femininity and domesticity. The film's popular uptake resisted identification with the monstrous image of Wuornos, instead imagining Theron as a feminine victim-heroine behind the screen. Ultimately, that visual substitution functions as a mode of popular affective fixation that restabilizes the fantasy of domestic security in an era of increasingly mobile gender spatial categorizations.

Monstrous mobility and serial violence

When Aileen Wuornos was arrested and charged with the murder of Richard Mallory, and implicated in the shooting deaths of six other Florida men, she was dubbed a serial killer. However, news reports stressed that she was not just any serial killer. *Newsweek* reported: "Florida has had its share of serial killers. Now it may have another, but with a twist: the accused is a woman."[1] The article implied that although serial killers are nothing new, Aileen Wuornos, as a female serial killer, is more surprising and more "twisted" than her male counterparts. Ignoring the small percentage of other female serial killers, many news reports depicted Wuornos as the first and only female serial killer in the nation. For example, the *CBS Evening News* said Wuornos had "earn[ed] a place in the annals of American crime as the first female serial killer."[2] This insistence that Aileen Wuornos was the first and only female serial killer marked a collective investment in disavowing women's violence. By marking Wuornos as an exception, the discourse about her protected an image of women as nonviolent, even passive. Even those who questioned her primacy as the first female serial killer displayed a similar investment in maintaining a domesticated image of women's violence. The *Washington Post* explained why Wuornos's case seemed so unique:

> While other women have been involved in multiple murders, none until Wuornos had killed in ways normally associated with male murder.

Wuornos worked alone and used a gun to kill strangers ... For the most part, other female murderers used poisons to kill victims they knew.[3]

Even though acknowledging that Wuornos is not the only female killer in history, these reports suggested that there was something peculiarly masculine that distinguished Wuornos from other murderesses. Serial murder experts explained that, like male serial killers, Aileen Wuornos enjoyed the power she felt over her victims: "being a serial killer is 'all about power.' And, maybe, about being a man."[4] The parallelism between "about power" and "about being a man" in this statement equates power with being a man, linking serial killing to both. Yet while the press depicted Wuornos as killing for power "like a man," they also took her serial killing as evidence of a hateful desire to overpower men. A serial murder expert, quoted in *USA Today*, explained: "It's like a hunter looking at a trophy to prove he was stronger, more powerful than his adversary. What you have here is a feeling of power and control over someone who is hated ...You don't have to be an $80-an-hour-doctor to see she had a hatred of men."[5] While the interviewee likened Wuornos to men to describe her as predatory and power-hungry—using the masculine pronouns "he" and "his" in the analogy—he stated at the same time that she hated men and wanted to overpower them.

Media reports linked manliness and man-hating in the female serial killer by emphasizing Wuornos's sexuality. The *New York Times* made this link most explicitly: "The press and especially the television tabloid shows had a field day with the story about what they called 'the man-hating murderer,' apparently because Ms. Wuornos was an admitted lesbian."[6] However, despite all the media hype, Aileen Wuornos was not an admitted lesbian. In interviews, she repeatedly refused the label "lesbian," explaining that she and Tyria Moore—the woman news reports consistently described as her "lesbian lover"[7]—were "like sisters" and "just tight friends."[8] Wuornos's biographer Sue Russell corroborated: "We'll never know the 'x-factor' that tipped her into serial murder, but the media's 'man-hating lesbian' label was off the mark."[9] The media's unexamined insistence that Aileen Wuornos killed men because she was a man-hating lesbian, despite her own repeated and widely publicized claims to the contrary, marks a popular investment in disarticulating heteronormative femininity from predatory violence. Through this articulation of lesbianism, man-hating, and serial killing, media reports affirmed the safety and non-violence of heterosexual domesticity organized by norms of female passivity.

What distinguished Wuornos from other female killers, according to mainstream discourse, was that her murders defied the domesticity and passivity that generally characterize women's violence. As Kyra Pearson argues, Aileen Wuornos troubled the existing gendered matrix of intelligibility:

"So saturated with domesticity is criminology's classification of female killers that Wuornos stumped serial killing [experts] because she acted violently in a non-domestic space and with strangers."[10] For example, a guest expert interviewed on MSNBC pointed to Wuornos's stranger killings as uniquely similar to male serial killers: "The only person who has ever even approached the parameters set for male serial killers is Aileen Wuornos. She killed in a way that male serial killers do, pretty much stranger to stranger."[11] Here, Wuornos's acts were unique for a woman, not because she killed multiple people, but because she killed them *strangely*: that is, she killed strangers in a random, predatory way outside the domestic space of the home. Pearson persuasively demonstrates how the so-called "highway hooker" troubles binary notions of privacy and publicity, manifested in Wuornos's case as a division between the home and the highway.[12]

In addition to problematizing the otherwise neatly intelligible spaces of domesticity and publicity, the figure of Aileen Wuornos reconfigured the public through a collective investment in defending domestic space. Wuornos received national attention as "America's first female serial killer" not only because she challenged normative divisions between the private and public spheres—killing strangers outside the domestic space of the home—but also because the story of her serial killings circulated publicly, producing a "relation among strangers" in the social imaginary.[13] As Michael Warner explains, publics emerge through "stranger sociability," in which individuals do not relate to each other directly, but instead are indirectly linked together by a shared, mediated relationship to a text that addresses them all.[14] In the case of Aileen Wuornos, that shared text was the film *Monster*.

Masking monstrosity through visual substitution

While the story of Aileen Wuornos has been the subject of several news articles, television shows, books, and documentaries over the last two decades, the film *Monster* was the most broadly circulated and elicited the biggest audience response. The film's motif of mirrors stages a visual identi-fication with Wuornos that had the potential to reorient viewers' investment in viewing her as an undomesticated monster. However, the overall uptake of the film in popular discourse—including blogs, newspaper articles, television interviews, and film reviews—indicates that many viewers focused exclu-sively on actress Charlize Theron, ignoring the visual identification with Wuornos that the film staged. Viewers' uptake of the film substituted Charlize Theron—who came to operate as a symbol of domestic security—for Aileen

Wuornos—a symptom of the undomesticated mobility of gendered violence. In this way, audience responses rhetorically re-contained gendered violence within restabilized boundaries of domestic space.

The initial reception of the film after its 2003 release focused on the compassion that viewers felt for the fictionalized version of Wuornos. As one of Wuornos's biographers wrote in a *Washington Post* editorial: "The audience, watching breathlessly, feels a rush of sympathy for her."[15] The movie produced this sympathy for Wuornos through visual identification. Reviews emphasized the scenes that featured the monster in the mirror, scenes in which the framing of the film positions the viewer to look into a mirror and see the face of Aileen Wuornos looking back. For example: "There are repeated moments when she catches sight of herself in the mirror and almost can't believe what she has seen. What impresses you most is how tragic the story is."[16] As this review indicates, the scenes in the mirror elicit viewers' sympathy for Wuornos. "At its best, the film has a concise visual logic that speaks for itself. After one murder, we get the briefest glimpse of Wuornos inspecting her bloodstained body in the mirror."[17] According to popular criticism, the scenes in front of the mirror functioned as an exemplary set of moments that characterize *Monster* in its audience's view.

The movie's mirror motif encouraged viewers to identify with Wuornos. In these mirrored scenes, the *Washington Post* reported, "the character seems most human and most like us."[18] Jacques Lacan uses the concept-metaphor of a mirror to explain this process of identification.[19] The mirror image constitutes the viewing subject by reflecting a stable, coherent image of the viewer back to himself or herself. However, this encounter with the mirror reflection is also alienating because that mirror image of the viewer is positioned outside himself or herself. In other words, the viewer looks at his or her reflection from the visual position of another person, viewing the reflected image of himself or herself as though it were someone else. The movie *Monster* shows its viewers an image of Aileen Wuornos as though it were a mirror image of themselves, creating an alienating identification with Wuornos and constituting themselves in the image of this monstrous other. Through this visual staging of identification, *Monster* encouraged the audience to view Wuornos sympathetically as a humanized victim. As a *Washington Post* reviewer explained: "Theron and debuting writer-director Patty Jenkins make it their mission to evoke the humanity in this woman and to make us realize that ... Aileen certainly isn't the monster."[20]

Yet while the film *Monster* initially alarmed critics by inviting viewers' identification with the monstrous image of Aileen Wuornos, it turned out that viewers were much more likely to focus their view on Charlize Theron. More than the movie's storyline, the film's viewers celebrated actress Charlize

Theron's portrayal of Aileen Wuornos. While *Monster* took in a respectable $35 million at the U.S. box office, most of the revenue was collected after Charlize Theron's Oscar nomination was announced—before the nomination, the box office take was only $3 million.[21] Theron's performance won both an Academy Award and a Golden Globe for Best Actress. Her performance also garnered several lesser-known awards, including Best Actress at the Film Independent's Spirit Awards, MTV Movie Awards, National Society of Film Critics Awards, and the International Press Academy Satellite Awards. Well-known movie critic Robert Ebert declared Theron's performance "one of the best performances in the history of cinema."[22]

Ebert's praise is illustrative of the general reaction to the film: while viewers found Theron's performance superlative, they were largely underwhelmed by the movie as a whole. One review described it as: "An okay movie made nearly great by one great thing: the bravura, mercilessly watchable performance of Charlize Theron."[23] Another critic even called *Monster* "[a] gruesome, helpless spiral barely saved by an actress locating humanity where few would have cared to bother."[24] The general audience made similar assessments. As one blogger wrote: "This was not an easy movie to like but I was so enthralled at Charlize Theron's makeover and performance that it took center stage over the story."[25] Critics and general audiences alike disparaged the film's narrative and focused instead on Charlize's performance.

The popular uptake of the movie *Monster* performed this substitution by largely ignoring the film's content and highlighting the physical appearance of Charlize Theron in the guise of Aileen Wuornos. Caroline Picart notes the "heavy media emphasis on ... the transmogrification of Theron's physical perfections into a grotesquely real simulation of the actual Wuornos," and distinguishes it from the content of the film itself.[26] Discussions of the film stressed the physical surface of Charlize Theron's body in her portrayal of Aileen Wuornos: "We have to just start with the surface stuff because it is so staggering."[27] Most reviews of the film mention the physical "transformation" of Wuornos, and many focus on it exclusively. The *New York Times* is illustrative of this repeated refrain: "Charlize Theron pulls off the year's most astounding screen makeover."[28] Often, reviewers described Theron's transformation into Wuornos as a double or a mirror: "an amazing physical copy" or a "a dead-on facsimile."[29] *USA Today* reported that: "Even Theron found herself unrecognizable when she looked in the mirror after being made up as Wuornos."[30] Theron explained: "[M]y biggest concern was that when I looked in the mirror, I would see her and not me."[31]

The metaphor of the mirror, in this way of looking, is not a reflection, but instead appears as an artificial image, a mask that seems to veil some deeper truth. Unlike the reflective mirror in which a viewer imagines and identifies with his own reflection, Lacan explains, the image of a mask or veil "incites him [the viewer] to ask what is behind it."[32] Rather than looking at the monster mirror as a reflection, much of the uptake of the film *Monster* treated the image of Aileen Wuornos as a mask, a mere covering surface that invited viewers to ask what was underneath. This way of watching *Monster* interrupts the reflexive circuit of viewer identification. Rather than being taken up as the viewer's image reflected in the mirror, the image of the monster is instead read popularly as a mask that the viewer tries to see through. Rather than reflexively looking at themselves as the object reflected in the *Monster* mirror, viewers instead looked to Charlize Theron as the "true" object behind the screen. By looking for Theron rather themselves in the monstrous image of Wuornos, viewers did not put themselves in Wuornos's place—instead, they replaced that monstrous image with the attractive actress who portrayed her.

Just as the uptake of the film emphasized Theron's make*over* into Aileen Wuornos, it located Charlize Theron *under* the surface of Aileen Wuornos. National Public Radio's "Fresh Air" predicts to listeners, "You'll spend the first few minutes searching for Theron under all that makeup."[33] This formulation envisions an audience seeking a Charlize Theron hiding underneath the guise of Aileen Wuornos. Repeatedly, articles detailed the body adornments and modifications used to make Theron look like Wuornos, including her weight gain, false teeth, haircut, brown contact lenses, and heavy makeup. The DVD version of the film includes a documentary, "The Making of a *Monster*," that explains and demonstrates the two-hour-long, step-by-step layering of makeup and costuming that make Theron disappear under Wuornos's face and body.[34] Wuornos's bodily surface functions as a role or disguise, underneath which Theron withdraws and becomes invisible. Visually depicting the figuration of Wuornos as a mask for Theron, *Bright Lights Film Journal* featured a cartoon in which Charlize Theron holds a mask of Aileen Wuornos's face in front of her own.[35] Reactions to the film suggested that viewers understood the monster as a mask, trying to look through or look beyond the mirror to a hidden interior, instead of seeing the surface of the mirror as reflecting back.

Imagining Wuornos's body as mask for Theron positions Theron as a true depth and Wuornos as a false surface. Aileen is the mask; Charlize is under the mask. Viewers are comforted that Charlize Theron is the beautiful actuality that exists underneath the horrific image of Aileen Wuornos. If Aileen Wuornos was actually Charlize Theron all along, her viewers are saved from identifying with the monster in the mirror. The figure of Charlize Theron functions as an alibi that keeps the viewer from reconsidering, let alone identifying with, the monstrosity of Aileen Wuornos. The film's popular uptake resisted identification with the character mirrored back at the viewer, as viewers looked through the mirror as a screen and imagined the smooth contours of Theron's face behind the distorted monster mask. The uptake of the film assured viewers that, not only was Wuornos a monster, she was also just a character in *Monster*—a character that Charlize Theron played very, very well. This allowed the image of Charlize Theron to function as a "real" substitute for the seemingly "fictional" life story of Aileen Wuornos. Identifying with Wuornos would have required viewers to recognize themselves in the monstrous image of gendered violence that Wuornos represented, and thereby recognize that violence as a public problem. However, substituting Theron for Wuornos allowed viewers to hold onto an idealized image of feminine domesticity. While Wuornos's story depicted the monstrous, mobile violence that could not be contained within the boundaries of the domestic sphere, commentators retold Theron's story in a way that allowed viewers to sustain a more traditional narrative of gendered violence relegated to the private interior domain of family intimacy.

Projecting the emotional interior of domestic space

Commentators suggested that Theron's widely acclaimed exterior performance could be attributed to her interior emotional life. More than just a physical transformation, many commentators noted that Theron's interior was also transformed. CNN reported that playing Aileen Wuornos "transformed [Charlize Theron] inside and out."[36] Viewers metaphorically projected their vision past the character's exterior to look inside Theron. From her bodily surface, audiences imagined her soul: Theron was credited with a "soul-searching performance"[37] and "emotional soul-baring."[38] Audiences suggested that, by animating Wuornos's appearance on the surface, Theron's performance enabled a visual projection beyond that appearance, a 'sneak peek' into her emotional interior, a Theron family secret beneath the surface.

The press attributed Theron's successful performance to her own encounter with intimate violence, when she watched her mother shoot and kill her abusive father. A reviewer on National Public Radio speculated: "Charlize Theron's empathy for the role may come from her own biography. When she was a teen-ager in her native South Africa, Theron was attacked and nearly raped by her father. Her mother shot and killed him in the act. She was tried and acquitted."[39] Theron's encounter with family violence, which many film reviewers emphasized, functioned as a more normative substitute for Wuornos's serial killings. As Pearson shows, Wuornos's serial murders fail to fit the norms of intelligibility for female violence and victimization: "prevailing conceptions of violent women rest on spatial and gender norms narrowly configured around white familial intimacy."[40] Theron's story, on the other hand, did fit within those spatialized norms of domestic privacy that render women's violence intelligible.

While Aileen Wuornos's threatened familial space from outside, Gerda Theron's violence defended it from inside. Understood as protecting her family, Gerda Theron's killing was intelligible as an act of self-defense, while Aileen Wuornos, whose serial killing threatened the image of the functional nuclear family, appeared as an unintelligible monster. ABC's *Primetime Live* tapped into the narrative of family intimacy in an interview with Theron the evening before the film *Monster* was released: "Charlize Theron has a complex and wrenching story all her own. She was just 15 years old, when her mother shot her father ... The story is not a simple mother–daughter fairy tale."[41] Though the family "fairy tale" was complicated by Theron's mother shooting her father, it none the less remained a viable framework for interpreting her mother's killing. By focusing on Charlize Theron to the exclusion of the Wuornos character she played, the popular uptake of the film recentered a normative narrative of women's violence contained within the boundaries of domestic space. This projection of Charlize Theron's interior transformation kept most viewers from encountering anything monstrous in *Monster*.

However, although the figure of Charlize Theron replaced the distorted monster in the popular uptake of the film, at times she became a sign of that monstrosity herself. While many praised her transformation into the Wuornos character, viewers sometimes worried whether Charlize Theron was too much like Aileen Wuornos. That is, the more convincing a copy she was of Wuornos, the less the monster seemed like a mere mask for a hidden interior. At times, viewers said that they could no longer distinguish between Charlize Theron and Aileen Wuornos. Reviews in the *New York Times*, the CBS *Early Show*, and the *Washington Post* all described Theron as "unrecognizable" in *Monster*.[42] Here, the discourse of masquerade, which clearly distinguishes Aileen Wuornos from Charlize Theron, gives way to a discourse of mimesis: there is no longer any recognizable distinction between the two.

Viewers who watched *Monster* and pictured Charlize Theron behind or beyond a Wuornos mask were often disturbed when their optic of "false" surface and "true" depth collapsed. One radio announcer disclosed: "Charlize Theron is not just persuasive, she's completely unrecognizable ... The resemblance to the real Wuornos is downright scary. I had to find a picture of Theron after the screening to remind myself what she really looks like."[43] When the film rendered Theron and Wuornos visually indistinguishable, this viewer is horrified, compelled to remind himself that Theron is not a repulsive monster. He tries to reinstall a distinction between Theron's "resemblance" and the "real Wuornos." Even further, he found a picture to establish what Theron "really looks like." This viewer is not alone. One *New York Times* review predicts that those "who were entranced by Charlize Theron's eerily accurate impersonation of Wuornos in 'Monster' will want to compare her performance with the real Wuornos,"[44] and another describes their similarity as "disturbing, uncannily accurate."[45] The accuracy of Charlize's mimicry evoked an urge to reinstate the distinction between surface and depth, and between falsity and actuality, between the troubling story of Wuornos's "predatory" violence and the normative story of women's victimization and familial protection that Theron came to represent.

Even film critic Roger Ebert expressed his discomfiture when the distinction between character Wuornos and actress Theron blurred: "There's the uncanny sensation that Theron has forgotten the camera and the script and is directly channeling her ideas about Aileen Wuornos. She has made herself the instrument of this character."[46] What makes Ebert's skin crawl is not only that Theron has forgotten the camera and the script, but that she has forgotten *herself*. It seems that Aileen Wuornos may be animating Theron's body: Theron's body is an instrument, a direct channel for Wuornos. What strikes Ebert as "uncanny" is that Theron might be possessed by Wuornos. Is it Theron—the victim-guardian of domestic space—or Wuornos—the monster-symptom of serial mobility—holding that gun?

The uptake of the film marked viewers' investment in projecting a vision of the "actual," beautiful, victimized interior of Charlize Theron from her "fake," ugly, and dangerous *Monster* mask. Tellingly, what frightens viewers about the film is not Wuornos's story, in which she was sexually abused by her family, raped and tortured by strangers, killed seven, and was put to death by the state. Nor is it Theron's story, in which she witnessed her mother kill her alcoholic and abusive father. Instead, the "downright scary" thing was that Wuornos and Theron's stories might be same. Viewers expressed the most anxiety about *Monster* when they could no longer see the beautiful, victimized "reality" of Theron underneath and distinct from the Wuornos character. *Monster* seemed truly monstrous when there was no longer a normative figure to forestall viewers' identification with the image of a man-hating, serial-killing, inhuman lesbian prostitute that threatened to undermine the privileged vision of gendered domestic space. Against the visual form of the film, which depicted the monstrous serial mobility of gendered violence outside the boundaries of domestic space, viewers' responses struggled to contain gendered violence inside—inside the interior space of the victim's emotional experience, inside the private sphere of the nuclear family, and ultimately, inside the heteronormative narratives of passivity and intimacy that domesticate gendered violence.

Notes

1 Ned Zeman, "A Case of Sex and Death in Florida," *Newsweek*, January 20, 1992, 6.

2 Giselle Fernandez and Juan Vasquez, "Accused Woman Serial Killer on Trial in Florida," *CBS Morning News*, CBS, January 16, 1992.

3 Henry Allen, "We Find the Defendant … Everywhere," *Washington Post*, February 12, 1992.

4 "Femme Fatale," *New York Times*, February 2, 1991.

5 Deborah Sharp, "'Damsel of Death' Trial Starts in Florida," *USA Today*, January 13, 1992.

6 Vincent Canby, "First the Murders, Then the Merchandising," *New York Times*, October 9, 1993.

7 Zeman, "A Case of Sex and Death in Florida," 6.

8 Montel Williams, "Serial Killers Revisited: Aileen Wuornos and Westley Allan Dodd," *The Montel Williams Show*, February 26, 2004.

9 Sue Russell, "Serial Killer Aileen Wuornos Chooses Execution," *Sue Russell Writes*, http://www.suerussellwrites.com/wuornos2.html/

10 Kyra Pearson, "The Trouble with Aileen Wuornos, Feminism's 'First Serial Killer,'" *Communication and Critical/Cultural Studies* 4 (2007): 259.

11 Jerry Nachman and Jeannie Ohm, *Nachman*, MSNBC, October 8, 2002.

12 Pearson, "The Trouble with Aileen Wuornos," 261.

13 Michael Warner, "Publics and Counterpublics," *Public Culture* 14, no. 1 (2002): 55.

14 Ibid., 52.

15 Sue Russell, "More of a Monster Than Hollywood Could Picture," *Washington Post*, February 8, 2004.

16 Allan Hunter, "Your Weekend Starts Here: Monster in Despair," *The Express*, April 2, 2004, 47.

17 Jonathan Romney, "Dying is an Art, and She Does it Very Well," *Independent*, April 4, 2004, 18.

18 Michael O'Sullivan, "Theron Holds 'Monster' in Her Grip," *Washington Post*, January 9, 2004.

19 Jacques Lacan, "The Mirror Stage as Formative of the *I* Function as Revealed in Psychoanalytic Experience," in *Écrits: A Selection,* trans. Bruce Fink (New York: W. W. Norton and Company, 2002), 76.

20 Desson Thomson, "'Aileen': How a 'Monster' Was Made," *Washington Post*, February 13, 2004.

21 Carl DiOrio, "'Monster' Mash," *Variety,* March 22, 2004, 5; "Business Digest," *New York Times,* February 2, 2004.

22 Roger Ebert, "Beyond Redemption: Charlize Theron Gives Meaning to 'Monster'," *Chicago Sun-Times*, January 1, 2004.

23 O'Sullivan, "Theron Holds 'Monster' in Her Grip."

24 Ty Burr, "'Monster' Role Makes Quite an Impact: Theron Turns Killer Role into True 'Monster'," *Boston Globe*, January 9, 2004.

25 Internet Movie Database, "Monster," http://www.imdb.com/title/tt0340855/maindetails/

26 Caroline J. Picart, "Crime and the Gothic: Sexualizing Serial Killers," *Journal of Criminal Justice and Popular Culture* 13, no. 1 (2006): 6.

27 Diane Sawyer, "Charlize Theron Actress Stars in 'Monster'," *Good Morning America*, ABC, January 8, 2004.

28 Stephen Holden, "A Murderous Journey to Self-Destruction," *New York Times*, December 24, 2003.

29 Denby, "Killer: Two Views of Aileen Wuornos," 84; Russell, "More of a Monster Than Hollywood Could Picture."

30 Donna Freydkin, "For Her: In These Roles, Beauty Does an About-Face," *USA Today*, December 29, 2003.

31 Ibid.

32 Jacques Lacan, *The Four Fundamental Concepts of Psychoanalysis*, ed. Jacques-Alain Miller, trans. Alan Sheridan (New York: W. W. Norton and Company, 1977), 112.

33 "Aileen Wuornos' Life Story Portrayed in 'Monster' and 'Aileen,' Both Worth Seeing," *Fresh Air*, National Public Radio, January 9, 2004.

34 *Monster*, DVD, directed by Patty Jenkins (Los Angeles, CA: Media 8 Entertainment, 2003).

35 Edward D. Miller, "Capturing the Beauty of the Beast," Bright Lights Film Journal, February, 2004, http://www.brightlightsfilm.com/43/monster.htm/

36 Kathleen Hays and Daryn Kagan, "Does 'Monster' Distort the True Story?" *The Flipside*, CNN, February 27, 2004.

37 Hilton Als, "Against Type," *The New Yorker*, February 2, 2004, 31.

38 Stephen Holden, "The Performances in Close-Up: Best Actress," *New York Times*, February 15, 2004.

39 "New Film 'Monster' Profiles Serial Killer Aileen Wuornos," *All Things Considered*, National Public Radio, December 29, 2003.

40 Pearson, "The Trouble with Aileen Wuornos," 258.

41 "Charlize Theron: New Movie Turns Actress into Monster," *Primetime Live*, ABC, January 8, 2004.

42 Stephen Holden, "Holiday Movies' Somber Embrace," *New York Times*, January 2, 2004; Rene Syler, "Charlize Theron Discusses Her Role in the Film 'Monster'," *The Early Show*, CBS, January 9, 2004; Thomson, "Inside the Skin of a Killer."

43 "New Movie 'Monster'," *All Things Considered*, National Public Radio, December 28, 2003.

44 Stephen Holden, "Real Life Behind 'Monster': A Serial Killer's Last Days," *New York Times*. January 9, 2004.

45 Holden, "The Performances in Close-Up: Best Actress."

46 Ebert, "Beyond Redemption: Charlize Theron Gives Meaning to 'Monster'."

6

Intersectionality bites:

Metaphors of race and sexuality in HBO's *True Blood*

Peter Odell Campbell

This chapter examines the television series *True Blood*[1] as a queer political text. The non-pejorative "queer" of everyday U.S. speech has come to denote an identity category grounded in sexual difference, dissidence, and "dishomogeneity"[2] that may be inclusive of, but also different from, the more specifically defined "lesbian," "gay," "bisexual," and "transgender" (LGBT). In a similar but not identical move, "queer" can also be used as an umbrella term to broadly and efficiently describe multiple specific categories of sexual minority identity at the same time. In both of these senses, the narrative and characters of *True Blood* represent queers and queerness with a frequency and centrality still uncommon to contemporary U.S. major media.[3] But here (focusing primarily on *True Blood*'s first season) I want to consider the series as a queer *text*—that is, to think beyond the question of the presence of queer characters in *True Blood*'s narrative in order to examine some of the ways in which the series functions as a vehicle for a particular kind of queer politics.

Vampires and queer metaphor in *True Blood*

In contrast to the assimilationist and state-focused activism of lesbian and gay "liberation" organizations,[4] "queer politics"[5] exposes and presents alternatives to institutionalized heteronormativity,[6] embraces difference, resists assimi-lation and institutionalization, and combats "disciplining, normalizing social forces"[7] in whatever form these might be encountered.[8] Precisely because "queer" is typically a refusal of specific identification, queer politics can have the ironic effect of effacing differences and diversity—particularly in terms of race and class—among those persons and political goals understood as "queer."[9] Consequently, in asking how and in what ways *True Blood* functions as a queer political text, I follow the feminist and queer of color theorist Cathy J. Cohen's 1997 call for a queer politics that moves beyond identity to define queer and queerness in terms of a fluid and contextual oppositional stance to "dominant norms" of sexuality, gender, race, and class.[10] "Queer" for Cohen should be understood in part as a radical political orientation against the *intersecting* oppressions of racism, sexism, classism, and heter-onormativity. Absent such an intersectional approach (which acknowledges and responds to the inevitable and inextricable overlap of different forms of identity and oppression), Cohen argues that queer and feminist politics tend to assumptively marginalize persons who experience identity and subjectivity in multiple, simultaneous, and overlapping forms.

True Blood is a show about monstrosity in general and vampires in particular, as well as the relationship of both to a troubled notion of what it might mean to be human. The vampire—and in particular the televisual vampire—is an ideal representational vehicle for queerness and queer politics.[11] Vampires are not just insistently present in culture,[12] but present as metaphors. Vampire-as-metaphor operates as a kind of catch-all for representations of distance from cultural norms in not only negative but ambiguous and intriguing form:[13] a producer of popular culture looking for a metaphorical vehicle to stand in for any "real" form of distance from the normative should find the vampire ideal. The vampire's liminal (in between, marginal, at once vital and dead) nature renders it available as a metaphorical figure for the representation of otherness in terms that are more complex than positive or negative. In their representation of varied and diverse similarities, differences, and distance from "human" norms of life and relation, the vampires of *True Blood* function metaphorically as a stand-in for queers, queerness, and queer politics in contemporary U.S. public life. *True Blood* is perennially lauded by the Gay and Lesbian Alliance Against Defamation (GLAAD) for not only the presence of its lesbian, gay, and bisexual characters, but also for the diversity of queer and queer of color experiences these mostly human characters represent—in particular, the Black queer human Lafayette.[14] It is in *True Blood*'s vampires, however, that not only the potential but significant limitations of its intersectional queer politics become clear.

In the United States, the anti-statist and assimilationist radicalism[15] of queer politics is increasingly belied by the selective appropriation and assimilation of certain forms of queer life and relation into the statist and heteronormative institutions and processes of U.S. public life. This process of appropriation and assimilation works in tandem with an increasingly pervasive "post-racial"[16] politics that works to deny the ongoing and significant presence of racial hierarchy and oppression in U.S. national culture. The post-racial normalization of queer identity comes at the expense of what Cohen calls the "secondary marginalization"[17] of certain queer—particularly woman, poor, working class, and queer of color—subjects within "mainstream" gay, lesbian, and queer activist politics.[18] As Jasbir K. Puar and Amit S. Rai argue, while it is true that "'the nation disallows queerness' … some queers are better than others."[19] The interaction between the various vampire characters and their human interlocutors on *True Blood* functions metaphorically for this dynamic; it is clear from the first episode of the series that, while all vampires hunger for human blood, some vampires are better than others. The early seasons of *True Blood* in particular frame trouble with certain vampires in part as a trouble with intersectionality—with the dangers inherent in a vampire subject's refusal to act in accordance with normal and singular notions of how both vampires and humans should perform their identities.

Vampires and the politics of intersectionality

Alan Ball's *True Blood* debuted on the Home Box Office Network (HBO) in 2008. The first season begins with the revelation that not only do vampires exist, but that in the United States they have decided to "come out of the coffin" and attempt to be assimilated into American human culture—a move made possible by "Japanese scientists'" discovery of an effective synthetic human blood substitute called "True Blood." Some vampires, more interested in assimilation than their fellows, drink True Blood and are safer than others. *True Blood* follows the adventures of Sookie Stackhouse (Anna Paquin), a waitress at Merlotte's Bar in sleepy and isolated Bon Temps, Louisiana. Sookie—secretly a telepath who suffers from her ability to hear the thoughts of everyone around her—meets and enters into a relationship with Bill Compton (Stephen Moyer), a vampire returning after a long absence to life in Bon Temps in order to try "mainstreaming" in the human community. Over the course of the first season, Bill, Sookie, Sookie's boss Sam Merlotte (Sam Trammell), her best friend Tara Thornton (Rutina Wesley), Tara's cousin, Sookie's friend and the bar's cook Lafayette Reynolds (Nelsan Ellis), and Sookie's brother Jason (Ryan Kwanten) deal with various difficulties related to human–vampire interactions.

First and second season episodes include interludes from talk shows discussing the question of "vampire rights." Beginning in the first season (and appearing more often in the second), anti-vampire religious moralists function as some of the *True Blood*'s primary villains. Given the timing of the series, the most obvious referent here is the U.S. gay and lesbian civil rights movement—in particular, the focus on gay and lesbian rights of access to major legal institutions such as marriage. In the first and second seasons, the placement of the controversial Sookie–Bill human–vampire relationship narrative against the backdrop of a national "vampire rights" debate aligns the queer politics of *True Blood* with the marginalizing and anti-intersectional focus of much of the "real" national campaign for gay and lesbian civil rights.[20]

Civil rights campaigners for gay and lesbian rights of access frequently appropriate historically race-focused equal protection arguments in support of the rights of gays and lesbians to marry and participate in other public institutions such as the military.[21] David Remnick echoes this trope when he declares in the *New Yorker*'s response to New York's legalization of same sex marriage that "the gay-rights movement has ... mirrored the black freedom movement, but in hyper-speed."[22] Just as Remnick does not acknowledge the possibility that this "mirroring" is the result in part of specific political and rhetorical choices, so it is in what Siobhan B. Somerville identifies as "a persistent critical tendency to treat ... shifts in the cultural understanding and deployment of race and sexuality as separate."[23] Where a relationship between race and sexuality is recognized, the assumption of separateness is maintained; relevant scholarship on the history and status quo of race and sexuality in the United States often reinforces the "separation [of race and sexuality]" through the production and reproduction of "analogies between race and sexuality and between racialized and sexualized bodies."[24] Understanding race and sexuality in this way clearly undermines attempts to conceive of an *intersectional* politics and scholarship that are at once racialized and queer, promoting and maintaining the "secondary marginalization" of queer people of color within queer scholarship and activism. Queer is naturalized as White (thus also re-naturalizing whiteness itself) and racialized identity as heterosexual.[25]

The critical race feminist Kimberlé Crenshaw speaks eloquently to the problem of anti-intersectional politics in modern U.S. civil rights movements—that is, politics that combat particular forms of oppression in a manner that erases the lives and reality of those who have explicit, conscious, multiple, and intersecting experiences of identity. Crenshaw focuses her critique on the "single-axis framework ... dominant" in both "antidiscrimination law" and "feminist theory and anti-racist politics."[26] This demand for radical anti-oppressive politics to always start from a consideration of how humans—some more than others—experience multiple forms of identity and oppression at the same time is what is meant by "intersectional" politics, or a politics of "intersectionality."[27]

The call for an "intersectional" politics is not a simple call for combination—that is, to speak always of multiple oppressions and identities at once. Rather, "the intersectional experience is greater than the sum" of its parts.[28] The "single-axis framework" allows human beings who experience identity in multiple simultaneous and overlapping ways to be only one thing at a time in public life—"Black women," in Crenshaw's example, tend to be excluded entirely within both single-axis (racist) feminist and single-axis (patriarchal/ sexist) anti-racist politics.[29] Similarly, the anti-intersectional politics of much of the U.S. gay and lesbian civil rights movement not only fails to include but actively marginalizes and oppresses queers of color and other queer subjects who are less recognizable to the heterosexual and heteronormative public as those "queers who are better than others."

True Blood offers the vampire *at once* as a representational vehicle for the intersectional nature of queer identity, *and* as a metaphorical reproduction and endorsement of Cohen's politics of "secondary marginalization." *True Blood*'s vampires are intersectionally raced and queer: their interaction with one another and with the human characters frames the vampires as at once and to varying degrees sexual and racial Others (even the vampires coded as heterosexual are marked as sexually different through their literally monstrous sexual preferences). In Crenshaw's terms, *True Blood*'s vampires—in a way that might be unique on television—are metaphorical representations of intersectional, at once "multiply-burdened"[30] and privileged ways of existing in contrast to a "single-axis" society. At the same time, *True Blood*'s narrative consistently frames those vampires who metaphorically stand in for particularly radical and anti-assimilationist queer politics as unsafe, especially monstrous, parochial, and cruel.

Safe vampires and the politics of marginalization

True Blood's simultaneous embrace of intersectionality and the politics of "secondary marginalization" are particularly evident in the first season. Bill Compton is initially presented as both a vampire and a protagonist through an insistent contrast between Bill, other vampires, and other male human characters. In "Strange Love,"[31] *True Blood*'s premier episode, Bill appears for the first time in Merlotte's Bar as Sookie is beset as always by the constant obscene babble in the minds of her customers. When Bill walks into the bar, only Sookie and Sam Merlotte notice the appearance of a vampire—Sookie because Bill's mind is quiet to her, and Sam because he is a shapeshifter who has the sensory abilities of a dog. Bill is thus immediately marked as different, but not for any reason that carries human racial or sexual connotations. He is very pale, but otherwise physically unnoticeable as a vampire, and he expresses as much by asking Sookie "am I that obvious?" after noticing her overly excited reaction to his presence.

Bill's identity as a vampire sets him apart, but in the first season—when Bill only drinks "True Blood" and makes every effort to behave as a human among humans—his difference only matters as long as both humans and vampires continue to insist on making it so. If Bill Compton the vampire metaphorically stands in for otherness in the real world outside the narrative, he is a representation of a particular form of difference from the norm that is unfairly marked as deviant or monstrous. Bill *is* a monster, but he is better than others. He is White. He retains the heterosexuality from his human past, consistently resisting both serious and mocking overtures from other vampires who are not so inclined. He is a strong believer in the value of romantic monogamy, in sharp contrast to many other vampires whose appetites appear to be both fleeting and more primarily physical (in later seasons of the series, Bill loses his singular focus, but this is presented as a bitter and *all too human* return to the sinful ways of his vampire past). Bill does not long or attempt to be human—he frequently reminds Sookie that he is not, in fact, alive—but he regrets the loss of his human past and attempts to function normally among humans in any way he can. Sookie—the only protagonist arguably presented as wholly morally unproblematic within the narrative—does everything that she can to help him.

Nearly every other vampire in the first season is defined primarily by his or her evident monstrosity. Bill's dress and gentlemanly manner would not mark him as particularly unusual in either the status quo or antebellum Bon Temps. The other vampires have no interest in fitting in, and tend to display an explicit contempt for human mores—a dynamic particularly evident in the third episode, "Mine," where Bill gets an unwanted visit from Malcolm, Liam, and Diane, hedonistic vampires that Bill palled around with in his pre-mainstreaming existence. Malcolm, Liam, and Diane mock Bill for being "Mr. Mainstream" and trying to "dress up and play human."[32] Bill has bought into the national political agenda of "coming out of the coffin," and protests "we have to moderate our behavior, now that we are out in the open." Malcolm—one of only two vampires in the first season who are presented as *homosexual* in the nature of their preference for both human and vampire sexual partners—responds by questioning the wisdom of coming out, and asking—rather coyly—"honey—if we can't kill people, what's the point of being a vampire?" Malcolm's particular vampirism—which includes a proclivity for risking the spread of the HIV/AIDS analog "Hep V," "the only blood-born pathogen that can harm vampires"—is thus a neat metaphorical stand-in for the "real" world characterization of anti-assimilationist queer identity as "gluttonous,"[33] "vampiric,"[34] dangerous, and immoral.[35]

True Blood's marginalization of the marked-as-deviant queer (both human and vampire) is marked by irresponsible drug use, unchecked and amoral hedonism, and sexual promiscuity—in contrast to the series' more normal and reasonable monsters' and human queers' efforts toward responsible consumption and monogamy. All vampires hunger for human blood; some are safer than others; and one—Bill—drinks "blood" in a manner that is as close an approximation of normal, human forms of consuming sustenance as possible. None the less, *True Blood* represents an important progression from other important vampire television shows[36] from the perspective of intersectional queer of color politics. In contrast to their network television antecedents and contemporaries, *True Blood's* vampires offer a complex representation of multiple intersecting identities, oppressions, and politics, even as certain embodied sites of intersection are presented more favorably than others.

True Blood and race politics

Part of what distinguishes *True Blood* from many of its vampiric contemporaries on film[37] and television is that the narrative and visual/scenic framing of the show make the inherently racialized politics of the series difficult to ignore. Race in *True Blood* functions as an explicit metonymic frame for all of the identity struggles in the series. The opening shot of "Strange Love" sets the tone for the visual setting of *True Blood*; the camera, taking on the perspective of a moving car, barrels down a winding, dark, southern road with blues/country music playing. The sets in *True Blood* are certainly consistent with televisual and cinematic tales of southern vampires, replete with darkness, mist, moss-laden trees, and graveyards,[38] but the series' introductory sequence also insistently invokes a racialized southern setting (to which I will return in a moment). Race and ethnicity is also a varied, explicit, and—at times and with certain characters—a foregrounded component of vampiric otherness, a narrative dynamic that is simply not present in most other vampire popular media.

The particular deviance of Malcolm, Liam, and Diane is presented as racial as well as sexual; Diane is Black and characterized by markers of a stereotypically African-American femininity. In "Mine," Sookie seems to find it disgusting that Bill and Diane were once lovers.[39] This disgust is not explicitly framed as a reaction to miscegenation, but the cause of Sookie's reaction is left open to interpretation. Sookie exclaims "what, gross! Bill, she's so ... they're all so mean, so ..." Bill finishes the sentence with "evil," but there is certainly something that is particularly disgusting to Sookie about Diane. The racial politics of inter-species sex between humans and vampires are made explicit throughout the series—Sookie's friends are generally shocked by her decision to sleep with a vampire—but they are especially apparent in "Mine"; while Sookie—after encountering Malcolm, Liam, and Diane—is deciding not to date Bill because of their fundamental species differences, her brother Jason is kicked out of his sometime lover's house because he cannot handle the fact that she has slept with a vampire.

As a vampire, Bill Compton finds in the first season that he is not only White, but that he is expected to explicitly perform his whiteness. This performance of whiteness is an actual and explicit racial component of Bill's character, and of the particular way that Bill-the-vampire functions as a metaphor for acceptable, "better than others" Otherness. Bill was the son of an antebellum Bon Temps plantation owner before being "made" (bitten and turned by a fellow vampire) while returning from fighting for the Confederacy in the American Civil War.[40] Sookie's Black friend Tara deploys Bill's racial past as a reason for why he would be bad for Sookie—not only is he a vampire, but he once owned slaves. When Bill gives a presentation to the local "Descendents of the Glorious Dead" society,[41] Tara is in the audience. Bill is framed in this scene as a kind and tragically human-like figure, but the viewer is also privy to Tara's clearly uncomfortable reaction to watching a former confederate soldier give a presentation to White descendants of civil war dead in a southern church. In contrast to the assumed and undiscussed whiteness of most vampire characters in film and television,[42] Bill's whiteness—and his particular connection to the history of whiteness in Bon Temps—is explicitly addressed in the narrative, and is acknowledged as a vital prerequisite to his efforts to gain inclusion and legitimacy in the public society of Bon Temps.

I do not mean to celebrate the racial politics in *True Blood*. The depictions of Black southerners in the opening credits sequence are limited to protesters getting beaten by cops and hyperbolic images of evangelical worship—scenes of Black women singing hymns are speeded up so that they appear frenetic and strange—and the Black female human characters in *True Blood* tend in earlier seasons to offer stereotypical and victimized versions of Black femininity. For example, Tara is subject to what the blogger and activist Gabrielle Korn describes as a directly proportional relationship between the depth and complexity of her character and the amount of abuse to which she is subjected in the narrative.[43] The werewolves that become increasingly significant to the narrative of later seasons are presented as almost entirely White, and the distinctions between the good werewolf who falls in love with Sookie and his malefactor fellows are crudely grounded in class stereotypes.[44]

Finally, during the explicit (human/vampire) miscegenation conflict in "Mine" and subsequent episodes, Tara and Sam (who is White) undertake a clandestine interracial relationship of their own—but unlike Sookie and Bill's inter-species relationship, at no time is there an explicit discussion of the racial political implications of the only human to human, and thus non-metaphorical, representation of interracial sex in the first season (an example of the *post-racial* politics of the series I discuss in the final section). *True Blood* may offer a complicated and perhaps unique metaphorical representation of intersectional identities and politics, but with the possible exception of Lafayette,[45] the series tends to shy away from addressing the *political* intersections of race and sexuality in literally human terms.

What is none the less important is that *True Blood* offers a representational vehicle for an intersectional politics of race and sexuality at all. While the vampire generally may be an inherently raced and sexualized metaphor for the non-White and the queer, with *True Blood*'s vampires it is refreshingly difficult to distinguish between and separate those moments when they serve as metaphors for non-normative racial and non-normative sexual identity. *True Blood*'s vampires can be read metaphorically in terms of Crenshaw's demand for an intersectional politics of identity that goes beyond simple "single-axis" combination: the complexity and difference inherent to what it *means to be a vampire* is a constant and foregrounded narrative trope throughout the run of the show. Attempts by certain individuals and groups of characters—both major and incidental—in the series to homogenize vampires, or homogenize the manner in which human–vampire difference is significant, are inevitably met with (sometimes spectacular and violent) failure.

The post-racial politics of *True Blood*

True Blood presents a significant tension between the potential for vampiric metaphor as a rhetorical vehicle for an intersectional politics of race and sexuality, and the role that particular vampire characters play in invoking an anti-radically queer politics of "secondary marginalization." If *True Blood*'s vampires metaphorically stand in for an intersectional range of marginalized subject positions in the U.S., the "hierarchies of value"[46] evident in the contrast between different vampires invoke an oppressive and limited ideal of intersectional politics. In part as a response to this tension, Lisa Nakamura, Laurie Beth Clark, and Michael Peterson argue "*True Blood* is socially conservative, gesturing towards a radical politics ... that it cannot ... deliver."[47] I want to conclude with a slightly different position: that the queer politics of *True Blood* do not reflect social conservatism so much as they participate in a newly prevalent "post-racial" ideal of queer and queer of color politics in U.S. public life.

Discourses of "post-race" and "color-blindness" have been prevalent in mainstream U.S. legal and political discourse for decades. "Post-racial," in particular, is an increasingly ubiquitous term in mainstream U.S. political discourse: a policymaker's invocation of a "post-racial" status quo or future ideal is the rhetorical strategy of blaming present racism on race-conscious attempts to address the ongoing effects of past and still-present racism in society.[48] Recent gay and lesbian politics of assimilation and access to major public institutions have been marked by a simultaneous move toward racial and national whitewashing in gay and lesbian political movements. The form of queer subjectivity promoted as ideal in most legislative and major organizational efforts at gay liberation is either explicitly presented as race-neutral, noticeably White, or both.[49]

True Blood's vampires stand in for a queer form of subjectivity that is radically intersectional even as it conforms to a post-racial ideal: the vampires embody difference in a way that is difficult or impossible to homogenize across the entire vampire population; but any over-emphasis of difference among vampires, or between vampires and humans, tends to have negative consequences. The most clearly sympathetic vampire characters tend to oscillate between post-racial politics of assimilation (problems between humans and vampires are the fault of members of either species who continue to insist that human/vampire differences are particularly significant) or blaming the other (anti-vampire sentiment is the fault of vampires themselves; vampires as a species will either learn to live harmoniously with humans or be guilty and deserving of their own destruction).[50]

In "The First Taste," Bill "calls on" Sookie at her grandmother's house; Jason and Tara, suspicious of the vampire's intentions, invite themselves over and do not comport themselves well. It is difficult to distinguish among the representations of heterosexism and racism in this scene. Jason's declaration that "we just don't think you [vampires] deserve special rights" carries historical present racist and heterosexist connotations, and the viewer knows from other scenes in the first season that Tara's reaction to Bill is not *only* a result of Bill coming from a slave-owning family, but also arises from her own prejudice against him as a vampire. Bill responds to Tara by fondly recalling the slaves that his "daddy"—not him—did own. Tara, however, is not only best friends with Sookie, but views Sookie's grandmother—an active and proud member of the "Descendants of the Glorious Dead" society—as a loved and unofficial surrogate parent. Tara objects much less—if at all—to the *present* racism implicit in the Glorious Dead society's ongoing activity than she does to Bill as an actual participant in that past. This is post-racial politics exemplified:[51] the greater sin is not racism per se; but rather the continued insistence that racial hierarchies continue to exist; and that past racial difference continues to matter. "The First Taste" invites the viewer to consider the hopeful possibility of a post-racial reconciliation of difference, given the fantastic scenario of a representative of past racist structures— Bill—actually reappearing in our status quo cultural institutions.

Throughout the series, it is Tara and Lafayette—the only recurring Black human characters in the run of *True Blood*—who continue to be tasked with the narrative role of insisting on the need to remain at least suspicious of any vampire as a representative of their inherently evil, untrustworthy, and unsafe species. *True Blood*'s two Black humans are presented as at once more racially savvy than the idealistic Sookie, and far less able to overcome their prejudicial reactions to vampires as a whole based on their frequent (and frequently their fault) negative interactions with vampiric individuals. Race problems in *True Blood* tend to be fomented by either people of color, monsters, or obscenely bigoted White humans (who are nearly always poor, and/or uneducated, and/ or caricatures of radical conservatives)[52] who are presented in explicit contrast to Sookie and Sam. Sookie, we find out eventually,[53] is a faerie (a mostly White race): a racialization of Sookie's character that suggests to me the post-racial rhetorical device of claiming a marginalized or threatened ethos[54] for whiteness as a means of re-sanctifying and normalizing whiteness as an ideal. Sookie's perseverance and ability to remain true to her mostly normal self in the face of danger and shocking personal revelation is particularly contrasted with Tara's flights of hysteria and despair. Tara is eventually "made vampire" at the beginning of the fifth and current season.[55] It seems likely that, in order for her character to finally find happiness in her identity, she also will need to learn an effective means of becoming a safer vampire than others.[56]

In "The First Taste," the criticism Tara does offer of Bill is explicitly connected to her (and Jason's) anti-vampire bigotry. To the extent that he is a sympathetic character, Bill in *True Blood*'s first season idealizes the post-racial transcendence of racism: as an antebellum plantation owner's son, he did not object to slavery; but may have acted well toward his father's slaves. After a vampiric life of sin and inequity, his gentlemanly desire to integrate into the post-racial society of Bon Temps is all that is needed for atonement. When this atonement fails in later seasons, it is not his racist past as a plantation owner, but his subsequent murderous past as a vampire that complicates Bill's efforts to distance himself from monstrosity. Bill the vampire contains in a single body the post-racial narrative of the evolution of U.S. politics and culture—from fighting a major war over slavery to the realization of the dream of a post-racial future.

The complex and differential relationship between humanity and vampirism in *True Blood* stands in for contemporary public debate over the appropriate place of White queers, queers of color, and queer life in U.S. public culture. The critic J. M. Tyree celebrates Lafayette in particular as a "dynamic gay character" of "disruptive intelligence," who in contrast to the "gay-friendly conservatism" suggested by the series' vampires "upends any neat parable of assimilation."[57] I agree—except that the complexity of Lafayette's character is belied by the series' depoliticization of his queer of color identity, and the numerous ways in which the radical representational potential of Lafayette's presence in the series is constrained within a post-racial critique of what happens when difference is taken too far. The actual queer humans in the series are not included as part of the first season's depictions of struggles for civil rights, relationship recognition, and so on—a narrative trend that remains fairly constant throughout the run of the show. As explicitly queer vampires become more common in *True Blood*—beginning at the end of the first season—their queerness in turn is not presented as complicating the debate over the wisdom of "coming out of the coffin." Vampires stand in for a "multiple-axis" politics of identity, but the complex diversity of vampiric identity is something the vampire community no longer appears to be interested in as a political question. *True Blood*'s vampires are post-racially queer.

Notes

1 Allan Ball, 2007, *True Blood*, Home Box Office Network.

2 Rachel Alsop, Annette Fitzimmons, and Kathleen Lennon, *Theorizing Gender* (Malden: Blackwell Publishing, 2002), 95.

3 See, for example, J. M. Tyree, "Warm-Blooded: *True Blood* and *Let the Right One In*," *Film Quarterly* 63, no. 2 (2009): 31–2, and Herndon Graddick, Matt Kane, Max Gouttebroze, Tanya Tsikanovsky, and Anthony Nget, "GLAAD 2011: Where We Are On TV," Gay and Lesbian Alliance Against Defamation *GLAAD. org* (Summer 2011), http://www.glaad.org/files/where_are_we_on_tv_2011.pdf/

4 Michael Warner, *Publics and Counterpublics* (Brooklyn: Zone Books, 2002), 209–10.

5 Warner, *Publics and Counterpublics*, 210.

6 The assumed normalcy and basic goodness of heterosexual modes of life and relation in public institutions.

7 Steven Seidman, "Identity and Politics in a 'Postmodern' Gay Culture: Some Historical and Conceptual Notes," *Fear of a Queer Planet: Queer Politics and Social Theory*, (ed.) Michael Warner (Minneapolis: University of Minnesota Press, 1993), 133.

8 The radical queer activist groups "ACT UP" and "Queer Nation" are two well-known and—to the extent there can be—representative examples. See, for example, Warner, *Publics and Counterpublics*, 209–11; Charles E. Morris III, "ACT UP 25: HIV/AIDS, Archival Queers, and Mnemonic World Making," *Quarterly Journal of Speech* 98, no. 1 (2012): 49–50; Lauren Berlant and Elizabeth Freeman, "Queer Nationality," in Warner (ed.), *Fear of a Queer Planet: Queer Politics and Social Theory*, 195.

9 Seidman, "Identity and Politics," 133.

10 Cathy J. Cohen, "Punks, Bulldaggers and Welfare Queens: The Radical Potential of Queer Politics?" *GLQ* 3 (1997): 438.

11 See for example, Dee Amy-Chinn, "Queering the Bitch: Spike, Transgression, and Erotic Empowerment," *European Journal of Cultural Studies* 8, no. 3 (2005): 314, and Allison McCracken, "At Stake: Angel's Body, Fantasy Masculinity, and Queer Desire in Teen Television," *Undead TV: Essays on Buffy the Vampire Slayer*, eds Elana Levine and Lisa Parks (Durham and London: Duke University Press, 2007), 116–20.

12 Eric Nuzum, *The Dead Travel Fast: Stalking Vampires from Nosferatu to Count Chocula* (New York: St. Martin's Press, 2007), 3.

13 Peter Day, "Introduction," *Vampires: Myths and Metaphors of Enduring Evil*, (ed.) Peter Day (Amsterdam and New York: Rodopi, 2006), xii, xiv.

14 Mike Thompson in Graddick *et al.*, "Where We Are On TV."

15 See for example Warner, *Publics and Counterpublics*, 209–11, and Barbara Smith, "Where's the Revolution?" *The Nation* (January 1, 1998) http://www.thenation.com/print/article/wheres-revolution/

16 Catherine Squires, "Running Through the Trenches: Or, an Introduction to the Undead Culture Wars and Dead Serious Identity Politics," in "What Is This 'Post-' in Postracial, Postfeminist … (Fill in the Blank)?" *Journal of Communication Inquiry* 34 (June 10, 2010): 211–12.

17 Cohen, "Punks, Bulldaggers and Welfare Queens," 437–65.

18 Judith Butler, *Undoing Gender* (New York: Routledge, 2004), 104–6. My particular use in this chapter of "queer" in opposition to "mainstream" "gay and lesbian" politics follows Shane Phelan's discussion in *Sexual Strangers: Gays, Lesbians, and Dilemmas of Citizenship* (Philadelphia: Temple University Press, 2001), 3, 108, 109. See also Peter Odell Campbell, "The Procedural Queer: Substantive Due Process, *Lawrence v. Texas*, and Queer Rhetorical Futures," *Quarterly Journal of Speech* 98, no. 2 (2012): 203, 205, 215–16.

19 Jasbir K. Puar and Amit S. Rai, "Monster, Terrorist, Fag: The War on Terrorism and the Production of Docile Patriots," *Social Text* 72, no. 20 (2002): 127.

20 Butler, *Undoing Gender*, 104–6.

21 See, for example, Russel K. Robinson, "Proposition 8, 'Hate' & 'Like Race' Arguments" (paper presented at the Northwestern University Queertopia! An Academic Festival conference, Chicago, Illinois, 21–2 May 2010).

22 David Remnick, "Comment: It Gets Better," *The New Yorker* (July 11 and 18, 2011): 31.

23 Siobhan B. Somerville, *Queering the Color Line: Race and the Invention of Homosexuality in American Culture* (Durham and London: Duke University Press, 2000), 3.

24 Somerville, *Queering the Color Line*, 4.

25 Jasbir K. Puar, *Terrorist Assemblages: Homonationalism in Queer Times* (Durham: Duke University Press, 2007), 131.

26 Kimberlé Crenshaw, "Demarginalizing the Intersection of Race and Sex: A Black Feminist Critique of Antidiscrimination Doctrine, Feminist Politics and Antiracist Politics," University of Chigaco Legal Forum (1989): 139.

27 Ibid., 140.

28 Ibid.

29 Ibid., 140, 143–5.

30 Ibid., 140.

31 "Strange Blood," *True Blood*, 2007.

32 "Mine," *True Blood*, 2001.

33 Andrew Sullivan, "Gluttony," *The Stranger* (1999): http://www.thestranger.com/seattle/Content?oid=606090/

34 Richard Kim, "Andrew Sullivan, Overexposed," *The Nation* (June 5, 2001): http://www.thenation.com/doc/20010618/kim20010605/

35 Kim, "Andrew Sullivan."

36 Such as *Buffy the Vampire Slayer* and *The Vampire Diaries*. A. Susan Owen, "*Buffy the Vampire Slayer*," *Journal of Popular Film and Television* 27, no. 2 (1999): 30; and Sayantani DasGupta, "White Vamps, Black Witches: Race Politics and Vampire Pop Culture," *Racialicious. com* (February 21, 2011), http://www.racialicious.com/2011/02/21/white-vamps-black-witches-race-politics-and-vampire-pop-culture/

37 See, for example, Timur Bekmambetov (dir) and Seth Grahame-Smith (wri), *Abraham Lincoln: Vampire Hunter*, Film, 105 m., June 22, 2012; Catherine Hardwicke (dir) and Melissa Rosenberg (wri), *Twilight*, Film, 122 m., November 21, 2008; Chris Weitz (dir) and Melissa Rosenberg (wri), *The Twilight Saga: New Moon*, Film, 130 m., November 20, 2009.

38 Tyree, "Warm-Blooded," 32.

39 "Mine," *True Blood*, 2007.

40 "Sparks Fly Out," *True Blood*, 2007.

41 Ibid.

42 Owen, "*Buffy,*" 30, and DasGupta, "White Vamps."

43 Gabrielle Korn, "The Trials, Tribulations, & Turning of *True Blood*'s Tara Thornton," *Autostraddle* (July 12, 2012), http://www.autostraddle.com/the-toils-tribulation-and-turning-of-true-bloods-tara-thornton-14116/

44 See, for example, "9 Crimes," "I Got a Right to Sing the Blues," and "Hitting the Ground," *True Blood*, 2010.

45 Tyree, "Warm-Blooded," 34.

46 Nikhil Pal Singh, *Black Is A Country: Race and the Unfinished Struggle For Democracy* (Cambridge. MA: Harvard University Press, 2004), 24.

47 Lisa Nakamura, Laurie Beth Clark, and Michael Peterson, "Vampire Politics," *Flow* (December 4, 2009): flowtv.org/2009/12/vampire-politicslisa-nakamura-laurie-beth-clark-michael-peterson/

48 Squires, "Running Through the Trenches," 211–12. See also James D. Anderson, "Race-Conscious Educational Policies vs. a 'Color-Blind Constitution': A Historical Perspective," *Educational Researcher* 36 (June/July 2007).

49 Puar, *Terrorist Assemblages*, xii–xiv.

50 See, for example, "I Will Rise Up," *True Blood*, 2009.

51 Puar, *Terrorist Assemblages*, 118. See also Squires, "Running Through the Trenches," 211–12; Neil Gotanda, "A Critique of 'Our Constitution is Color-Blind,'" *Stanford Law Review* 44 (1991): 2; and Stevens, J., dissenting, *Parents Involved in Community Schools v. Seattle School District No. 1*, 551 U.S. 701, 551 U.S. ___ (June 28, 2007): 2, available at http://www.law.cornell.edu/supct/pdf/05-908P.ZD.

52 See, for example, "Burning House of Love," *True Blood*, 2007.

53 "I Smell a Rat," *True Blood*, 2010.

54 For an example of this strategy, see Opinion of Roberts, C. J., *Parents Involved in Community Schools v. Seattle School District No. 1*, 551 U.S. 701, 551 U.S. ___ (June 28, 2007): 26, available at http://www.law.cornell.edu/supct/pdf/05-908P.ZO.

55 "Turn! Turn! Turn!" *True Blood*, 2012.

56 See, for example, "Whatever I Am, You Made Me," *True Blood*, 2012.

57 Tyree, "Warm-Blooded," 34.

7

Gendering the monster within:

Biological essentialism, sexual difference, and changing symbolic functions of the monster in popular werewolf texts

Rosalind Sibielski

"**E**ven a man who is pure in heart and says his prayers by night may become a wolf when the wolfsbane blooms and the autumn moon is bright." So goes the legend that sets in motion the 1941 film *The Wolf Man* (George Waggner), one of the iconic representations of the werewolf in U.S. popular culture. Although tales of lycanthropy date back to Greek and Roman mythology, *The Wolf Man* is credited by Creed[1] and du Coudray[2] with establishing the conventions that continue to structure werewolf narratives, not just in terms of cinema, but in terms of television, literature, and comic books as well. If werewolves still transform "when the wolfsbane blooms and the autumn moon is bright," however, how this metamorphosis is represented differs depending on the sex of the character. In contemporary werewolf texts, lycanthropy is inscribed upon the body according to biological sex in the same way that gender is. It is not merely that the ways in which monstrosity manifests differ according to gender, but rather that monstrosity itself is gendered, with the forms that it takes reproducing hegemonic discourses surrounding sexual difference by proposing that male and female lycanthropy—much like masculinity and femininity—are not just rooted in the body, but also in the bodily differences between women and men.

This essay examines the gendering of monstrosity in recent werewolf narratives. As du Coudray notes, it has long been a convention of werewolf stories that "[male] lycanthropy finds expression primarily in the murderous hunger for flesh and blood, while for female werewolves, the opposite is true: lycanthropy is essentially a release for sexual hunger." [3] This representational practice simultaneously appeals to and reasserts notions of biological essentialism by invoking Western discourses that position the tendency toward violence as an inherently masculine trait and the tendency towards wantonness as an inherently feminine trait. The gendering of lycanthropy along these lines therefore does more than just draw on "the pervasive cultural association of femininity with nature, embodiment and biology" in order to make monstrosity appear "more 'natural'" in women than in men, as du Coudray suggests.[4] Ultimately, it functions on a symbolic level to make gender itself appear "natural," essentializing sexual difference by linking the different forms in which lycanthropy manifests between male and female characters to the anatomical differences between the sexes upon which hegemonic theories of sexual difference are premised and substantiated.

While the representational conventions used to gender lycanthropy in this way originate in nineteenth-century gothic literature,[5] since the 1980s they have assumed a more central narrative focus, to the point where the adoption of gendered behaviors and desires is now as much a consequence of the werewolf curse as the ability to transform from human to wolf. The foregrounding of this aspect of werewolf lore in the post-Women's Liberation, post-Gay Liberation era is significant when considered alongside both the surge in werewolf narratives in U.S. popular culture at the turn of the millennium and the concomitant infiltration into the cultural mainstream of feminist, queer, and transgender discourses rejecting the biological grounding of gender identity. Indeed, it suggests that the insistence on the gendering of monstrosity within these narratives can be read as a response to recent challenges to culturally-entrenched notions concerning how—and by whom—masculinity and femininity can be authentically and correctly performed.

This is not to suggest that reconceptualizations of gender have been embraced within dominant U.S. culture any more than deviations from hegemonic performances of gender are viewed as anything other than "unconventional" (if no longer exactly pathological) behavior. However, understandings of both gender and sexuality as causal effects of biological sex have been contested at a number of sites within the cultural mainstream in recent years. This contestation informs current political and legal battles over anti-bullying legislation, gay and transgender civil rights, the overturn of the U.S. military's "don't ask, don't tell" policy, and continuing efforts to repeal the Defense of Marriage Act, as well as legalize gay marriage. It also underpins the increasing cultural visibility of individuals whose gender identification does not "match" their biological sex. This has been pronounced in popular media, from MSNBC's 2007 documentary series *Born in the Wrong Body*, to the LOGO Network's reality program *RuPaul's Drag Race* (2009–), to the publicity surrounding Chas Bono's gender reassignment surgery and the subsequent controversy over his selection as a contestant during the 2011 season of ABC's *Dancing With The Stars*. The public debates surrounding these issues have moved "alternative" conceptions of gender from the margins to the center of U.S. culture, opening up spaces to imagine performances of gender that transverse the gender binary, even if that binary remains intact.

The most widespread responses within dominant culture to this questioning of gender norms have been reactionary in nature. Hence the small number of popular representations of performances of gender outside those norms have been met with an insistent retrenchment of hegemonic enactments of gender in a much larger number of mainstream popular culture texts. This includes novels like Stephenie Meyer's *Twilight* saga,[6] in which the protagonists fervently conform to orthodox gender roles, as well as television series such as *Men of a Certain Age* (TNT, 2009–11), *How to Be a Gentleman*, (CBS, 2011), and *Last Man Standing* (ABC, 2011–), the plots of which revolve around characters struggling to reassert those roles. It also includes films like *Forgetting Sarah Marshall* (Nicholas Stoller, 2008), *The Hangover* (Todd Phillips, 2009), and *Crazy, Stupid, Love* (Glenn Ficarra and John Requa, 2011), all of which are about men (re)claiming their patriarchal manhood in the post-feminist era.

This essay argues that the popular resurgence of werewolf narratives from 2000 onward can be read within the context of this larger ideological retrenchment, with the figure of the werewolf functioning as another discursive site at which hegemonic constructions of sexual difference can be reasserted. As a consequence of this, the cultural uses of monsters within those narratives have shifted. Tales of monstrosity have frequently been deployed to give expression to cultural fears concerning the blurring of the boundaries between the masculine and the feminine by representing the breakdown of gender categories as "monstrous." In twenty-first-century werewolf texts, however, tales of monstrosity are instead deployed to shore up cultural meta-narratives of biological essentialism by insisting that sexual difference is so deeply ingrained that even monstrosity is governed by it.

The horrors of sexual difference

Given the extent to which sexual difference is a source of horror within patriarchal culture, it is perhaps not surprising that it figures as a central thematic
concern within the horror genre, which, as Grant asserts, is "preoccupied
with issues of sexual difference."[7] The monsters haunting horror texts are
often interpreted as projections of the dominant constructions of gender
"haunting" the cultures in which they are produced. Such interpretations
are heavily informed by psychoanalytic theory, in which the cultural dread
occasioned by sexual difference is linked to castration anxiety, and tales of
monstrosity are interpreted as expressions of that anxiety. Accordingly, Neale
argues that male monsters embody the specter of phallic lack "central to the
problematic of castration,"[8] which is rooted in men's fears of being stripped of
phallic power, and thus becoming "like women." Conversely, Creed suggests
that tales of female monstrosity give expression to fears of the patriarchal
male subject being "unmanned" in a different way—namely, through men's
supposed vulnerability to the power women possess via their ability to arouse
and fulfill heterosexual desire.[9]

Such readings of monsters inadvertently expose the paradoxical nature
of patriarchal anxieties surrounding sexual difference. It is not the bodily
differences between the sexes, after all, that lie at the heart of the castration
threat within the psychoanalytic schema,[10] but rather the fear that through
the loss of the phallus the differences between men and women can be
erased, rendering them *similar to* one another. As such, the crisis occasioned
by sexual difference that the scholars above see as fundamental to the horror
genre can be understood as deriving less from a dread of difference than a
dread of an absence of difference, in the face of which men's and women's
respective—and hierarchical—places within the symbolic order are collapsed.

Consequently, if horror narratives are preoccupied with sexual difference,
there are instances in which that preoccupation stems from efforts to
reassert it rather than to disavow it. Indeed, within the contradictory logic of
patriarchal culture it is only by reasserting sexual difference that the dread
it inspires can be dissipated. This is because the "fact" of sexual difference
serves as both verification and guarantor of the supposedly inherent and
immutable differences between the sexes upon which the patriarchal order
is predicated. This is arguably what is accomplished through the gendering
of lycanthropy in werewolf narratives. In invoking the trope of the "monster
within" to equate monstrosity with the surfacing of latent impulses that find
expression in the guise of the monstrous double, the turn to monstrosity
is often represented in horror texts as a manifestation of the id, the primal

instincts that make up human beings' "essential" nature.[11] Because lycanthropy manifests differently between male and female characters in werewolf narratives, its representation as an embodiment of the id therefore serves to confirm that men and women possess essentially different natures.

Gendering the monster within

In werewolf narratives, the ontological horror occasioned by the transformation from human to wolf is compounded by the desires that characters act upon while in wolf form, which are attributed to aspects of the id unleashed through the werewolf curse. Significantly, while Freud ascribes to the id an instinctual impulse toward the gratification of (primarily) libidinous and aggressive drives,[12] there is a sexed division between which of these drives surface as a consequence of lycanthropy, so that the turn to monstrosity nearly always engenders libidinous behavior in women and aggressive behavior in men.

Thus, from the nineteenth century onward, male characters are consistently overcome by a single-minded compulsion to kill while in wolf form, characterized by uncontrollable bloodlust. Conversely, although it is generally acknowledged that female werewolves also kill, the loss of impulse control they experience is centered on a compulsion towards sexual gratification. For them, irrepressible sexual lust either accompanies or overrides whatever bloodlust is awakened by the werewolf curse. Marsha in *The Howling* (Joe Dante, 1981), for example, is only ever depicted having sex whilst in wolf form. Meanwhile, in *The Curse* (Jacqueline Gary, 1999), Frida transforms and kills during sex, with the act of killing serving as a means to sexual pleasure rather than a pleasure in-and-of-itself.

In tying these respective urges to kill and to copulate to the return of the repressed, werewolf narratives gender expressions of the "monster within" in ways that essentialize sexual difference by attributing the sexed division between those urges to the workings of the unconscious, and through it, men's and women's ostensibly differing psychic makeup. This is made explicit in the scene in the *Buffy the Vampire Slayer* episode "Wild at Heart"[13] in which Oz confesses that in his wolf form he desires to be "free to kill," while Veruca attributes to her "wolf within" the freedom to indulge her sexual desires. Veruca's insistence that the "wolf within" is a part of them rather than something separate establishes an association between the "wolf within" and the id. This, in turn, positions the gender-specific urges they experience in wolf form as an effect of inherent—but also inherently different—instincts that ostensibly differentiate the sexes from one another. At the same time, because of the lupine forms that they assume when they transform, these desires are equally positioned as an effect of the natural order.

This has long been a theme in werewolf narratives. However, "Wild at Heart" also illustrates a shift in werewolf texts at the turn of the millennium whereby the gendered forms in which lycanthropy manifests become a central narrative focus rather than just an incidental aspect of werewolf lore. Consequently, while the representational conventions through which lycanthropy is gendered remain the same, the cultural uses of those represen-tations change significantly. In drawing attention to gendered manifestations of lycanthropy as at once a biological imperative and an effect of the laws of nature, werewolf stories are not deployed in twenty-first-century popular culture to disavow the castration fears supposedly provoked by the fact of sexual difference. Instead, they are deployed to disavow the fact that sexual difference is a cultural construct.

This shift in the symbolic function of the werewolf is also reflected in the alteration to werewolf lore in twenty-first-century texts whereby the change from human to wolf is only one of several transformations characters undergo as a result of their lycanthropy. Unlike earlier werewolf narratives, in these texts becoming a werewolf also causes changes to characters' human personalities and their human bodies in the time outside the full moon. These changes are likewise divided along the axis of sexual difference, prompting the adoption of behaviors and modes of bodily presentation that conform to hegemonic models of gender according to biological sex. In this way, too, twenty-first-century representations of the werewolf are deployed to reinforce conceptualizations of sexual difference rooted in biological essen-tialism, since lycanthropy does not just manifest in gendered terms, but also results in the embodiment of gender norms.

For men, the werewolf curse prompts hyper-aggressive behavior while in human form. Tyler in *The Vampire Diaries* (The CW, 2009–) is represented as hotheaded and volatile as a result of his lycanthropy, while Jacob in both the novel and film versions of the *Twilight* saga is subject to uncontrollable rages.[14] Similarly, Jimmy in *Cursed* (Wes Craven, 2005) and Isaac in MTV's *Teen Wolf* (2011–) become more assertive, but also more prone to fighting, after contracting lycanthropy. Meanwhile, in both the film (Rod Daniel, 1985) and television versions of *Teen Wolf*, the "killer instinct" awoken in Scott translates into ruthless competitiveness on the athletic field.

This acquisition of toughness extends to most male protagonists, who gain physical strength as well as the capacity to both inflict and withstand physical pain as a side effect of their lycanthropy. It also underpins the changes to their human bodies, which manifest most often in terms of the "bulking up" of their physiques. For example, in the case of Derek in MTV's *Teen Wolf* or Alcide in *True* Blood (HBO, 2008–), both of whom begin the narrative as werewolves already, their lycanthropy is signified by their bulging biceps and washboard abs. Conversely, in the case of Jacob, for whom the ordeal of becoming a werewolf forms the basis of the plot in *New Moon*, the progression of his lycanthropy is tracked through the alteration of his body, which in both the novel[15] and film (Chris Weitz, 2009) becomes noticeably more muscled.

These physical changes involve the embodiment of secondary sex characteristics that are used to differentiate male bodies from female bodies within Western culture, much as the proclivity towards aggression mirrors personality traits that are culturally coded as markers of hegemonic masculinity. In this way, just as lycanthropy and gender are inscribed upon the psyche in mutually reinforcing ways, they are also inscribed upon the body in ways that similarly mark it as "properly" masculinized. The same is true of werewolf narratives featuring female protagonists, except in those texts the changes they undergo mark them as "properly" feminized.

For women, the werewolf curse triggers hypersexual behavior in human form. Ginger in *Ginger Snaps* (John Fawcett, 2000) goes from being uninterested in sex to only being interested in sex as a result of her lycanthropy. She also acquires enhanced seduction skills, as well as an increased capacity for experiencing and giving sexual pleasure. In addition to a heightened libido, female lycanthropy also tends to result in the shedding of sexual inhibitions. In *The Dresden Files* episode "Hair of the Dog,"[16] Heather's werewolf nature causes her to become so carried away by passion that she knocks Harry off balance when she kisses him. Likewise, Madison, who appears in the *Supernatural* episode "Heart,"[17] is so overcome by desire for Sam that she slams him into a wall and tears at his clothing in her eagerness to make love to him.

The sexual aggression manifested by these characters provides a gendered corollary to the violent aggression manifested by male characters by similarly appealing to cultural discourses that code sensuality as a quintessentially feminine attribute and toughness as a quintessentially masculine attribute. In linking female lycanthropy to the development of insatiable sexual appetites, female werewolf narratives also incorporate aspects of the trope of the monstrous-feminine, a representational paradigm within the horror genre that Creed interprets as an expression of patriarchal anxieties surrounding female desire.[18] To the extent that this is an exclusively *female* incarnation of monstrosity, however, its invocation simultaneously serves to maintain the gendered divide between manifestations of lycanthropy by ensuring that it is only ever expressed in gender-appropriate forms.

This is also true of the changes to their human bodies that female characters experience, which foreground secondary sex characteristics used to designate bodies as anatomically (and normatively) female. While their male counterparts develop muscles, women develop more voluptuous physiques. Likewise, their style of dress alters to emphasize their altered bodies. Ginger trades oversized sweaters and peasant skirts for tight-fitting tops and mini-skirts, while Ellie in *Cursed* exchanges her power suits for slinky dresses and stilettos, and in MTV's *Teen Wolf* Erica's frizzy hair and frumpy attire are replaced by teased hair and plunging necklines.

In this way, lycanthropy manifests in terms of the embodiment of gendered body ideals as well as gendered behaviors: men gain physical strength while women gain heterosexual desirability. There are, of course, exceptions to this representational convention, but they tend to reinforce the overall pattern of representation rather than critique it. For example, Leah in the *Twilight* saga may not become "sexier" as a result of her lycanthropy, but instead she becomes a nagging shrew. This mobilizes another form of feminine-coded aggression that genders the expression of her monstrosity every bit as much as the sexual aggression displayed by the characters discussed above. On the other hand, in *Blood and Chocolate* (Katja von Garnier, 2007), Vivien's lycanthropy grants her the courage and strength of character to rebel against the patriarchal structure of her pack, eventually proving herself to be the prophesized figure destined to lead them into "a new age of hope and glory." However, while Vivien may escape hypersexualization, the other female characters do not. Vivien thus becomes the exception that proves the rule. Her "unconventional" performance of lycanthropy/femininity becomes just one more thing that marks her as unique, with the result that it is ultimately represented as an aberration from—rather than alternative to—patriarchal models of femininity.

The emphasis on the embodiment of gender norms as a byproduct of lycanthropy in contemporary werewolf texts is a recent development. In gothic literature, while the hungers awakened by the werewolf curse are gendered along the same lines, they do not carry over to characters' human personas. Likewise, while female characters are sometimes described as having otherworldly beauty, and male characters are sometimes described as "fierce" in appearance, these physical traits are represented as reflections of their monstrosity rather than direct effects. This begins to shift in the latter half of the twentieth century in texts like *The Howling*, in which Bill's transformation from sensitive, new-age vegetarian to red-meat-craving macho-man signals the onset of his lycanthropy. However, is not until the proliferation of werewolf narratives in early twenty-first-century popular culture that the positioning of the body as the locus for reciprocal expressions of both gender and monstrosity becomes an established narrative convention.

This, too, marks a shift in the symbolic function of monsters when it comes to twenty-first-century werewolf texts. While, as discussed above, tales of monstrosity have long been used to give expression to cultural anxieties surrounding sexual difference, male monsters traditionally have been defined by their deviation from gender norms, while female monsters have been defined by their perversion of gender norms. In twenty-first-century werewolf narratives, however, monstrosity is characterized instead by the embodiment of gender norms. Indeed, although lycanthropy is almost always gendered according to the conventions outlined above, there are no instances in which those conventions cross gender lines. Jimmy in *Cursed* and Scott in both versions of *Teen Wolf* gain sexual prowess as a result of the werewolf curse, but it is only their compulsion toward violence that threatens to overwhelm them; their sexual desires remain under their control. Likewise, in Charlaine Harris's *Southern Vampire Mysteries* series,[19] the female werewolves Debbie and Jannalynn are prone to violent tendencies, but this is in addition to their uncontrollable sexual appetites not in place of them. There are no texts in which male lycanthropy manifests as a loss of sexual inhibition, or in which female lycanthropy manifests solely as bloodlust. Thus, whereas stories about monsters traditionally have served to give expression to cultural anxieties surrounding the erasure of sexual difference, since the turn of the millennium werewolf narratives have instead served to combat those anxieties by (re) affirming the immutability of sexual difference.

Body horror and embodiments of sexual difference

The other place in werewolf narratives where this essentializing of sexual difference is evident is the depiction of the transformation from human to wolf. For men, this metamorphosis involves a bloody and violent breach of bodily borders. Such representations have been interpreted as castration metaphors because the abjection that characterizes them ostensibly serves to "feminize" the male body. Creed argues that the male werewolf's loss of power over his body as he transforms invokes a loss of phallic power, while simultaneously invoking comparisons to the female body in so far as he is effectively represented "giv[ing] birth to himself, by turning himself inside out."[20] Alternately, Badley suggests that the foregrounding of the spectacle of the male body in extremis in horror texts constitutes a fetishization of abjection that mirrors the fetishization of female bodies as erotic objects in classical Hollywood cinema.[21]

However, while exhibitions of suffering on the part of the male werewolf certainly constitute moments of spectacle, it does not automatically follow that those moments signify emasculation just because men are rendered objects of the cinematic gaze, or that male bodies are automatically feminized because they are positioned as embodiments of the abject. Nor do depictions of the male body in agony always serve to signify a loss of phallic power. Jeffords proposes that the simultaneous abjectification and objectification of the male body during scenes of torture in action films actually serves to reaffirm phallic power by invoking the endurance of physical suffering as a guarantor of patriarchal manhood.[22] This is arguably the same function that scenes of lycanthropic transformation serve in male werewolf texts, since what is emphasized is not loss of control over the body as much as mastery over that loss of control.

This is accomplished most explicitly through the narrative focus on the male werewolf's mastery over physical pain. Although there are a handful of contemporary texts in which the transformation from human to wolf is quick and painless, in the majority it is marked by unrelenting anguish. In the *Vampire Diaries* episode "By the Light of the Moon,"[23] it takes several hours for Tyler to undergo his first transformation, during which he experiences continuous torment as his bones break and his body contorts into impossible positions. Likewise, in the episode "Tully" from the British version of *Being Human*,[24] George's transformation is accompanied by a voice-over in which Mitchell details the excruciating pain that George feels as he transforms, which is compounded by the tearing and reforming of muscles and the shrinking of internal organs—all of which, Mitchell confides, should kill him, but instead "drags him through fire and keeps him alive, and even conscious, to endure every second."

The emphasis in these texts on the ability to both endure and survive extreme physical damage becomes another way of testifying to the toughness male characters acquire through lycanthropy. This carries over even into texts in which the change itself is painless. For example, Jacob's accelerated healing causes his bones to begin to mend before they can be properly set in *Eclipse*, necessitating that he submit to having them re-broken without the aid of painkillers since his body metabolizes them too quickly to have any effect. In the film version (David Slade, 2010), the sound of his off-camera screams as he undergoes this ordeal underscores the magnitude of his agony. However, as in the case of the scenes of lycanthropic transformation discussed above, his ability to bear this agony attests to his toughness. To the extent that such toughness equates with phallic power in Western culture, it also suggests that, far from a failure of masculinity, what is signified through such representations is instead the triumph of masculinity over that which threatens to strip protagonists of their patriarchal manhood.

This is also suggested through the mastery over their physical transformation that male characters demonstrate by disciplining themselves to control it. In *The Vampire Diaries*, these issues are connected, as Tyler must practice until he is able to initiate and halt his transformation at will, but also without pain. A similar conditioning is suggested in *Underworld* (Len Wiseman, 2003), where the experienced Lycans possess this ability, while Michael does not. In other texts, controlling the transformation is tied to gaining control over other aspects of the werewolf curse. For both Jacob in the *Twilight* saga and Scott in MTV's *Teen Wolf*, the transformation is triggered by anger, so that gaining control over it requires them also to gain control over the aggression engendered by their lycanthropy. Alternately, in the U.S. version of *Being Human* (The SyFy Channel, 2011–), while Josh is unable to control his physical transformation, his quest to reclaim the career and the romantic relationship destroyed when he became a werewolf (and, thus, to reclaim his manhood) similarly requires that he learn to assert control over his monstrous nature.

The arduous conditioning that allows these characters to curb their lycanthropic impulses further attests to their phallic power by demonstrating the "mastery over the individual's dangerous desire for aggression" that Freud identifies as the cornerstone of both patriarchal manhood and Western Civilization.[25] In achieving control over their physical transformations, which amount to an involuntary reflex, they also exercise power over their bodies through sheer force of will, thus demonstrating a capacity to exert "mind over matter" that is also a masculine ideal. In this way, such representations equally serve to affirm characters' masculinity by appealing to Western understandings of sexual difference rooted in the belief that men possess absolute control over their bodies and their emotions, while women are entirely controlled by theirs.

Following that logic, it is perhaps not surprising that for female werewolves the transformation is represented in terms of a perverse revelry in the total loss of control over the body that accompanies it. In *Ginger Snaps*, the frenzied writhing of Ginger's body as she transforms is depicted in ways that suggest a hedonistic pleasure-in-pain rather than suffering. Alternately, both Veruca in *Buffy the Vampire Slayer* and Heather in *The Dresden Files* are depicted experiencing something closer to orgasm. Such representations invoke the archetype that Kristeva terms the "unbridled woman," whose bodily appetites and excesses signify the "wild, obscene, and threatening femininity" at the heart of patriarchal constructions of womanhood.[26] In this way, much as the bodies of male werewolves are masculinized via their ability to exert control over their physical transformation, the bodies of female werewolves are feminized by their lack of control, but also the abandon with which they give themselves over to it.

This lack of control extends to other aspects of their lycanthropy as well. Ginger, Veruca, and Joanie in *Cursed* all refuse to regulate either their physical transformations or their lycanthropic impulses, which is a large part of what codes them as villains. Conversely, Heather, Madison, and Nina (who appears as a recurring character in the fifth season of *Angel* [The WB, 1999–2004]), are all incapable of managing their lycanthropy, requiring them to rely on male experts on the werewolf curse to manage it for them. Even Debbie in *True Blood*, who *is* able to control her transformation, cannot stop herself from acting on her emotions and desires, often quite irrationally. In this way, the lack of self-control demonstrated by these characters serves a reciprocal symbolic function to the self-control demonstrated by male characters. It equally serves to gender manifestations of lycanthropy according to patriarchal constructions of sexual difference by marking lycanthropy on the body according to biological sex.

The association of pain—or alternately, pleasure-in-pain—with lycanthropic transformation that makes this possible is also a recent development. In gothic literature the only pain accompanying the werewolf curse is existential, while in classical Hollywood cinema the transformation from human to wolf is accomplished via a series of dissolves, during which characters seamlessly shift form. It is not until *The Howling* and *An American Werewolf in London* (John Landis) in 1981 that this changes, although the gory characterizations of lycanthropic transformation in these films have been an established convention ever since. Badley situates this change within the larger trend toward "body horror" in U.S. popular culture in the 1980s, as well as advances in special effects technology that made possible cinematic representations of monstrosity not previously achievable.[27] However, technological advances alone do not explain this shift in representation when it comes to werewolf narratives—in part because it introduces a significant alteration to werewolf lore, and in part because depictions of pain and/or bodily excess were still possible within the limitations of earlier special effects technologies (and certainly in the case of literature).

At the same time, while the bodily abjection that characterizes lycanthropic transformation in twenty-first-century werewolf texts certainly incorporates aspects of the body horror subgenre, the texts also depart from the conventions of that subgenre in significant ways. As Badley notes, within body horror narratives, "embodiment [is] the horror," made manifest in depictions of the human body mutated, mutilated, contaminated, or deformed.[28] However, embodiment is only horrific in such narratives because it is imagined in terms of occupying what are culturally designated as "Othered" bodies, bodies that are pathologized in various ways. For example, Creed interprets the alien queen in *Alien* (Ridley Scott, 1979) as a metaphor for the maternal body,[29] while Badley points out that the scientist-turned-monster in David Cronenberg's 1986 remake of *The Fly* is often read as a metaphor for the body infected by the AIDS virus.[30]

The monsters who appear in stories outside of the body horror subgenre also possess abnormal bodies, from the sutures stitching together the limbs of the monster in *Frankenstein* (James Whale, 1931) to the razor blades protruding from the fingertips of Freddie Kruger in *A Nightmare on Elm Street* (Wes Craven, 1984). Even the vampires in the *Twilight* saga possess physical anomalies, even if those anomalies are not grotesque. In contrast, while the body of the werewolf is certainly rendered abnormal in twenty-first-century werewolf narratives at the moment of transformation, because lycanthropy otherwise manifests in terms of the embodiment of gender norms, the physical changes to protagonists' human bodies that result from the werewolf curse actually serve to normalize those bodies rather than to pathologize them.

This marks another departure in twenty-first-century werewolf narratives from older horror texts, although in this case it does not signal a shift in the cultural function of monsters, but rather in the representational practices through which that function is carried out. The physical abnormalities that define the monstrous body in horror texts serve the ideological purpose of reaffirming dominant cultural conceptions of what constitutes a "normal" body. This is one way in which using monsters as metaphors for Othered bodies also serves to maintain their status as "Other." The gendering of monstrosity in twenty-first-century werewolf narratives also serves this cultural function, in that while it affirms the biological grounding of gender, it also affirms the cultural criteria through which normative expressions of gender are defined. The difference is that in these texts the monstrous body is deployed to uphold gender norms by embodying those norms rather than by providing a contrast to them.

This points to what is perhaps the most significant difference in representational practices in twenty-first-century werewolf narratives. Tales of monstrosity traditionally have been stories of what it is to be Other, with monsters often serving as metaphors for members of culturally marginalized groups.[31] In some cases, the demonizing of the monster serves the ideological function of demonizing those who fall outside of socially dominant identity categories. In more radical deployments, the figure of the monster serves to reconfigure understandings of identity and difference in order to envision "new categories and ways of being" outside of Western patriarchal constructions.[32] Either way, tales of monstrosity are one of the few places within mainstream popular culture where Othered identities are given representation. This is not the case in contemporary werewolf texts. Instead, because of the ways in which lycanthropy is gendered in these texts, even the monsters end up reproducing cultural norms (at least where performances of gender are concerned). Ultimately, then, while contemporary werewolf narratives mobilize tales of monstrosity to assuage cultural anxieties surrounding sexual difference by insisting on its biological grounding, in doing so they also deny that there is any way in which gender can be performed outside of hegemonic models, even when it comes to monsters.

Notes

1 Barbara Creed, *Phallic Panic: Film, Horror, and the Primal Uncanny* (Melbourne: Melbourne University Press, 2005).

2 Chantal Bourgault du Coudray, *The Curse of the Werewolf: Fantasy, Horror and the Beast Within* (London: I. B. Tauris, 2006).

3 Ibid., 114.

4 Ibid., 112.

5 Ibid., 114.

6 Stephenie Meyer, *The* Twilight *Saga* (New York: Little, Brown, and Company, 2005–8).

7 Barry Keith Grant, "Introduction," in *The Dread of Difference: Gender and the Horror Film*, ed. Barry Keith Grant (Austin: University of Texas Press, 1996), 1.

8 Stephen Neale, *Genre* (London: British Film Institute, 1980), 43.

9 Barbara Creed, *The Monstrous-Feminine: Film, Feminism, Psychoanalysis* (New York: Routledge, 1993).

10 In psychoanalytic theory, the threat of castration is conceptualized in terms of literal (genital) castration, as well as symbolic forms of castration rooted in fears of men losing the power they are granted in patriarchal culture by virtue of their anatomical difference from women.

11 Sigmund Freud, *The Ego and the Id* (New York: W. W. Norton and Company, 1960).

12 Ibid.

13 The WB, November 9, 1999.

14 While it is revealed in *Breaking Dawn* that Jacob is a shapeshifter rather than a werewolf, this revelation comes at the end of the final novel in the *Twilight* saga, when it is too late to have any effect on the narrative except retroactively. Because Jacob is represented as a werewolf throughout the series, he is included in this analysis.

15 Stephenie Meyer, *New Moon* (New York: Little, Brown and Company, 2006).

16 The SyFy Channel, February 11, 2007.

17 The CW, March 22, 2007.

18 Creed, *The Monstrous-Feminine*.

19 Charlaine Harris. *The Southern Vampire Mysteries* (New York: Ace Books, 2001–).

20 Creed, *Phallic Panic*, xiii.

21 Linda Badley, *Film, Horror, and the Body Fantastic* (Westport: Greenwood Press, 1995).

22 Susan Jeffords, *Hard Bodies: Hollywood Masculinity in the Regan Era* (New Brunswick: Rutgers University Press, 1994).

23 The CW, December 9, 2010.

24 BBC Three, February 1, 2009.

25 Sigmund Freud, *Civilization and Its Discontents* (New York: W. W. Norton and Company, 1961), 84.

26 Julia Kristeva, *Powers of Horror: An Essay on Abjection* (New York: Columbia University Press, 1982), 167.

27 Badley, *Film, Horror, and the Body Fantastic*.

28 Ibid., 7.

29 Creed, *The Monstrous-Feminine*, 16–30.

30 Badley, *Film, Horror, and the Body Fantastic*, 128.

31 Robin Wood, *Hollywood from Vietnam to Reagan … and Beyond* (New York: Columbia University Press, 2003), 63–84.

32 Elaine L. Graham, *Representations of the Post/Human: Monsters, Aliens and Others in Popular Culture* (New Jersey: Rutgers University Press, 2002), 54.

PART TWO

Monstrous technologies

8

Abject posthumanism: Neoliberalism, biopolitics, and zombies

Sherryl Vint

The posthuman has been a provocative site of theoretical enquiry for at least the last 20 years, establishing connections between science fiction (sf) scholarship and wider academic explorations of fragmented, postmodern subjectivity. Key texts have used the figure of the posthuman to prompt us to imagine subjectivity beyond the constraints of liberal humanism and its rapidly outdated ideal of the autonomous self. Katherine Hayles's *How We Became Posthuman* reassessed our understanding of subjectivity, consciousness, and embodiment through an interrogation of cybernetics, making a powerful argument that the self was more than information and that in embodiment we might find the key to another kind of being. Similarly, Donna Haraway's "A Manifesto for Cyborgs" celebrated this figure of hybridity precisely because it refused discourses of purity and origin, opening up a space to think otherwise about our "joint kinship with animals and machines"[1] and suggesting a way out of "the maze of dualisms in which we have explained our bodies and our tools to ourselves."[2] Both of these influential figures of the posthuman promised an expanded horizon for thinking about the human, a new discursive approach rooted in partial and fragmentary identities, multiple standpoints of knowledge, and politics of affinity. Refusing key binaries of the Western philosophical tradition, these potent figures promised much.

Yet as early as 1990, in an interview with Andrew Ross and Constance Penley, Haraway was already questioning the emerging mythology of cyborg figures in popular culture as compared to her vision.[3] The hypermasculine, armed, and relentlessly single-minded cyborgs of the *Terminator* (1984–2009) franchise, for example, hinted at a politics exactly in opposition to Haraway's deconstructive trickster. Things have changed even further in the twenty-first century. From the more-than-human subject dialectically interrogated and embraced in sf texts such as Octavia Butler's *Patternist* (1976–84) series or Iain M. Banks's *Culture* (1987–2010) novels, we have moved into an era in which posthumanity is a generalized condition. New and abject posthumans raise anxieties about massification and material collapse that emblematize our current state of neoliberal crisis and biopolitical governance. This version of the posthuman bears little relation to Haraway's ironic cyborg and instead partakes of the experiences of exclusion and abjection epitomized by Agamben's *homo sacer*, the one who can be killed but not sacrificed because this figure is constituted only by the bare life of existence, not full human being. These abject posthuman figures—most evident in the reconfiguration of zombies from the living dead to the infected living—deconstruct the binary of living and death: surviving but not but really alive, they persist in a future without hope, a paradoxical future without a future.

The prevalence of such images in our cultural imagination suggests, as the title of one of Zizek's works proclaims, that we feel we are living in end times. Zizek identifies as the "four riders" of our ongoing apocalypse "ecological crisis, the consequences of the biogenetic revolution, imbalances within the system itself, ... and the explosive growth of social divisions and exclusions."[4] As he, among others, points out, although it is urgent that we change systems of global capitalism, today we find it "easier to imagine a total catastrophe which ends all life on earth than it is to imagine a real change in capitalist relations."[5] We revel in the imagination of apocalyptic disaster in recent popular culture for this reason. This fascination is so pronounced that a recent review in *Time* magazine, commenting on the zombie colonization of much popular culture beyond the horror film, declared them "the official monster of the recession."[6]

Zombi(e)s, labor, neoliberalism

The relationship between zombies and abjection is well established in the critical tradition, often focused on issues of labor, thereby acknowledging the connection to a pre-Romero mythology of the zombi[7] as someone compelled by voodoo to rise from the grave and work. Although post-Romero zombies are more commonly associated with images of overwhelming consumption, the capitalist dialectic of production and consumption links these states. As David McNally argues in *Monsters of the Market*,[8] such creatures are ways of working through the alienation of capitalist extraction of surplus value: they mirror how humans' living labor is turned into a dead thing, a commodity. The frequent images of dismemberment in monster texts, McNally contends, revisit the traumatic violence of historical moments like the enclosures of land through which peasants were forced into dependence on a wage, now repeated in the predations of neoliberal globalization and reflected in the rise of such mythologies in Sub-Saharan Africa. Capitalism is damaging beyond physical suffering, Marx insists: it destroys the spirit or essence of the human, transforming creative energies and full being into interchangeable units of work via its equivalizing logic. The interchangeability of zombies, who appear always as a mass, whose inhumanity is emblematized by this very failure to be distinct individuals, suggests something of their appropriateness as a symbol for disenfranchised labor.

Workers everywhere are now reduced "to the lowest common denominator, to a disposable cost, compelling them to compete with sweatshops,"[9] and this new, more generalized condition of abjection is reflected in texts that at times ask us to sympathize with rather than—or, better, in addition to—fear the zombie. Hints of such a change are present in Romero's shifting mythology, from the implication that reactionary law enforcement is just as happy to execute an out-of-place black man as they are to dispatch ghouls in *Night of the Living Dead* (1968), to what Mohammed Silem has diagnosed as "a permanent state of crisis for two competing 'class' structures, the privileged but besieged living and the disenfranchised but ever-more organized Undead"[10] in *Land of the Dead* (2005), to the metafictional blurring of film and reality in *Diary of the Dead* (2007) that ends by asking whether humanity is worth saving given its wanton brutality. In popular culture more widely, the shifting position of the zombie is indicated by films that blend zombie apocalypse with other genres, such as comedy in *Shaun of the Dead* (Wright 2004), the buddy film *Zombieland* (Fleischer 2009), or satire in *Fido* (Currie 2006).

Our obsession with the living dead speaks also to our episteme of biopolitics in which the boundary between the living and the dead is precisely what is at issue politically and philosophically. While "the right of sovereignty was the right to take life or let live," the new right established with the modern security state is "the right to make live or to let die."[11] Crucially, there are two aspects to the new exercise of biopower. Not only are certain kinds of lives fostered and shaped through its disciplinary institutions, while others are let expire through neglect or design, but also—and more importantly—this new biopower establishes a logical connection between the making-live and letting-die that institutes a paradoxical logic. The metaphor of the body politic shifts from taking as its referent the body of the sovereign to the aggregate body of the population whose "health" is now the object of good governance. One of the ways of fostering this body is by expelling or excising that which is unhealthy: thus letting die is integrally bound up with making live. As Foucault documents, the shift of sovereign power toward biopower was concomitant with a shift toward membership within a nation-state being understood as a matter of biology or race. Racism allows what is homogenous (the human species) to be conceptualized as divided between the "good," healthy citizens and the "bad," unhealthy specimens, construed as fundamentally different from the human/citizen. Thus, Foucault argues, the political project of liberation focused on protecting the aggregate population from the excesses of the sovereign state turned into a politics of medical-hygienic conformity and the defense of society from biological dangers. The enemy is no longer "the race that came from elsewhere or that was, of a time, triumphant and dominant," but "a race that is permanently, ceaselessly infiltrating the social body, or which is, rather, constantly being re-created in and by the social fabric."[12]

This context of biopolitics is crucial for understanding why the image of the zombie in many recent films has shifted from the living-dead to the infected-living: zombies emerge more clearly as our possible selves, as abjected and expelled parts of the body politic—just as labor is expendable to global capital and migrant laborers as people are unwanted by many nation states. The threat of these new zombies is double, to be incorporated literally by being consumed, or to be incorporated by infection. Further, global capitalism has made monsters of us all, reproducing the kind of subjectivity that guides corporate decisions that privilege profit above people, an ironic turn from corporations having the legal status of persons to organic people behaving with the utter self-interest characteristic of corporate personhood. Henry Giroux calls this a zombie politics that "views competition as a form of social combat, celebrates war as an extension of politics and legitimates a ruthless Social Darwinism in which particular individuals and groups are considered simply redundant, disposable."[13] The world of such laborers whose physical bodies but not human subjectivities are required by capital parallels the subjectivity produced by what Achille Mbembe, discussing the non-human status of slaves, calls necropolitics, where the subject is "kept alive but in *a state of injury*, in a phantom-like world of horrors and intense cruelty and profanity."[14]

Giorgio Agamben's biopolitical work on the distinction between *zoe* (the simple fact of living) and *bios* (the proper human life, infused with essence or spirit) is also pertinent, repositioning as it does the human/animal boundary to a caesura *within* the human that reveals how contingent is the category of *bios*. A number of philosophers have been concerned with the ease with which biopolitics thus becomes thanatopolitics, a governance of life inevitably producing massive death in a model that finds its ultimate exemplar in the Nazi regime. Although it is important to preserve a distinction between the thanatopolitical "letting die" of liberal biopolitics and the "making die" of totalitarianism, it is nonetheless valuable to trace their connections as well. Indeed, Timothy Campbell contends that "this distance grows ever smaller under a neoliberal governmentality" which is concerned with a reduction of persons to things, or rather with the attempt "to crush the person and thing, to make them coextensive in a living being."[15]

Campbell goes on to outline the original Greek distinction, which also informs Agamben's work, by which a quality called "charisma" or "grace" was understood to separate the mere living of *zoe* from the fully human existence of *bios*, marking those humans who had sufficiently separated themselves from the animal within. Under neoliberalism, he concludes, "the 'truth' of the market, becomes the final arbiter of who has made sufficient moves toward deanimalization."[16] Zombies, with their historical ties to abject labor, and who combine a human form with signs that it has been robbed of grace—reduced to decomposing flesh—thus epitomize the crisis of subjectivity today. The speed of many of these new infected living zombies only makes them more dangerous, reflecting the vicissitudes of an unstable, globalized labor market in which we all could quickly and catastrophically slip from the *bios* of being gainfully employed to the *zoe* of economically irrelevant biological life.

Danny Boyle's film *28 Days Later* (2002), which popularized the new zombie paradigm, exemplifies the most negative aspects of our neoliberal order figured as zombie future. It establishes a number of motifs that have become staples of the genre: the protagonist, Jim (Cillian Murphy), wakes from a coma, enabling the representation of the transformation as a single, decision shift;[17] the many scenes of him wandering around an abandoned London feed our fascination with images of a world depleted of humans; the rapidity of the change from human to infected, requiring the surviving humans to turn instantly upon their fellows, embodies neoliberalist ethics; and the violence, both the rapid and animal-like movements of the infected, and the splatterpunk aesthetic of their dispatch, indulge a dehumanization of all, both infected and human. Although the film ultimately concludes on a hopeful note for rescue and suggests the restoration of the heteronormative family at the end, early scenes work to challenge our faith in restoration rather than transformation as key to a better future. The state of normality before and after the disaster, we are reminded, is "people killing people," and black actors Naomi Harris (who wields a machete) and Marvin Campbell, an infected soldier kept as an experiment, both evoke the image of Haitian rebellion against slavery and the injustices of the "civilized" order before.

Infected-living, biopolitics, contagion

In their critique of the fantasy of restoring "normal" civilization via the abject bodies of slaughtered zombies, recent zombie narratives challenge us to rethink life beyond the anthropocentrism of the liberal subject. In *Remnants of Auschwitz*, Agamben suggests that biopolitics requires a theory that moves beyond the binary of making-die/letting-live or making-live/letting-die, a theorization that is adequate to a situation in which "man's animal functions survive while his organic functions perish completely."[18] Building on his example of someone in a persistent comatose state, Agamben offers the new formulation of "*to make survive*" to capture the "decisive activity of biopower in our time [that] consists in the production not of life or death, but rather of a mutable and virtually infinite survival."[19] Biopower works to separate *within the individual subject* that which is human (*bios*) from that which is merely living (*zoe*), to keep what it can make into a thing and exploit (labor-power) and jettison what is inconvenient, inefficient, and irrelevant (the full human subject). Biopolitics produces a kindred creature to the infected-living zombies. Like capital's fantasy of labor-power without human workers, the infected-living persist, *survive* as biological bodies without human subjectivity. Foucault also connects the biopolitical divisions of the modern state to economic shifts of neoliberalism, which increasingly turned to managing populations and territories, rather than disciplining individuals, requiring new regimes of statistical governance in which things such as scarcity, starvation, and unemployment are no longer problems to be solved, but rather rates to be calibrated to ensure each occur in sufficient quantity to preserve the health of the overall system of capitalist circulation.

Agamben's contention that the concentration camp is the paradigmatic expression of late modernity, and his writings on the figure of the *Muselmann*, are perhaps the myth for this new and more sinister posthuman. The *Muselmann* is not only or "not truly a limit between life and death," he tells us, "rather, he marks the threshold between the human and the inhuman."[20] The *Muselmann* is a particularly horrifying figure because he continues to live after the limit of life, showing "the insufficiency and abstraction of the limit"[21] we have set to the category of the human. What is uniquely horrifying about such figures, Agamben observes, is not that "their life is no longer life," a condition of degradation suffered by all camp inhabitants, but instead that "their death is no longer death."[22] Drained of all affect and denied the possibility of communication, these figures die as human beings before their physical deaths.

Zizek suggests something similar in his discussion of the dispossessed and stateless subjects of contemporary biopolitics, figures similarly stunned into a shuffling semblance of human existence. These victims of natural disasters and global economic collapse are the new living dead, alive but without place in the life-worlds of neoliberal governance. Such figures cannot rightfully be described using the familiar language of post-traumatic stress disorder, Zizek insists, because trauma has become the normalized rather than the disruptive condition. What is also true, but which Zizek does not explore, is that this more generalized condition is not new but rather is newly extended to many subjects who previously saw themselves as protected from such damage by the discourse of liberal humanism and its state institutions. I call these new zombie narratives ones of abject posthumanism in which humanity becomes split between surviving "real" humans and infected, dangerous posthumans (the zombies; the infected), a literalization of what Foucault has termed the racism of modern biopolitical governance.

Viruses, which are both "natural" and manufactured as a technology of warfare, are an apt image for this abject posthuman, another kind of living-dead/infected-living. They are alive but incapable of reproduction on their own, and so they take over the functions of "healthy" cells, forcing them to reproduce the virus and become more agents of infection. This is precisely the trajectory of the abject posthumans who prey on surviving humans. Yet, as Priscilla Wald points out, the image of contagion does not have only pejorative associations. The word originally was used to describe the rapid circulation of ideas, not disease, and even the virus itself, although it often results in death, is not inherently about killing but rather about *changing*. Intrinsic to the idea of the virus is not only the model of the invading outsider, but also the transmission of shared immunity and thus group belonging. Contagion, Wald points out, "dramatizes the dilemma that inspires the most basic of human narratives: the necessity and danger of human contact."[23]

Similarly, Roberto Esposito seeks to think about biopolitics that does not inevitably become thanatopolitics, and uses the paradigm of immunity to explore the dialectical relations between self and community that are captured in the body's biological defenses. He characterizes post-9/11 America as a society suffering from an autoimmune disorder, in which the possibility for community is destroyed by a too-vigilant mechanism for detecting and annihilating infection,[24] a dynamic that is also operative in recent zombie narratives. For example, the AMC series *The Walking Dead* (2010–) is an extended meditation on the problems of community and individuality. It partakes equally of zombie and post-apocalyptic traditions and is about what kind of human community will be built on the ashes of the pre-infection world as much as about the flight from zombie attack.

The show is ambivalent in its depiction of zombies as *zoe* or *bios*: on the one hand, in the many and familiar scenes of zombie hordes converging on our protagonists, the zombies are represented simply as monstrous threat and are killed in volume and with violent abandon; on the other, and in contrast to *28 Days Later*, when one of the core group, Amy (Emma Bell), becomes infected, the group is divided between those who want to dispatch her immediately and those willing to allow her sister, Andrea (Laurie Holden), time to grieve. In her phase of zombie infection, death, and rebirth as monstrous, then, Amy occupies a space in which she is not human and yet also not *fully* Other. In the end, her death is deemed inevitable and thus this moment of hesitation does not offer a way to think through community and contagion in new ways, but it nonetheless treats the community's autoimmune responses as a difficulty, something questioned as well as naturalized. The series shifts further toward a reactionary us–them binary in the second season when the hope for reversal, promised by the CDC, has been destroyed. Its narrative arc concerns the differences in leadership style between Rick and his second-in-command, Shane Walsh (Jon Bernthal). Shane quickly adapts to the harsh new realities of the post-apocalyptic world, willing to sacrifice human lives as easily as zombie ones if it proves advantageous to those he identifies as *his* community, a narrow group that does not extend to their entire collective. Shane puts himself at risk but only for those in his self-identified family, whereas Rick strives to be the leader for the entire group and is willing to risk himself to help any people they encounter.

The first half of season two is taken up by a long search for a missing child, Sophia (Madison Lintz), whom they finally discover in the conclusion of "Pretty Much Dead Already" (November 27, 2011). In the episode's final moments Rick and his group confront Hershel (Scott Wilson) and his family, the owners of the farm where they are staying, over the infected that Hershel has kept quarantined in the barn rather than killed. Hershel insists upon seeing the zombies as ill rather than monstrous. Rick disagrees but has sufficient investment in the old order to respect Hershel's autonomy. Shane repeatedly insists that the old world is dead and, to survive, they must embrace new, harsher values. This debate over how to interpret the zombies—as within or beyond human community—is abruptly ended when Shane begins shooting, releasing the penned-up zombies and continuing the massacre until the final one—the missing Sophia, now changed—emerges from the barn. Crucially, it is Rick, not Shane, who kills her, representing his reluctant capitulation to the values Shane epitomizes. Sophia's change is an outcome they could easily— yet tellingly did not—predict, undermining the surface narrative's support of Rick's kinder, gentler post-apocalyptic regime. *The Walking Dead* shares with Rick a desire for a sense of humanity that can persist beyond the zombie apocalypse—an investment in ideals of community, a condemnation of the autoimmune disorder that will sacrifice all for the sake of the self. Yet the narrative simultaneously endorses Shane's perspective that this dream is not only impossible but also dangerous, a liability in a world understood to have peeled away the veneer of community and revealed the "true" state of nature as a war of all against all. The series tries to balance these two impulses by vilifying Shane (who is killed for his crimes by the end of this season) and by making Rick loath to change: yet change he does, implying that the division of community into full and less-than human subjects is inevitable rather than a result of human political and economic systems.

The abject posthuman in *The Walking Dead*, then, is ultimately less the monstrous zombies than it is the monsters that the human community must become to survive in a world founded on such rapacious values. Shane is representative of the ethos of the neoliberal order, a discourse that acts on the population "to make survive," in Agamben's terms, but one that simultaneously dehumanizes and makes monstrous these survivors. This is true both of the zombies in the series, reduced to endless walking and consuming, and of those humans able to adjust themselves to the new order, to draw a narrow circle of community and demonize all those outside it. This perspective reflects the logic of neoliberalism that fragments human subjects across geographic, ethnic, and class boundaries, and its refusal to allow one to recognize that survival is often at a cost for and of others.

In "The Imagination of Disaster," Susan Sontag analyzes the dehumanization in formulaic 1950s disaster films and argues that films such as *Them!* (Douglas 1954) and *Invasion of the Body Snatchers* (Siegal 1956) provide their audiences with the "fantasy of living through one's own death and more, the death of cities, the destruction of humanity itself,"[25] seeing in their repeated motifs an effort to come to terms with the violence of contemporary technology and pervasive xenophobia. Such films rely on an unacknowledged similarity between the dehumanized invaders and the logical and impersonal values of the savior-scientists, resulting in narratives that deny rather than enable social critique. Such films, Sontag contends, are an "*inadequate response*" to the problems they narratize, texts complicit "with the abhorrent" since they neutralize it and "perpetuate clichés."[26] Just as the soulless and hyper-rational aliens of 1950s disaster movies reflected limitations of the contemporary political ethos, the recent films of zombie infections, in their depictions of the "necessary" extremes of human violence to counter this threat, similarly demonstrate an unacknow-ledged homology between their antagonists and their heroes. Texts such as *The Walking Dead*, which seem to question the exclusion of abject posthumans, only to insist on the necessity of their annihilation, enact a similar bad faith. They maintain that the split between abject and human subjects, between *zoe* and *bios*, is "natural" rather than made by contingent human choice, and thereby normalize and naturalize the competition of capitalism and its dehumanization.

Contradictions, profanations, the promises of monsters

I want to conclude by asking whether it is possible to think of the abject posthuman in ways other than as the monstrousness of bare life detached from the protections of the subject/citizen. In thinking about the posthuman infected-living zombies, can we recover anything of contagion's roots in shaping shared immunity/community?[27] Life should be "pure relation and therefore absence or implosion of subjects in relation to each other: a relation without subjects,"[28] Esposito contends. It is the logical categories of modernity (identity, causality, non-contradiction) that create a situation in which the impulses of life turn on themselves: such categories "construct barriers, limits, and embankments with respect to that common *munus*."[29] When humans refuse to be what liberal philosophy has constituted as "the human," new possibilities emerge, including new models of the relationship between individual and community. Campbell describes Esposito's biopolitics as a "philosophy of the impersonal,"[30] drawing on the work of Simone Weil and the idea that what is sacred in a person is precisely what disrupts the self-focused individual and prevents the immune response from coming into play. To develop this idea of impersonal *bios*, Campbell returns to Agamben and his idea of profanation. If something becomes sacred by removing it from the realm of ordinary human activity and separating it to the supernatural, then the reverse process, to profane, restores "to common use what sacrifice had separated and divided."[31]

Agamben refers to this reverse action as "a profane contagion"[32] and further contends that capitalism introduces this division with the commodity form that "splits into use-value and exchange-value."[33] Capitalism separates the human spirit from the human body, requiring that humanity does not work to live (that is, produce use-values to reproduce itself) but rather lives to work (that is, produce surplus-value for capital). In order to profane, in Agamben's sense, we must remove objects from this service to capital and return them to service to humanity, via embracing the same actions emptied "of their sense and of any obligatory relationship to an end."[34] Campbell suggests that humor is one way that we might separate our actions from a given or obligatory end and thus restore them to the human realm of profanation. The Argentinean film *Fase 7* (Nicolás Goldbart 2011) uses humor to redirect the zombie narrative to a new end, reading the world of zombie capital from the point of view of those subjects damaged rather than enriched by neoliberalism. *Fase 7* profanes the zombie narrative.

Fase 7 is a zombie film without any zombies. It begins with our unlikely hero, Coco (Daniel Hendler), who is shopping with his pregnant girlfriend

Pipi (Jazmín Stuart). Although crowds rush through the street in a panic as these two load their groceries and go home, they are oblivious and carry on bickering about quotidian tasks. Later that evening, as they eat dinner, we overhear a television news report talking about the virus having spread to the U.S., Canada, Mexico, Spain, and the U.K., concluding that Argentina may now be under threat. When the broadcast shifts to a W.H.O. representative explaining the risk, it simultaneously shifts from Spanish to the representative's English. Most of the film follows Coco and Pipi as their apartment building is quarantined by hazmat-suited agents who speak to them through megaphones and continually defer answering their questions. Rather than fleeing zombie hordes or learning to kill, Pipi and Coco play board games, bicker, make ration lists, and otherwise settle in for a boring apocalypse. We learn of the outbreak only through occasionally overheard bits of dialogue from television broadcasts, and most of this information continues to be in English.

When violence does break out, it begins as an attack on one of the building's residents, Zanutto (Fredrico Luppi), whose persistent cough has turned the others, organized by the paranoid Horacio (Yayo Guridi), against him. Horacio tries to involve Coco in these plots, but the inept, bumbling, and generally well-meaning Coco resists and even tries to warn Zanutto. The war among residents that breaks out is represented as a series of comic escapades, as Zanutto emerges not as a vulnerable old man but rather as a stylized, larger-than-life action hero. The death toll mounts, but the killing is entirely by paranoid residents turning on one another, a parody of the new ethos promoted by zombie narratives. Coco is given a mysterious videotape by Horacio that offers a conspiracy theory about the manufacture of the virus as part of a plot to implement "a new world order that guarantees the status of corporations, the ones responsible." We never see the full video but overhear parts of its narrative, including excerpts from George Bush's New World Order speech of 1991 given after the first U.S. invasion of Iraq. In the dénouement, almost everyone is killed except Coco and Pipi, who leave the building and head north.

Fase 7 is simultaneously a playful and a serious film. It mocks the easy capitulation to the zero-sum-game ethics of neoliberalism naturalized in many other zombie films, and reminds us of the connections between such fictional new world orders and the material one constructed for us by American hegemony and global capital. In leaving the city, Coco and Pipi refuse Bush's New World Order, revealing the emptiness of the supposed "rule of law rather than the law of the jungle,"[35] and seek a different kind of future than the hypocrisies of U.N. interventions that have made the world safe for global corporations. Throughout, Coco has retained his humanity and refused to adopt the new ethos of generalized killing; he remains committed to community rather than individuality, and his escape with pregnant Pipi at the end suggests a possibility for the birth of something new. Pipi and Coco escape with Horacio's paranoid survivalist supplies but with their own plan to live a rural life beyond the pressures and pace of the city. Although this film cannot undo the dominant thanatopolitical theme of zombie narratives, it nonetheless offers a glimpse at how such images might otherwise be deployed: a way of seeing that the end times can also be those of new beginnings.

Notes

1 Donna Haraway, "A Cyborg Manifesto: Science Technology, and Socialist-Feminism in the Late Twentieth Century," in *Simians, Cyborgs and Women: The Reinvention of Nature* (New York: Routledge, 1991), 154.

2 Ibid., 181.

3 Donna Haraway, "The Actors are Cyborg, Nature is Coyote and the Geography is Elsewhere: Postscript to 'Cyborgs at Large'," in *Technoculture*, eds Constance Penley and Andrew Ross (Minneapolis: University of Minnesota Press, 1991), 21–6.

4 Slavoj Zizek, *Living in the End Times*, rev. edn (London: Verso, 2011), x.

5 Ibid., 334.

6 Lev Grossman, "Zombies are the New Vampires," *Time*, April 9, 2009. http://www.time.com/time/magazine/article/0,9171,1890384,00.html (accessed January 10, 2012).

7 Gerry Canavan, "Fighting a War You've Already Lost: Zombies and Zombis in *Firefly/Serenity* and *Dollhouse*," *Science Fiction Film and Television*, 4, no. 2 (2011): 173–203. This is an excellent overview of the distinctions and similarities between zombis and zombies and their relevance to capitalist critique.

8 David McNally, *Monsters of the Market: Zombies, Vampires and Global Capitalism* (Leiden: Brill, 2010).

9 Jean Comaroff and John Comaroff, "Alien-Nation: Zombies, Immigrants, and Millennial Capitalism," *The South Atlantic Quarterly* 101, no. 4 (2002): 784.

10 Mohammed K. Silmen, "Zombies Rest, and Motion: Spinoza and the Speed of Undeath," *Zombies, Vampires and Philosophy: New Life for the Undead*, eds Richard Greene and K. Silem Mohammad (Chicago: Open Court, 2006), 94.

11 Michel Foucault, *Society Must be Defended*, trans. David Macey (New York: Picador, 2003), 241.

12 Ibid., 61.

13 Henry A. Giroux, *Zombie Politics and Culture in the Age of Casino Capitalism* (New York: Peter Lang, 2010), 2.

14 Achille Mbembé, "Necropolitics," trans. Libby Meintjes, *Public Culture* 15, no. 1 (2003): 21.

15 Timothy Campbell, *Improper Life: Technology and Biopolitics from Heidegger to Agamben* (Minneapolis: University of Minnesota Press, 2011), 72.

16 Ibid., 94.

17 I am thinking of the parallels between the insertion of the protagonist and viewer quickly *in media res* of the new world of zombie politics, and the strategies of neoliberalism that utilize a rhetoric of urgency and crisis to compel people to accept rather than question rapid changes of policy. See Naomi Klein, *The Shock Doctrine: The Rise of Disaster Capitalism* (New York: Picador, 2007).

18 Giorgio Agamben, *Remnants of Auschwitz: The Witness and the Archive*, trans. Daniel Heller-Roazon (New York: Zone Books, 2002), 155.

19 Ibid.

20 Agamben, *Remnants*, 55.

21 Ibid., 70.

22 Ibid.

23 Priscilla Wald, *Contagious: Cultures, Carriers and the Outbreak Narrative* (Durham: Duke University Press, 2007). Kindle LOC 55.

24 Roberto Esposito, *Bios: Biopolitics and Philosophy*, trans. Timothy Campbell (Minneapolis: University of Minnesota Press, 2008).

25 Susan Sontag, "The Imagination of Disaster" [1965], in *Science Fiction: Stories and Contexts*, ed. Heather Masri (New York: Bedford, 2009), 1005.

26 Ibid., 1014.

27 Other scholars have found liberating possibility in the figure of the zombie, a subject that refuses individuation and one whose excessive, unchannelled energy may partake of the spirit of the multitude. See Simon Orpana, "Spooks of Biopower: The Uncanny Carnivalesque of Zombie Walks," *Topia* 25 (Spring 2011): 153–76; and Sarah Juliet Lauro and Karen Embry, "A Zombie Manifesto: The Nonhuman Condition in the Era of Advanced Capitalism," *boundary 2* (Spring 2008): 85–108. Orpana sees in the popular celebration of zombies a model for collectivity premised on notions other than a mutually beneficial contract among otherwise distinct individuals, but notes as well that such a "collective constellation ... only appears as a threatening, monstrous Other to those still trapped within the individualist, bourgeois paradigm" (158). Similarly, Larou and Embry argue that the zombie's very lack of subjectivity is precisely what makes it a fitting image of the posthuman, "a subject that is not a subject" (96).

28 Esposito, *Bios*, 89.

29 Ibid., 90.

30 Campbell, *Improper*, 66.

31 Ibid., 52.

32 Giorgio Agamben, "In Praise of Profanation," *Profanations*, trans. Jeff Fort (New York: Zone Books, 2007), 74.

33 Ibid., 81.

34 Ibid., 86.

35 This line is a direct quotation from Bush's speech. In the film's final sequence, as the survivors drive out of the apartment's garage, we hear a voiceover of this speech (in Bush's voice) as we view them leaving.

9

Monstrous technologies and the telepathology of everyday life

Jeremy Biles

A good part of monstrosity ... is just that: ... our scientific means, our knowhow, progress all take an uncontrollable, inhuman dimension.

JEAN BAUDRILLARD

Man has, as it were, become a kind of prosthetic God. When he puts on all his auxiliary organs he is truly magnificent ... but ... they still give him much trouble at times.

SIGMUND FREUD

Killing the masters

Those familiar with the critically acclaimed 2003 re-imagining of the television series *Battlestar Galactica* will not forget its dramatic opening. A series of title cards reveals that the Cylons—a race of cybernetic entities—"were created by Man ... to make life easier on the Twelve Colonies." But the Cylons rebelled, determining to "kill their masters." Following an armistice, the Cylons disappeared for over 40 years. As the title cards continue to frame the epic drama about to unfold, we see a Colonial officer calmly perusing files at a desk on a "remote space station" that had been built to accommodate "diplomatic relations" with the long-absent Cylons. The decades of quiet are, however, about to come to an explosive end.

The doors to the space station open, and the startled officer looks up from his papers to find a pair of menacing robotic Cylon Centurions. These mechanical soldiers stand aside to make way for the entrance of a Number Six, one of a line of humanoid Cylons that has "evolved" since the armistice. The copy known as "Caprica Six," played with sultry verve by fashion model Tricia Helfer, is a far cry from her cold and patently robotic relatives. This curvaceous Cylon, by all appearances indistinguishable from a human, brims with sexual energy. She approaches the fearful but enchanted officer, leans in seductively, and asks him, "Are you alive?" She then engages the officer in a sensual kiss as a Cylon missile strikes the space station, engulfing it in flames. Enacting what they take to be a divinely ordained plan, the Cylons initiate a full-scale nuclear assault on the Twelve Colonies, with the intent of wiping out the humans, whom they regard as physically, intellectually, and morally inferior beings. Humanity is overtaken in a nuclear apocalypse, eradicated by technological monsters of its own creation.

Sex and death, biology and technology, religion and violence thus converge and clash in the opening moments of *Battlestar Galactica*. If "popular culture is like a mirror, reflecting who we are," we would do well to ask what this television series reveals about us.[1] In the following pages, I want to take *Battlestar Galactica* as a touchstone in considering our cultural moment, a time in which humans are becoming increasingly intimate with technology, penetrated by and absorbed into the technological realm in an unprecedented manner.[2] Combining biological and technological attributes, the Cylons are at once seductive and lethal, and thus a source of simultaneous fear and fascination for the television audience. In this way, they dramatically attest to a widespread cultural ambivalence regarding the pervasiveness and possibilities of technology, as well as the transformation—or eradication—of humanity that attends those possibilities.

This essay inquires into what accounts for such collective ambivalence—simultaneous technophilia and technophobia—and the surprising religious dimensions it displays. It argues that the anxious and exhilarated attitude toward technology is a response to the dual destiny announced by our technological horizon. On the one hand, technology promises perfection and victory over death; robotic bodies will ensure corporeal immortality, while the ability to upload human minds into networked computers heralds boundless consciousness, infinite interconnectedness. On the other hand, the overtaking of human biological bodies by robotic, technologized bodies points toward the demise of the human species in its present form.[3] The trajectory of developments in artificial intelligence, robotics, and networked computing thus portends what some thinkers refer to as an "apocalypse": a death of the imperfect human coincident with a technological resurrection.[4] The "salvation" promised by this vision of technology simultaneously elevates and erases the human; immortality and death coincide. From this point of view, the very technology that promises perfection and immortality is a sacred monster that kills its master.

Anatomy of a Cylon: Immortality in the age of robotics

One of the great innovations of the re-imagined *Battlestar Galactica* is the introduction of sexy Cylons.[5] Virtually indistinguishable from humans, even at the cellular level, humanoid Cylons like the Number Six are a far cry from their metallic ancestors. The erotic charisma of this model in particular plays a key role in the series. Caprica Six uses her sexual prowess in order to manipulate humans. This is most notably the case with the Cylon-smitten genius, Gaius Baltar, whom Caprica Six seduces in order to obtain access codes to a Colonial military network subsequently rendered ineffective, allowing the Cylons successfully to launch their attack. Number Six may be a machine, but she is a passionate (and very shrewd) machine who incites desire, sometimes to fearful ends.

The combination of seductive power and lethal intent is just one point of ambivalence encapsulated in the Cylons. There are others. In fact, as we will see, the Cylons are monstrous, not just in their capacity for genocidal violence, but in their embodiment of qualities that are typically held to be incompatible, or at least in tension with each other: biology/technology, human/machine, life/death. Fictional monsters often figure coincidences of opposites, mingling characteristics that human minds want to keep distinct; as "boundary objects" straddling and blurring the borders between seeming opposites, monsters thus embody ambivalent attributes.[6] In this regard, Cylons are quintessential sci-fi monsters.

More specifically, Cylons, or "Cybernetic Lifeform Nodes," are monstrous *cyborgs*. In her seminal "Cyborg Manifesto," Donna Haraway claims that cyborgs are "monstrous" in their intractable hybridity. The cyborg is a "a cybernetic organism, a hybrid of machine and organism, a creature of social reality as well as a creature of fiction."[7] As hybrids of "animal and machine,"[8] Cylons are the "perfect examples of cyborgs," dramatizing the "tension between their existence as machines and their existence as organic life forms."[9] As a commentator has noted, many of *Battlestar Galactica*'s characters—on both the human and Cylon sides—are "obsessed with the fate of the machine–human hybrid. ... [I]t is the destiny of the two races to be melded together."[10]

Such melding holds out the promise of the virtual immortality of the body. In the miniseries that launched the re-imagined program, William Adama, commander of the eponymous spacecraft, finds himself locked in hand-to-hand combat with a male humanoid Cylon. Though outmatched by the Cylon's superior physical strength, Adama none the less manages to dispatch of his enemy. Before he is able to do so, however, the Cylon tells Adama, "I can't die. When this body is destroyed, my memory, my consciousness, will be transmitted to a new one. I'll just wake up somewhere else"—the cathedral-like Resurrection ship—"in an identical body." We will return to the Cylons' ability to transmit consciousness later. For the moment, we can consider the prospect of virtual bodily immortality dramatized by the Cylons.

The Cylons partake of a kind of immortality afforded by their status as cyborgs.[11] As one critic points out, "Cylon bodies are ... at a minimum part-organic, but have a superior integration with technology."[12] In fact, Cylon bodies are "factory-made"; complete body copies are mass manufactured and ready for use. If a conscious Cylon's body is destroyed, another copy is there to house its memory and consciousness, thereby ensuring virtual immortality. In this way, the Cylons figure what some thinkers believe to be the destiny of the human, namely, to achieve such perfect integration with robotic technology that the corruption, damage, or loss of a body part will simply require replacement with another identical part. If all biological, and thus corruptible, body parts are replaced by robotic parts, decay and injury will no longer entail mortality.

This optimistic scenario concerning the technological overcoming of bodily death is one facet of what religion and technology scholar Robert M. Geraci calls "Apocalyptic AI." Geraci discerns a distinctively apocalyptic dimension to the work of futurists, roboticists, and artificial intelligence experts like Ray Kurzweil, Hans Moravec, and Marvin Minsky, who believe that advances in robotics and computer technologies will transcend "the human body's limited intellectual powers and inevitable death."[13] According to Kurzweil and other futurists, it is the "destiny" of humans to merge ever more intimately with their technologies.[14] Human bodies will be replaced by robotic parts, and human minds will be scanned and uploaded into networked computers, ensuring undying and boundless consciousness.[15] Artificial intelligence will achieve "Singularity," exceeding human biological intelligence, and enjoying transcendent "spiritual experience."[16] Much as traditional Jewish and Christian apocalyptic narratives portray an end-time in which the mortality that marks and mars the present world will be overcome, so do Apocalyptic AI theorists envision a "radically transcendent future where we forsake our biological bodies" and "upload our minds into robotic bodies in order that we will no longer become ill, die, or suffer mental decline."[17] Geraci sees this apocalyptic scenario being ushered in with the "Age of Robots," in which robotic technologies will guarantee immortality through incorruptible, replaceable bodies reminiscent of the Cylons' "resurrected" bodies.[18]

There is, however, a dark side to the optimistic eschatology propounded by the Apocalyptic AI thinkers. Rather than seeing the replacement of human bodies with robotics as a form of "salvation," some see it as a threat—not the promise of immortality but a harbinger of death. Hypotheses about the eventual usurpation of the authentically human, biological body brings to mind philosopher Martin Heidegger's suspicious assessment of technology. In a prescient essay treating "The Question Concerning Technology," Heidegger claims that the essence of technology is "ultimately a way of *revealing* the totality of beings." This way of revealing, however, also menaces humans, threatening to "overwhelm [humans ...] and all other possible ways of revealing."[19] The menace lies in the fact that humans run the risk of failing to master technology, of being mastered by technology—of becoming *technologized*. Succumbing to what he calls the "enchantment" of technology presents the threat of "unrestrained domination of machination."[20] Even as we want to lay claim to immortality, then, we are driven to a kind of death through a merging with the inorganic realm of technology, which Heidegger aptly describes as the "gigantic"—a "monstrous" immensity.[21]

The "apocalypse" is thus ushered in by the intractable encroachment of technology and the concomitantly increasing intimacy of human bodies and machines. The human body in its biological form gives way to technologization, replaced by incorruptible plastic, metal, and other synthetic parts. Subject to technological perfectibility, the organic body is revealed to be obsolete. Herein lies the ambivalence underwriting the forfeiture of the biological body: it derives from a *wish* to die and a *desire* to be resurrected *as immortal*.

The drive toward the inorganic manifest in the quest for technological apotheosis is a contemporary iteration of what Sigmund Freud called the death drive. According to Freud, the human subject contains opposed energetic flows: the sex drive and the death drive. The pleasure principle that governs life, according to Freud, comes in moving from a state of greater tension to one of lesser. The death drive, however, is beyond life and thus "beyond the pleasure principle," to the effect that "instincts tend towards the restoration of an earlier state"[22]—a state of undifferentiated "inorganic stability."[23] The death drive, in short, is the instinct that seeks to turn the human subject into inanimate matter, indistinct from its inanimate environs. Though Freud theorizes the death drive as a "return" to a pre-animated state without tension, today the death drive is turned in a different direction; it may be reconceived as a drive toward the inorganic in the form of technology itself. This is the death drive not as a reversion to a prior state, but as movement toward a future possibility. The drive toward technology, the drive toward the immortality of the technologized body, is, in this specific sense, concurrent with the death drive.

The coincidence of opposites in play here is marked by a profound ambivalence of the sort notoriously associated with what scholars of religion term "the sacred." Classic theories of the sacred from the likes of Emile Durkheim and Rudolph Otto see the sacred in radically ambivalent terms. Durkheim believes that the sacred exhibits opposing aspects: beneficent and destructive, light and dark, the forces of life and the powers of decay. As we will see, religious rituals reflect the ambivalence of the sacred, at once exalting and dissolving an individual's everyday sense of self. Similarly, Otto develops a phenomenology of the sacred encapsulated in the famous phrase *"mysterium tremendum et fascinans."* The sacred is a mystery that is both terribly powerful, or tremendous, and deeply desirable, or fascinating. Both the wellspring of life and the bringer of death, the sacred is at once attractive and repellent, magnetic and repulsive, exalting and deadly.

A compelling eroto-mystical force animates this drive toward the inanimate, this allure of the technological. French thinker Georges Bataille's distinctive theory of eroticism and mysticism helps illuminate a mystical current drawing humans toward their technological destiny. Inflected by Freud's theory of the death drive as well as Durkheim's concept of the ambivalence of the sacred, Bataille's theory regards eroticism and mysticism as entailing experiences of the dissolution of the self. In this manner, Bataille's understanding of mysticism clearly resonates with accounts of many traditional mystics, who, through ascetic and meditative practices, seek to eradicate their individual egos in merging with the divine totality, the godhead, culminating in what Bataille describes as an experience of sacred "continuity." Similarly, Bataille sees erotic activity as proceeding through a "death, the rupture" of the individual in union or continuity with the erotic partner.[24] "The whole business of eroticism," writes Bataille, "is to destroy the self-contained character" of the participant, allowing for the "blending and fusion of separate objects."[25] The death of the self demanded by eroto-mystical experience is both thrilling and terrifying, elevating and depleting, and thus, according to Bataille, "monstrous."[26]

This monstrous combination of pleasure and anguish clearly recalls the ambivalence of the sacred as described by Durkheim and Otto. But Bataille's vision of religious experience is also beyond the pleasure principle, opening onto the Freudian death drive. The death that Bataille describes has the discrete, self-contained individual dissolved in an experience of what he calls "continuity" or "communication," that is, a sense of connection and convergence with something greater than the individual. Erotic partners experience this connection as orgasmic rupture and flow, with subjects uniting in love. Traditional mystics experience the loss of ego as union with the divine, with Being itself. Similarly, today's technological subjects, I would suggest, are seduced by the prospect of a death of the human in its present, biological form—a death that is coincident with bodily immortality. The replacement of the human body by robotics carries with it the promise of merging with the technological "immensity," the inorganic but immortal.

Walter Benjamin once referred to the "sex appeal of the inorganic."[27] Caprica Six would seem to literalize this sex appeal of the inorganic— not only because she uses her factory-made curves to titillate *Battlestar Galactica's* human characters as well as its human audience, but because her erotic presence announces the eroto-mystical allure of a bodily immortality achievable only by loss in the technological immensity. This is an immortality that demands the forfeiture of the biological body, the death of the human as presently constituted. The inorganic, the robotic, the technological: these present us with a death that is also a preservation—a demise that would ensure immortality. It is a destiny in which the death drive is "[transvalued] ... as the very principle of self-preservation, indeed of self-exaltation."[28]

Total communication: The telepathology of everyday life

The anxious prospect of intense continuity or communication is foregrounded in the opening episode of *Battlestar Galactica*, where the ship that gives the show its title is described by the characters as "antiquated," a "relic," a "museum." Its computers and communications systems are outmoded and offline, and its fleet of Viper fighter craft have long since seen any active combat. But this superannuated vessel remains protected from the Cylons, who have infiltrated and rendered defenseless the Colonial networked defense system. Having learned from previous experience of the Cylons' ability to exploit networked computers, Commander Adama is adamant: "I will not allow a networked computerized system aboard this ship while I'm in command!"

But networks are not all bad. Though networked computers endanger the Colonial population, they protect and promote the lives of Cylons. As "cybernetic lifeforms nodes," Cylons can plug into computers directly, allowing for immediate connectivity and communication across vast distances. And as we noted above, the contents of Cylons' minds can be uploaded into computers, allowing for their consciousness to be archived and disseminated across the network. This feature not only grants immediate access to information; it is also another component of the virtual immortality enjoyed by the Cylons. From the outset, then, *Battlestar Galactica* dramatically portrays both cultural hopes and anxieties surrounding computer networks and telecommunications technologies.

The conjunction of technophobia and technophilia dramatized in the treatment of networks on *Battlestar Galactica* was already being considered decades ago by media theorist Marshall McLuhan. McLuhan discerns this pervasive ambivalence regarding networks in terms that will further limn their curious religious dimensions. Much as *Battlestar Galactica*'s Gaius Baltar succumbs to the erotic caresses of the cyborg lover who threatens the survival of the human species, the human sensorium, claims McLuhan, is "massaged" by technology in a manner at once pleasurable and pernicious; technological mediums "work us over,"[29] stroking, soothing, and ravishing our senses, thereby drawing us into a "fatal fascination" with technology.[30] McLuhan conceives of technology as a kind of prosthetic "extension of biology." In particular, electronic communications networks represent an "exteriorization" or amplification of the human nervous system.[31] "With the arrival of electric technologies," writes McLuhan, "man extended, or set outside himself, a live model of the central nervous system itself."[32] But as McLuhan explains, this exteriorization has a dangerously captivating effect on those who behold it; we are "hypnotized by the extension ... of [our] own being in a new technological form," for humans are ineluctably "fascinated by any extension of themselves in any material other than themselves."[33]

This "fatal fascination" lies in the fact that, according to McLuhan, any technological extension or amplification of the nervous system, while granting pleasure, is in some sense traumatic; exteriorization of the senses entails vulnerable exposure, and thus the need for protection. Amplification of the nervous system is only "bearable ... through numbness or blocking of perception."[34] This "suggests a desperate and suicidal autoamputation, as if the central nervous system could no longer depend on the physical organs to be protective buffers against the slings and arrows of outrageous mechanism."[35] Our biological humanity is deadened, such that technological self-extension is concurrent with autoamputation. Extrapolating from McLuhan, we find that we ever more closely resemble the "lifeless"—robotic, inorganic—material with which we are merging. This is the "suicidal" side of the technological massage, the intensifying convergence with the inorganic and mechanical.

And yet, as *Battlestar Galactica* suggests, cyborgs, at least as they are imagined in the form of Caprica Six, are not cold, lifeless, and bereft of spiritual depths. Rather, these amalgamations of organic life and machinic technology are passionate and spiritual—and McLuhan's genuinely ambivalent position acknowledges such possibilities. In fact, as Lewis H. Lapham points out, by McLuhan's account, "unifying networks of electronic communication might restore mankind to a state of bliss not unlike the one said to have existed within the Garden of Eden." Lapham describes this tendency as a "mystical component" of McLuhan's thought, for it envisions, in McLuhan's words, a "spiritual form of information" that would "make of the entire globe, and of the human family, a single consciousness."[36]

Similarly, McLuhan claims in *The Global Village* that "robotism"—which includes human immersion in the milieu of electronic networks—"is the capacity to be a conscious presence in many places at once."[37] Robotism, in other words, is "decentralizing," and engendering a culture "organized like an electric circuit: each point in the net is as central as the next."[38] Again, McLuhan sees this eventuality in ambivalent terms. The "good news," he claims, is that the connected subject will "enjoy an illusionary sense of a well-defined identity"; the plugged-in person will feel shored up by her immediate access to information. But "the bad news is that all persons, whether or not they understand the processes of computerized high-speed data transmission, will lose their old private identities. What knowledge there is will be available to all." We find here again a simultaneous elevation and evacuation of individual consciousness that bespeaks a state in which "everybody is nobody"; we become connected but anonymous, uplifted and dissolved.[39]

McLuhan's description of the transformation of human inner experience in a culture of robotics and electronic network communications resonates tellingly with Durkheim's account of religious experience. Durkheim observes that for the religious person, the world is divided into two opposed realms: the sacred and the profane. As opposed to the profane, which Durkheim identifies with everyday life and individual needs, the sacred is the realm of collective life. Religious rituals instigate experiences of intense social connectivity, experiences that bring to mind McLuhan's description of culture as an electronic circuit promoting a state in which "everybody is nobody."

In fact, Durkheim uses of the metaphor of electricity to describe the energies that unify the social collective, at once exalting and dissolving ritual participants.[40] In ritual situations, social energies circulate like electrical currents, surging and coursing through the collective. The manner in which energy circulates culminates in a bubbling-up of intense emotions, which Durkheim refers to as collective "effervescence." The proximity of others in such ritual situations

... acts as an exceptionally powerful stimulant. When [participants] come together, a sort of electricity is formed by their collecting which quickly transports them to an extraordinary degree of exaltation. Every sentiment expressed finds a place without resistance in all the minds, which are very open to outside impressions; each re-echoes the others, and is re-echoed by the others.[41]

Though Durkheim is here describing the ecstatic rituals of traditional societies, his remarks apply with surprising aptness to today's intensifying network culture. Much as McLuhan describes the loss of individuality in electric networks as a succumbing to the allure of "[jumping] out of my skin," or "going out of my mind,"[42] so does Durkheim find in the "electricity" of intense religious experiences a pronounced element of ecstatic self-loss. The social collective becomes a kind of superorganism shot through with a force that dissolves individuals' everyday senses of self, bringing them together as a social collectivity at once cohesive and fluctuating. The intense "sensation of sacredness" in such rituals puts participants "quite outside" themselves.[43]

Being outside of oneself—ecstatic—through immersion in the infinity of the net is both the dream of self-extension and the nightmare of self-loss. As network technologies—the Internet, cloud computing, etc.—evolve, we may foresee a totally globally integrated communications system in which each individual becomes a node in a network of connections, or a "terminal of multiple networks," as Baudrillard puts it.[44] Similarly, theologian Mark C. Taylor has noted that the self in network culture is "a node in a complex network of relations." "In the midst of these webs, networks, and screens," he goes on, "I can no more be certain where I am than I can know when or where the I begins and ends. I am plugged into other objects and subjects in such a way that I become myself in and through them, even as they become themselves in and through me."[45]

Boundaries between inside and out, oneself and another, become blurred, crossed, sometimes erased. Such technologically interconnected minds are imminently susceptible to external (or are they internal?) impressions, each mind "echoing and re-echoing the other," to use Durkheim's phrase. Taylor claims that "both natural and sociocultural systems are fundamentally informational and communicational processes, which are always already taking place in such a way that it is no longer clear where to draw the line between mind and matter, self and other, human and machine. *Mind is distributed throughout the world.*"[46] The resulting situation is one in which, as philosopher of religion Thomas A. Carlson remarks, "distributed networks of intelligence and agency think and act through me as much as I through them, and with effects that can seem mystical."[47] Carlson's recent work has helpfully charted the "delocalizing effect of this technologically networked culture, which seems to yield a collective humanity that ... may well signal a trace of the mystical in modern and contemporary culture."[48]

There may be more than a "trace" of the mystical in network culture. To be sure, the emptying out or interpenetration of the discrete self in relation to other minds through networks recalls Bataille's conceptualization of the erotic subject in the experience of communication. One may extrapolate from Bataille in furthering Taylor's and Carlson's insights. The advancement of today's network culture presages the conditions for an emerging technological mysticism. As network communications become increasingly prevalent, the proximity that Durkheim understood as necessary to ritual efficacy gives way to pure immediacy. Humans inevitably merge with the network, their consciousnesses emptied into the fluctuating totality of connections. Self-loss and self-extension coincide: the discrete self dissolves into the technological milieu as bounded individual consciousness becomes coextensive with boundless networked consciousness.[49]

Such developments invite technophilic and technophobic responses. Intimating both the pleasure of proximity and the sacrifice of self, they set the stage for what might be called the "telepathology of everyday life." The phrase is an allusion to Freud's famous essay "The Psychopathology of Everyday Life," in which its author discusses the quotidian pathologies that haunt humans' daily existences: slips of the tongue, forgetfulness, and the like. I want to preserve that sense of the quotidian in my phrase. The monstrously hybridic term "telepathology" encapsulates and contracts "telepathy" and "pathology," both of which should be held in mind here.[50] In this context, *telepathy* represents the dream of networked computers and communications systems: it is the communication of minds or the transmission of thought by means other than our usual sensory apparatus, sometimes over great distances, and often with a sense of simultaneity between the communicating minds. *Pathology* refers not to a psychological disease in the usual sense, but rather to the cultural dis-ease that accompanies the drive toward networked consciousness and immortal robotic bodies.

As attested by *Battlestar Galactica* and countless other examples from popular culture, a pervasive cultural anxiety underlies the exhilarating prospect of increasingly perfectible bodies and immediate communication. The sci-fi Cylons evoke the attraction and fear produced by the possibilities of immortal, "purified" bodies and networked consciousness—both of which, the futurists assure us, are on our own very real technological horizon. The dis-ease lies in the disturbing ambivalence that attends these developments; it is the anxious and elated desire for the death of the self, the loss of the human in the technological immensity. "Telepathology" thus captures something of the fierce ambivalence produced by computer network and robotic technologies, and the loss of self they portend. It names the psychological underpinnings of the various aspects of technological mysticism we have noted in these pages.

Telepathology contains a further meaning. "Pathology," which we have connected with the ambivalent dis-ease produced in the face of technologization, comes from the Greek *pathos*, for suffering, feeling, or emotion. Telepathy—*tele-pathos*—has to do with communicating not only notional content, but also emotional experience. Durkheim, as we observed, spoke of a collective effervescence arising in moments of intense communication. His metaphor for describing the energetic flow produced by ritual activities was electricity, which takes on particular significance in the present context. Today, social networking technologies on the Internet provide electronic contact with other minds, and facilitate the production and delivery of frequent emotional charges, in a kind of distribution of effervescence across the network. The result of this pleasurable stimulation, this electronic massage, is a sense of compulsion. A felt need arises to be constantly *concurrent*: both telepathically simultaneous with, and participating in the emotional currents of, every other nodal point in the network.[51] The seductiveness of today's electronic communications systems—television, email and the Internet, cell phones, etc.—is such that their users often exhibit addictive behaviors. Like certain drugs, technology is enchanting and addictive, promising pleasure and threatening enslavement.[52]

Networked communications technologies thus generate intractable ambivalence, granting at once a sense of gratifying pleasure in the form of emotional stimulation and connectedness, even as they invite an ever greater (dis)integration into the network itself. In this way, the telepathology of everyday life evidences a new form of collective effervescence, one in which virtual connections replace the proximity of bodies, promoting a communication at once globally distributed and immediate. And thus the sphere of the sacred extends to, and is even becoming coextensive with, the technological sphere.[53]

Technological mysticism dramatically enacts both an anxious and an ecstatic loss of the self, a dissolution within the technological milieu. And it expresses the simultaneously tremendous and fascinating prospects of perfect bodies and boundless consciousness. It evinces an aspiration for immortality even as it is propelled by the death drive's orientation toward the inorganic. This technological mysticism is, then, both a sickness and a blessing—a telepathology in which the subject is "evacuated and elevated at once."[54] What it announces is that the immortality of the species coincides with the end of the human, which will be dissolved in and through the monstrous technologies it has created. If *Battlestar Galactica*'s Cylons reflect something about us, it is this: we are seduced by what is killing us, and fear what we long to immerse ourselves in—technology itself. Dying and rising in waves of anxiety and ecstasy, we are making way for our technological apotheosis, inhuman and more than human: a perfectly monstrous possibility, and the possibility of the monstrously perfect.

Notes

1 Bruce David Forbes, "Introduction: Finding Religion in Unexpected Places," in *Religion and Popular Culture in America*, (ed.) Bruce David Forbes and Jeffrey H. Mahan (Berkeley: University of California Press, 2000), 5.

2 Mark Seltzer speaks of the "intimacy" of human bodies and machines in *Serial Killers: Death and Life in America's Wound Culture* (New York: Routledge, 1998). Ray Kurzweil discusses the fact that humans are growing "more intimate with our technology" in *The Singularity Is Near: When Humans Transcend Biology* (New York: Viking, 2005), 309. As we will see, Georges Bataille uses the term "intimacy" in describing mystical communication.

3 Though this chapter is structured around the categories of "body" and "mind," no Cartesian dualism is intended by this structure.

4 See Robert M. Geraci, *Apocalyptic AI: Visions of Heaven in Robotics, Artificial Intelligence, and Virtual Reality* (Oxford: Oxford University Press, 2010). For a discussion of religion, technology, and perfection, see also David F. Noble, *The Religion of Technology: The Divinity of Man and the Spirit of Invention* (New York: Penguin, 1999).

5 As critics have noted, female Cylons appear generally more sexually appealing than their male counterparts. The present discussion of "sexy Cylons" gestures toward questions concerning gender and the technological feminine that, though urgent, are beyond the scope of this essay.

6 Geraci refers to robots as "boundary objects" in *Apocalyptic AI*, 142.

7 Donna Haraway, "A Cyborg Manifesto: Science, Technology, and Socialist-Feminism in the Late Twentieth Century," in *Simians, Cyborgs and Women: The Reinvention of Nature* (New York: Routledge, 1991), 149–81.

8 Haraway, "A Cyborg Manifesto," 149.

9 Paul Booth, "Frak-tured Postmodern Lives, Or, How I Found Out I Was a Cylon," in *Battlestar Galactica and Philosophy: Mission Accomplished or Mission Frakked Up?*, (ed.) Josef Steiff and Tristan D. Tamplin (Chicago: Open Court, 2008), 23.

10 Ibid.

11 Scholars like Donna Haraway believe that humans are in fact already cyborgs, amalgams of organic bodies and technology; things as commonplace as simple tools, eyeglasses, and medication are technologies from which we are practically inseparable.

12 Shana Heinricy, "I, Cyborg," in Steiff and Tamplin (eds) *Battlestar Galactica and Philosophy*, 101.

13 Geraci, *Apocalyptic AI*, 9.

14 Ray Kurzweil describes the Singularity as the "destiny" of humanity, in the documentary *Transcendent Man*, dir. Robert Barry Ptolemy, Ptolemaic Productions, 2009.

15 Ray Kurzweil, *The Age of Spiritual Machines: When Computers Exceed Human Intelligence* (New York: Penguin Books, 1999). See especially pp. 124–31.

16 See Kurzweil, *The Age of Spiritual Machines*, especially pp. 151–3.

17 Geraci, *Apocalyptic AI*, 9, 31–2.

18 Ibid., 9.

19 David Farrell Krell's gloss in Martin Heidegger, *Martin Heidegger: Basic Writings*, ed. David Farrell Krell (San Francisco: HarperCollins, 1993), 309.

20 Heidegger, cited in Thomas A. Carlson, *The Indiscrete Image: Infinitude & Creation of the Human* (Chicago: University of Chicago Press, 2008), 45.

21 See Heidegger's "The Question Concerning Technology" and Krell's introduction to the essay in *Martin Heidegger: Basic Writings*, 309.

22 Sigmund Freud, *Beyond the Pleasure Principle*, the Standard Edition, trans. and ed. James Strachey (New York: W. W. Norton and Company, 1961), 44.

23 Freud, cited in J. Laplanche and J.-B. Pontalis, *The Language of Psycho-analysis* (New York: W. W. Norton and Company, 1973), 98.

24 Georges Bataille, *Erotism: Death and Sensuality* (San Francisco: City Lights Books, 1962), 19.

25 Ibid., 17, 19, 25.

26 Ibid., 37.

27 Walter Benjamin, *The Arcades Project*, trans. Howard Eiland and Kevin McLaughlin (Cambridge, MA: Harvard University Press, 1999).

28 Hal Foster discusses the death drive in relation to the work of Filippo Tomasso Marinetti, claiming that Marinetti sought to "extrapolate the human toward the inorganic-technological" even as he sought to "define the inorganic-technological as the epitome of the human." *Prosthetic Gods* (Cambridge, MA: The MIT Press, 2004), 123.

29 Marshall McLuhan, *The Medium Is the Massage*, 26.

30 Arthur Kroker, "Digital Humanism: The Processed World of Marshall McLuhan," in *Digital Delirium*, (ed.) Arthur Kroker and Marilouise Kroker (New York: St. Martin's Press, 1997), 106.

31 Kroker, "Digital Humanism," 90–1.

32 Marshall McLuhan, *Understanding Media: The Extensions of Man* (Cambridge, MA: The MIT Press, 1998), 43.

33 Ibid., 11, 41.

34 Ibid., 42–3.

35 Ibid., 43.

36 Lewis H. Lapham, "Introduction" to McLuhan, *Understanding Media*, xviii, xvii.

37 Marshall McLuhan and Bruce R. Powers, *The Global Village: Transformations in World Life and Media in the 21st Century* (New York: Oxford University Press), 83.

38 Ibid., 92.

39 Ibid., 129.

40 Robert Geraci also notes the electricity in Durkheim's account of effervescence, arguing that cyberspace provides a new domain in which such religious experience is possible. See *Apocalyptic AI*, 90–5.

41 Emile Durkheim, *The Elementary Forms of the Religious Life*, trans. Joseph Ward Swain (New York: Free Press, 1915), 246–7.

42 McLuhan, *Understanding Media*, 42.

43 Durkheim, *Elementary Forms*, 245, 246.

44 Jean Baudrillard, "The Ecstasy of Communication," in *The Anti-Aesthetic: Essays on Postmodern Culture*, ed. Hal Foster (Seattle: Bay Press, 1983), 128.

45 Mark C. Taylor, cited in Carlson, *The Indiscrete Image*, 18.

46 Taylor cited in ibid., 17.

47 Carlson, *Indiscrete Image*, 19.

48 Ibid., 77.

49 See, for example, Kurzweil, *The Age of Spiritual Machines*, 124.

50 In addition to forms of pathology, forms of telepathy or "thought transference" also occupied Freud. See, for example, "Dreams and Occultism," in *New Introductory Lectures in Psychoanalysis*, trans. and (ed.) James Strachey (New York: W. W. Norton and Company, Inc., 1965), 31–56.

51 Unplugging from computers, cell phones, television, and other technologies, meanwhile, can result in withdrawal symptoms similar to those accompanying withdrawal from drugs. See, for example, Richard Gray, "Facebook Generation Suffer from Withdrawal Syndrome," *The Telegraph*, January 2, 2011 (http://www.telegraph.co.uk/technology/news/8235302/Facebook-generation-suffer-information-withdrawal-syndrome.html).

52 On technological enslavement, see, for example, Bill Davidow, "Technology Addiction Will Lead to Our Evolution—Or Enslavement," in *The Atlantic*, January 6, 2012 (http://www.theatlantic.com/health/archive/2012/01/technology-addiction-will-lead-to-our-evolution-or-enslavement/250951/).

53 "Cyberspace is sacred space," as Geraci claims in *Apocalyptic AI*, 13.

54 Hal Foster, *The Return of the Real: The Avant-Garde at the End of the Century* (Cambridge, MA: The MIT Press), 168.

10

Monstrous citizenships:

Coercion, submission, and the possibilities of resistance in *Never Let Me Go* and *Cloud Atlas*

Roy Osamu Kamada

In book seven of *The Prelude*, William Wordsworth recounts a visit to London during St. Bartholomew's Fair in 1802.[1] David Simpson describes Wordsworth's historical moment as one where "the modern world according to Horkheimer and Adorno was beginning to take on a recognizable profile but was not yet fully formed."[2] Simpson cites noted features of modernity in Wordsworth's world and work[3] (a world war, the rise of industrialism and free market capitalism, and the growing alienation of the worker); in particular Simpson cites Wordsworth's invocation of *spectacle*, which "underpins so much of the aesthetics of modernity ... an apt association that affiliates the spectacle with the commodity."[4] Wordsworth's early nineteenth-century experience of the modern metropolis anticipates more contemporary accounts in illuminating and telling ways. Contrasting the city's bustling crowds with the idyllic quiet of the country, Wordsworth describes it as "a hell for eyes and ears ... din/Barbarian and infernal ... [full of] far-fetched, perverted things,/All freaks of nature .../This parliament of monsters."[5] Overwhelmed by the urban diversity and unable to properly situate this landscape in the metaphysical function of the Wordsworthian sublime,[6] Wordsworth recoils from "The slaves unrespited of low pursuits,/Living amid the same perpetual flow/Of trivial objects, melted and reduced/To one identity by differences/ That have no law, no meaning."[7] For Wordsworth to describe the seething diversity of the urban cosmopolis as monstrous and "melted and reduced/ To one identity," during this visit to London, indicates that, even during the early years of the Industrial Revolution, familiar modern formulations of otherness, monstrosity, and legal forms of citizenship were in place. What Wordsworth calls "This parliament of monsters" is more than a dizzying array of attendees at St. Bartholomew's Fair; his allusion to the "unrespited" slaves does more than indicate a certain economic or racial diversity present in the streets of London at the time. Wordsworth's conclusion that these slaves embedded in the "perpetual flow/Of trivial objects, [are] melted and reduced" to singular identities (the category of the enslaved as opposed to an individual subjectivity) points to the arbitrary and contingent nature of that particular ontological status. Arguing that the reduction of the individual to the status of slave is the result of "differences/That have no law, no meaning," Wordsworth points to the capricious and haphazard logics animating the economic and juridical distinction of citizenship and belonging. And lastly, for the purposes of this chapter, Wordsworth also points to the linkages between traditional ideas of monstrosity, cultural otherness, and marginal citizenship.

In reading the traditional function of the figure of the monster, Martha Nussbaum asserts that "we need a group of humans to bound ourselves against, who will come to exemplify the lines between the truly human and the basely animal."[8] Jeffrey Cohen describes the figure of the monster as "an abjecting epistemological device basic to the mechanics of deviance construction and identity formation."[9] While these perspectives certainly assert the utility of the discourse of the monstrous other as a critical concept, I would like to suggest that the monster might be more than "an embodiment of difference."[10] Wordsworth's articulation of the monstrous anticipates Nussbaum's and Cohen's understanding of the social function of the monstrous and offers the start of a critique of the arbitrary logics animating terms of citizenship and belonging. However, where Wordsworth only briefly alludes to the urban spectacle that David Simpson argues is emblematic of an oncoming modernity, I would like to turn toward more contemporary and full-throated formulations of postmodern monstrosity in contemporary literature. Specifically, I argue that particular articulations of the postmodern monster might illuminate previously occluded aspects of the contemporary global citizen. This article considers two recent novels that invoke the figure of the clone as a particular kind of ghostly monster. The clone, as a specific manifestation of postmodern monstrosity, gestures toward the partial and incomplete components of subjectivity. Where the monstrosity of modernity is embodied in a figure such as Victor Frankenstein's creature, the monstrosity of the postmodern is more accurately embodied in a figure such as the clone—a figure whose ontological difference from the human is insisted upon even as that difference remains mysterious and nearly inarticulable. The clones in David Mitchell's *Cloud Atlas* (2004) and Kazuo Ishiguro's *Never Let Me Go* (2005) offer discursive formulas for interrogating contemporary flexible formulations of citizenship and for reconsidering the ways in which any given subject is regarded as part of or in exile from the national body.

Aihwa Ong notes that "in the era of globalization, individuals as well as governments develop a flexible notion of citizenship and sovereignty as strategies to accumulate capital and power."[11] She goes on to suggest that "'Flexible citizenship' refers to the cultural logics of capitalist accumulation, travel, and displacement that induce subjects to respond fluidly and opportunistically to changing political-economic conditions. In their quest to accumulate capital and social prestige in the global arena, subjects emphasize, and are regulated by, practices favoring flexibility, mobility, and repositioning in relation to markets, governments, and cultural regimes."[12] However, where Ong's argument ultimately articulates cultural and economic logics that animate a specific kind of transnationality, one that is particularly available to citizens of industrialized countries, I would like to extend the idea of flexible citizenship to subjects whose citizenship and forms of affiliation to dominant social and national groupings are less legible, less determined, and less inscribed in the juridical and cultural discourses.

Utopian formulations of cosmopolitanism, with its connotations of transgression and transnational identity, can obscure issues of historical materiality in favor of images of an almost poststructural mobility that evacuates subjectivity of its constitutive historicity. Triumphalist formulations of the cosmopolitan such as Pico Iyer's "global soul" imply a cosmopolitan subject who traverses the globe unanchored to the past in any traumatic way. Commenting on this formulation of cosmopolitanism, Gayatri Spivak notes that "when we speak of transnationality ... we think of global hybridity from the point of view of popular public culture, military intervention, and the neo-colonialism of multinationals."[13] Paul Gilroy critiques uncritical constructions of cosmopolitanism that are simply "built upon foundations supplied by enlightenment anthropology ... [He notes that] secreted inside the dazzling rhetoric of universal inclusion ... there is another paradigmatic and hierarchical anthropology that can ... be comfortable ... with the commonsense wisdoms that produce race as a deep fracture in culture, capacity, and experience."[14] Certain transnational subjects, on the other hand, lack the ability to be a cosmopolitan in this sense. As Sheldon Pollock, Homi K. Bhabha, Carol Breckenridge, and Dipesh Chakrabarty note in their introduction to *Cosmopolitanism*, "A cosmopolitanism grounded in the tenebrous moment of transition is distinct from other more triumphalist notions."[15] Critical (and vernacular) formulations of cosmopolitanism, then, articulate the fractures between cultural identity and historical materiality where the past, like all ghosts, exists in the margins.

Using recent invocations of the figure of the specter, I would like to theorize an uncanny mode of citizenship that might help to unpack and articulate a more critical formulation of cosmopolitanism. This uncanny mode of citizenship draws from Freud's essay on the uncanny where he defines the uncanny as "everything ... that ought to have remained hidden and secret, and yet comes to light."[16] In his study of the uncanny, Nicholas Royle remarks that it is something more than just the "particular commingling of the familiar and unfamiliar"[17] that Freud suggests in his 1919 essay, "Das Unheimliche." Freud writes that "the unhomely is that species of the frightening that goes back to what was once well known and had long been familiar [and where] the familiar can become uncanny and frightening."[18] Royle suggests that it "can consist in a sense of homeliness uprooted ..."[19] Royle goes on to describe the uncanny as "the revelation of something unhomely at the heart of hearth and home ... a strangeness of framing and borders, an experience of liminality ... as a foreign body within oneself, even the experience of oneself *as* a foreign body."[20] Situating this concept in a political and historical context, Homi K. Bhabha notes that "the unhomely is a paradigmatic colonial and post-colonial condition." [21] Bhabha goes on to note that, in the condition of postcoloniality, "The recesses of the domestic space become sites for history's most intricate invasions. In that displacement, the borders between home and world become confused; and, uncannily, the private and the public become part of each other, forcing upon us a vision that is as divided as it is disorienting."[22] By parsing the haunted experience of the cosmopolitan with the uncanny, we are able more precisely to articulate the ways in which the past is never quite just prologue, but is always present in its own fraught way for the cosmopolitan subject. The uncanny is a technology which helps to articulate the simultaneous experience of belonging and estrangement that constitutes the lived reality for citizens deemed marginal, liminal, or even illegal; citizens who are at once part of a national body and yet whose difference is arbitrarily formulated and insisted upon. I use the frame of haunting, of the figure of the specter, to further articulate the specific contours of this form of flexible citizenship.

As my citations of Nussbaum and Cohen indicate, monstrosity is frequently configured as an absolute category of otherness, albeit one frequently configured along ideological fault lines, an action which implicitly concedes the arbitrary and contingent formation of the category. However, as Avery Gorden, Pheng Cheah, Hershini Bhana Young, Bianca Del Villano, Bishnupriya Ghosh, and Jacques Derrida have all remarked, the idea of haunting, of the ghostly specter, is one that carries particular utility in this postmodern, postcolonial, transnational age. In 1997 Avery Gorden posited haunting as a way to supplement the available (and failed) critical vocabularies "to communicate the depth, density, and intricacies of the dialectic of subjection and subjectivity ... of domination and freedom, of critique and utopian longing."[23] Indeed, Derrida suggests that haunting and the figure of the specter function ontologically: "It is necessary to introduce haunting into the very construction of a concept. Of every concept, beginning with the concepts of being and time. That is what we would be calling here a hauntology."[24] He goes on to detail the consequences of this innovation: "The spectro-genic process corresponds therefore to a paradoxical incorporation. Once ideas or thoughts ... are detached from their substratum, one engenders some ghost by giving them a body. Not by returning to the living body from which ideas and thoughts have been torn loose, but by incarnating the latter in another artifactual body, a prosthetic body, a ghost of spirit."[25] In many ways this is an elaboration of Derrida's earlier treatments of supplementarity; however, in this case, his focus is on specifically embodied aspects of being. We have, then, the spectral monster, the liminal figure who stands at the divide between human and nonhuman, being and nonbeing, and citizen and alien.

In my focus on the clone characters in Ishiguro's and Mitchell's novels, I want to suggest that the figure of the clone functions in much the same way as the figure of this uncanny specter. In the tradition of early twentieth-century dystopian novels such as *1984* and *Brave New World*, *Never Let Me Go* and *Cloud Atlas* explore the experience of being and belonging in a postmodern and transnational world. Ishiguro's and Mitchell's novels, like thoae of Orwell and Huxley, function as cautionary tales against the promise of unrestrained scientific development and/or economically motivated bioproduction. Simultaneously, they work to articulate and critique the boundaries of belonging and affiliation that go with the simultaneous acts of enfranchisement and disenfranchisement that the clones suffer over the course of the novel's narratives, even as the narrative logic of both novels ultimately suggests the likely failure of such critiques.

In tales of monstrous reanimation such as Mary Shelley's *Frankenstein* (1818) the specific origin of the constituent parts that comprise the reanimated creatures remains unnarrated and obscure. Shelley only notes that Victor Frankenstein cobbled together the body parts for his creature from charnel houses and suggests, in part, that the creature's fatal flaw was always already a fundamental part of its inalterable nature—a nature pre-determined by its debased physical origin. Such suggestions lend credence to readings of the creature as a racialized figure framed within the discourses of colonialism. Noting Shelley's own certain engagement with issues of race and empire, critics such as Allen Lloyd Smith and Gayatri Spivak have advanced arguments suggesting that Frankenstein's creature can also function as a figurative metaphor for the stitched-together body of the British Empire itself. In these readings, even as the Empire is comprised of and maintained by materials (mineral resources and products of cheap labor) imported or smuggled into the metropolitan center of empire, and even as empire itself is a lumbering monstrosity, so too is Frankenstein's creature constituted by body parts that have a debased and uncertain point of origin. However, whereas in Shelley's novel the nature of these body parts obscenely assembled by a madman can be read through such allegorical lenses, in more contemporary narratives the affect of body parts is quite literal; no longer do they stand as metonyms for the exploited resources of colonial landscapes, we now face the atomization of the human alongside the commodification of parts of the human body. This process is, typically, performed along racial, gendered, cultural, and economic fault lines.

In a number of contemporary and popular films (such as Stephen Frears's *Dirty Pretty Things* (2002), Damjan Kozole's *Spare Parts* (2003), and Darren Lynn Bousman's musical, *Repo! The Genetic Opera* (2008)) as well as in the real-world sociological research of Nancy Scheper-Hughes, the various modes of organ trafficking and their connections to the legacies of (post)colonialism and globalization have been explored. As Sheper-Hughes has noted, "[i]n these troubling new contexts the commodified organ becomes an object of desire for one population and a commodity of last resort for 'the other' and socially disadvantaged population."[26] Kazuo Ishiguro's novel, *Never Let Me Go*, under the sign of Shelley's novel, returns the interrogation of the ethics of organ trafficking to the fictional and speculative realm. Ishiguro's novel seemingly evacuates the characters of any concrete historical contexts in favor of ahistorical identities that seem to exist outside of political contexts. Drawing on theories of postcolonialism and critiques of cosmopolitanism, this chapter argues that, like so many of his other characters, these clones in Ishiguro's novel function as ghostly echoes of empire and as metaphors indicating the impossibility of the cosmopolitan, who is unavoidably invested in a traumatic and fraught past, and ultimately is unable to achieve any legible status as a normative subject in the larger, dominant culture.

Like Mary Shelley's *Frankenstein*, *Never Let Me Go* obliquely invokes themes of race and the role that racial Others play in the constitution of the national body. The novel takes the form of a speculative memoir, set in an alternative late twentieth-century world, written in the voice of a clone whose entire life has been over determined by her pre-destined fate to be a source of "extra parts" for the "human" population. Kathy, the narrator of the novel, tells the story of growing up in a community of boarding students at an exclusive school in the English countryside. What initially appears to be a kind

of traditional *bildungsroman*[27] reveals itself to be a piece of macabre speculative fiction that situates the scene of education as a scene of coercion. It is
at their school, Hailsham, that the clones are most fully "educated" into their
destined futures. This is an education that is absolute in its coercive power.

Scenes of education have frequently been scenes of indoctrination and
coercion, as Terry Eagleton notes: "[i]t is within this [educational] apparatus
that the ideological function of literature—its function, that is to say, in reproducing the social relations of the mode of production—is most apparent."[28]
The clones are, even as children, made subtly aware of their destiny and
function within the larger schema of society. But the mode of this education
is insidious. Ishiguro writes: "Tommy thought it possible the guardians had,
throughout all our years at Hailsham, timed very carefully and deliberately
everything they told us, so that we were always just too young to understand
properly the latest piece of information. But of course we'd take it in at some
level, so that before long all this stuff was there in our heads without us
ever having examined it properly."[29] Additionally, what lends these scenes of
education such power is precisely the allegorical mode in which the whole
novel functions. While the clones are inscribed within the narrative logic of
the novel as a different order of being, the narrative itself is actually ambivalent about this fact. They are hybrids who are always almost fully legible
and legal subjects, but who are always consigned to the margins by what is
revealed to be the arbitrary convention of their point of origin. However, unlike
V. S. Naipaul's Ralph Singh, Salman Rushdie's Saladin Chamcha, and Kirin
Desai's Jemubhai Patel, these clones operate under a different sign of race
and difference than postcolonial theory generally allows for.

Like many of his other works, *Never Let Me Go* articulates issues of race,
empire, and culture without necessarily invoking the traditional signifiers
of racial or cultural difference. In an article on *Remains of the Day*, Meera
Tamaya notes that, while "elliptically alluded to, never directly mentioned,
historical events are the powerful absences which shape the characters and
narratives ... of Ishiguro's novels."[30]

Ishiguro's fiction is frequently shaped by many such "powerful absences."
In the case of *Never Let Me Go*, race fills this role. While the clones in the
novel clearly belong to an underclass of society whose larger destiny is
predetermined, they are not marked by any traditional physical signs of racial
or cultural difference. However, they do display some of the internal signifiers
of a group of people who have been subjected to a deliberate and perpetual
process of abjection. Early on in the novel, Kathy notes how the students
were aware of their own abject status of difference. Speaking of the headmis-
tress of the school, Kathy notes: "Madame was afraid of us. But she was
afraid of us in the same way someone might be afraid of spiders. We hadn't

been ready for that. It had never occurred to us to wonder how we would feel, being seen like that, being the spiders ... it's like walking past a mirror you've walked past every day of your life, and suddenly it shows you something else, something troubling and strange."[31] And later, speaking of their "models," the original human beings from whom they were cloned, Ruth declares: "We're modeled from trash. Junkies, prostitutes, winos, tramps ... If you want to look for possibles [the original humans from which the clones were cloned], if you want to do it properly, then you look in the gutter. You look in rubbish bins. Look down the toilet, that's where you'll find where we all came from."[32]

The reaffirmation of the clones as subalterns is especially important, as the notion of the clones as racialized figures might almost disappear under their less traditional signifiers of racial abjection. Additionally, while the clones certainly are subaltern subjects within the logic of the narrative, they are also liminal subjects whose abjection isn't conventionally inscribed upon them. What I mean to propose here is that the clones, in addition to being clearly subaltern subjects, are also inscribed under a spectral sign of the citizen. In this particular case, the denotation of the citizen as a spectral sign allows for a certain application of the term "citizen" without necessarily invoking the proscriptive aspects of that term. The ghost, or the specter, functions as a useful figure for considering how something like historical trauma or enlightenment subjectivity or even citizenship might be dispersed but still possess a kind of presence. Citing Derrida, Bishnupriya Ghosh remarks that "ghosts bear witness to erasures in the 'living present'."[33]

In David Mitchell's *Cloud Atlas*, Somni-451, a fabricant living in a futuristic super-capitalistic Korea, learns to question her status and imagines the possibilities of resistance. In both this and Ishiguro's narrative, however, the status of the clone as an Other, as a monstrous and subordinate figure, is revealed to be arbitrary and subject to a contradictory logic. In the case of Ishiguro's teen clones, their function as organ donors to "real" humans radically undermines the oppositional logic dividing the human from the synthetic. For even as the "real" humans integrate the cloned organs into their own bodies, they immediately and irreparably become figures of otherness themselves, thus undoing the logic of the real vs. the fake. In Mitchell's novel, the biological differences are more extreme, but less central to the logic dividing the real humans from the synthetic ones. Rather, the apparent motivating mechanism of difference is economic, but an economics grounded in biological difference. Here the clones are subordinate subjects not only because they are biologically synthetic but also because they were created to serve the biologically "real." They become subordinate subjects because their biological difference is completely implicated in a capitalist system that requires a biological logic to formulate class. The novel's narrative seems to focus on the possible acts of resistance to such a logic, and foregrounds the arbitrary nature of the initial designation as nonhuman. However, in a cruel twist toward the end of this section, the whole act of resistance is revealed to be a Foucauldian plot that doesn't allow any true resistance, as the whole revolutionary movement is revealed to be part of the larger culture's plan to contain revolutionary elements in the society.

In an early section of the novel, entitled "An Orison of Somni-451," the rebellious clone Yoona-939 asks: "[W]hy were fabricants born into debt but purebloods not?"[34] (This logic undergirds the asymmetrical power relationships—the fabricants are the working class, forever consigned to labor.) Her simple question interrogating the normative order of being in this world is quickly classified as "blasphemous hubris." Like the world of Ishiguro's novel, the clones (fabricants) have been educated into a state of absolute submission by their world: Somni declares that Yoona risks being in violation of Catechism Six and that she would "pray to Papa Song to heal my friend" on her behalf. This indoctrination is framed in language that is simultaneously totalitarian and religious. Even the title of the chapter, "An Orison of Somni-451," indicates that the testimony she gives over the course of the chapters constitutes a kind of prayer. Even as the children at Hailsham are educated into subjection, so too is the entire belief system of Mitchell's fabricants woven into every aspect of their lives, physically and metaphysically.

The conditions of possibility surrounding the imagined resistance of the clones are articulated but mostly likely dismissed in the narrative. While Somni offers cogent critiques of the logic of the corporatized government, her logic seems a slight rebellion in the face of the brutal machinery that converts the bodies of the fabricants into the literal fuel of this empire. Somni argues: "[T]o enslave an individual troubles your consciences ... but to enslave a clone is no more troubling than owning the latest six-wheeler Ford, ethically. Because you cannot discern our differences, you believe we have none. But make no mistake: even same-stem fabricants cultured in the same wombtank are as singular as snow-flakes."[35] Then later, Somni describes the full function of the overdetermined status of her own being as liminal: "Try this for deviancy: fabricants are mirrors held up to purebloods' consciences; what purebloods see reflected there sickens them. So they blame you for holding up the mirror."[36] And later she demands that "the consumer must understand that fabricants are purebloods [too]."[37]

However, this section nears its conclusion with Somni witnessing the brutal slaughter of thousands of fabricants who had been told they were on their way to a Hawaiian retirement. Somni witnesses their bodies literally slaughtered and torn into component parts and then converted into foodstuffs that are consumed by the working fabricants as well as by the citizens. Remarking that "it is a perfect food cycle," Somni reflects on the absolute nature of a system of domination that uses the labor of the fabricants to fuel its economy and then uses the corporeal bodies of those same fabricants to fuel the making of more fabricants and the feeding of the whole society, pureblood and fabricant. And then finally the section concludes with Somni being informed that the entire sequence of events beginning with her initial discovery of class consciousness was engineered by the corporate government in order to draw out any possible rebellious elements in the culture and then contain them.

Like the bio-logic of Ishiguro's clones that emphasizes the arbitrary nature of their designation as marginal subjects, the bio-logic of the corprocratic system of Nea So Copros emphasizes the same ultimate absence of difference. Even as the purebloods of Mitchell's futuristic dystopia consign the fabricants to a life of service and labor, in their frenzy for consumption (a consumption that Mitchell cleverly notes is legally required of pureblood citizens) they consume not only the labor of the fabricants but their very bodies. The purebloods, like the "normal humans" of Ishiguro's world, are ultimately constituted by and biologically the same as the fabricants. The logic of separation is purely contingent, and yet the structure of the society (figured as a pyramid) requires this logic to parse out essential and absolute differences between differing levels of citizenship. Or, as Somni asks, "what if the differences between social strata stem not from genomics or inherent xcellence (sic) or even dollars, but merely differences in knowledge? Would this not mean the whole pyramid is build on shifting sands?"[38]

I would like to close by referring to an incident in Ishiguro's novel that illustrates this ghostly form of citizenship. This incident takes place near the novel's end, well after the children have left Hailsham. At this point in the novel, Ruth and Tommy have grown up and begun their roles as donors, and Kathy has become a carer. When Kathy and Ruth plan a visit to Tommy, the subject of a wrecked fishing boat comes up. The boat becomes an object of obsession for Ruth and eventually the destination of an excursion for the three friends: "It's supposed to be this old fishing boat. With a little cabin for a couple of fishermen to squeeze into when it's stormy."[39] The boat itself acquires an ambivalent symbolic meaning that isn't made explicit in the narrative logic of the novel. Once they get to the boat, "sitting beached in the marshes under the weak sun," Ruth's response is quite ecstatic: "It's really beautiful." Tommy then mysteriously remarks: "maybe this is what Hailsham looks like now."[40]

While at first it is difficult to understand the logic behind Tommy's statement, his observations open the door for an understanding of the vexed relationship the children had to the scene of their education and coercion.

By understanding the wrecked boat as analogous to the desiccated grounds of their former school, the clones map a number of meanings onto their understanding of that school. They see it, in retrospect, as a place of refuge that provided woefully insufficient safety; they also see it as a wreck itself. Additionally, the boat, functioning as a more abstract symbol, expresses a particular understanding they have about their own nature. Even as the boat is a now-useless vessel that once served a viable function, the clones can see themselves in the same way. Even as a sea-going vessel is stranded on dry land and as such its very nature is ambivalent, so too are the clones, very much in human form and yet not allowed to behave as fully human subjects. The boat is a figure of partial being; of a subject unable to fully emerge into its own ontology. Even as the clones might want to be fully human, might want to be normative citizens of the British Commonwealth, they can never be. For all that they share the form of the human and the citizen, they are forced into this category of monstrosity, of being unable to fully be. Similarly, Somni-451 might accurately identify the haphazard and arbitrary logics determining her status as monstrous Other, but she is unable, in the end, to undo their effect. Granted access to only partial and incomplete states of being and citizenship, Somni-451, Kathy, Tommy, and Ruth can only exist in the uncanny space in between states of ontological and juridical being. Unable to become fully enfranchised members of their biological or national families, they remain, in Mary Shelley's words, monstrous progeny.[41]

Notes

1 St. Bartholomew's Fair was one of the city's major fairs sanctioned by Royal Charter. Held in London starting from 1133, it was abolished in 1855. Richard Cavendish notes that, by the early seventeenth century, "the fair had become far more of a carnival than a business function. Puppet-shows, wrestlers, fire-eaters, dwarfs, dancing bears, performing monkeys and caged tigers vied for attention with contortionists and tight-rope walkers. Astrologers cast horoscopes and miraculous medicines were hawked. Proprietors of food and drink, beer and tobacco, bellowed for custom amid a miasma of roast pork." Eventually, the fair attracted too many thieves and muggers, and the city authorities shut it down in 1855. See Richard Cavendish, "London's Last Bartholomew Fair: September 3rd, 1855," *History Today* 55: 52.

2 David Simpson, *Wordsworth, Commodification and Social Concern: The Poetics of Modernity* (London: Cambridge University Press, 2009), 119.

3 William Wordsworth (1770–1850) was a major British poet. Along with Samuel Taylor Coleridge, Wordsworth wrote *Lyrical Ballads*, frequently seen

as the foundational collection of Romantic Poetry. Wordsworth also wrote *The Prelude*, an autobiographical poem that linked together the tradition of the epic with intimate personal narrative and explored the growth of the mind of the poet from an early age.

4 Simpson, *Wordsworth*, 120.

5 William Wordsworth, *The Prelude: A Norton Critical Edition*, (eds) M. H. Abrams, Stephen Gill, and Jonathan Wordsworth (New York: W. W. Norton and Company, 1979), Book VII: 659–92.

6 Wordsworth, building on the aesthetic tradition of the sublime (see Longinus, Edmund Burke, etc.), imagined an aesthetic category (the sublime) that offered more than sensual delight; along with others (Immanuel Kant, for one), he suggested that the sublime was a particularly powerful aesthetic category capable of inducing moral as well as sensual revelations.

7 Wordsworth, *Prelude*, Book VII: 700–4.

8 Martha Nussbaum, *Hiding from Humanity: Disgust, Shame, and the Law* (Princeton: Princeton University Press, 2004), 107.

9 Jeffery Cohen, "Preface: In a Time of Monsters," in *Monster Theory*, (ed.) Jeffery Cohen (Minneapolis: University of Minnesota Press, 1996), ix.

10 Ibid., x.

11 Aiwa Ong, *Flexible Citizenship: The Cultural Logics of Transnationality* (Durham, NC: Duke University Press, 1999), 6.

12 Ibid.

13 Gayatri Spivak, "Diasporas Old and New: Women in the Transnational World," in *Class Issues: Pedagogy, Cultural Studies, and the Public Sphere*, (ed.) Amitava Kumar (New York: New York University Press, 1997), 89.

14 Paul Gilroy, *Postcolonial Melancholia* (New York: Columbia University Press, 2005), 63. This is not to say that there are not critical formulations of the cosmopolitan. In *When Borne Across* (New Brunswick: Rutgers University Press, 2004), Bishnupriya Ghosh discusses "cosmopolitical" writers who challenge "both the forms of nationalism reinforced by global flows and the pernicious globalism surfacing in dispersed local contexts" (5)

15 Carol Breckenridge, Sheldon Pollock, Homi K. Bhabha, and Dipesh Chakrabarty (eds), *Cosmopolitanism* (Durham, NC: Duke University Press, 2002), 5.

16 Sigmund Freud, *The Uncanny*, trans. David Mclintock (New York: Penguin Books, 2003), 376.

17 Nicholas Royle, *The Uncanny* (New York: Manchester University Press, 2003), 1.

18 Freud, *The Uncanny*, 124.

19 Royle, *The Uncanny*, 1.

20 Ibid., 1–2.

21 Homi K. Bhabha, *The Location of Culture* (London: Routledge, 1994), 13.

22 Ibid.

23 Avery Gordon, *Ghostly Matters: Haunting and the Sociological Imagination* (Minneapolis: University of Minnesota Press, 1997), 8.

24 Jacques Derrida, *Specters of Marx: The State of the Debt, the Work of Mourning, and the New International* (New York: Routledge, 1994), 161.

25 Ibid., 125–6.

26 Nancy Scheper-Hughes and Loïc J. D. Wacquant, *Commodifying Bodies* (London: Sage Publications, 2002), 2

27 *Bildungsroman* (literally, "formation novel") is the term for coming-of-age novels or narratives depicting the upbringing and growth of a young person. Wordsworth's *Prelude*, Charlotte Bronte's *Jane Eyre*, as well as J. D. Salinger's *Catcher in the Rye* are some well-known examples of the *bildungsroman*.

28 Terry Eagleton, *Marxism and Literary Criticism* (Berkeley: University of California Press, 1976), 56.

29 Kazuo Ishiguro, *Never Let Me Go* (New York: Alfred A. Knopf, 2005), 82.

30 Meera Tamaya, "Ishiguro's *Remains of the Day:* The Empire Strikes Back," *Modern Language Studies* 22, no. 2 (1992): 45.

31 Ishiguro, *Never Let Me Go*, 35–6.

32 Ibid., 166.

33 Ghosh, *When Borne Across*, 207.

34 David Mitchell, *Cloud Atlas: A Novel* (New York: Random House, 2004), 192.

35 Ibid., 187.

36 Ibid., 222.

37 Ibid., 346.

38 Ibid., 222.

39 Ishiguro, *Never Let Me Go*, 216.

40 Ibid., 224.

41 In her introduction to the 1831 revised edition of *Frankenstein*, Mary Shelley referred to the original edition of the novel as her "monstrous progeny."

11

On the frontlines of the zombie war in the Congo:

Digital technology, the trade in conflict minerals, and zombification

Jeffrey W. Mantz

Perhaps no other genre has proven as imaginative or exhaustive in speculating end times scenarios as zombie literature and film. Depending on what social anxiety may preoccupy a captive audience at a particular moment, zombies have been reanimated by space debris, radiological and bacteriological agents, viral outbreaks, neurotoxins, and sorcery. And the explosion in gaming technology and zombie film has offered a space within which these possibilities can be explored further, having the odd effect of making those who spend countless hours in these virtual worlds both better equipped to deal with a hypothetical zombie horde and at the same time more reclusive and withdrawn (strangely, in fact, like zombies) from a material reality that continues to fester persistently about us. Yet none of this would have been possible had it not been for a real zombie apocalypse that has already been unfolding for more than a decade and that has gone largely unnoticed. Ground Zero for this conflict has been the remote eastern region of the Democratic Republic of the Congo. Minerals abundant in the eastern Congo have been essential to the revolution in digital technology. Perhaps two-thirds of the world's supply of coltan, for example, can be found there. Coltan, short for columbite-tantalite, a compound from which one can refine tantalum, is an amazingly efficient conductor ideal for digital devices such as mobile phones and gaming consoles; it has been referred to as the "holy grail" of the digital age. Unfettered global demand for these minerals has helped finance a war that, with at least 5–6 million dead, is the deadliest since World War II, and is plagued by some of the most harrowing atrocities (epidemic gang rape, mutilations, incidents of cannibalism) in recent human memory.

The persistence of this war continues to be haunted by a cruel calculus: the more rapacious and expansive the global demand for digital products has become, the worse the fight has become for the Congolese, culminating finally in the fact that the availability of mobile phones in the Congo has been what has allowed militias to coordinate effective attacks on mining villages. The zombie apocalypse, as it has manifested in the eastern Congo, thus has a dual meaning: first in the sense that our digital technology revolution has created the conditions of possibility for real human terror, and second in the sense that use of these technologies has subjected its users to forms of social disengagement and disembodiment so advanced that they are most aptly termed zombification. The zombie metaphor is prescient, especially as the unfolding global drama surrounding this commodity chain mirrors that commonly found in zombie apocalyptic narratives, where a small group of survivors struggles against an ever-expanding horde. Here, our Congolese heroes, a group largely composed of small-scale artisans who manage to persevere outside the purview of militias, as well as those trying simply just to eke out a living and survive in the context of a devastating war, are pitted against a much larger, and exponentially expanding, faceless multitude of digital technology consumers, facilitators, and racketeers. What we regard as extraordinary and "post-apocalyptic" in contemporary film and literature—the improvisation of ordinary means of subsistence in the absence of any kind of infrastructure, the forging of networks and informal methods of exchange with other survivors, the confronting of moral questions about the value of life and its protection and the duties owed to others—is simply ordinary in the case of the eastern Congo. The zombie war can thus, I contend, be understood as a powerful device for explaining both the spacious divide that has tended to separate Congolese producers and consumers of digital technologies, and the necropolitics that have come to dominate their relations.

This chapter begins with an account of the origins of the conflict in the Congo, with an aim toward explaining how the extraction and circulation of blood minerals essential to the digital technology explosion have contributed to *zombification*. They have done this in two ways: first, on the ground in the Congo, through regimes of production and circulation that have tended to radically impact the corporeal and philosophical experience of eastern

Congolese struggling within them; and second, through the proliferation of products developed from these minerals that have increasingly fostered modalities of detachment among consumers in the most industrialized and economically developed nations of the world. Next, this chapter considers the different ways in which zombies have manifested throughout various cultural and folkloric traditions, with the aim of locating the conflict mineral trade within the larger frame of anxieties and social tensions that tend to give new life to the undead. The chapter then considers how the kind of zombies that have emerged within the twenty-first century, at the time that the Congo has been harvested for its technology minerals, have created a digital divide, in which survivors in the Congo (as elsewhere in the least affluent areas of the world) attempt to negotiate the rapidly expanding horde of zombified consumers, who are still mostly located in the industrialized, most economically advanced areas of the world. The methods of creativity, improvisation, and innovation deployed by Congolese responding to the philosophical challenges they must engage with everyday mirror the social dramas and moral lessons one finds in the best of post-apocalyptic narratives. I contend that we should best look to these experiences to gain a sense of the most effective strategies for winning any zombie war.

Congo and the origins of zombification

Since the mid-1990s, the eastern provinces of the Democratic Republic of the Congo have been the site of one the world's most protracted and violent conflicts. Officially, there have been two military exchanges—the First Congolese War (1996–7), which significantly involved the overthrow of the dictator Mobuto Sese Seko; and the Second Congolese War (1998–2003), which involved a much more complicated conflict between the Congo and a number of other African interests in the region. The origins and persistence of conflict in the eastern Congo are in fact much more complicated.[1] To fully grasp the context of these myriad conflicts, it is necessary to discuss two variables: the various personnel deployed militarily (both within the Congolese and neighborhood nation armies, and through non-state militias) through the region, and the degree to which the international community has met this region of Africa with a high level of ambivalence.

Tensions between various groups in the eastern Congo owe many of their origins to land and resource scarcities that emerged as a product of Mobuto Sese Seko's brutal dictatorship (1965–97) over the nation. The U.S. bolstered Mobuto with billions of dollars in aid, with which he mostly absconded. His kleptocracy was tolerated so long as he proved to be a major African ally against the Soviet Union. When the Cold War ended and American aid dried up, Mobutu's influenced waned. The decline of Mobuto's internal and regional influence coincided with a massive influx of refugees from neighboring Rwanda between June and August of 1994. These refugees were composed mostly of ethnic Hutus who feared reprisals from the Rwandan Patriotic Front, a Tutsi-led liberation army that had wrested control of the country from Hutu militants (the *interahamwe*). The *interahamwe* had for the previous three months engaged in wholesale genocide of most of the nation's Tutsi minority, and a sizeable number of Hutu moderates who had resisted: in total, somewhere between a half a million and over a million deaths.[2]

News footage showing the *interahamwe* systematically hacking unarmed civilians to death with machetes was broadcast widely to North American and European households. That something terrible had been happening was widely acknowledged, yet the international community stood idly by and allowed the massacres to envelop that entire nation until as much as 20 percent of its population had been eradicated. That there was an inexcusable wave of diplomatic and military paralysis as the genocide occurred has been admitted by just about everyone who had some role in monitoring it. President Clinton acknowledged his failure to intervene as one of the great regrets of his presidency. General Roméo Dallaire, who commanded a small U.N. peacekeeping group in Rwanda with almost no support, some of whom were also massacred, suffered from such depression in the aftermath that he attempted suicide.

A parallel set of circumstances would emerge in the eastern Congo in the years to follow, beginning late in 1994 as refugees from Rwanda flooded in, but with tensions reaching critical levels through the two wars, and continuing up to the present day. Mobutu had let in hundreds of thousands of *interahamwe* with the Hutu refugees, who subsequently assumed leadership roles in the refugee camps. After he was deposed in the First Congolese War, forces loyal to the new Rwandan government broke up the refugee camps, sending those Hutu militants into the forests. The next several years were characterized by the emergence of a litany of competing militias: a Rwandan-backed occupation force that would terrorize supposed eastern Congolese sympathizers; equally horrific Hutu militants (now organized into a group called the FDLR) who would brutalize Congolese ethnic Tutsi among others; various Congolese nationalists who saw themselves as resisting Rwandan occupation; and so on. Various neighboring nations would back the Congolese government, or one or another militia, until enough of the continent was involved to characterize it as Africa's World War. The Congo's rich supply of resources—gold, diamonds, copper, cobalt, uranium, and timber—financed much of that military activity, and certainly drove regional interests in controlling the eastern provinces of the DRC.

Soon it was discovered that the Congo also held sizable reserves of minerals (columbite-tantalite, or coltan, was among the most important; tin and tungsten would also become significant) necessary for the production of electronic goods in the rapidly expanding global market for digital commodities. Various militias would fight for control of these mines, and force rural Congolese to work as miners or porters. With the proceeds, they would purchase arms to continue their campaigns of violence and terror, dispossessing people of their agricultural produce, raiding their cattle (which are significant in this part of Africa for marriage and other socially significant transactions), gang raping women so as to render them unmarriageable (and thus, to borrow Orlando Patterson's[3] phrasing, socially dead), conscripting children into armies as soldiers and sex slaves, and otherwise forcing surviving Congolese into servitude for their causes. By 2001, some observers were noting that there was a direct connection between the expansion of markets in mobile phones and other digital technologies and the spread of conflict in the eastern Congo. A large international peacekeeping force (now numbering about 20,000) was deployed in the Congo beginning in 2000, but most of the international community was completely unaware of the conflict until a series of international organizations began to cluster their campaigns around building awareness of the epidemic of gang rape in the region.

This history has manifested what I regard to be a "zombie apocalypse" in two ways. First, the trade in conflict minerals has forced the encounter between a group of rural Congolese struggling to survive in a difficult terrain, and a much larger, expanding horde of global consumers, and their unabating demand for commodities produced through mining. Second, those global consumers continue to be increasingly disengaged from the perils faced by rural Congolese. This *zombification* of the consumer through the rapacious use of digital technology goes beyond mere estrangement or alienation of the consumers from the vagaries of the production process; it also includes the processes through which such commodity flows tend to bifurcate experiences in such a way that makes mutual empathy quite difficult. So while the mobile phone summons sentiments about the freedom of movement and the openness of information to those living in more affluent societies, it might be quite hard for a Congolese miner living in a village occupied by a militia, being forced into slave labor, and having had his own methods of communication curtailed by the militia, to conceive of the mobile phone as much more than an inconvenient technology that enables their persecution. That is particularly acute when the miner is aware that the efficacy of militia control is contingent upon the monopolization of mobile technology and its use in the occupied area, and also that the very product he is mining makes it possible to fabricate such technology.

Zombification here goes beyond being merely a useful metaphor for the personal detachments that have tended to accompany the purported hyperconnectivity-associated globalization in the digital age. I contend that the zombie is an ideal figure for discussing the politics of production and consumption of digital-age technologies for two reasons. First, so much analysis and literary representation of the Congo has traditionally centered on the semiotics and politics of death. The Congo's historic association with cannibalism, for example, barely needs mention. It was most significantly popularized in Joseph Conrad's famous *Heart of Darkness* (1902),[4] but is exigent in much of the historic literature about the Congo. Reports of cannibalism (as a tactic of intimidation and terror) committed by militias such as the Lord's Resistance Army and the Mai Mai are often depicted as continuous with these believed historical practices (in both cases, it is more rumor than reality that gave these accounts their power). In the case of Haiti, well into the twentieth century, it was widely reported to American audiences that "voodoo" (the Americanization of the Haitian religion Vodou) engaged extensively in cannibalism and sacrifice.[5] There is a long historical legacy of treating the Caribbean as a source of cannibalism; even the name Caribbean derives from a term the Taino (the original inhabitants of Haiti) used to refer to outsiders from the east (Caribs, which in Taino cosmology were thought to be cannibals). So Columbus and his Spanish financiers comfortably propagated a myth that to this day is still accepted as conventional wisdom, despite the fact, as the historian William Keegan has noted, that under this same cosmology, Columbus and in fact all Europeans were by definition "cannibals."[6] Turning the tables to situate the zombie problem as a creation of the North Atlantic (here I am referring to those nations in Western Europe and North America that have been responsible for fostering economic inequalities between nations for the last several centuries) would thus seem to be only fair, especially in light of my second main reason for relying on this zombie metaphor. The digital age has been built on a set of tragedies that mirror common tropes found in narratives of zombie apocalypse. Most accounts of zombie apocalypse depict a scenario where some manmade catalyst—a bacteriological agent, a viral outbreak, a military weapon gone awry—aggressively attacks human hosts at an exponential rate, attenuating humanity physically and spiritually, as we observe our demoralized survivors succumb to their repressed carnal instincts, sense of ethical purpose, and finally corporeally to the zombie horde itself. Along the radical digital divide that simultaneously connects and separates the Congo from the affluent global north, Congolese miners extract minerals under physically perilous conditions to fuel a technological revolution that permits its consumers to experience accelerating senses of physical disconnection from both themselves aand others. This "zombification" of consumers living in disproportionately affluent areas of the world feeds on the labor and lives of Congolese, who, because of the carnal desires that feed the expanding zombie horde, must constantly face the kinds of physical dangers, moral and ethical quandaries that one might expect a group of apocalyptic survivors to encounter.

Zombie typologies: Toward a taxonomy of the undead

Despite all of the emphasis on authenticity in their appropriation of the name "zombies," the characterizations upon which the contemporary (post-1968, with the release of Romero's modern classic *Night of the Living Dead*) cinematic and literary traditions depend are decisively distinct from the figures associated with Haitian and West African folklore from which the term derives.[7] In the case of the latter, those figures are not necessarily undead at all (in the sense of representing revenant corpses). In the case of Haiti, these *zombi*[8] more broadly characterize a range of categories pertaining to individuals whose soul (or more accurately, "souls"—in Haitian folklore there is a dual conception of the soul, and in fact two types of "zombies": the bodiless soul and the soulless body) has been appropriated by *bokor* (a special category of priest in Haitian Vodou) and subjected to his control.

In any case, the contemporary cinematic and literary zombie has either abdicated (or never appropriated to begin with) the central importance of servitude found in the *zombi* of Caribbean and African folklore, in favor of a zombie that is undirected, predatory, cannibalistic, and whose true terror is realized by its presence within a larger horde of collaborative undead[9]. This is not a zombie that can be understood in terms of the political relations of control between two categories of individuals (e.g. master and slave), but rather is better understood in terms of a hydraulic relationship between humanity and something else that feeds on it. Our decomposition (both physically, and in terms of our effectiveness in social relations; that is, our ability to cooperate with one another to ward off throngs of undead) is what composes the zombie horde. In cases where human beings are able to remain composed, the zombie horde ubiquitously decomposes, albeit at radically variant rates.

In their contemporary meaning, it is not unusual to see such a range of zombies used to underwrite explanations for the socioeconomic relations between the rich and poor, colonial and colonized, or the global north and south. Jean and John Comaroff have described "occult economies",[10] where reports of organ thefts, Satanic practices, and other species of nocturnal creep are deployed to make sense of political economic and ecological change, disruptions to the family and kinship, immigration through narratives that "[express] discontent with modernity and dealing with its deformities."[11] This draws upon a critical analysis of capitalism's influence in social and moral transformation that emerged most seminally in the late nineteenth century with the publication of Karl Marx's *Capital*. Marx describes relations of production as vampire-like, since capital (and its "dead labor") survives by preying on the labor of the living.[12] In his well-known discussion of use and exchange values, he describes the "mystical" nature of the commodity as one "abounding in metaphysical subtleties and theological niceties."[13] Some literary analysts have even suggested that *Capital* could be read as a gothic novel,[14] in the tradition of Mary Shelley who, in creating *Frankenstein*, gave us a modernist version of a zombie of "artificial" origin.[15] Harman has suggested that the lessons of late capitalism teach us that "capitalism as a whole is a zombie system, seemingly dead when it comes to achieving human goals and responding to human feelings, but capable of sudden spurts of activity that cause chaos all around."[16]

Within the field of anthropology, there are numerous accounts identifying the significant role played by the undead in various autochthonous rationalizations of social and economic change. Luise White has discussed how the invocation of the undead has been essential to the memory of colonialism in East and Central Africa.[17] Haitian *zombis* are often presented as having explanatory power for the narratives of enslavement and the loss of will that they embed. Isak Niehaus[18] discusses zombies and zombie-keepers in the context of South African witches and witchcraft, a case that he similarly suggests involves "the loss of individual freedom implied by enslavement, and 'expedition of the dead'."[19] Metaphors for social struggle, particularly against major socioeconomic changes, are well represented elsewhere in South African understandings of immigration,[20] as well as within the folkloric traditions of the eastern Caribbean[21] and Surinamese maroon society.[22]

Zombies in the digital age: Necropolitics and post-apocalyptic struggle

Zombies have experienced something of a popular culture explosion in the first decade of the twenty-first century. There is substantial speculation about what factors might be contributing to their current infamy, which for the sake of space I will not address here except to note that this has coincided with the massive expansion of digital technology into all aspects of business and leisure in the more affluent, economically developed nations of the world. The zombies in film, literature, and videogames that have been afforded new terrains within which to gormandize, none the less share many of the common characteristics seen across different cultural and folkloric traditions. Here, I want to take up the question of where to fit the digital-age zombie within the field of undead taxonomy.

Lauro and Embry, in their seminal "Zombie Manifesto" (2008)[23] have also developed a tripartite categorization of the undead, composed of the zombi, zombie, and zombii. The zombi draws upon the classic figure in Haitian cosmology, a "body raised from the dead to labor in the fields"[24]; one could conceivably broaden this category to include other types of folkloric zombi that emerge through some sort of mystical confluence of this-worldly and otherworldly powers. The zombie, by contrast, is more that figure found in the contemporary film and video game genres of the industrialized world (e.g. North America, Western Europe, more affluent parts of Asia and Western Pacific), a "nonconscious, consuming machine"[25] that typically emerges from some kind of non-supernatural agent. A fictional scientist in *Night of the Living Dead*, for example, speculated the reanimation of the dead was the result of radioactive contamination from an exploded space probe. In the first film of the *Resident Evil* series, we are informed that an infective agent is the source of the zombie outbreak; a widely influential but sinister pharmaceutical company called the Umbrella Corporation, which also apparently invests heavily in a covert genetic engineering division, developed this T-virus in one of its many underground labs.

For Lauro and Embry, zombies are a "monstrous figure of global capitalism [that] fed on the labors of the impoverished 'third world' labor force. The zombie has thus transitioned from a representation of the laboring, enslaved colonial body, to a dual image of capitalist enslavement: the zombie now represents the new slave, the capitalist worker, but also the consumer, trapped within the ideological construct that assures the survival of the system. *This ravenous somnambulist, blindly stumbling toward its next meal, is a machine that performs but two functions: it consumes, and it makes more consumers.*"[26] What they are describing then is the emergence of a kind of synergistic relationship between humans and zombies, in which the decomposition of humans (in both a corporeal sense, and a psycho-social sense) contributes to the composition of an ever-expanding zombie horde.

Zombii represent a future in which this horde expands to constitute a totality, "a truly consciousless posthuman."[27] As an alternative to the cyborg developed by Donna Haraway,[28] Lauro and Embry urge us to consider the zombie as a better-suited model for posthumanity, "because of its indebtedness to narratives of historical power and oppression ... [plus the fact that it destroys borders and categories of opposition, such as] ... living and dead, subject and object, slave and slave rebellion."[29] They continue: "[T]he zombie presents a posthuman specter informed by the (negative) dialect of power relations rather than gender."[30] If the cyborg is a hybrid of the divide between subject and object, the zombie basically disrupts this distinction in its entirety by simultaneously rejecting both subject and object. Zombii thus represents the ultimate expression of human fears about our own decay and the accompanying decay of our own consciousness.

As we know, the expansion of this horde has been aided in no small way by the relationships that have unfolded for the last decade and a half in the Congo. Minerals such as tantalum, tin, and tungsten, all in abundance in the eastern Congo, have provided the raw materials that have enabled the digital industry to expand so dramatically in the twenty-first century.[31] Coltan (columbite-tantalite, the ore from which tantalum is produced) has been heralded by some in the scientific community as the "holy grail" of the digital age. There is no question that Congolese minerals have been essential to digital products ranging from mobile phones to gaming consoles to improved processors that edge us closer to a technological singularity, the consumption of which has created the condition of possibility for the emergence of the posthuman zombii. Moreover, the modes of disengagement endemic to zombii have been cultivated in roughly direct proportion to the technological advances propelled by conflict minerals.

Interestingly, the vernacular used by many outsiders to describe the Congo's exploitation evokes a supernatural rather than an artificial register.[32] It is now common to characterize Congo's abundance of minerals, their subsequent pilfering, and the subjugation and exploitation of its subjects as a "resource curse."[33] It is not clear which sorcerers inflicted this curse, but it is certainly the case that the Congo has been delegated to the shady side of a global digital divide. Thus, whereas the cyborg argument had focused on North Atlantic experiences and anxieties about (or more precisely, the anxious complacency with which one engages) the relinquishing of corporeal autonomy with advances in technology, we should turn more to the ways in which the digital age has disparately affected those outside of this consumptive space, to the broader political economic circumstances that have permitted such "troubling" consumption even to take place.

Based on what we have observed above, we could say that Congolese struggles with the indulgences of a surfeit global north provide ample evidence for the kind of ravenous somnambulists that Lauro and Embry describe. But I want to emphasize that the struggle is as much one about the meanings of humanity—about what a loss of consciousness or the capacity for engagement really means—as it is about some abstracted ideas about exploitation or appropriation. Achille Mbembe[34] defined much of this type of relationship as one characterized by necropolitics, a set of practices marked by "contemporary forms of subjugating of life to the power of death."[35] Congolese persist much like the survivors in *The Walking Dead*, the graphic novel and television series in which the zombies are set more or less as a backdrop of despair against the human struggle for some sense of hope in a post-apocalyptic environment. The characters are constantly challenged about what kind of person they have become in the face of such adversity. What sort of things must one do in order to survive? What sort of moral challenges does one find presented in an increasingly ordinary and quotidian manner? "Survival" connotes something quite different when its provoca-teurs meander somewhat reluctantly through the embers of a hell on earth. We see in this struggle a gradual human decomposition, in both a mental and a corporeal sense. It is a representation that strays radically from that seen in the spate of video games and films (many of which are based on these video games) that have come to dominate the iconography of the zombie in Western popular culture in the twenty-first century. Common to these adrenaline-infused, virtualized excursions is a tendency for the characters to be mentally and emotionally flat, and for physical decomposition to be externalized along a very unambiguous us/them divide. Something like the *Resident Evil* franchise simply leaves no space to develop the kind of tempo intrinsic to the dirge of the post-apocalyptic human drama. I would submit that the true appeal of the original Romero films is in their capacity to embrace the human–zombie relationship as refractive, rather than antagonistic. The narrative power of *Night of the Living Dead*, to take a genre-defining example, exists not in the aesthetic of the slow zombie per se, but rather in its focus on the human struggle between the main characters, who unnecessarily bicker and fail to effectively collaborate in the face of common threat looming at every angle around them. The decomposition of human social relations, and eventually of those humans themselves, is complemented by the aura of decay all around them.

On the other side of the digital divide, Congolese face daily challenges to their corporeal and mental experiences of humanity. And most of this struggle has taken place around the ways each Congolese person has had to struggle with their corporeality. Will I have food today? Will I get any kind of protein this week? If I run away from this militia into the forest, will I succumb to malaria before I can find any treatment? If I stay here, will I die of cholera? How likely is this militia to rape or murder, compared to the militia that they are fighting?

How much longer can my body continue to take this abuse from mining? Will it be long enough for me to make some money to get to a city?

Ordinary Congolese have proven incredible innovators in these very physically and mentally challenging contexts. In addition to being a site of exploitation, mines and the trade in minerals have also been one of the only sources of income for an economically thrashed region. The artisanal mines that employ hundreds of thousands of rural Congolese are marked by astonishing creativity in their design and execution; I have referred elsewhere to these innovations as "improvisational economies."[36] Congolese have been able to develop systems for trafficking minerals over vast distances, across unfriendly terrain, without roads. New economies, political and social relationships, and methods of communication have emerged throughout the region, without the benefit of anything vaguely resembling venture capital. Thus, while the gradual sink into zombii may plague the global north, the Congo stands out for its consciousness of the political, economic, and social relationships underlying the digital age, and for its capacity for creativity on a playing field that is far from level.

Epilogue: Winning the zombie war

What becomes the successful survival strategy in this world increasingly organized around the politics of death? If Congolese are indeed afflicted by a kind of resource curse, how might they prevail through developing systems of countersorcery that enable them to combat the curse and make mineral trades profitable for themselves? Congolese survivors find themselves at something of a crossroads. International concerns about whether one's iPad or mobile phone was causing violence in the Congo have resulted in one major legislative change. In 2010, the United States passed the Wall Street Financial Reform Act (known popularly as the Dodd-Frank Act), which included a section that would require American corporations to demonstrate that they were not obtaining minerals from morally questionable sources. Though at the time of this writing the act (known as "Obama's Law" to Congolese) was still not being enforced by the SEC, it would seem that this change would provide some much needed relief to struggling rural Congolese. I am not so sure. It is true that Congolese need systems for monitoring mineral traffic, perhaps through the use of technologies such as RFID tagging, which would track the GPS signal of minerals. Unfortunately, none of the pilot reforms being pursued in the Congo appear to involve Congolese stakeholders in the monitoring of the mineral trade. Often, in fact, they have such a poor understanding of how the overwhelming majority of minerals are illegally trafficked that they develop regulatory and policing systems that are harassing, inefficient, and serve only to bolster more troublesome routes of exchange. The illicit trade, largely unaccounted for in these models, has sophisticated systems for mineral laundering, such as illegally transporting minerals to Rwanda and retagging them as originating from there, that have actually benefited from greater regulation of the Congo.[37] The trouble with Dodd-Frank enforcement has been that it has transformed the concern about conflict minerals into a debacle about how best to the police the "natural," violent inclinations of the Congolese, who are believed by international intermediaries to be engaged in age-old ethnic hatreds that the mineral trade has only enabled.

If the political and economic transformations taking place in the economically developed areas of the world are stripping us of our capacity for creativity, consciousness, and corporeality, perhaps we should start paying some attention to the actual innovators. In the Congo, for example, relying on Congolese stakeholders in the mineral trade to document the trade—perhaps through forums patterned on traditional methods of African civic engagement, or through the use of social media[38]—offers far more promise than turning to the zombies to solve the problems of the apocalypse.

Notes

1 John Frank Clark (ed.), *The African Stakes of the Congo War* (New York: Palgrave Macmillan, 2002); Stephen Jackson, "Making a Killing: Criminality & Coping in the Kivu War Economy," *Review of African Political Economy* 93/94 (2002): 517–36; Jeffrey W. Mantz, "Improvisational Economies: Coltan Production in the Eastern Congo," *Social Anthropology* 16, no. 2 (2008): 34–50; Jeffrey W. Mantz, "Blood Diamonds of the Digital Age: Coltan and the Eastern Congo," *Global Studies Review* 4, no. 3 (2008): 12–14; Celine Moyroud and John Katunga, "Coltan Exploitation in the Eastern Democratic Republic of the Congo," in *Scarcity and Surfeit: The Ecology of Africa's Conflicts,* (ed.) Jeremy Kind and Kathryn Sturman (Pretoria: Institute for Security Studies, 2002); Georges Nzongola-Ntalanja, *The Congo: From Leopold to Kabila, A People's History* (New York: Zed Books, 2002); William Reno, *Warlord Politics and African States,* (Boulder, CO: Lynne Reiner, 1999); James H. Smith, "Tantalus in the Digital Age: Coltan ore, temporal dispossession, and 'movement' in the Eastern Democratic Republic of the Congo," *American Ethnologist* 38, no. 1 (2011): 17–35; James H. Smith and Jeffrey W. Mantz, "Do Cellular Phones Dream of Civil War?: The Mystification of Production and the Consequences of Technology Fetishism in the Eastern Congo," in *Inclusion and Exclusion in the Global Arena,* (ed.) Max Kirsch and

June Nash (New York: Routledge, 2007); Thomas Turner, *The Congo Wars: Conflict, Myth, and Reality* (New York: Zed Books, 2007).

2 Philip Gourevitch, *We Wish To Inform You That Tomorrow We Will Be Killed With Our Families: Stories From Rwanda* (New York: Farrar, Straus and Giroux, 1998); *Mahmood Mamdami, When Victims Become Killers: Colonialism, Nativism and Genocide in Rwanda* (Princeton, NJ: Princeton University Press, 2002).

3 Orlando Patterson, *Slavery and Social Death: A Comparative Study* (Cambridge, MA: Harvard University Press, 1985).

4 Joseph Conrad, *Heart of Darkness* (Edinburgh and London: W. Blackwood and Sons, 1902).

5 See, for example, Spenser St. John, *Hayti or the Black Republic* (Edinburgh/ London: Smith, Elder and Co., 1884), 182–228 (this covers Chapter 5, "Vaudoux Worship and Cannibalism"). For an excellent critique of St. John, see Leslie G. Desmangles, *The Face of the Gods: Vodou and Roman Catholicism in Haiti* (Chapel Hill, NC: University of North Carolina Press, 1992).

6 William F. Keegan, "Columbus was a Cannibal: Myth and the First Encounters," in *The Lesser Antilles in the Age of European Expansion*, ed. Robert L. Paquette (Gainesville, FL: University Press of Florida, 1996): 17–32.

7 For further discussion of the origins of the term, see Hans-W. Ackermann and Jeannine Gauthier, "The Ways and Nature of the Zombi," *The Journal of American Folklore* 104, no. 414 (1991): 466–94. The term *zumbi* (translated from Kikongo as "fetish"; on a related note, contemporary Congolese use the French word *fétiche* to describe many forms of sorcery) is one suggested origin, as is the Kikongo *nzambi* (or Kimbundu *nzúmbe*, meaning variously spirit of a dead person, or almighty). These explanations would make sense as a large proportion of the slaves brought to Saint Domingue/ Haiti in the late eighteenth century (just prior to the 1791–1804 revolution) were taken from the Congo. Others have suggested that the origins might be from the French *les ombres* (meaning "shadows"), or even from the Taino word *zemi*.

8 I use the truncated term *zombi* here to denote the figure associated with folklore; and distinguish it from the zombie popularized in American cinema. The section that follows provides a more nuanced discussion of the rationality behind this dichotomy.

9 Max Brooks, *A Zombie Survival Guide: Complete Protection from the Living Dead* (New York: Three Rivers Press and Random House, 2003) provides an interesting rationalization of the difference between the Haitian zombies and viral zombies, acknowledging that both exist, but the true threat to humanity is from the viral zombie, which cannot be controlled (and in Brooks's universe, attempts to do so have been tragic).

10 Jean Comaroff and John L. Comaroff, "Occult Economies and the Violence of Abstraction: Notes from the South African Postcolony," *American Ethnologist* 26, no. 2 (1999): 279–303.

11 Ibid., 284.

12 Karl Marx, *Capital: a critique of political economy, Volume I*, trans. B. Fowkes (New York: Penguin Books, 1976 [1867]): 342; see also Mark Neocleous, "The Political Economy of the Dead: Marx's Vampires," *History of Political Thought* 24, no. 4 (2003): 668–84.

13 Marx, *Capital*, 161.

14 Ann Cvetkovich, "Marx's Capital and the Mystery of the Commodity," in *Mixed Feelings: Feminism, Mass Culture, and Victorian Sensationalism* (New Brunswick, NJ: Rutgers University Press, 1992)

15 Manuel Vargas, "Dead Serious: Evil and the Ontology of the Undead," in *The Undead and Philosophy: Chicken Soup for the Soulless*, (ed.) Richard Greene and K. Silem Mohammad (Chicago, IL: Open Court Press, 2006): 39–52.

16 Chris Harman, *Zombie Capitalism: Global Crisis and the Relevance of Marx* (Chicago: Haymarket Books, 2010): 11.

17 Luise White, *Speaking With Vampires: Rumor and History in Colonial Africa* (Berkeley: University of California Press, 2000).

18 Isak Niehaus, "Witches and Zombies of the South African Lowveld: Discourse, Accusations and Subjective Reality," *The Journal of the Royal Anthropological Institute* 11, no. 2 (2005): 191–210.

19 Ibid., 192.

20 Jean Comaroff and John L. Comaroff, "Alien-Nation: Zombies, Immigrants and Millennial Capitalism," *The South Atlantic Quarterly* 101, no. 4 (2002): 779–805.

21 Jeffrey W. Mantz, "Enchanting Panics and Obeah Anxieties: Concealing and Disclosing Eastern Caribbean Witchcraft," *Anthropology and Humanism* 32, no. 1 (2007): 18–29.

22 H. U. E. Thoden Von Zeldon, "Revenants that Cannot Be Shaken: Collective Fantasies in a Maroon Society," *American Anthropologist* 97, no. 4 (1995): 722–32.

23 Sarah J. Lauro and Karen Embry, "A Zombie Manifesto: The Nonhuman Condition in the Era of Advanced Capitalism," Boundary 2 35, no. 1 (2008): 85–108.

24 Ibid., 87.

25 Ibid., 99.

26 Ibid.

27 Ibid., 90.

28 Donna Haraway, "A Cyborg Manifesto: Science, Technology and Socialist-Feminism in the Late Twentieth Century," in *Simians, Cyborgs and Women: The Reinvention of Nature* (New York: Routledge, 1991): 149–81.

29 Lauro and Embry, 91.

30 Ibid.

31 Jeffrey W. Mantz, "Improvisational Economies: Coltan Production in the Eastern Congo," *Social Anthropology* 16, no. 2 (2008): 34–50; Jeffrey W.

Mantz, "Blood Diamonds of the Digital Age: Coltan and the Eastern Congo," *Global Studies Review* 4, no. 3 (2008): 12–14; James H. Smith, "Tantalus in the Digital Age: Coltan ore, temporal dispossession, and 'movement' in the Eastern Democratic Republic of the Congo," *American Ethnologist* 38, no. 1 (2011): 17–35; James H. Smith and Jeffrey W. Mantz, "Do Cellular Phones Dream of Civil War?: The Mystification of Production and the Consequences of Technology Fetishism in the Eastern Congo," in *Inclusion and Exclusion in the Global Arena*, ed. Max Kirsch and June Nash (New York: Routledge, 2007).

32 Vargas also suggested a tripartite classification of the undead: supernatural, in which a zombie is created through some form of sorcery (similar to Lauro and Embry's zombi); artificial, in which the undead subject emerges through the intervention of some kind of non-magical agent (similar to the modern zombie); and natural, where the undead subject is spawned through some form of mutation (meaningful more in speaking about the origin myths of other undead figures like vampires); Vargas, *Dead Serious*, 43–5.

33 Richard M. Auty, *Sustaining Development in Mineral Economies: The Resource Curse Thesis (London: Routledge, 1993);* Macartan Humphreys, Jeffrey D. Sachs and Joseph E. Stiglitz (eds), *Escaping the Resource Curse* (New York: Columbia University Press, 2007); Jeffrey D. Sachs and Andrew M. Warner, *Natural resource abundance and economic growth*, NBER Working Paper #5398 (Cambridge, MA: National Bureau of Economic Research, 1995); Jeffrey D. Sachs and Andrew M. Warner, "Sources of slow growth in African economies," *Journal of African Economies* 6 (1997): 335–76.

34 Achille Mbembe, "Necropolitics," *Public Culture* 15, no. 1 (2003): 11–40.

35 Ibid., 39. For our purposes, I am interested less in Mbembe's ideas about a state of exception and governmentality, and more with a concern for how to understand resource extraction as a global, political economic process.

36 Jeffrey W. Mantz, "Improvisational Economies: Coltan Production in the Eastern Congo," *Social Anthropology* 16, no. 2 (2008).

37 Jeffrey W. Mantz, "From Digital Divides to Creative Destruction: the Congolese 'blood mineral' trade and the fashioning of digital age knowledge economies," under review for *The Politics of Instability: Sexual Violence, Political Corruption, and International Complicity in the Democratic Republic of the Congo*, eds Timothy Scarnecchia and Monika J. Flaschka (Kent, OH: Kent State University Press, n.d.).

38 Ibid.

12

Monsters by the numbers:

Controlling monstrosity in video games

Jaroslav Švelch

"This game is an atrocity," a middle-aged woman says in a T.V. ad entitled *Your Mom Hates Dead Space 2*.[1] She is one of the two hundred "moms" selected for fake focus testing sessions, during which they were shown some of the most disturbing and violent scenes from the 2011 survival horror game. All of them feature *necromorphs*, grotesque monsters made out of recombined parts of human corpses. "Moms" scream when a monster jumps into view. When asked about their opinions of the game, they find the footage—which includes impalement and vomiting—disgusting. They wonder "why anybody would make something like this." They "hate it."[2]

The ad was a part of a more elaborate marketing campaign for *Dead Space 2*. Marketing an M-rated title as something gamers' mothers will hate, the campaign was rather predictably criticized for its reliance on gender and generational stereotypes. While concentrating on these issues, the critics have overlooked an even more important instance of manipulation. The women are not *playing* the game; they are merely spectators. They are not allowed to face the monsters in the same way their supposed "sons" are— with a plasma cutter, javelin gun, or grenades. Without gameplay experience, their disgust and lack of understanding is much more pronounced.

The players, on the contrary, do know why somebody would make something like this. Much of the pleasure of the game stems from the interaction with the monsters—one of the reviewers notes that the "limb-shredding precision of the plasma cutter is wonderful."[3] As the players progress through the game, they discover strategies that will help them defeat the *necro-morphs*. Rather than celebrating gore, the descriptions of monsters on the *Dead Space* wiki pages resemble systematic zoological accounts:

> The act of strategically removing the limbs from the creatures is dubbed "Strategic Dismemberment" by the *Dead Space* game team. Each creature has its own strategies when it comes to dismemberment: some creatures will simply die after enough limbs have been removed, some creatures will die instantly if a specific limb is cut off, while some creatures will become even more of a threat if shot in the wrong place.[4]

Whereas the "moms" see (or are made to see) the monsters as scary, gooey abominations, the strategizing player sees them as challenges—as targets that follow certain rules, and that can be taken apart using a suitable method.

The players' view represents a kind monstrosity that is specific to the medium of video games. Although video game monsters may *look like* the ones we know from genre films, they also move and act within simulated worlds, following the rules laid out by game designers. Driven by a constant demand for action and challenge, video games present us with monsters that can be analyzed and defeated. The medium's computational and procedural nature makes monstrosity fit into *databases* and *algorithms*.[5]

This is not an isolated process; in the twenty-first century, more and more aspects of our lives and cultures are being digitized and ordered into databases, allowing for more efficient control over information flows as well as movement and actions of individuals. Deleuze describes these changes as a shift to *societies of control*, characterized by numerical evaluations and computing.[6] As video games are from the ground up designed to be controlled, they are a testing ground for the logic of the new societies; according to Galloway, they are "allegories for our contemporary life under the protocological network of continuous *informatic control*."[7] Video game monsters, therefore, exemplify the way in which societies of control deal with and take advantage of enmity, threat, and challenge.

The reactions of "moms," on the other hand, represent traditional under-standings of monstrosity based on the monsters' transgressive qualities. Carroll defines the monster as "any being not believed to exist now according to contemporary science."[8] In his view, monsters are impure, because they transgress the categories and rules we use to understand the world around us.[9] The *necromorphs*, for example, provoke the emotions of "disgust" or "awe,"[10] because they are both alive *and* dead and they are both one *and* many. They represent a fantastic, non-existent biology.

FIGURE 12.1 *Shooting necromorphs in* Dead Space 2. © *2011 Electronic Arts, Inc.*

Kristeva approaches horror using the concept of the *abject*, arguing that the cause of abjection is "what disturbs identity, system, order. What does not respect borders, positions, rules. The in-between, the ambiguous, the composite."[11] She distinguishes the *abject* from an *object*—the former is not "definable," it is not "an ob-ject facing me, which I name or imagine."[12]

Video games, however, make the player face the monsters. These creatures do become objects of the player's actions; their rules are clearly defined and ready to be scrutinized. What we are witnessing is a major shift in our conceptualization of monstrosity. The logic of informatic control has now colonized even the things we fear: our monsters, previously deemed to be inscrutable and abject.

This chapter argues that video games, the major new media form that has broken into the mainstream in the twenty-first century, produce and propagate a new type of monstrosity which follows the principles of informatic control. In order to understand this new monstrosity, we must go beyond visual and narrative analysis of the creatures and investigate them as objects of play and interaction, embedded within the designed systems of video games.

This new monstrosity is shaped by the fundamental features of video games. Video games are *rule-based* phenomena and their rules are encoded in the games' software. This makes the new monstrosity knowable and unambiguous. Video games emphasize *action* and its effects in the game worlds. Their monsters therefore become targets of the player's agency and are defeatable. Video games include elements of both *free-form play* and *pre-designed challenges*. While the former renders monstrosity manageable and controllable, the latter turns the monsters into problems or puzzles that have their solutions. In the following sections, I will examine the effects of these features on video game monstrosity and investigate how this new monstrosity relates to the conditions of the societies of control.

Rule-based: The origins of video game monsters

The first feature of the new type of monstrosity actually predates computers. Rules were one of the defining features of games investigated by the pioneers of the study of games in the mid-twentieth century. Already in 1959, Caillois pointed out that the "orderly" and "spectacular" nature of games is at the expense of mystery, secrecy, and doubt—notions that we traditionally connect with monstrosity:

> Without doubt, secrecy, mystery, and even travesty can be transformed into play activity, but it must be immediately pointed out that this transformation is necessarily to the detriment of the secret and mysterious, which play exposes, publishes, and somehow *expends*. In a word, play tends to remove the very nature of the mysterious.[13]

By turning monsters into objects of play, the game dispels their mystery. But could this not be said about monster narratives, too? How are games, in this respect, different from traditional linear media?

Literature is able to keep the secrets concealed thanks to *indeterminacy*, most famously conceptualized by Iser. According to Iser's theory of literary reception, the reader concretizes an image of a fictional world based on the clues she is given in the text;[14] the image is however perpetually incomplete.[15] This indeterminacy allows for a blurred and contradictory portrayal of monstrosity. Consider the following (non-)description of a monster by H. P. Lovecraft:

> The Thing cannot be described—there is no language for such abysms of shrieking and immemorial lunacy, such eldritch contradictions of all matter, force, and cosmic order.[16]

While widely used in fiction,[17] indeterminacy cannot be utilized within the rule systems of games.

Juul theorizes games as hybrids of *rules* and *fiction*. The rules define what is possible in the fictional game spaces, including the actions of the player character and the monsters, while the fiction part contains background narratives, images, dialogs, and other pre-designed content. Taking *Dragon Age: Origins*, a role-playing video game with relatively transparent rules, as an example, I contend that while the fiction is likewise indeterminate—we cannot know every detail of the dragon–human relationships in the fictional world of the game—the rules are complete, clear-cut, unambiguous, and apply to all players. Juul sums this up by saying that rules are *real*, while fictions are not.[18] Whereas the killing of a dragon by an elf mage is a fictional event, subtracting hit points[19] from a variable in a data array assigned to a "dragon" is a real event. The rules that govern the behavior of video game monsters are thus indeed knowable—if not always known—by the player.

Monsters that obey the rules have been around longer than video games. Their precursors can be found in medieval bestiaries, in which fantastic creatures were described similarly to the *necromorphs* on the *Dead Space* wiki: the manticore "is a beast found in India, with a triple row of teeth, the face of a man, and grey eyes ...; it stings like a scorpion and has a hissing voice. It is a powerful jumper, and it delights in eating human flesh."[20] Medieval bestiaries were also predecessors of informatic control—they catalogued both real and fictional monsters and re-interpreted them as allegories of Christian morals.[21]

It does not come as a surprise that the "monster manuals" of the early role-playing games were made to resemble these medieval bestiaries, only with more precise figures. In the original *Dungeons & Dragons* pen-and-paper role-playing game's *Monster Manual*, the dragon—a monster laden with centuries' worth of meanings and interpretations—is described using a table of numbers. We can learn that a green dragon has a "breath weapon" that can create a 5" x 4" cloud of "chlorine gas," has seven to nine hit dice and a 55 percent chance of being able to talk.[22] The monster manual is, in fact, monstrosity squeezed into a database.

Whereas medieval bestiaries attempted to situate unknown creatures within what was the known system of nature, games like *Dungeons & Dragons* created simulated natures of their own and populated them with creatures that followed their artificial laws and conditions. This is even more pronounced in video games, where rules are encoded in software and the referee—the computer—is consistent and unrelenting. The rules that uphold video games are based on logical operations and numerical representation. Video game monsters therefore cannot be contradictory or blurred—the medium renders monstrosity knowable and objective.

Action and challenge: Motivation for elimination

Before I start analyzing video game monsters, it is important to identify their function in the video game medium. I have already stated that video game monsters become objects of the player's actions.[23] Video games are in fact a cultural form that presupposes action; they are an "action-based medium."[24] As *agency*—the "satisfying power to take meaningful action and see the results of our decisions and choices"[25]—is one of the main draws of games and other virtual environments, it comes as no surprise that so many games are built around destruction, which is a striking example of agency.

Monsters, however, are not static targets. The player is supposed to beat, outsmart, or otherwise overcome them using her logical or motor skills—challenge being one of the most basic and widespread design elements of video games.[26] A steady rhythm of incoming challenges contributes to the experience of *flow*,[27] a psychological concept revered by many game designers.[28]

Games have used monsters to challenge the player since the early arcade titles like *Space Invaders*.[29] Design-wise, they have certain advantages over computer-controlled human enemies. While the latter[30] may be expected to behave according to the current notions of what is "realistic," monster enemies allow for more freedom. They can relentlessly follow simple rules like the aliens from *Space Invaders*, or provide elaborate challenges like the *necromorphs*. Using monsters as foes also alleviates concerns about morality of in-game action,[31] because killing non-humans is likely to be considered less morally questionable than killing people.[32]

The player has a range of motivations to eliminate monsters. It allows her to progress in the game, accomplish its missions, and eventually beat it. In games like *Dragon Age: Origins*, the player is also rewarded by experience points (XP)—which can be used to improve the character's "stats" (such as strength) or "skills"—or loot, that may include in-game money or equipment that improves the character's chances in upcoming battles. In the process, the monster is transformed into in-game capital. When more capital is required, the player may turn to the practice of *farming*—accumulating XP and loot by means such as fighting unchallenging monsters.[33] Given how much this activity resembles work, it is no wonder that in multi-player games, *gold farming* has become a job for thousands of people in the developing countries who sell in-game capital for real money.[34]

Elimination of monsters can also earn the player trophies recognized outside of the game. Some of these involve completing arbitrary challenges unrelated to the game's primary goals. In the zombie survival game *Dead*

Island, one can for instance receive a trophy called "Hack & slash" for "killing 250 zombies using edged melee weapons."[35] The trophy is then published on the player's public gamer profile for other players to see, turning the achievement into *gaming capital*.[36]

In this section, I have explored how video games' focus on action and its effects shapes their new brand of monstrosity. In order to maintain the level of challenge, games tend to provide a continuous influx of identical monsters.[37] Video game monstrosity is conquerable and can be processed into in-game or out-of-game profit. In this respect, video games mirror the inner workings of contemporary corporations, in which "challenges" and "contests" allow for dynamic evaluation of individual performances.[38]

Emergence: Experimenting with monsters

Besides being challenges and opportunities for action, video game monsters become objects of play.[39] To cut through the web of meanings associated with the word *play*, I will once again rely on Caillois, who differentiated between two modes[40] of play: *paidia*, which involves spontaneous improvisation and "primitive joy in destruction and upset," and *ludus*, which involves "reaching a solution" of an "arbitrarily designed problem."[41]

The concept of *paidia* is essential to so-called *sandbox* games, in which the player can experiment with the game world without having to follow a strict narrative. The design of such games takes advantage of the principle of *emergence*. In the language of game analysis, emergence is the process in which a number of relatively simple rules combine to produce game events or chains of events unforeseen by the player and the developer.[42]

An example of emergence is the swarming behavior typical for one of the most famous monsters that blindly follows simple rules (or *a* rule)—the zombie.[43] Zombies continue to be among the video games' most favorite monsters, as is evident from mainstream titles like *Dead Rising*,[44] *Dead Island*,[45] and *Left 4 Dead*,[46] all released within the last decade, and their existing or planned sequels.

Swarming has been traditionally seen as monstrous;[47] the non-localized anti-individualistic swarm defies our notions of sovereignty and has been used as a "metaphor for the opposite of Western liberal democracies."[48] But while this emergent behavior has been considered threatening because it can slip out of control, zombie games are all about *performing* crowd control—or, better, *horde* control. In *Left 4 Dead*, the following tactic is recommended to fight the zombies:

If you know where a Horde is coming from, throw the Molotov at a choke point between the Horde and your teammates. Try to throw the Molotov just as they reach the choke point in order to increase the likelihood of burning the entire Horde before the flames expire.[49]

As is the case with emergence-based games in general, much of the pleasure of zombie games resides in the exploration of what can be done. Zombies can be lured into a trap and set on fire; to stop them from approaching, one can shoot their legs off. In *Dead Rising 2*, a game that borders on parody, they become objects of over-the-top experiments in violence. The main character can kill them using various improvised weapons including a *heliblade*, a combination of a toy helicopter and a machete. Given the zombies' slow movements[50] and softness of flesh, the effects of the player's agency are spectacularly vivid. The destruction of zombies' anatomy tends to be simulated in great detail—limbs are cut off; heads explode. *Dead Island* boasts that "layers of muscle and meat" are rendered beneath each foe, enabling for realistic "slicing and dicing" effects.[51]

Whereas the narratives of zombie games often tackle the biological and personal horrors of a zombie infection, zombies themselves become objects of play and experimentation; the "joy of destruction and upset" dominates the gameplay.[52] It is telling that George A. Romero described the more carefree and action-packed remake of his *Dawn of the Dead*, which featured many creative ways of killing zombies, as "more of a video game."[53]

To sum up my arguments in this section, zombie games play with the tension between emergence and control. But while the two seem to be fundamentally opposed, Galloway and Thacker argue that global networks brought forth a "new alliance between *control* and *emergence*," enabled by the protocol, which allows for distributed, non-hierarchical control.[54] Typical video game zombies represent emergence that is designed for the joy of control and agency, enabled by the underlying rules. In emergence-based video games, monsters become playthings.

Algorithm: The monster as a puzzle

While the *paidia* principle turns monsters into objects of player experimentation, *ludus* turns them into pre-designed challenges. In the introduction, I argued that traditional conceptualizations of monstrosity saw monsters as strange and unfathomable; as epistemological challenges. This section will focus on bosses—monsters that strive to retain some of this challenge by requiring the player to defeat them in new and unique ways. I will show that even these follow the logic of informatic control.

Bosses, like other monsters, are driven by algorithms that are contained within the rule systems of the games and encoded in software.[55] However, they are usually tougher, unique within the game, and exhibit more complex behavior. The player is expected to grasp their algorithms, discover their weak spots, and avoid their special attacks. Consider the following description of *Ganon*, a boar-like demon and the final boss of 1986's massively influential title *The Legend of Zelda*:[56]

> Ganon will attack while invisible. Avoid his fireballs and swing the Magical Sword at where he appears to be. While many believe his movement pattern is random, close observation of his fireball's starting positions will reveal semi-circular, counter-clockwise patterns, which shift when a circuit is completed. [The main character] must use this to his advantage when predicting where Ganon will next be positioned. After he is hit a few times, he will turn red and be paralyzed. [The character] must shoot him with a Silver Arrow to finish him off.[57]

Ganon is a prototypical boss: He has special attacks (fireballs), special abilities (invisibility), and a weakness (vulnerability to silver arrows). As the player is learning of these, she is identifying the rational rules behind the seemingly "random" patterns of behavior and designing a strategy to defeat the monster.[58]

Similar puzzle-like boss monsters feature in contemporary action games. In the recent tongue-in-cheek action game *Shadows of the Damned*,[59] the game's main character—a demon hunter—eliminates one of the bosses, a horseman demon named George Reed, in the following manner: First, he must avoid Reed's attacks and wait for his horse to excrete horseshit that emanates an aura of darkness. The darkness reveals a weak spot on Reed's back, suddenly made visible. When Garcia shoots the spot, the horse rears, exposing another weak spot that has to be penetrated. This procedure has to be repeated several times before Reed dismounts from the horse and eats it, marking a beginning of the next phase of a multi-part boss battle.

While unique within the individual title, the algorithms of boss monsters tend to follow design conventions. In her close reading of the action game *Castlevania: Symphony of the Night*,[60] Fernández-Vara finds that Dracula, the game's main villain, has, on the level of rules, nothing to do with either Stoker's nor Lugosi's vampires—rather, that he is a stereotypical video game boss:

He does not bite or suck blood, he avoids contact with our hero, and throws fireballs, summons fire spirits and thunder whenever he opens his cape. ... Fighting Dracula follows a stock videogame routine of hits and misses and of summoning powers.[61]

While bosses receive special treatment from game designers, their behavior tends to follow the "video game routine," which consists of elements suitable for easy computational implementation. They let themselves be examined, revealing their weak spots, "telegraphing"[62] their special attacks and repeating their patterns of action. No matter whether the design of the monster's algorithms is creative or stereotypical, the player is expected to devise and perform a winning strategy. This strategy usually involves a carefully choreographed sequence of moves, adjusted in real time to react to the monster's actions.[63]

Unsurprisingly, the player's strategy itself resembles an algorithm. As Manovich puts it, "the similarity between the actions expected from the player and computer algorithms is too uncanny to be dismissed."[64] As opposed to traditional monstrosity, which was considered unintelligible, video game bosses can be defeated if the player discovers and internalizes their algorithms. Both the monster and the player are eventually subject to the algorithmic logic.

It is therefore possible even for the unique bosses to be *figured out* and, in Caillois's words, "published."[65] Like the author of the *Ganon* article cited above, the player can literally publish the solution on a wiki page and share it with others. The temporarily unknown then becomes knowledge, neatly organized in the form of a database.[66] Monstrosity is under (informatic) control.

Conclusion

Traditionally, monsters were taken to represent "tokens of fracture within the human psyche"; they were supposed to be "unnatural, transgressive, obscene, contradictory, heterogeneous, mad."[67] Video games, however, make us think that we can indeed *know our enemy*. Monstrosity is now under the control of the empowered player. Although video game monsters are still made to *look* disgusting or awe-inspiring, their behaviors are dictated by algorithms that can be analyzed and described. They are slain by the hundreds and turned into rewards and mementoes of players' efforts and skills. Metaphorically speaking, they are ready to be "strategically dismembered," just like *Dead Space 2*'s *necromorphs*.

This is due to both the numerical nature of the medium, and the principles of play it follows. According to Galloway and Thacker, games are:

[...] training tools for life inside the protocological network, where flexibility, systemic problem solving, quick reflexes, and indeed play itself are as highly valued and commodified as sitting still and hushing up were for the disciplinary societies of modernity.[68]

If video games are indeed training grounds for our lives in control societies, they teach us that even monstrosity, formerly relegated to the fringes of human experience, can be made visible and manipulable. In video games, like in surveillance systems, the hidden is to be revealed and the dangerous is to be eliminated.[69] This should concern cultural critics more than video game violence and the "disgusting" monsters.

Galloway and Thacker argue that games should be investigated not as "a liberation from the systems of production and exchange," but as "the very pillars that prop those systems up."[70] Being allegories of the societies of control, they do in many respects mirror their all-encompassing logic, under which the unknown must be conquered.

At the same time, I believe that they also provide opportunities to question this logic, although these have been largely untapped.[71] The allegory does not necessarily have to be *in agreement* with the values of the society of control. As the player learns about the rules and algorithms of the game, she may realize that the real foe—the actual monster—is the game itself; the game that makes us kill all these beasts in exchange for the promise of achievement and fun. But before the medium can address the monstrous in a way that does not reduce it to cannon fodder, game designers, players, and critics must realize how deeply entrenched in the logic of the twenty-first century informatic control video game monstrosity is.

Acknowledgments

The research for this chapter was supported by the Specific Research Program of the Ministry of Education of the Czech Republic no. 265 501. I would like to thank Matt Weise, Clara Fernández-Vara, Nikolaus König, Sabine Harrer, Honza Švelch, Jakub Šmíd, and Iveta Hajdáková for inspiring discussions about the topic that generated many of the ideas in this chapter.

Notes

1 *Your Mom Hates Dead Space 2* (Electronic Arts, 2011) http://www.youtube.com/watch?v=nKkPFDEiC6Q&feature=relmfu/

2 *Your Mom Hates Dead Space 2 Behind-the-Scenes* (Electronic Arts, 2011), http://www.youtube.com/watch?v=jri8LFci4xQ&feature=relmfu/

3 Jim Sterling, "Review: Dead Space 2," *Destructoid*, January 24, 2011, http://www.destructoid.com/review-dead-space-2-192306.phtml/

4 "Necromorphs," *The Dead Space Wiki*, n.d., http://deadspace.wikia.com/wiki/Necromorphs/

5 According to Manovich, computer programming reduces the world "to two kinds of software objects which are complementary to each other: data structures and algorithms." Lev Manovich, *The Language of New Media* (Cambridge, MA: The MIT Press, 2001), 223.

6 Gilles Deleuze, "Postscript on the Societies of Control," *October* 59, Winter (1992): 3–7.

7 Alexander R. Galloway, *Gaming: Essays on Algorithmic Culture* (Minneapolis: University of Minnesota Press, 2006), 106. Italics mine.

8 Noël Carroll, *The Philosophy of Horror, or, Paradoxes of the Heart* (New York: Routledge, 1990), 27–8.

9 Carroll, *The Philosophy of Horror*.

10 Timothy K. Beal, *Religion and its monsters* (New York: Routledge, 2002), 7.

11 Julia Kristeva, *Powers of Horror: An Essay on Abjection* (New York: Columbia University Press, 1982), 4.

12 Ibid., 1.

13 Roger Caillois, "The Definition of Play and The Classification of Games," in *The Game Design Reader: a Rules of Play Anthology*, (ed.) Katie Salen and Eric Zimmerman (Cambridge, MA: The MIT Press, 2006), 124.

14 Wolfgang Iser, "Indeterminacy and the Reader's Response in Prose Fiction," in *Aspects of Narrative*, (ed.) J. Hillis Miller (New York: Columbia University Press, 1971).

15 Lubomír Doležel, *Heterocosmica: Fiction and Possible Worlds* (Baltimore: Johns Hopkins University Press, 1998).

16 H. P. Lovecraft, *Tales of H.P. Lovecraft*, (ed.) Joyce Carol Oates (New York: HarperPerennial, 2007), 74.

17 Indeterminacy is also present, perhaps to a lesser extent, in film. In *Night of the Living Dead*, we receive plenty of visual information about zombies, but we can only see them from a limited number of viewpoints, selected by cinematography and montage.

18 Jesper Juul, *Half-real: Video Games Between Real Rules and Fictional Worlds* (Cambridge, MA: The MIT Press, 2005).

19 *Hit points* are a numerical representation of health condition, for both player characters and monsters.

20 Debra Hassig, *Medieval Bestiaries: Text, Image, Ideology* (Cambridge: Cambridge University Press, 1995), 121.

21 Hassig, *Medieval Bestiaries*.

22 Gary Gygax and Dave Arneson, *Dungeon & Dragons Volume 2: Monsters & Treasure* (Lake Geneva, WI: Tactical Studies Rules, 1974), 11.

23 *Actions* include more than the button-mashing frenzy of "action" games. Moving units or characters around the battlefields of strategy and role-playing games is also action.

24 Galloway, *Gaming*, 3.

25 Janet Murray, *Hamlet on the Holodeck: the Future of Narrative in Cyberspace* (Cambridge, MA: The MIT Press, 1998), 126.

26 The pervasiveness of challenge has been criticized by some independent game designers, including the Belgian studio *Tale of Tales*, known for their meditative titles such as *Graveyard*. See Auriea Harvey and Michaël Samyn, "Over Games," *Tale of Tales*, 2010, http://www.tale-of-tales.com/tales/OverGames.html/

27 Mihály Csíkszentmihályi, *Flow: The Psychology of Optimal Experience* (New York: HarperPerennial, 2008).

28 Raph Koster, *A Theory of Fun for Game Design* (Scottsdale, AZ: Paraglyph Press, 2005).

29 Taito, *Space Invaders*, Arcade (Taito, 1978).

30 Human enemies in games—especially action games—are quite often on the verge of becoming monstrous themselves; to be able to "play by the rules" of the genre, they carry guns and other devices that give them superhuman powers.

31 For more about video games and ethics, see Jaroslav Švelch, "The Good, the Bad, and the Player: The Challenges to Moral Engagement in Single-Player Avatar-Based Video Games," in *Ethics and Game Design: Teaching Values Through Play*, ed. Karen Schrier and David Gibson (Hershey, PA: Information Science Reference, 2010), 52–68; Miguel Sicart, *The Ethics of Computer Games* (Cambridge, MA: The MIT Press, 2009).

32 In some versions of the 1997 vehicular combat game *Carmaggedon*, pedestrians were replaced by zombies (and red blood by green blood) to appease rating agencies. "Pedestrian," *Carmageddon Wiki*, n.d., http://carmageddon.wikia.com/wiki/Pedestrian/

33 While the term originated in the multiplayer environment, it has expanded into the domain of single-player games. It is an umbrella term for a number of activities; killing low-level monsters is sometimes called *hunting*. See Richard Heeks, "Current Analysis and Future Research Agenda on 'Gold Farming': Real-World Production in Developing Countries for the Virtual Economies of Online Games," *Development Informatics: Working Paper Series*, no. 32 (2008), http://www.sed.manchester.ac.uk/idpm/research/publications/wp/di/documents/di_wp32.pdf/

34 Ibid.

35 Techland, *Dead Island*, PlayStation 3 (Deep Silver, 2011).

36 For more about achievements, see Mikael Jakobsson, "The Achievement Machine: Understanding Xbox 360 Achievements in Gaming Practices," *Game Studies* 11, no. 1 (2011), http://gamestudies.org/1101/articles/jakobsson/. The concept of *gaming capital* was introduced by Consalvo, who defined it as a complex of "knowledge, experience, and positioning" of a particular player, which is recognized by the wider subculture: Mia Consalvo, *Cheating: Gaining Advantage in Videogames* (Cambridge, MA: The MIT Press, 2009).

37 This is now also possible in film, thanks to CGI. The monstrosity brought about by CGI is actually very similar to video game monstrosity, mainly due to their shared tendency to make monsters visible and spectacular.

38 Deleuze, "Postscript on the Societies of Control," 4.

39 In this chapter, I use the word *game* to describe the artifact and the word *play* to describe the activity.

40 Video games utilize both of these modes. Although they are not mutually exclusive, games tend to favor one of them.

41 Caillois, "The Definition of Play and The Classification of Games," 141–2.

42 The foremost examples of games based on emergence are simulation games such as *SimCity* or *The Sims*. See: Juul, *Half-real*.

43 Already popular in horror film, zombies easily crossed over into the video game medium. This is not surprising given that already the early zombie films, such as *Night of the Living Dead*, had exhibited a strong focus on emergence—they were video games waiting to happen. In Romero's 1968 film, one zombie is scary but can be easily avoided, but when dozens of them mob a country house, the emergent results are horrifying. Classic zombie films focus on the efforts of men and women who are defending themselves against a zombie onslaught, imminent and relentless as if driven by unstoppable computer algorithms. See George A. Romero, *Night of the Living Dead*, 1968.

44 Capcom, *Dead Rising*, Xbox 360 (Capcom, 2006).

45 Techland, *Dead Island*.

46 Valve Corporation, *Left 4 Dead*, PC (Valve Corporation, 2008).

47 Carroll, *The Philosophy of Horror*.

48 Alexander R. Galloway and Eugene Thacker, *The Exploit: A Theory of Networks* (Minneapolis: University of Minnesota Press, 2007), 114.

49 "Molotov," *The Left 4 Dead Wiki*, n.d., http://left4dead.wikia.com/wiki/Molotov/

50 While *Dead Rising*'s zombies are slow, *Left 4 Dead*'s are fast; *Dead Island* has both slow and fast ones.

51 Josh, "Dead Island Announcement Trailer (Xbox 360, PS3, PC)", February 17, 2011, http://www.videogamesblogger.com/2011/02/17/dead-island-announcement-trailer-xbox-360-ps3-pc.htm/

52 Although not finished yet, the independent zombie survival simulation *Project Zomboid* offers another take on the zombie apocalypse, aiming to simulate its societal effects, such as "starvation, illness, loneliness, depression, alcoholism, drug addiction, suicide, insanity, trust issues." Similarly, the game mod *DayZ* (unofficial expansion of the *Arma II* army simulation game) is a complex simulation of individual survival in a zombie-infested landscape. As opposed to mainstream zombie games, it does not avoid frustrating the player. Indie Stone Studios, *Project Zomboid*, PC, 2012; Dean Hall, *DayZ*, PC (Bohemia Interactive, 2012).

53 Simon Pegg, "Simon Pegg Interviews George A Romero," *Time Out London*, September 8, 2005, http://www.timeout.com/film/news/631/

54 Galloway and Thacker, *The Exploit: A Theory of Networks*, 22. Italics mine.

55 While artificial intelligence is slowly but steadily gaining ground in game design, most monsters continue to follow arbitrary sets of rules designed for a desired level of difficulty. For more about AI in games, see Michael Mateas, "Expressive AI: Games and Artificial Intelligence" (presented at the Level Up: Digital Games Research Conference, Utrecht, 2003), http://users.soe.ucsc.edu/~michaelm/publications/mateas-digra2003.pdf/

56 Nintendo, *The Legend of Zelda*, Nintendo Entertainment System (Nintendo, 1987).

57 "Ganon," *Zelda Wiki*, n.d., http://www.zeldawiki.org/Ganon/

58 There may be more than one winning strategy. Also, the player does not necessarily proceed by way of rational reasoning. Rather often, players try to defeat the monster in a trial-and-error fashion.

59 Grasshopper Manufacture, *Shadows of the Damned*, PlayStation 3 (Electronic Arts, 2011).

60 This is in fact one of the many games to feature the character of Dracula. Konami, *Castlevania: Symphony of the Night*, Sony PlayStation (Konami, 1997).

61 Clara Fernández-Vara, "Dracula Defanged: Empowering the Player in Castlevania: Symphony of the Night," *Loading* 4, no. 6 (2010): 8.

62 A term used in the video game slang to describe the signal a monster gives when it is about to attack.

63 Encounters with boss monsters resemble Bollywood dance sequences—they take place in closed-off spaces and they need to be well choreographed and performed.

64 Manovich, *The Language of New Media*, 222.

65 Caillois, "The Definition of Play and The Classification of Games," 124.

66 Before the *wiki*, this information was published in gaming press and on dedicated websites. See Consalvo, *Cheating*.

67 Richard Kearney, *Strangers, Gods, and Monsters: Interpreting Otherness* (London and New York: Routledge, 2002), 4–5.

68 Galloway and Thacker, *The Exploit: A Theory of Networks*, 115.

69 For further discussion of informatic control and surveillance, see Galloway and Thacker, *The Exploit: A Theory of Networks*; Mark Andrejevic, *iSpy: Surveillance and Power in the Interactive Era* (Lawrence, KS: University Press of Kansas, 2007).

70 Galloway and Thacker, *The Exploit: A Theory of Networks*, 115.

71 There are already a number of games that challenge typical video game monstrosity. The horror adventure game *Amnesia: The Dark Descent* obscures the monsters by making them virtually unbeatable. As the main character becomes "insane" when looking at a monster, the game dissuades the player from getting close to them, let alone examining them. The critically acclaimed game *Shadow of the Colossus* questions the ethics of monster-slaying. At the beginning, a mysterious voice promises its protagonist that after destroying 16 huge monsters—colossi—in a deserted fantastic land, his dead love will come back to life. The colossi, however, are not portrayed as evil, but as wonderful and solitary forces of nature. There are also no other foes in the game besides the colossi, which breaks the convention of the constant flow of challenge and makes the game a series of majestic boss battles. The colossi can be defeated as typical puzzle-monsters, with the twist of the hero being able to climb their towering bodies. His victories are, however, presented in a decidedly non-heroic way. As he is keeps killing the colossi, his appearance deteriorates and he ultimately becomes a pale shadow of his former self. His—and the player's—urge to kill monsters is questioned and it becomes clear that he had been tricked by the voice, just like the player had been tricked by the game. Frictional Games, *Amnesia: The Dark Descent*, PC (Frictional Games, 2010); Team Ico, *Shadow of the Colossus*, Sony Playstation 2 (Sony Computer Entertainment, 2005).

13

Killing whiteness:

The critical positioning of zombie walk brides in internet settings

Michele White

Introduction

Most contemporary Western viewers are familiar with conventional wedding images, which are now widely available in Internet settings. In the most common version of these representations, women in white wedding gowns and men in tuxedos pose stiffly in places of worship. There are also images of demure brides, couples performing cake cutting and other rituals, and attendees jumping in unison or casually arranged. Such photographs almost always convey conventional ideas about heterosexual unions and gendered identities.[1] Feminine beauty, delicateness, and whiteness, which ordinarily make allusions to race, are perpetuated through wedding cultures and photographs. In loosely related Internet representations, zombie brides wear versions of traditional bridal garb while participating in zombie walks. In these public events, which developed in the twenty-first century, people enact undead roles as a means of exploring different forms of consciousness, embodiment, identity, and relationships.

Zombie walk brides (zombie brides at zombie walks) evoke different versions of gender, race, and sexuality than traditional brides. A Flickr image

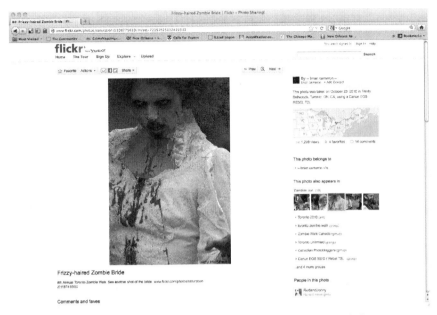

FIGURE 13.1 -- *brian cameron* --, *"Frizzy-haired Zombie Bride," Flickr.*
October 23, 2010 (http://www.flickr.com/photos/saturation/5108775610/in/set-
72157625102419331)

of the tipped-down face of a zombie walk bride should convey decorous femininity, but she looks at viewers with hooded and dark-ringed eyes, bares her red-stained teeth, and dribbles someone's blood down her chin and dress, or at least what functions as blood.[2] Georgie_grrl argues that the zombie bride in another Flickr image "got left at the altar ... maybe she ate the groom" and challenges the monogamous heterosexuality associated with brides.[3] Zombie bride Helen would present a more languorous figure except she has a torn, bloodied, and bruised face.[4] The groom is missing from this Flickr image but bridesmaid Emma stands against Helen and hangs her arm in a similar pose. The photographer entitles the image "Undead Wedding" and makes these women into a couple. Such portrayals of dirty fluids and social breakdowns reference and reorder the familiar features of wedding cultures. These zombie brides' skin is not just pale, their dresses are not white, and they do not ordinarily support traditional marriages.

Flickr has abundant images of individuals at zombie walks, including zombie brides. This Internet site provides hosting and sharing features, was designed in 2004, and is now owned by Yahoo! Flickr is often mentioned as a key example of social media and thus as an exemplary instance of twenty-first-century technology.[5] The site offers "new ways of organizing photos and video," indicates that photography albums are "in desperate need" of "retirement," and distinguishes itself from older media and the accompanying organizational and photographic histories where white children are transformed into heterosexual couples, get married, and have families of their own.[6] Flickr claims to have reconceptualized imaging and relationships but its favicon, the specially designed icon that appears in the browser's URL bar and stands in for the site, pairs a blue and pink dot, or a male and female together. The site's texts also feature blue and pink and binary gender and heterosexual references. The depictions of zombie brides on Flickr, with their once white wedding dresses, are a version of these blue and pink pairings and a critical reminder of the ways people are rupturing such models of femininity, heterosexuality, and whiteness.

Zombie walk brides can be understood as monstrous and critical twenty-first-century technologies because people produce these gruesome characters through makeup and Internet sites in order to engage with contemporary identity categories. My reading of zombie brides as a critical method is related to cultural understandings of zombie representations. We "love zombies so much," writes Doug Gross, because they help "reflect whatever our greatest fears happen to be at the time."[7] Steven Schlozman "will always love" the "original *Dawn of the Dead*" because it has "great social commentary."[8] A number of texts on zombies address how George A. Romero's *Night of the Living Dead* (1968) is a reminder of civil rights struggles.[9] However, there are only a few considerations of the racial positions of human characters in other contemporary zombie films and almost no writing about the gender, race, and sexuality roles associated with zombie embodiment and behavior. The political implications of zombie walks and the ways zombie cultures and representations have been extended and transformed in Internet settings have also been vastly understudied.[10]

Depictions of zombies deserve further critical analysis because they appear along with more conventional representations and yet pose radically altered conceptions of selfhood, identity, and embodiment. For Sarah Juliet Lauro and Karen Embry, zombies engage two sorts of terror: fear of being devoured, which is directed mainly at the physical body, and dread of having one's individual consciousness absorbed by the horde.[11] Contemporary zombies challenge conceptions of biology and science by seeming to function beyond expectations for human physiology. Female zombies' disruptions are particularly visceral since society often associates women with biological reproduction. For instance, zombie brides distort ideas about pure and virginal brides when they appear with aborted or zombified babies.[12] Zombies' bodies are torn and liquid; skin is peeling, rotting, and extremely dark and pale; and skeletal structure is twisted, visible, and partially missing.

Identification with these disordered bodies and states occurs because characters and viewers imagine becoming zombies. In Romero's *Dawn of the Dead* (1978), humans look out at the encroaching zombies, theorize that they are all drawn to the mall for similar reasons, and one of the characters declares, "They're us." Contemporary viewers and critics perpetuate these forms of recognition in Internet settings. Gavon Laessig's "Undead Like Me" post indicates, "People identify with the zombie because the zombie is us."[13] On sites like Flickr, photographers recognize themselves in zombies. Aimeesque provides a picture of a zombie photographer angling his camera at the attending photographer and identifies the experience as "the twilight zone when the photographer and zombie in him met."[14] It is not unusual for viewers to recognize their zombie portrayals, name themselves, and become further enmeshed with zombie positions. suezq1342 posts an image of "a zombie guy" who "asked his zombie girlfriend to be his zombie bride in front of at least 2000 people" and RedandJonny respond with a "Whoa ! Thats us!!!"[15] Viewers also make out their social positions, sexual and familial relationships, corporeality, and futures mirrored and threatened by zombies. These forms of recognition and revision have been theorized as aspects of Internet settings, including the ways people produce versions of themselves through avatars and profiles. Sherry Turkle argues that character-based new technologies provide people with methods for working through their identities and relationships.[16] People form their own version of twenty-first-century hybrid monstrosity, and of extended and empowered corporeality, when they identify with the computer hand-pointer and their reflections combine with images of people on the screen.[17]

Zombies' connections to humanness and reordering of selfhood, identity, and embodiment are condensed in the figure of the zombie bride. Brides ordinarily support heterosexuality, monogamous coupling, familial and reproductive futures, consumerism, and whiteness. The overwhelmingly white racial composition of people at zombie walks, which is conveyed in Internet depictions, is worrying. Yet zombie walk brides also rework their whiteness and physiognomy. In Internet representations, they wear filthy and torn dresses, have broken bodies and reddish-brown scabbed skin, are drenched in blood and gore, brandish bits of other people, and reach out to eat individuals. Their bodies are a record of violence against women (or perhaps aggression against humans), which is all too resonant in contemporary society. However, zombie brides also manage to remain active and agentive while killing or otherwise losing their living husbands. While there are troubling aspects of this murderous position, it has critical applications and suggests how identities and relationships are being restructured in the twenty-first century. Zombie brides tend to represent uncoupling and a different model than Flickr's heterosexual ethos. These women shift the white monogamous heterosexuality that helps produce traditional brides, weddings, and women's roles towards a bloody and blood-colored cannibalistic polyamory. They support Michael Hardt and Antonio Negri's indication that monsters disrupt normative power and its structures.[18] Zombie walk brides challenge authority, including the continuing role of the family in articulating contemporary roles and norms.

Zombie walks

Zombie walks are organized public gatherings where people perform as zombies. They are held in urban settings, happen around Halloween, collect funds for charities, and incorporate horror film screenings. Zombie walks have happened on most continents and are widely represented in Internet settings. The earliest zombie walk was called "The Zombie Parade" and was held in 2001 in Sacramento, California, as part of a midnight film festival.[19] The first event that was labeled a "zombie walk" occurred in 2003 in Toronto, Ontario. The 2010 zombie walk in Brisbane, Australia, attracted around 10,000 participants.[20] All of these events are documented, commented upon, and reimagined in Internet settings. For instance, photographers use Flickr's "sets" to organize and advertise zombie images. Flickr's "group" option allows photographers to bring together their images, think about specific zombies in discussion boards, and provide a visual and textual history of zombie walks. It also provides a different formation than Flickr's references to family and heterosexual coupling.

Zombie walks offer people opportunities to enliven the undead, disrupt everyday social spaces and mores, and envision different identifications and connections. Margaret Robinson tells a reporter at a zombie walk, "We are all zombies tonight, we are all undead."[21] Her vision of zombie unification celebrates the horde rather than hierarchical structures but she also promises a parity that is not available to all people. In these Internet settings, participants identify their interests in the physicality and shock value of zombie walks, where other individuals are likely to unexpectedly encounter fleshy and staggering hordes, and consider the recrafted skin tone, facial physiognomy, and figure of undead participants. Through these Internet practices, participants begin to think about and reshape their identities, including their racial position. Early academic and popular texts often describe Internet settings as places where identities can be produced and remade, but forum participants suggest a more ambivalent position in foregrounding their traditional identities through images and other means, changing their racial position with makeup and blood, and thinking about becoming something else.[22] This position is imagined as eternal and often persists through Internet images, but the corporeal manifestations of participants' zombie presentations are usually temporary.

The critical possibilities of zombie walk brides

The zombie walk bride is identified as a key type, a figure of fascination and delight, and something that can further tie zombie culture to the contemporary world. For instance, sniderscion believes that "It just wouldn't be a Zombie walk without at least one Zombie Bride in her wedding dress."[23] dr_dustbunny advises that "Everyone needs the ever soo hawt 'Bride Zombie', saw around ten of those."[24] "There is always a bunch of Zombie brides and Prom Queen Zombies at any Zombie gathering," writes grayd80. "They must be especially vulnerable!"[25] These posters assert the importance of brides in zombie culture and that these figures are appealing because they are recognizable, continue some features of dyadic gender, reference feminine beauty and appeal even as they move beyond these strictures, and are susceptible and thus available for transformation. Most zombie walk photographers continue this focus, and support the centrality of brides in wedding cultures, by including images of brides in their Flickr sets. For instance, david anderson's set of six images includes two zombie brides. He credits zombie brides with "the best poses of the evening" and went to the zombie walk "hoping to find some corpse brides."[26] This interest forwards alternative conceptions of brides and, as the comment about "hot" brides suggests, constitutes monstrous women as erotically appealing. Images of grotesque zombie brides offer an antidote to the mandates for brides, and women more generally, to be conventionally attractive. Yet they also continue the association of women with abjection, including the idea that women are too filthy and fluid.

People generally believe that there have been significant positive changes in Western women's roles since the second wave of the women's movement. However, Sherril Horowitz Schuster argues that the position of the bride "seems virtually untouched by the change in the directed attainments of women."[27] Even women who do not ordinarily participate in traditional feminine behaviors, as Chrys Ingraham's research illustrates, embrace conventional femininities "in order to have the wedding they've been imagining" since childhood.[28] Zombie walk photographers and participants present brides but reject the ordinary mandates to portray white and pristine dresses and loving, demure, and slender brides. Photos by Mavis imagines a bride saying, "I've devoured my groom and most of my bridesmaids, now what can I eat? Burp."[29] Tom Grinsfelder "can't believe she ate the whole thing! BRAINS!!!"[30] These zombie brides' carnivorous gazes and readiness to eat and incorporate everyone threaten traditional bridal roles, "the one" monogamous and heterosexual relationship, and the controlling looks of grooms and other viewers. Zombie walk brides also retain some aspects of binary gender, whiteness, and heterosexuality because their practices require that they are recognizable under the rage and stains. It is worth considering the possible function of unrecognizable brides and instances where "that's not me" encourages critical reflection.

The bridal features of these zombies become altered when their dresses are another color because of the blood and filth, their manner deviates from traditional roles, and photography cannot convey their characteristics. This transformation occurs in a Flickr image by vanBuuren, which has the groom's mouth pressed against the side of the bride's face and is entitled "kiss the bride."[31] The picture could establish the primacy of heterosexual romance. However, the photographer inquires whether the zombie groom is "Kissing? or sucking her brains through a headwound?" In doing this, he challenges

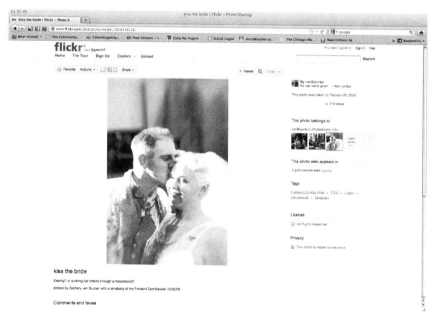

FIGURE 13.2 *vanBuuren, "kiss the bride," Flickr. October 26, 2008 (http://www. flickr.com/photos/bunnytek/2978549155/)*

the heterosexual coupling that is centered by the action and forwards non-normative and barely alive whiteness. The bride shifts from extremely pale to dissolving because of the tonal qualities of the image and the bride's light skin, blonde hair, and white veil. For example, the overexposed white veil "eats" into her hair and dress. This image thus undoes the white body by absorbing it back into the blank white surface around the depiction. The groom sucks out her brains and the light eats away at her body. Thus, the varied processes enacted in this image consume whiteness while troubling female subjects.

Zombie walk commentary combines heterosexual coupling with the homosocial and potentially same-sex erotics of women's wedding cultures. Zombie brides Loran and Krystle, according to photographer Ian Aberle, "were on their way to the Bridal Show when the Zombie Apocalypse happened."[32] "Now they just eat the brains of the men they will never wed." Loran and Krystle are prevented from having weddings, which are usually imagined as women's dream day and focused on conventional gender roles, and they punish the now unavailable suitors by consuming them. Aberle provides a history of frustrated white heterosexual unions, and presumably foiled white reproduction, but the images suggest a more queer future in which zombies engage in varied sorts of pleasures and relationships. In the images, Loran and Krystle kiss and propose that zombie identities replace heterosexuality with gay and lesbian sexual attachments.[33] reynolds.james.e offers the related indication that he "didn't see any grooms" at the zombie walk.[34] This leads him "to believe that zombies may be more socially progressive in some areas than we tend to be" and that the brides are lesbians. Zombie brides reference lesbian identities and traditional wedding cultures and disturb contemporary investments in stable roles and categories. Like the Internet's amalgamation of diverse technologies, texts, and parts, zombies are a compendium of what they physically and conceptually consume and process, including skin.

The politics of zombies and race

Contemporary zombies' conceptual debt to filmic depictions of Haitian zombies, tendency to derive from white people, extreme paleness, and undeadness make them troubled white subjects who have mixed-race histories. Zombie walk participants and their Internet representations, particularly zombie brides, quote and complicate these layers of whiteness. This is significant since, as Ingraham argues, white wedding dresses and media representation of couples getting married, which almost always represent

FIGURE 13.3 *ian, "Kissing Zombie Brides," Flickr. May 1, 2010 (http://www. flickr.com/photos/ianaberle/4577128483/in/set-72157623865916387/)*

them as white, make weddings "code for whiteness."[35] By critically using the term "white," scholars highlight some of the ways power is produced. My intent in deploying the term is to emphasize how the whiteness of wedding dresses, conceptions of purity, and the purported whiteness of people's faces are interlocked; the privileges that come with these often unstated connections; and the failure and continuance of the term as an identifier of color, innocence, and hierarchy in the twenty-first century.

Scholars study whiteness as a means of interrogating racial categories, the people who are raced, and the production and extension of racial inequalities.[36] Ruth Frankenberg sees whiteness as a "construct or identity almost impossible to separate from racial dominance."[37] George Lipsitz identifies whiteness as "the unmarked category against which difference is constructed."[38] Whiteness is relational, rather than distinct and stable, and deployed by whites as a method of articulating their difference from racial and ethnic "Others." Such studies of whiteness show that, even when not racist, whites gain advantages from many social, institutional, and governmental operations because of their skin color. For instance, white individuals and racial positions are forwarded in Internet settings through such devices as images of light-skinned people and graphics of white hands, even though these technologies are often believed to enable everyone to equitably engage.[39] Thus, narratives about twenty-first-century technologies have resulted in situations where racial inequalities are perpetuated even as people are told that the categories and hierarchies that produce such situations no longer exist. Zombie walk participants and their representations offer some remedies to this because they point to ways of acknowledging the production of race. They also propose that whiteness is associated with monstrosity and deadness rather than the more usual links to beauty, empowerment, and aliveness.

Richard Dyer describes how the undead in films connect whiteness to death. White society "feeds off itself" in the form of vampires consuming white victims, and "threatens to destroy itself."[40] This is also the case with zombie films, which frequently assert "whiteness as death."[41] White people in zombie walks paint on whiteness as an additional layer of color and skin, link whiteness to death, and thereby trouble the usual racial hierarchies and help indicate that race is constructed. Some of the people who structure zombie whiteness thus begin to acknowledge the role of skin color as an organizing principle in social and cultural relations. For example, the dialog between halfgeek and kenndubeau highlights zombie skin. kenndubeau notes that the couple is "so proud to be" portrayed in halfgeek's "Mr & Mrs Zombie" photograph.[42] They identify the image as "Great" because halfgeek "really brought out the decay in" their "skin". halfgeek replies, "I brought out the decay? Wow … I'm … honored, I think ;)."[43] halfgeek's ironic hesitation recalls the standards of wedding photography, including the practice of making brides appear slender, beautiful, and unblemished, and the ways zombie images deviate from these norms.[44] The couple is excited about their skin breaking down, shifting away from white, and having an unstable position. In expressing this, they begin to peel back skin, and material versions of this process are suggested by the consequence of decay and examine its physical and ideological layers. The effects and colors that they incorporate into their faces encourage an interrogation of what whiteness and other racial positions mean.

halfgeek entitles another image from this series "Nice Day for a White Wedding," and conveys clothing that is not that white.[45] This and sebastien. barre's references to white weddings evoke Billy Idol's "White Wedding" song and challenging of the whiteness, morality, and purity associated with these events.[46] Idol sings that there is nothing fair or pure in this world. Blondeness is also compromised by zombies' filthy and stained state. For instance, the lightness of a zombie bride's dress, face, and blonde hair are undone by the scabbed sores that cover most of her features.[47] As Julie Burchill indicates, there are problems with notions of racial purity because the greatest blondes

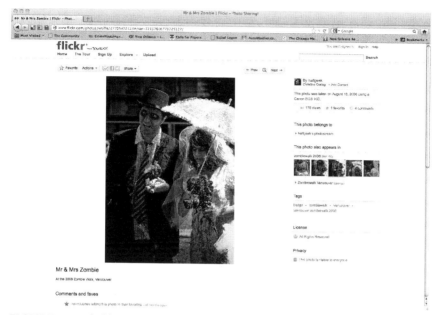

FIGURE 13.4 *halfgeek, "Mr. & Mrs Zombie," Flickr. July 31, 2012 (http://www. flickr.com/photos/wolfie/2770597212/in/set-72157606779725127/)*

in film have all been brunettes. Thus, "we are not as white as we think."[48] There tend to be dark roots at the base of blonde-whiteness. Produced code is also a kind of base for Internet texts, including images of white people.

sebastien.barre foregrounds the production of color in his "re-contrasted cutout," which is a highly mediated image. The zombie bride is presented in extremely saturated color, the dress illuminated white, and the background all grays.[49] The brightness of the dress is contrasted with the dark red-purple of the white bride's face (or, she seems to be white because of the skin showing through the sheer sleeves and the photographer's comments). White gowns almost always make white brides look darker than the fabric. However, the photographer's aesthetic decisions and the seemingly bruised and bloody qualities of the bride's face provide a proposal for white brides where weddings are not a code for whiteness and white women cannot really be white. After death, "the skin is discolored by livor mortis," the "purple-red discoloration from blood accumulating in the lowermost (dependent) blood vessels."[50] Zombie brides quote these deathly features and make their images proposals for whiteness as deadness.

FIGURE 13.5 *sebastien.barre, "Zombie Walk – Saratoga Springs, NY – 07, Sep – 30," Flickr. September 1, 2007 (http://www.flickr.com/photos/99706198@ N00/1847604474/)*

Conclusion: Dead white in the 21st century

Internet-facilitated images of zombie brides connect whiteness, weddings, and technologies (including zombie brides' cosmetic technologies and the hi-tech failures that are associated with zombie apocalypses) to death and the undead. However, the Internet, like television, is imagined to be a site where things are alive because the technologies, including webcams and instant messaging, seem to deliver content in real time and thus a form of liveness.[51] Flickr claims to facilitate similar experiences with its "Share your life in photos" tagline.[52] It suggests that photography and other technologies facilitate life. People's descriptions of "dead" computers can be part of this animation of technologies and their association with lifecycles, but the political possibilities of undead technologies and bodies, which do not follow expected cultural scripts and norms, are more promising. Internet-facilitated zombie brides are dead white, do not meet traditional beauty standards, and do not have a stable color and thus challenge normative gender categories, heterosexual relationships and rituals, and the hierarchical structures of race. They literally peel back the usual forms of white skin and femininity (such as disordering wedding dresses) and encourage viewers to do the same.

Whiteness has formal and ideological problems in Internet settings. Zombie brides and their Internet representations illustrate the ways that whiteness is visually and ideologically compromised. For instance, in vanBuuren's image, the distinctions between the white zombie bride's body and other parts of the website are unclear.[53] Whiteness is usually the privileged state, but images of white people are more likely to dissipate in Internet settings because they blend with and, in a gesture that is related to zombies, are consumed by the white page. The Internet and related technologies are imagined to be alive, and thus a variety of stereotyped representations are understood as authentic, real, and animate. However, any careful view of whiteness in these settings, and admittedly this issue remains largely unaddressed in writing on new media, indicates that it cannot be fully distinguished or supported. This is somewhat different than whites getting to ignore their racial position and privilege. Zombie walk brides and their Internet representations remind viewers of the other colors enmeshed in whiteness and of the abject aspects of whiteness, which includes this white bleeding, and thereby function as monstrous and critical twenty-first-century technologies.

Acknowledgments

This chapter was written with support from the Carol S. Levin Fund, Newcomb College Institute, and Tulane University. I greatly appreciate Marina Levina's and Diem-My Bui's thoughtful engagement in the project.

Notes

In the Internet references in this chapter, such detailed information as the unconventional capitalization, punctuation, and spelling choices from websites are included. Some of the references list only the last access date because no specific "publication" date for comments to Flickr and some other sites are indicated.

1 Charles Lewis, "Working the Ritual: Professional Wedding Photography and the American Middle Class," *Journal of Communication Inquiry* 22, no. 1 (January 1998): 72–92.

2 -- brian cameron --, "Frizzy-haired Zombie Bride," Flickr, October 23, 2010. http://www.flickr.com/photos/saturation/5108775610/in/set-72157625102419331/ (accessed July 30, 2012).

3 Georgie_grrl, "Undead and Undead Bride," Flickr. http://www.flickr.com/photos/saturation/5108741655/in/set-72157625102419331/ (accessed July 30, 2012).

4 sjnewton, "Undead Wedding," Flickr, October 27, 2007. http://www.flickr.com/photos/77844986@N00/1779429957/ (accessed July 30, 2012).

5 David Beer and Roger Burrows, "Sociology and, of and in Web 2.0: Some Initial Considerations," *Sociological Research Online* 12, no. 5 (2007). http://www.socresonline.org.uk/12/5/17.html/ (accessed July 30, 2012); Bruce W. Dearstyne, "Blogs, Mashups, and Wikis, Oh, My!" *The Information Management Journal* 41, no. 4 (2007): 24–33.

6 Flickr, "About Flickr," June 2, 2012. http://www.flickr.com/about/; Shawn Michelle Smith, "'Baby's Picture Is Always Treasured': Eugenics and the Reproduction of Whiteness in the Family Photograph Album," *Yale Journal of Criticism* 11, no. 1 (1998): 197–220.

7 Doug Gross, "Why We Love those Rotting, Hungry, Putrid Zombies," CNN, October 2, 2009. http://articles.cnn.com/2009-10-02/entertainment/zombie.love_1_zombie-movie-encyclopedia-white-zombie-peter-dendle?_s=PM:SHOWBIZ/ (accessed July 30, 2012).

8 Steven Schlozman, as quoted in Carol Memmott, "Novelist Lets Us in on 'Secret' about Zombies," CNN, March 25, 2011. http://www.usatoday.com/life/books/news/2011-03-25-zombie_ST_N.htm/ (accessed July 30, 2012).

9 Stephen Harper, "Night of the Living Dead: Reappraising an Undead Classic," *Bright Lights Film Journal* 50 (2005). http://www.brightlightsfilm.com/50/night.html/ (accessed July 30, 2012); Adam Lowenstein, "Living Dead: Fearful Attractions of Film," *Representations* 110, no. 1 (2010): 196–200.

10 Bryce Peake, "He is Dead, and He is Continuing to Die: A Feminist Psycho-Semiotic Reflection on Men's Embodiment of Metaphor in a Toronto Zombie Walk," *Journal of Contemporary Anthropology* 1, no. 1 (2010): 49–71.

11 Sarah Juliet Lauro and Karen Embry, "A Zombie Manifesto: The Nonhuman Condition in the Era of Advanced Capitalism," *boundary 2* 35, no. 1 (2008): 85–108.

12 johnnytreehouse, "Wow …," Flickr, October 10, 2010. http://www.flickr.com/photos/johnnytreehouse/5071600124/ (accessed July 31, 2012).

13 Gavon Laessig, "Undead Like Me," Lawrence.com, October 27, 2008. http://www.lawrence.com/news/2008/oct/27/undead_like_me/ (accessed July 31, 2012).

14 aimeesque, "the twilight zone when the photographer and zombie in him met …," Flickr, June 11, 2011. http://www.flickr.com/photos/aimeesque/5831214815/in/photostream/ (accessed July 31, 2012).

15 suezq1342, "Toronto Zombie Walk 2009," Flickr, October 25, 2009. http://www.flickr.com/photos/suezq1342/4042990701/in/set-72157622535809385/ (accessed July 31, 2012); RedandJonny, "Toronto Zombie Walk 2009," Flickr. http://www.flickr.com/photos/suezq1342/4042990701/in/set-72157622535809385/ (accessed July 31, 2012).

16 Sherry Turkle, *Life on the Screen: Identity in the Age of the Internet* (New York: Simon and Schuster, 1995).

17 Michele White, *The Body and the Screen: Theories of Internet Spectatorship* (Cambridge, MA: The MIT Press, 2006).

18 Michael Hardt and Antonio Negri, *Multitude: War and Democracy in the Age of Empire* (New York: Penguin, 2004).

19 Wikipedia, "Zombie walk," June 4, 2011. http://en.wikipedia.org/wiki/Zombie_walk/

20 *Brisbane Times*, "Thousands of Undead Dance and Shuffle through Brisbane," October 25, 2010. http://www.brisbanetimes.com.au/queensland/thousands-of-undead-dance-and-shuffle-through-brisbane-20101025-16ziq.html/ (accessed July 31, 2012).

21 Margaret Robinson, as quoted in Urmee Khan, "Zombie World Record Broken in Nottingham," *The Telegraph*, October 31, 2008. http://www.telegraph.co.uk/news/newstopics/howaboutthat/3333085/Zombie-world-record-broken-in-Nottingham.html/ (accessed July 31, 2012).

22 Turkle, *Life on the Screen*; Peter Steiner, *The New Yorker* 69, no. 20 (July 5, 1993): 61.

23 sniderscion, "Toronto Zombie Walk 2008–6222," Flickr, October 19, 2008. http://www.flickr.com/photos/sniderscion/3003562957/ (accessed July 31, 2012).

24 dr_dustbunny, "the_infected: ZOMBIE WALK 2005," LiveJournal, August 28, 2005. http://community.livejournal.com/the__infected/14334.html/ (accessed July 31, 2012).

25 grayd80, "Zombie Bride!" Flickr, October 18, 2008. http://www.flickr.com/photos/22490363@N02/2957373462/ (accessed July 31, 2012).

26 david anderson, "Watch it burn ... together," Flickr, October 31, 2010. http://www.flickr.com/photos/venndiagram/5136832863/ (accessed July 31, 2012); david anderson, "Zombie bride," Flickr, October 31, 2010. http://www.flickr.com/photos/venndiagram/5133593724/in/set-72157625166586881/ (accessed July 31, 2012).

27 Sherril Horowitz Schuster, "Here Comes the Bride: Wedding Announcements and Bridal Norms," *Sociological Focus* 30, no. 3 (1997): 280.

28 Chrys Ingraham, *White Weddings: Romancing Heterosexuality in Popular Culture* (New York and London: Routledge, 1999), 100.

29 Photos by Mavis, "bride," Flickr, October 24, 2009. http://www.flickr.com/photos/portland_mike/4195260787/ (accessed July 31, 2012).

30 Tom Grinsfelder, "Messy Eater," Flickr, October 24, 2009. http://www.flickr.com/photos/grinsfelder/4043130594/in/set-72157622669588816/ (accessed July 31, 2012).

31 vanBuuren, "kiss the bride," Flickr, October 26, 2008. http://www.flickr.com/photos/bunnytek/2978549155/ (accessed July 31, 2012).

32 Ian Aberle, "Zombie Brides and Cool Rides (Dark)," Zombie Ambience, August 12, 2010. http://zombieambience.com/2010/08/zombie-brides-and-cool-rides-dark/ (accessed July 31, 2012).

33 ian, "Kissing Zombie Brides," Flickr, May 1, 2010. http://www.flickr.com/photos/ianaberle/4577128483/in/set-72157623865916387/ (accessed July 31, 2012).

34 reynolds.james.e, "Zombie Brides," Flickr, October 30, 2007. http://www.flickr.com/photos/revjim5000/1804831243/ (accessed July 31, 2012).

35 Ingraham, *White Weddings*, 139.

36 John Hartigan, Jr., "Establishing the Fact of Whiteness," *American Anthropologist* 99, no. 3 (1997): 495–505.

37 Ruth Frankenberg, "Introduction: Local Whitenesses, Localizing Whiteness," in *Displacing Whiteness: Essays in Social and Cultural Criticism*, (ed.) Ruth Frankenberg (Durham, NC: Duke University Press, 1997), 9.

38 George Lipsitz, "The Possessive Investment in Whiteness: Racialized Social Democracy and the 'White' Problem in American Studies," *American Quarterly* 47, no. 3 (1995): 369.

39 White, *The Body and the Screen*; Michele White, *Buy It Now: Lessons from eBay* (Durham, NC: Duke University Press, 2012).

40 Richard Dyer, *White* (London: Routledge, 1997), 210.

41 Dyer, *White*, 211.

42 kenndubeau, "Mr. & Mrs Zombie," Flickr. http://www.flickr.com/photos/wolfie/2770597212/in/set-72157606779725127/ (accessed July 31, 2012).

43 halfgeek, "Mr. & Mrs Zombie," Flickr. http://www.flickr.com/photos/wolfie/2770597212/in/set-72157606779725127/ (accessed July 31, 2012).

44 Jeffery Sobal, Caron Bove, and Barbara Rauschenbach, "Weight and Weddings: The Social Construction of Beautiful Brides," in *Interpreting Weight: The Social Management of Fatness and Thinness*, (ed.) Jeffery Sobal and Donna Maurer (New York: Aldine de Gruyter, 1999), 113–35.

45 halfgeek, "Nice Day for a White Wedding," Flickr, August 16, 2008. http://www.flickr.com/photos/49503138525@N01/2773204681/ (accessed July 31, 2012).

46 sebastien.barre, "Zombie Walk – Saratoga Springs, NY – 07, Sep – 30," Flickr, September 1, 2007. http://www.flickr.com/photos/altuwa/1847604474/in/set-72157602513733201/ (accessed July 31, 2012); Billy Idol, "White Wedding (Part One)," On *Billy Idol* [CD]. UK: Chrysalis Records, 1982.

47 killer blythes, "Zombie Bride," Flickr, October 10, 2009. http://www.flickr.com/photos/killerblythes/4001898893/ (accessed July 31, 2012).

48 Julie Burchill, *Girls on Film* (New York: Pantheon Books, 1986), 103.

49 sebastien.barre, "Zombie Walk – Saratoga Springs, NY – 07, Sep – 30," Flickr, September 1, 2007, http://www.flickr.com/photos/99706198@N00/1847604474/ (accessed July 31, 2012).

50 Kenneth V. Iserson, "Rigor Mortis and Other Postmortem Changes," Encyclopedia of Death and Dying. http://www.deathreference.com/Py-Se/Rigor-Mortis-and-Other-Postmortem-Changes.html/ (accessed July 31, 2012).

51 Jane Feuer, "The Concept of Live Television: Ontology as Ideology," in *Regarding Television: Critical Approaches – An Anthology*, (ed.) E. Ann

Kaplan (Los Angeles: The American Film Institute, 1983), 12–22; Michele White, "Television and Internet Differences by Design: Rendering Liveness, Presence, and Lived Space," *Convergence: The International Journal of Research into New Media Technologies* 12, no. 3 (2006): 341–55; Mimi White, "The Attractions of Television: Reconsidering Liveness," in *Mediaspace: Place, Scale, and Culture in a Media Age*, (eds) Nick Couldry and Anna McCarthy (New York: Routledge, 2004), 75–91.

52 Flickr, "Welcome to Flickr – Photo Sharing," May 19, 2012. http://www.flickr.com/ (accessed July 31, 2012).

53 vanBuuren, "kiss the bride," Flickr, October 26, 2008. http://www.flickr.com/photos/bunnytek/2978549155/ (accessed July 31, 2012).

PART THREE

Monstrous territories

14

Zombinations:

Reading the undead as debt and guilt in the national imaginary

Michael S. Drake

Ulrich Beck[1] has controversially used the metaphor of the zombie to refer to analytical categories of social science that no longer have an effective material basis in what he calls "second modernity." However, Beck's use of the concept has come under criticism for its premature diagnosis of the redundancy of categories such as class, nation, and the family for the analysis of contemporary society.[2] These forms appear to be evolving and even flourishing, rather than disappearing from society. This chapter will examine, as a test case, one category which seems particularly robust, that of nation.

My argument is that both Beck and his critics misunderstand the concept of zombie. This popular fictional figure actually provides us with a key concept for understanding contemporary social phenomena. "Zombies" are not inert husks, but get up and walk, creating mayhem, actively seeking to devour the flesh of the actual living members of society. In this sense, we can understand the self-conscious construction of neo-nationalisms in the age of globalization as zombification in a more exact sense. These nationalisms are "pure imaginaries," since the concept as a motivating force has become emancipated from the material conditions (mass society) which underpinned the "imaginary community" of modern national identity.[3] As a consequence, today's nationalists are fully aware of the performative character of their ideology, yet do it anyway.[4] Where modern nationalism as the expression of social and political conditions was, regardless of our value-judgments, extraordinarily productive, today's nationalisms consume the very society they misrepresent. Neo-nationalisms are all the more virulent because they are not expressions of underlying social formations and structures, but are only sustained by performative assertion. They fill the void that is left as globalization erodes the material conditions for the modern imagination of national community. Violence and destructiveness, rather than governance and productiveness, thus becomes their mode of operation.

Beck's metaphorical deployment of the concept of the "zombie" fails because he draws on an outdated anthropological understanding of the term emanating from the outward gaze of "first modernity,"[5] or industrial society, which perceived the world outside itself as primitive, atavistic, doomed, and pathetic. This concept of the zombie understands it as husk, all but inanimate and lacking vitality. It corresponds to the way that modern people perceived pre-modern societies, as inadequate, ossified, irrelevant, a danger only in so far as they could be mobilized by modern experts turned deviant or demonic, such as the ideologues of fascism or communism

In contrast, Beck's "second modernity"[6] has produced a more reflexive concept of the zombie, beginning with George Romero's 1968 movie and coming into sharper focus in the 1978 *Dawn of the Dead*, an analogy of the "risks" or anxieties which consumer society presents to itself, developing through to films such as *28 Days Later* with its accelerated zombies reflecting the increasingly desperate hyper-consumers of terminal credit-based capitalism,[7] or Wright's spoof parody of the (at least in Romero's case) already deliberately self-parodic genre, *Shaun of the Dead*,[8] with its critically reflexive observations on contemporary British culture and masculinity, and also literary representations such as Lindqvist's *Handling the Undead*,[9] with its zombie telepathy as an analogy of contemporary social networking.

The concept of zombie as empty husk motivated by a controlling *expert* master articulates the fears of a modernity characterized by dependence on specialist expert knowledge.[10] Beck's use of the zombie metaphor thus stays close to an analysis of his own *first* modernity, failing to recognize the *independent* life of these fictions in the popular social imagination of his second, reflexive, modernity, where the material conditions of "zombie categories" have eroded away but the appeal of their fiction is more powerful than ever. Beck thus neglects the actuality, the political effect (regardless of validity) of "zombie concepts."

Zombie genealogy

David Inglis[11] recently situated shifting conceptions of the zombie in the context of cultural and intellectual history. He focuses on the failed attempts of the anthropologist Wade Davis "to redefine the zombi such that it would be seen not as a folkloric figment of the imagination but rather as a living reality," on the basis of his fieldwork in Haiti (conducted in the 1980s context of widespread belief that AIDS had been introduced from that island, associated with bloody Voodoo ceremonies, into the U.S.A.). Inglis argues that the failure of Davis's intellectual endeavor illustrates "general Western cultural resistance to the possibility of taking zombi(e)s too seriously."[12] Tracing the concept of the zombi(e) back to its historical roots in Haitian society, Inglis points out the striking differences between the figure in the Vodou belief system and that of our popular culture, "The Haitian fear is not *of* zombis ... the fear is instead of becoming a zombie ... the zombie very much expresses ex-slaves' fear of a return to the horrors of an enslaved condition."[13] The concept thus arises from and expresses a particular "social-cultural-legal constellation" and the collective memory of a society that had emancipated itself from slavery in a revolutionary but highly insecure and isolated form. The obvious question to ask is can we not, then, read the zombies of contemporary popular cultures as equally insightful analogies of particular societal constellations and their fears and collective memory? Inglis in fact sketches such insights in discussing how white Western appropriations of the figure of the zombi in pulp fiction and horror movies (in which it became the zombie), resonated with "the dehumanising and deadening effects of large-scale factory labour ... of the 1930s and 1940s," and simultaneously bore racist and culturalist connotations of the danger inherent in supposedly primitive, emotionally unrestrained, and irrational exoticism of black (Afro-)Caribbean bodies and culture.[14]

Critical studies of the revived zombie genre from the seminal 1968 release of George Romero's *Night of the Living Dead* have extensively analysed the subsequent series of Romero's films, and the wider genre that has proliferated infectiously around the figure of an increasingly accelerated and aggressively anthropophagic risen dead, as a satirical analogy of consumer capitalism of the late twentieth and early twenty-first centuries. Critical perspectives have spread from academia into an increasingly reflective popular culture itself, where they have become recommodified, with the effect that the genre has ossified, its ironic critique blunted with self-conscious and deliberately signposted allusions, so that zombie films and novels are clearly and explicitly produced to capture a niche market in satirical representation, as with the novel *World War Z*.[15] which was enthusiastically adopted as course text for security studies in one English University because it so accurately depicts real plans and likely outcomes of governmental securitizing responses to national emergency, while zombie mash-up rewritings of classics, such as *Pride and Prejudice and Zombies*[16] seem aimed at the market of the high school and undergraduate English literature students who are compelled to dissect and ingest the original texts.

The zombie genre is thus inherently critically parodic, an ironic reflection on the conditions of critique itself as an academicized production that has achieved successful cross-over into popular culture. However, it is in precisely this form, acknowledging this in all its reflexivity, that we can begin to re-read the genre for insights into our own, ironically reflexive social conditions and collective consciousness. The proliferation of Beck's use of the term as critical shorthand for an empty category has passed into global media with its widespread deployment to describe "zombie economy," "zombie politics," and even "zombie war." Such journalistic usage remains relatively close to Beck's, but popular culture has itself inventively taken up the term in more reflexively critical ways. Typing "Beck zombie" as keywords into an online search engine produces results that include Diane Reay's use of the concept to designate the persistence of social class inequalities in the English educational system—"a potential monster that grows in proportion to its neglect"[17]—in a straight-faced critique of Beck for abandoning the classical categories of nineteenth-century sociology, alongside hits for Howie Beck's spoof emo-singer-songwriter recording ("Zombie Girl"), and links to an online video game in which you can kill a zombie avatar of U.S. Republican Tea Party spokesperson Glenn Beck ("Tea Party Zombies Must Die"). The spoofing element in the genre has inspired "zombie walks" and street theater protests on a global scale. In the U.K., the Freedom of Information Act has been used to debunk the securitizing paranoia of contemporary governmentality by requiring local authorities to divulge what plans they have made to respond in case of zombie attacks, a critical-satirical strategy that bureaucracy has only been able to deal with at face value, inevitably invoking resultant public ridicule.[18]

I suggest that the contemporary zombie concept and genre, as both a reflection and an active, constructive part of our contemporary political strategies, can, following Inglis, provide us with insights into our own "socio-cultural-legal constellation," particularly into aspects of the cultural conditions of national identity in a globalizing world where the material foundations of the classical conception of nationalism, as analyzed by Anderson,[19] have eroded. I want to undertake this exercise through an analysis of one novel which, to some extent, subverts the zombie genre itself, acting as an auto-critique even of the reflexivity of the contemporary figure, and therefore representing an anticipation of the terminality of the twenty-first-century implosion of both zombie critique and credit-consumer society, where postmodern irony and reflexivity turn parasitic upon themselves.

The reliving, debt, and *ressentiment*

John Ajvide Lindqvist's novel *Let the Right One In*, and the Swedish movie of the novel,[20] are about the dangers of the abnormal and the horror of everyday normality from a child's point of view. Lindqvist's *Handling the Undead*, in contrast, deals with adult intimacy, emotional parenthood, and the inner life, turned suddenly into something almost (but not entirely) alien, repulsive yet irresistible. It is a novel about the perversity and futility of hope. It is also about debt. Published in Swedish in 2005, it offers us an unconscious reflection on debt and the impossibility of ever repaying indebtedness from the spectacular vantage of the time of the global credit-fueled boom, illuminated by the dancing pyres of the *auto-da-fé* of the commodity form, the rave which at one climactic point is emulated by the undead to unheard music by the eerie lights of a suburban dormitory housing complex. At one level, the novel is about the debt we owe the dead and how life is lived and the self is continuously constructed on credit we appropriate to ourselves, and what happens when we are confronted with payback time as the dead call for their due, not in the rabidly flesh-consuming form of the mainstream contemporary zombie genre, but by playing on our needs and our desires, calling us from within, from the mortgaged heart, from our emotional avarice, our inflationary need for satisfaction, for validation, for affirmation of *me*. The (risen) dead around whom the novel revolves are not only the parents, the older generation, but also spouses and even a child, indicating how the self of the credit-consumer society drew not only on the accumulated sacrifices of the past, but also mortgaged a future we assumed to be ever-increasingly bountiful. The grief ensuing on the reappearance of these dead, albeit as merely semi-animated insensate and dessicated respiring relics evokes at first a torrent of guilt, then anger. This is Nietzschean debt, procuring *ressentiment* in which resentment against perceived oppression becomes moralized as good and evil,[21] spilling over into violence that magnifies itself, refracted through the dead themselves, in which abjection becomes a virulent, malevolent destructiveness. It is our resentment of ourselves for our over-consumption of credit, and our *ressentiment* of our parent's generation for bringing us up to expect that everything was always going to get better, and then our anger at being made to feel guilty when we (the 99 percent identified by the Occupy

Movement) feel we did no evil, but only acted as good consumers, as we all-too-eagerly assumed we were expected to.

In Lindqvist's novel the emotive force is not, as in the mainstream zombie genre, the resentment of the undead against the living, but rather the *ressentiment* of the living for the undead, who represent the socially marginal, those unable to consume independently, in their guilt-invoking neediness, their apathetic helplessness. In the climactic scene of the novel the undead, dancing under the phosphorescent glow of the street lamps in their forlorn and otherwise abandoned housing complex, are attacked by a group of yuppie-type young men armed with the ubiquitous weaponry of consumerist violence, pool cues and baseball bats. It thus turns out to be not the dead, but the living, in particular young professional men, who are brutal, imbued with a lust for the entertainment to be had in destructive consumption of this demanding, needy, non-productive, uninstrumentalizable flesh, which fills them with revulsion as the Other to their own half-lived lives and totally commodified selves. Unlike the zombies of Romero and the contemporary mainstream genre, Lindqvist's undead are anything but animated; they are rather radically decelerated, initially entropic rather than dynamic. However, while the mainstream zombie is animated by a lust to devour living flesh, Lindqvist's undead (or reliving as they are also called by a society searching for a morally positive terminology) are animated by the affective force of those around them.

The novel shifts its viewpoints between a cast of characters, pursuing simultaneous narratives calibrated in the text by intervening date–timed official and media reports. Following some freak weather and inexplicable electrical effects in the Stockholm area, it is discovered that the recently deceased have arisen from their graves, deathbeds, and mortuaries, though without any restoration of the body, so they appear bearing all signs of the cause of their death and the effects of any subsequent bodily decomposition. Romero's film figured the dead as consumers, notable in the comments of one of the living characters in response to the question of why so many zombies appear at an out-of-town shopping mall that it is "as if they were programmed to come here, a sort of folk memory imprinted in the body."[22] In Lindqvist's novel the undead head for home, unerringly loyal in their reanimated life to their domesticity, to *Heimat*, to the myth of a Scandinavian consumerism oriented toward quality of life rather than the quantificatory consumption of the American dream. Just as Romero's zombies seek living flesh in the malls associated with consumerism, and Wright's zombies apparently seek it in the pub as similarly emblematic of the consumption of nostalgia of a remembered past, so Lindqvist's undead seek their affective charge in the heart of a heartless world, the domestic home (which is also of course itself emblematic of the consumption of Scandinavian and especially Swedish identity, globally marketed in Ikea's displacement of Laura Ashley as the iconic domestic design of the "new capitalism").

The undead Other

Among his textual strategies in *Handling the Undead*, Lindqvist employs batteries of standard sci-fi/horror tropes which in themselves are indicative of contemporary cultural anxieties (such as T.V.s that won't turn off but broadcast messages that seem to exert some control over those watching them, especially the housebound). However, while in classic sci-fi such phenomena constitute the narrative, in *Handling the Undead* these are merely devices, deployed like the gadgets we use in everyday life to connect up to a global communicative consciousness, as plug-ins, making of ourselves another modality, another modulation in the flow of communicative energy. One of the most significant novelties of Lindqvist's de-exoticized (and hence post-colonial, domesticized) undead is their telepathy, an attribute which extends as a field in their vicinity, much like wi-fi. In the presence of the undead, the living can hear each other's thoughts as well as sense the presence of these newly risen. However, the undead express no desires. It is assumed that they should be guided to rehabilitation, normalization, or, in the model of multiculturalism, a recognition of Otherness which results in their eventual ghettoization.

The most disturbing element of immigration for liberal societies (or at least for those elements of them that are not prepared to abandon their long-cherished egalitarian humanism and collapse into atavistic fantasy), is the sense of unease that ethnic, rather than racial, ideological, or sociological difference creates for the liberal conscience itself. The confrontation of the liberal abstraction of the Other with its embodied actuality has produced politically excessive reaction in precisely those national communities most traditionally committed to liberal inclusivism, most notoriously in the massacre committed by Anders Breivik in Norway in 2011, but also in the deliberately provocative rhetoric of the mainstream libertarian right in Denmark and the Netherlands, and of the Tea Party in the U.S.A. The undead are the manifold Other of the liberal conscience: ethnic minority, irreformable underclass, proletariat of the past, spoiled consumers, and ultimately the echoing, telepathized voice of contemporary self-consuming society itself. It is in the *crise de conscience* invoked by the undead Other, Lindqvist tells us, that we come to confront the *ressentiment* lurking at the heart of liberal good conscience. The relation of the living to the dead thus moves across the novel from the initial articulation that "Ultimately, this is about love,"[23] through hope, frustration, fear, and finally the stark alternatives of pity or violence. The virtual approximation to telepathy that is effected by the intensive use of social networking sites such as Facebook, a shared stream of consciousness, has shown that learning of the impulsive desires (or disgust) of others does not produce a happy consciousness, but the unhappy consciousness of mutually-shared self-loathing consequent on turning the inside out. The zombie telepathy in *Handling the Undead* evokes and explores this adeptly, revealing that what becomes shared in the empathic telecommunication to which Facebook approximates is not a deliberating cosmopolitan consciousness, the thinking of globalized philosophy,[24] but simply information about individuals' states of mind. Contrary to cosmopolitan hopes, the network society privileges affect over reason, affront over empathy.

Lindqvist's risen, the reliving or undead, personify the past both as dead weight and as the conscience of the living, who are connected by their presence at a level beyond normal communication. In this sense, the telepathy produced by the undead recalls the classical nationalist consciousness imagined by Herder and further refined by subsequent ideologists of the *volk*, the nation that is a naturally integrated entity at once biopolitical, cultural, and cognitive. In modernity, of course, that connectivity between citizens was manifest in social structures and national communicative infrastructures, in the provision of services, postage stamps, currency, newspapers, in the entire apparatus of the state and most of commerce too. The "imagined community" of the nineteenth and much of the twentieth century was a reality as well as an actuality. In the modern ideology of nationalism, that connectivity was imagined as natural; today, Lindqvist's novel suggests, such connectivity can only be imagined as *super*natural, as a telepathy between individuals and contending consciousnesses, rather than as a singular common consciousness of the nationalist masses.

Lindqvist's novel thus also hints, through its implicit analogy between telepathy and social networking, at the shift in the site of nationalist construction, of the imaginary itself, from the streets and broadsheets of the modern public sphere to the blogs, tweets, comments postings, websites, and network pages of the virtual public sphere of today, which is a public space of privatized, individualized consumers, where public pronouncement serves private interests. In Lindqvist's account of a Sweden that is alienated to itself, the ethnoscapes of the nation are transformed into their opposite, so the islands of memory and the reproduction of heritage become the haunts of a malevolent nightmare rather than the slow dreamtime of imagined tradition, while the welfare clinic-cum-housing estate becomes a concentration camp, converting rational hygiene into fearful quarantine.

Ethnoscapes and the repressed of national consciousness

It is interesting that Lindqvist's novel reaches its dual dramatic denouement in two settings emblematic of Scandinavian—and in particular Swedish—cultural identity; on the one hand in the archipelagic islands of the Scandinavian Baltic's fjordline coast, the *hemland* of cultural memory where the two characters who have absconded with their reliving undead child take refuge in their family summer house, in a flight from the state that is uncalculated, chaotic, and spontaneous, analogous to the flight of the middle classes from the urban environment of state-interventionism, and ultimately tragically catastrophic. The other climactic setting is the socio-psycho-sanitarily integrated housing complex of the welfare state, where the "reliving" (it is initially hoped) will be studied, made to yield up their secrets through the disciplinary apparatus of benign specialists in normalisation—clinicians, psychologists, social workers, speech therapists, etc., and at least "cared for," in the sense that the state always takes care of the bodies entrusted to its biopolitical expertise. However, when the state realizes it can do nothing for the undead, they are abandoned. In a militarized evacuation, the living exit from the secluded housing complex, just as the neoliberalized state abandons (often under the auspices of criminalization and cultural demonization) the long-term unemployed, the lumpen underclass who have proven resistant to 50-plus years of welfare state intervention. *Handling the Undead* thus simply accelerates the logic of the latent liberalism at the heart of social democratic strategies of social reform. Ultimately, *these* undead burn in a conflagration lit by yuppie hooligans, but which they themselves have unwittingly and nihilistically provoked.

Opposed to that logic, and to the violent *ressentiment* of the yuppie attackers, Lindqvist observes only a directionless, emotive moralism, as in the political resistances of our time, in the Anti-War campaigns and the Occupy movement, ultimately dependent on the *deus ex machina* of a higher, saving power to restore the world to moral order in which the dead stay dead. The novel's denouement among the archipelagic islands provides another incisive insight, perhaps even bleaker because devoid of redemption, into the soul of post-national cultural identity.

Left alone on the island, because her father has, after a furious disagreement, gone for fuel (the sub-scene itself a critical commentary on gender roles in the face of crisis), the mother of the undead boy is terrorized by a monster risen from the depths, the resurrected body of a drowned sailor. The idyllic archipelago of imagined cultural memory then becomes a template for the nightmarish return of the repressed of the national past it represents, the forgotten body of the dispensable proletariat, on whose labor the luxurious lifestyles of today are built, but which is unacknowledged in the national-cultural imaginary entertained as the heritage of a conspicuously consumerist generation for whom access to a summerhouse on the sea islands has become an unquestioned right, an aspect of their self-identification. The very texture and fabric of that culturally selective memory, so crucial to its totalizing integrity—the textural grain of wood, the frames of windows, planks, stoves, pipes, slates, and the flora and microgeography of the islands, renowned through their evocation in cult-status work such as Tove Jansson's *Summer Book*, or the films from Ingmar Bergman's Fårö island studios—become instead the elements of nightmare, as if the screen on which we project the dreams of the present is suddenly ripped in half to reveal a horror beneath. That horror, moreover, is animated by the fearfulness of the undead boy's mother, the seeker of condolence and security in cultural memory.

The fear of the young professional men at the repulsive emotive affect invoked by the needy, hapless undead had motivated the ageing cadavers to become almost reluctant vigilantes of their own secluded degeneration, and the mother's fear of the vast, mutilated, bloated white corpse of the drowned proletarian motivates it to destructive frenzy akin to the riots of our recession era. Significantly, the undead mariner kills not the mother, but her father, when he returns, without fuel, and adopts a masculine strategy of aggressive defense to protect his daughter and his reliving grandson, but slips and falls, rendering himself helpless to the proletarian monster's more adept reflection of his own aggressivity in its enactment of violent revenge upon the morally self-righteous middle class.

The resistant remainder

In the book's other, narrative thread, the helplessness, or at least the neediness, of the reliving dead also indicates their function as the conscience of the nation, a tangible reminder of the nationally-definitive welfare state project of Sweden under social democratic hegemony for much of the twentieth century. From the initial confusion produced by the appearance of the reliving dead, a consensus rapidly emerges in the impulse to normalize the anomaly they represent. At both individual and institutional levels, everything that is discovered about the reliving becomes framed in these terms. The aim becomes that applied to all deviant categories within the inherently normative societies of a welfare state that infers the needs of its subjects: to approximate all deviations to a norm, regardless of the result becoming a grotesque parody of the normal. Previously applied to the physically and mentally disabled, especially when young, this same logic of course is currently extended to another category of bodies analogous to the reliving of Lindqvist's novel, Alzheimer sufferers "treated" within complexes which purportedly restore the presence of this anomalous category of bodies within society to a semblance of normality, at least as long as the doors of the institutions housing them are kept closed, a normalization of abnormalization which empties out the moral significance of welfare.

Moreover, when the reliving dead (the resurrected remainder of the recipients of welfare) are left to themselves, when the state withdraws, "abandoning" them in the complex built to sequester them from society, they begin to manifest a "culture" of their own, a mysterious macabre dance of the undead that is witnessed by a psychic character in the novel. The efforts of this would-be salvationist to offer empathy are frustrated not by the state (whose barriers around the complex are more symbolic than physical, as though a kind of magical exclusion which makes social problems simply disappear), but by representatives of the laddish, yobbish, extra-professional culture of credit capitalism and its "corporate entertainment" itinerary of bars, strip joints, and the liminal bodies and spaces of the night-time economy. Their aim is to engage in some "recreational" baseball-bat-wielding bloodsports against the helpless, dependent dead, who, with the nihilistic viciousness of the downtrodden, oblige by quite literally biting back, fulfilling every prejudice of those who came to beat and mock them even as they resist their imposed role as passive object of sadistic entertainment.

Conclusion

Lindqvist's novel thus offers us an example of the way that the zombie metaphor is a more powerful analytical tool than is acknowledged by either Beck or his critics, who share the dismissive conception of the concept as an empty category. Lindqvist's mobilization of the concept reveals how popular culture, with its deployment of analogy, metaphor, simile can provide us with insights that are simply overlooked by literal-minded sociological analysis. Metaphors, like that of the zombie, resonate in a popular culture that repro-duces itself and knowledgeably constructs the identities it represents, aware of its own strategies and effects. The zombie is of course a fiction, but that gives its deployment in strategies of protest and resistance, and as a concept for critical analysis, such perspicacity for a globalizing, liquid world in which the imaginary has come to stand in for the material anchors of consciousness in modernity.

The contemporary popularity of the zombie genre may also reflect fears of de-individualization produced in the context of the perceived insecurity of individualization processes analyzed by Beck and others.[25] Ours is not an especially insecure age, but industrial society's fearful fantasies of totalitarianism and ideological mind-control have perhaps today been displaced by fantasies of depersonalization, which have been rendered more fraught by the implosion of credit-card capitalism in the twentieth century, as unquestioning access to secure systems has increasingly brought more and more elements of consumer society, not merely the dispossessed, up against the foreclosure of expected opportunities. The erosion of that disciplinary order produced apparently irreversible emancipation processes and the hyper-individualization of global consumer society.[26] but the loss of the certainties of the past produced by disciplinary apparatuses in which each knew their place is now experienced both as nostalgia and as nightmare, encapsulated in the concept of the zombie, or, in Lindqvist's novel, the reliving undead. In the attention that the novel is able to give to the exploration of the inner life of characters, it functions more effectively than the sweeping macro-sociology of Beck or indeed the methodologically handicapped microsocial approaches of interpretive sociology, proving more adept in tracing the inner workings of nostalgia and terror, guilt and fear, through to their implosion in violent *ressentiment*, whether in the form of cultural fantasy of affect or social democratic-liberal rationalization. Zombie then becomes simply the name we can give to an illness of which we suffer the symptoms.

Notes

1 Ulrich Beck and Elizabeth Beck-Gernsheim, *Individualization: Institutionalized Individualism and its Social and Political Consequences* (London: Sage Publications (in association with Theory, Culture & Society), 2002).

2 For instance, Daniel Chernilo, *A Social Theory of the Nation State: The Political Forms of Modernity Beyond Methodological Nationalism* (London: Routledge, 2007); and Diane Reay, "The Zombie Stalking English Schools: Social Class and Educational Inequality," *British Journal of Educational Studies* 54 (2006): 288–307.

3 Benedict Anderson, *Imagined Communities: Reflections on the Origins and Spread of Nationalism* (London: Verso, 1983).

4 Slavoj Zizek, "Invisible ideology: political violence between fiction and fantasy," *Journal of Political Ideologies* 1 (1996): 15–32.

5 Ulrich Beck and Christoph Lau, "Second modernity as a research agenda: Theoretical and empirical explorations in the 'meta-change' of modern society," *British Journal of Sociology* 56 (2005): 525–57.

6 Beck and Lau, "Second modernity," passim.

7 Richard Sennett, *The Culture of the New Capitalism* (Connecticutt, NJ: Yale University Press, 2006).

8 Edgar Wright (dir.), *Shaun of the Dead*. London: Universal Pictures (UK), 2004.

9 John Ajvide Lindqvist, *Handling the Undead*, trans. Ebba Segerburg (London: Quercus, 2009).

10 Ulrich Beck, *Risk Society: Towards a New Modernity* (London: Sage, 1992); and Anthony Giddens, *Modernity and Self-identity: Self and Society in the Late Modern Age* (Cambridge: Polity Press, 1991).

11 David Inglis, "The Zombie from Myth to Reality: Wade Davis, Academic Scandal and the Limits of the Real," *SCRIPTed* 7 (2010): 351–69.

12 Inglis, "The Zombie," 353.

13 Inglis, "The Zombie," 354.

14 Inglis, "The Zombie," 355–7.

15 Max Brooks, *World War Z* (London: Gerald Duckworth, 2007).

16 Jane Austen and Seth Grahame-Smith, *Pride and Prejudice and Zombies* (Philadelphia: Quirk, 2009).

17 Reay, "The Zombie," 289.

18 BBC News, June 10, 2011, "Leicester City Council 'not ready' for zombie attack," http://www.bbc.co.uk/news/uk-england-leicestershire-13713798 (accessed February 23, 2012); and Steven Morris, "When zombies attack! Bristol City Council ready for undead invasion," *The Guardian*, July 7, 2011, http://www.guardian.co.uk/society/2011/jul/07/when-zombies-attack-bristol-city-council-undead-invasion (accessed February 23, 2012).

19 Anderson, *Imagined Communities*.

20 Tomas Alfredson, *Let the Right One In*, Momentum Pictures, 2008.

21 Friedrich Nietzsche, *On the Genealogy of Morality and Ecce Homo*, trans. Walter Kaufmann (New York: Vintage Books, 1990).

22 George Romero, *Dawn of theDead*, United Film Distribution Company, 1978.

23 Lindqvist, *Handling the Undead*, 128.

24 Ulrich Beck, *Cosmopolitan Vision* (Cambridge: Polity Press, 2006).

25 Ulrich Beck, Anthony Giddens, and Scott Lash, *Reflexive Modernization: Politics, Tradition and Aesthetics in the Modern Social Order* (Cambridge: Polity Press, 1994).

26 Anthony Giddens, *Runaway World* (London: Profile Books, 1999).

15

The monster within:

Post-9/11 narratives of threat and the U.S. shifting terrain of terror

Mary K. Bloodsworth-Lugo and Carmen R. Lugo-Lugo

Tales of a battle between good and evil must depict the world as a threatening or even terrifying place, full of monsters. That alone would be enough to make people feel insecure. But there is more. The stories always imply (and often say quite openly) that the monsters can never be destroyed. The best to hope for is to build a stout defense against them, one strong enough to keep them from destroying us. The monsters may be contained. But their threat will never go away.[1]

Terror and vigilance: Post-9/11 monstrous constructions

Taken from *Monsters to Destroy: The Neoconservative War on Terror and Sin* by Ira Chernus, the opening epigraph speaks to both historical and contemporary (post-9/11) articulations of the quintessential conflict between good and evil as they are embedded within U.S. ideologies. Within the post-9/11 era, the (American) battle with evil entails a conflict with the (un-American) monstrous or "terrorist" body. We can locate formulations, and ideological articulations, of the constant—but ever-changing—battle described by Chernus within the rhetorical techniques deployed by former President George W. Bush during his time in office. Rhetorical strategies of the Bush administration are of central importance to the present discussion, since their immediate articulation and consistent deployment as a response to the events of September 11, 2001 helped to shape the post-9/11 American lens. In fact, this lens still informs the American landscape and provides an enduring feature of our national discourse, even in the wake of the country's election of its "first Black president," Barack Obama, and a change of national leadership in 2008–9.[2]

As we argue elsewhere, the repetition of an "us versus them" discourse, initiated by President Bush and his administration but continuing beyond it, promoted a pattern of discourse linking perceived "outside" threats (namely, Muslim extremists and countries "harboring terrorists") with perceived "inside" threats (namely, same-sex couples and "illegal" immigrants).[3] This language not only merged otherwise separate and distinct issues, it reinforced a series of oppositional pairings (for example, inside/outside and safety/threat), enabling the American public to conceive of the United States as a vulnerable place in light of the events of September 11, 2001. The discourse likewise constructed the American people, the country, and even (Western) civilization itself as requiring vigilant protection.[4] Security and protection became synonymous with containing threats—threats residing in uncertain places ("lurking in shadows") and potentially harming from within ("lingering among us").

After several years of diligent enemy construction during his administration, President Bush warned in his 2007 State of the Union Address: "By killing and terrorizing Americans, [our enemies] want to force our country to retreat from the world and abandon the cause of liberty. They would then be free to impose their will and spread their totalitarian ideology."[5] He added: "It remains the policy of this government to use every lawful and proper tool of intelligence, diplomacy, law enforcement, and military action to do our duty, to find these enemies, and to protect the American people."[6] September 11, 2001 was dubbed "The day that changed America," and the change that America endured became synonymous with a specific perception and response to perceived threats. Keeping with Chernus, we could say that the construction of these very threats captured and promoted a certain conception and perception of post-9/11 monsters for the American public.

President Bush's speeches, throughout his time in office, convey this monster as a cruel opponent of freedom—placing no value on life and aiming to impose an empire of oppression with brutal rulers to terrorize and kill Americans. According to Richard Jackson, "the [Bush] administration was quick to identify the terrorists as 'evil,' 'savage,' 'cruel,' 'cowardly,' 'inhuman,' 'hate-filled,' 'perverted,' and 'alien'."[7] Jackson identifies two central features of this monstrous narrative pertinent to the present chapter: first, the suggestion of "a massive, global terrorist threat against Americans and their way of life," as well as civilization more broadly construed; and second, the invocation of the "notion of 'the enemy within'," implying that the American public "should remain watchful of fellow citizens, and that measures designed to restrict liberties, increase surveillance on U.S. citizens and immigrants, and further militarize American society were necessary to counter the threat of these internal enemies."[8] We will return to Jackson's notion of "the enemy within" shortly, as it specifically informs our analysis of films in the present chapter.

Post-9/11 films have developed their narratives within this context. Many of the unfolding stories within these films reflect American fears and anxieties even if the films themselves do not directly address the events of September 11, 2001. Thomas Pollard argues that filmmakers responded to the events of September 11, 2001 "by producing some of the most pessimistic, violent, cynical movies of all time," while simultaneously projecting "powerful fantasy heroes capable of redressing all wrongs."[9] This state of affairs leads Pollard to conclude that, "apparently, widespread fear engenders strong characters, pessimistic moods, critical examinations of intelligence agencies, and a cynical perspective on a variety of social institutions including U.S. corporations, military, and government."[10] Jonathan Markovitz suggests: "Hollywood has a long history of turning widespread fears into cinematic spectacles, but never before has the source of those fears been so singular, so easily isolated, or so thoroughly disseminated to national and international audiences."[11] And Kyle Bishop argues, "The terrorist attacks of September 11, 2001 caused perhaps the largest wave of paranoia for Americans since the McCarthy era. Since the beginning of the war on terror, American popular culture has been colored by the fear of possible terrorist attacks and the grim realization that people are not as safe and secure as they might have once thought."[12]

These and other critical media scholars point out that post-9/11 films have developed the discourse and ideology of "9/11," as well as critiques of this framework, without specifically referencing the events of September 11, 2001. Post-9/11 films have examined American anxieties in the wake of a "changed America," including how Americans might respond to and ultimately cope with an increasing number of post-9/11 "monsters," while simultaneously relegating September 11, 2001 itself to an unspoken background. Antonio Sanchez-Escalonilla notes that, in the fictional works of Hollywood, "though direct references to the tragic day are avoided, there is a hypothetical discourse of contribution to the political debate, and often solutions are suggested to alleviate the social fractures, but always in the guise of entertainment."[13] Jackson claims that "[actions and events] take on different kinds and levels of meaning for a political community through processes of interpretation and social narration, usually by the powerful symbolic actors authorized to speak on behalf of the whole community."[14]

In this chapter, we explore connections between post-9/11 articulations of monstrosity and their representation in recent Hollywood films. We agree with Bishop's view, when commenting on post-9/11 zombie films, that, while central "plot elements and motifs are present in pre-9/11 zombie films, they have become more relevant to a modern, contemporary audience." We maintain that, while "genre protocols" may offer consistency pre- and post-9/11, ways of managing fears and anxieties assume a particular relevance to post-9/11 American audiences. We focus our analysis on three films: *Flightplan*,[16] *Lakeview Terrace*,[17] and *The Brave One*.[18] Each film presents a specific post-9/11 "problem," as well as an enacted "solution," that underscore themes of terror and vigilance in a post-9/11 world.

Keeping with Jackson, we link an examination of "the enemy within" to post-9/11 monstrosity in two particular ways: the monster as "person" and the monster as "place." We note a movement, or a transformation, from familiar terrain (knowledge of oneself, expectations around the role of authority figures, or the look and feel of one's city or neighborhood) to unfamiliar territory (becoming a stranger to oneself, being threatened by those with authority, or facing insecurity within one's typical place of comfort). Moreover, we observe a betrayal of borders and boundaries—an invasion of the familiar—within these and similar films. This betrayal demonstrates new anxieties (or a new inflection to particular fears and anxieties) within a post-9/11 United States.[19]

Flightplan: The monster on board

The film *Flightplan* develops the uncertainty of threats "lurking in shadows" and "lingering among us" in relation to an American mother, Kyle Pratt (Jodie Foster), who is attempting to protect and recover her six-year-old daughter, Julia, from an amorphous threat on board an airplane. Pratt, a propulsion engineer, is returning her dead husband's body to the United States from Germany when she loses her daughter on an Airjet—the "biggest plane of them all." Mirroring post-9/11 rhetoric of threats, the film presents a danger that is difficult to identify in so far as its source is unclear. Pratt spends the majority of the film attempting to determine the exact nature and cause of the threat, knowing only that her child is missing when she (Pratt) awakens from a nap.

The fact that Pratt is highly knowledgeable regarding the Airjet's structure and equipment casts her uncertainty about the daughter's whereabouts on the plane as all the more terrifying for audiences, since even within Pratt's familiar environment there lurks an undetected and ominous danger. To place the Airjet in the role of a post-9/11 United States, the plot suggests that citizens and even leaders of a country might be unable to account for threats lurking in the recesses of its borders, since monsters often have incomprehensible designs and sinister intentions. Pratt, and the film in general, attend to the perceived threat of any and all Muslims/Arabs as obvious post-9/11 sites of monster construction. As Manohla Dargis remarks, the film contains "some shameless nods to September 11."[20] This is displayed when the airplane's male Middle Eastern passengers are targeted, by Pratt, for her daughter's disappearance. Pratt conveys to the Air Marshall, Gene Carson (Peter Sarsgaard), after confronting one of these men, "I don't give a shit about being politically correct! I think they're highjacking the plane. I think my daughter's a hostage."[21]

While anxiously searching for her daughter, Pratt herself is turned into a safety threat given post-9/11 rules concerning airline passenger conduct. Carson is first to position Pratt this way when she attempts to barge into the cockpit after realizing her daughter is not in the passenger areas of the plane. Carson restrains Pratt and tells her, "I'm sorry I had to do that, but your behavior was constituting a threat to the safety of this aircraft."[22] Pratt then asks to enter the plane's cargo hold—again, knowing the plane's layout quite well and not seeing her daughter in the passenger areas. Carson offers to accompany her, but Captain Rich (Sean Bean) dismisses this suggestion, stating: "Mister Carson, I'm responsible for the safety of every passenger on this plane, even the delusional ones."[23] When Pratt voices her impatience with the Captain and crew, Captain Rich remarks: "There are 425 passengers on this flight who are NOT receiving any attention at the moment because every one of my flight attendants are [sic] looking for a child that none of them believe was ever on board."[24]

Pratt is declared mentally unstable after the crew searches for the girl within the plane's infrastructure, yielding no results. The Captain is handed an official document stating that the child was killed, along with Pratt's husband, when they both fell from the rooftop of their house in Germany. The paperwork, combined with the fact that Julia is not listed on the passenger manifest and no one remembers seeing her board the plane, convinces the Captain and crew that the child was never actually present. Instead, they infer that Pratt is suffering from extreme anxiety and grief, rendering her delusional. In turn, it is this delusion and its attendant behavior that constitute a threat. As Carson conveys, "I'm responsible for anything that might become a threat to the safety of this flight. Women with imaginary children qualify."[25]

Near the end of the film, the audience learns that the Air Marshall himself (along with a crew member accomplice) has kidnapped Pratt's daughter, hid her within the cargo hold of the plane, fabricated the paperwork deleting the child from the passenger manifest and documenting that she had died, and smuggled in explosives. Once Pratt realizes that Carson is the cause of her daughter's disappearance, she takes matters into her own hands. Pratt locates the child and the explosives in the avionics (where she has always thought the child was being hidden). After the plane has landed and she, her daughter, and the other passengers are secure, Pratt allows the explosives to detonate with Carson still inside the plane. We see Pratt transformed, during this one flight and its attendant ordeal, from an anxious and grieving widow/mother into a person capable of destroying a plane with someone else on board. Prior to her exit, Carson asks, "What are you gonna do? Blow us both up?" Pratt cooly and calmly responds, "No, just you."[26]

This film conveys to post-9/11 audiences that familiar spaces can quickly and radically transform into unfamiliar sites. With this transformation, one's sense of familiarity gives way to unfamiliarity—evoking a monstrous response. Carson is easily identifiable as the film's "bad guy" (at least, by the end of the film), and his "badness" is made all the more salient given the Air Marshall's role to protect the plane's passengers. This sort of danger "lingering among us" is one way in which the post-9/11 narrative has unfolded. However, it is Pratt's own transformation—from loving and grieving mother to person capable of destroying what she had designed (the plane) with Carson on board—that demonstrates an even more disturbing example of the "monster within." Unlike Carson who is killed at the end of the film (Pratt enacts a "solution" to his threat), Pratt's own monstrous transformation remains unresolved with the film's end.

Lakeview Terrace: The monster next door

Similar to *Flightplan*, *Lakeview Terrace* develops the notion of threats "lurking in shadows" and "lingering among us," primarily in relation to two characters. These characters are a police officer, Abel Turner (Samuel L. Jackson), and a supermarket chain executive, Chris Mattson (Patrick Wilson). With the tagline, "What could be safer than living next to a cop?"[27] the film is set in a suburban neighborhood in Southern California, and the plot is replete with racial and racist innuendo involving Turner who is Black, Mattson who is White, and Mattson's wife, Lisa (Kerry Washington) who is Black. Unlike Carson in *Flightplan*, who is only unveiled as a threat at the end of the film, the threat that Turner poses especially to Chris and Lisa—who have just moved in next door—is demonstrated early on. *Flightplan* and *Lakeview Terrace* are similar in that the person assigned to be protector (Air Marshall and police officer) instead transform into the monster they were supposed to guard against.

The audience receives a clear indication of Turner's views on racial mixing, the locus of his threat to the mixed-race couple, in an opening scene of the film. Here, Turner is detaining an informant (an overweight, white-looking man), and when the informant refers to Turner as "brother," the following exchange ensues:

Turner: Brother? Clarence, we ain't brothers. We didn't even crawl out of the same evolutionary pool. What are you, anyway? You know, always wondered about that. You a Euro-Mexi-Japa-Chine-stani or what? You don't even know, do you? Ain't got a clue.

Informant: Watch yourself.

Turner: You're a weed, that's what you are. A junkyard weed. Spray your ass with some Roundup.

Informant: I'm 1/7th Cherokee, bitch!

Turner: Yeah, and the other 93% wigger. Can you do the math on that, dumb ass?[28]

On Turner's first encounter with Mattson, it is Mattson's taste in music that grounds Turner's negative racial commentary. The audience sees that, as Mattson returns home from work, he is playing loud hip hop music in his car. After walking over to the car, introducing himself, and making a few crude remarks, Turner finally tells Mattson, "Say, you know, you can listen to that noise all night long, but when you wake up in the morning, you'll still be white."[29] And somewhat later in the film, while giving Mattson a tour of the neighborhood, Turner bluntly says, "You know, I got nothing against you. Or her. LAPD. I work with all kinds. I'd lay my life down for those guys. But that's where I work. This is where I live."[30]

Turner's desire for the couple to leave *his* neighborhood is expressed on multiple occasions and in ever-more threatening ways as the film progresses. The film highlights the escalating conflict between Turner and Mattson, as Mattson attempts to claim his role as protector of his family (Lisa is pregnant) and to reposition his authority as a white man within society. While the notion of a Black man posing a threat to a White person is not new (for example, historical notions of Black men as brutes or savages), what is new in *Lakeview Terrace* is the post-9/11 construction of this particular threat. Turner "resides within" the fold of the law, as cop, but uses that location and role to wield his own agenda—and that agenda plays out in the "nice" suburban neighborhood in which he and the couple live. As a Black cop making a threat against a mixed-race couple (primarily the White character, Mattson), the film's presentation of threat suggests an uncertainty given a sort of familiarity. That is, the threat resides in relation to a presumed protector and within one's own neighborhood. Additionally, the film implies that White Americans are on their own, in charge of protecting themselves and their families from the danger "lurking in the shadows of suburbia."[31] Here, suburbia is transformed from a familiar and safe place (for White folks, especially) into one that is housing monsters—monsters "lingering among us"—as close as next door.

Interestingly, the film also inverts history, since the threat that Blacks have faced at the hands of Whites dates to colonial times. This suggests that, in a post-9/11 America, White Americans—in particular—have experienced an unsettling territory in new ways. Like Kyle Pratt (discussed above) and Erica Bain (discussed below), Chris Mattson is himself transformed into something monstrous through his "solution" to the unfolding "problem." While he does not shoot and kill Abel Turner within the film, he is none the less quite ready to do so. Instead, Mattson allows Turner's colleagues to take the shot for him, resulting in Turner's death near the film's end. Mattson and his wife must find a way to "move on" after this "solution," leaving the ways in which Mattson has been transformed unresolved.

The Brave One: The monster inside

In *The Brave One*, the main character, Erica Bain (Jodie Foster), describes New York as "an organism that changes, mutates."[32] In a narration opening the film, she conveys:

> I'm Erica Bain. And as you know, I walk the city. I bitch and moan about it. I walk and watch and listen, a witness to all the beauty and ugliness that is disappearing from our beloved city. Last week took me to the gray depths of the East River where Dmitri Panchenko swims his morning laps, like he has every morning since the 1960s. And today I walked by the acres of scaffolding outside what used to be the Plaza Hotel. And I thought about Eloise. Remember Kay Thompson's Eloise? ... Stories of a city that is disappearing before our eyes. So what are we left of those stories? Are

we going to have to construct an imaginary city to house our memories? Because when you love something, every time a bit goes, you lose a piece of yourself.[33]

At the end of the narration, we learn that Bain has a radio show, "This is Erica Bain, and you've been listening to Streetwalk on WKNW."[34]

Bain's fiancé is beaten to death during a night-time stroll, with their dog, as the couple discusses their plans for marriage. Like the September 11, 2001 attacks on the city, the attack on the couple arrives "out of the blue," on a beautiful and otherwise normal day, with the sound of a passing airplane foreshadowing the horror of the event. With this event, Bain devolves into a "vigilante" killer—someone "fearing the place [she] once loved" and acting to protect the city and herself. She finds herself transformed into a stranger that both enacts justice for the death of her fiancé (killing eight men, including the three men who attacked her and her fiancé) and develops a close friendship with a detective, Mercer (Terrence Howard), who is investigating the deaths. Bain discovers in herself a monstrous inside to match a monstrous outside. She also faces an uncertain future involving an expanding array of monsters to destroy. However, she finds in herself a power she did not know existed.

Discussing the film, Claire S. King conveys how the trauma experienced by Bain can also be seen as an allegory of sorts invoking, constructing, and making sense "of national history and identity, framing 9/11 as a culturally traumatic event."[35] King continues:

Bain's assertions of mastery perform a fantasy of national resilience, and her transformation enacts the nation's attempts to convert itself from a feminized victim to a (re)masculinized agent. With her search for victims and stalking of predators recalling President Bush's commitment "to hunt down, to find, to smoke out of their holes" the terrorists he held responsible for 9/11, Bain's ability to remain "brave" rewrites the nation's response to perceived trauma and redresses what has been framed as weakness, or paternal failure, on the part of America …[36]

For our purposes, it is not the traumatic event (which can be described as "the day that changed Erica forever"), or her actions afterward (the ones that transformed her into "the stranger"), but Bain's understanding of and struggle with her own transformation that is most significant. The audience receives glimpses into her struggle throughout the film. For instance, Bain states: "It is astonishing, numbing to find that inside you there is a stranger. One that has your arms, your legs, your eyes. A sleepless, restless stranger who keeps walking, keeps eating, keeps living."[37] Upon returning to work, she conveys to her radio listeners:

I always believed that fear belonged to other people. Weaker people. It never touched me. And then it did. And when it touches you, you know that it's been there all along. Waiting beneath the surfaces of everything you loved. And your skin crawls, and your heart sickens, and you look at the person you once were walking down that street and you wonder will you … will you ever be her again?[38]

Bain conceptualizes the stranger as a thing. After killing her fourth victim, she remarks: "There is no going back to that other. She is gone. This thing, this stranger is all you are now."[39] At the end of the film, she repeats this statement with a slight modification: "There is no going back to that other person, that other place. This thing, this stranger, she is all you are now."[40] Bain's understanding of her own transformation, which turns her into a thing, "a monster," and places her somewhere else (for it is not the same city), is key, for it places the monster within a particular setting. Bain is not the same person, because New York is not the same city. When confronting her fiancé's killer, who had taken the couple's dog during the attack, she demands, "I want my dog back!"[41] in the way someone might remark, "I want my life back." In other words, "I want things restored to the way they were." While this restoration is not fully possible, the monster's enacting of revenge works to stabilize Bain's world. When facing a second of her assailants (who called Bain "bitch" during the assault, and re-named her stolen dog "Bitch"), Bain asks, as she shoots him, "Who is the bitch now?"[42]

The monster within: Concluding thoughts

The three films discussed above channel some of the anxieties developed by Americans after the events of September 11, 2001. *Flightplan*, *Lakeview Terrace*, and *The Brave One* can all be conceptualized as post-9/11 films, both in relation to their release dates (after 2001) and with respect to the issues central to their plots (threat and danger in a post-9/11 world). These films develop the discourse and ideologies of "9/11" without specifically addressing the events of September 11, 2001. By so doing, the films explore American anxieties in the wake of a "changed America," including how Americans might respond to and ultimately cope with an increasing number of post-9/11 "monsters." These films offer racialized and gendered lessons involving a post-9/11 United States, including issues of borders and boundaries as they engage with notions of American security and citizenship. All three films address instances in which things familiar (a plane one designed, the neighborhood in which one lives, a city one thinks one knows) transform into sources of fear and threat. The individuals in these films must take matters into their own hands, fighting various "monsters to destroy." As Chernus conveys, "monsters are not real—unless you believe in them. Monsters exist only in fictional stories. But if you really believe in the stories, you will believe in the monsters. Then the monsters will have very real effects. That's how monsters become real."[43]

Flightplan highlights the uncertainty or ambiguity of threats, as it simultaneously questions taken-for-granted understandings of reality. The film conveys to audiences that no one is safe under any circumstances and that "protectors" can pose a threat to one's safety and security as readily as more typical monsters. Kyle Pratt and her family suffer the consequences of a world in which people are not able to easily discern threats, where they are not able to trust authority, and where authority dismisses one's insecurity or reveals itself as the actual source of that anxiety. The only recourse a person might have, in such a context, is to blow up the monster after it is revealed. However, with this "solution" comes a transformation of one's self—a transformation into someone or something unrecognizable and (ironically, perhaps) itself monstrous.

Lakeview Terrace presents a scenario in which places that should offer security (one's neighborhood, one's home), reveal themselves as both physical and psychical battlegrounds. The film suggests that there is no safe haven, and, like *Flightplan*, implies that an authority figure and person assigned to one's safety and security might unleash a monster instead—a monster living next door, within one's presumed safe environment. Importantly, in contending with this monster, one is positioned to be transformed—transformed into something unsettling and unfamiliar. And while "external" threats might receive a sort of resolution within these films, the "monster within" continues beyond the final scenes of these post-9/11 movies.

The Brave One posits a certainty to threats and proposes that some actions might be justifiable in response to them, even if those actions (because of their horrific nature) irrevocably change the individual actors themselves. Erica Bain is transformed into an avenging monster herself. Even more unsettling, she comes to understand what she has become and knows there is no way back to her former self. This irrevocable change parallels the change that Americans see for themselves in the wake of September 11, 2001—a "day that changed America." Within this storyline, we see an unfolding of the Bush narrative and its continuing impact on a post-9/11 United States. The suggestion is that threats are everywhere and a heightened state of vigilance is required in the face of a changed America—an America that becomes "changed," we might add in conclusion, in part via one's response to and construction of post-9/11 "monsters."

Notes

1 Ira Chernus, *Monsters to Destroy: The Neoconservative War on Terror and Sin* (Boulder: Paradigm Publishers, 2006), 4–5.

2 Mary K. Bloodsworth-Lugo and Carmen R. Lugo-Lugo, *Containing (Un) American Bodies: Race, Sexuality, and Post-9/11 Constructions of Citizenship* (New York: Rodopi Press, 2010).

3 Ibid.

4 Ibid.

5 George W. Bush, "Address to the Nation," *The White House*, January 3, 2007, http://www.presidentialrhetoric.com/speeches/01.23.07.html (accessed January 3, 2012).

6 Ibid.

7 Richard Jackson, "The 9/11 Attacks and the Social Construction of a National Narrative," in *The Impact of 9/11 on the Media, Arts, and Entertainment: The Day that Changed Everything?*, (ed.) Matthew J. Morgan (New York: Palgrave Macmillan, 2009), 27.

8 Ibid.

9 Thomas Pollard, "Hollywood 9/11: Time of Crisis," in Morgan (ed.) *The Impact of 9/11 on the Media*, 206.

10 Ibid.

11 Jonathan Markovitz, "Reel Terror Post 9/11," in *Film and Television after 9/11*, (ed.) Wheeler Winston Dixon (Carbondale: Southern Illinois University Press, 2004), 201.

12 Kyle Bishop, "Dead Man Still Walking: Explaining the Zombie Renaissance," *Journal of Popular Film and Television* 37, no. 1 (2009), 17.

13 Antonio Sanchez-Escalonilla, "Hollywood and the Rhetoric of Panic: The Popular Genres of Action and Fantasy in the Wake of the 9/11 Attacks," *Journal of Popular Film and Television* 38, no. 1 (2010), 11.

14 Jackson, "The 9/11 Attacks," 25.

15 Bishop, "Dead Man Still Walking," 20.

16 *Flightplan*, DVD, directed by Robert Schwentke (2005; Berlin, Germany: Buena Vista Home Entertainment, 2006).

17 *Lakeview Terrace*, DVD, directed by Neil LaBute (2008; Hawthorne, CA: Sony Pictures Home Entertainment, 2009).

18 *The Brave One*, DVD, directed by Neil Jordan (2007; Brooklyn, NY: Warner Home Video, 2008).

19 Thank you to Marina Levina and Diem-My Bui for their careful editing of this chapter and useful suggestions throughout the piece.

20 Manohla Dargis, "Hunting for a Child No One Believes is There," *New York Times*, September 23, 2005, http://movies.nytimes.com/2005/09/23/movies/23flig.html (accessed January 6, 2012).

21 *Flightplan*, "Chapter 7," 45:06.

22 Ibid., "Chapter 5," 29:32.

23 Ibid., "Chapter 6," 39:23.

24 Ibid., 39:55.

25 Ibid., 35:58.

26 *Flightplan*, "Chapter 12," 126:25.

27 Ibid., DVD jacket.

28 Ibid., "Chapter 4," 12:33.

29 Ibid., "Chapter 5," 16:48.

30 Ibid., "Chapter 10," 33:08.

31 A. O. Scott, "Lurking in the Shadows of Suburbia, a Menacing Neighbor with a Gun," *New York Times*, September 19, 2008, http://movies.nytimes.com/2008/09/19/movies/19terr.html (accessed January 5, 2012).

32 *The Brave One*, "Chapter 11," 39:49.

33 Ibid., "Chapter 1," 0:58.

34 Ibid., 2:55.

35 Claire S. King, "The Man Inside: Trauma, Gender and the Nation in *The Brave One*," *Critical Studies in Media Communication* 27, no. 2 (2010): 111.

36 Ibid., 123.

37 *The Brave One*, "Chapter 11," 39:00.

38 Ibid., "Chapter 12," 43:40.

39 Ibid., "Chapter 18," 60:00.

40 Ibid., "Chapter 30," 60:57.

41 Ibid., "Chapter 28," 60:42.

42 Ibid., 60:50.

43 Chernus, *Monsters to* Destroy, 1.

16

The heartland under siege: Undead in the West

Cynthia J. Miller and A. Bowdoin Van Riper

Introduction

The North American West has traditionally been framed as a site laden with social and cultural meaning. Once described by Frederick Jackson Turner as "the meeting point between savagery and civilization,"[1] the Western frontier plays multiple roles: as a point of encounter between all that is "human" and the "wild"; as a setting for morality tales, told in the service of mainstream values and ideals; and as the country's heartland, the focal point for traditional national identity. Cinematic representations of the West, from the silent era to the present, have portrayed these multiple and intersecting roles in increasingly complex ways, and these portrayals have been complicated further still by the presence of the undead—mummies, vampires, zombies, and lost souls—entities that terrify the living, and exist in tension with many of the traditional meanings and functions of the West. At first glance, the undead present vicious, repugnant threats to humanity, terrorizing good and evil alike; on closer examination, however, their existence in the West, in relentless pursuit of the living, calls into question basic assumptions regarding the nature of humanity, the power of the moral order, and long-cherished notions of national identity.

While the undead first began to menace the West in the late 1950s, with Edward Dein's *Curse of the Undead* (1959), they did not truly begin to proliferate until the close of the twentieth century was near. *From Dusk Till Dawn* (1996), along with its 1999 sequel and prequel, laid the groundwork for the undead's twenty-first-century invasion of the frontier and ushered hordes of vampires, zombies, mummies, and ghosts into the new millennium. In the years that followed, films such as *Bubba Ho-Tep* (2002), *Western Zombie* (2006), *Seven Mummies* (2006), *The Quick and the Undead* (2006), *Dead Noon* (2008), *Deadwalkers* (2009), and *Devil's Crossing* (2010), created a convergence of twenty-first-century moral panics, situated in the heartland, even as genres converged in order to critique and comment on the Western tradition and its ascribed norms and values.

This careful positioning of the undead in the West is no accident. In the absence of urban infrastructure, industrialization, and technologization, the undead attack humanity in one of its most elemental regions, at one of its most elemental levels—the heartland of traditional American values and identity—at a time when rapid social change has called all fundamental elements of existence into question. This chapter, then, explores the many tropes and themes through which undead Westerns make those inner plagues and demons visible, and lay siege to a frontier tied to myths of freedom, independence, strength, ingenuity, that comprise not only individual identities, but collective national identity as well.

Putting the 'Wild' back in the West

The frontier, or more accurately, the process by which it was conquered, is seen as one of the defining elements in American national identity—the catalyst and proving ground for the courage, individuality, and dynamism of the American character—the "dominant individualism" that Turner saw as a hallmark of American character.[2] The frontier was, for many, the "wellspring of the independent, indomitable American spirit."[3] It was the land of Manifest Destiny—of conquest—and the farmers, ranchers, schoolmarms, saloon girls, entrepreneurs, and adventurers who settled the West represented a progressive force that carried the beacon of change to the wilderness that existed, only temporarily, beyond civilization's reach.

Beginning with the silent film *The Great Train Robbery* (1903), Western films became a mainstay of entertainment in the United States and flourished for decades, achieving its "Golden Age" in the 1930s–1950s.[4] Classic Western films, with titles like *Rough Riders Round-up* (1939), *Pals of the Silver Sage* (1940), and *Don't Fence Me In* (1945), were brought to life by characters who reinforced social norms, mainstream values, and conventional gender roles of the times.[5] These traditional Westerns emphasized the establishment of law and order, and presented an essential and ritualistic conflict between civilization and savagery, with plot elements that were constructed into various oppositions—East versus West; light versus dark; social order versus anarchy; community versus individual; town versus wilderness; cowboy versus Indian; school marm versus dancehall girl—and were manifested externally, in the landscape, and internally, in the community.[6] The boundaries that existed between these positive and negative poles were clearly signposted for all to see, with symbolic markers displayed in characters' dress, speech, and morals. Heroes and villains played out familiar roles, according to well-established rules of engagement, and transgressions—of the laws of man or nature—were ultimately answered by similarly well-established consequences.

Heroes of the traditional West have long been recognized as "guardians" of civilization—positioned with one foot in the "wild" and one foot in the civilized world—bearing the responsibility for maintaining the boundaries between order and chaos, civilization and barbarism. Agents of right and reason, Western heroes balanced frontier independence with concern for the common good, and tempered the need for violence with a mandate for restraint. They were champions of the moral order, and icons of national identity, playing a leading role not only in the taming of the West, but in expanding and extending mainstream American values and ways of life across borders, boundaries, and ideologies. Gunslingers, cattle rustlers, warriors and *bandidos* all ultimately succumbed to the hero's campaigns on behalf of bringing the frontier and its inhabitants under the control of civilized law.

In the late 1960s, a revisionist trend began to shape the genre, bringing a dark realism to the cinematic West. These revisionist Westerns, such as *The Wild Bunch* (1969) and *McCabe & Mrs. Miller* (1971) called the genre's taken-for-granted binary oppositions into question by challenging the use of violence, complicating interpersonal and intergroup relationships, providing a more sympathetic treatment of Native Americans and Mexicans, and creating disaffected heroes—"saviors" who battled their own demons and struggled against crises of conscience, checkered pasts, and resistance to civil authority's unreflexive notions of right and wrong. The relevance of the classic Western's uncomplicated moral messages also came into question, and from the revisionist era forward, frontier men on both sides of the moral divide evidenced a stronger identification with "the wild" than their more "civilized" counterparts, troubled embodiments of a vanishing way of life.

Frontier life, however, had begun to vanish much earlier. Even as the Golden Age of Western films spun its tales of the Wild West, its wildness had already been tamed, and the cinematic West had become a West of myth and legend—a West that was no longer. After a period of dormancy, however, the genre experienced a revitalization, as post-9/11 America sought certainty in tradition. In a decade that, as Kyle Bishop notes, is "so clearly looking to the past for narratives to express contemporary stresses and anxieties," it is no surprise that the foundational texts of national identity would provide reassurance in their themes of perseverance, individuality, and the triumph of moral order over chaos.[7] Through contemporary uses, appropriations, and adaptations of well-known icons, symbols, and tropes of the classic West—particularly in compound-genre and hybrid films that blend the world of the frontier with elements of horror or science fiction—its moral, ethical, and philosophical messages and meanings continue. Those messages and meanings take on new significance and face even greater challenges, however, as the undead put the "wild" back in the Wild West. As Brendan Wayne, Western actor and grandson of cinematic icon John Wayne, observes, genre mash-ups such as these serve to "revitalize" the genre and create a new, contemporary fan base among those who see the frontier as belonging to their cultural "others"—an older, outmoded generation.[8] At the same time, these narratives continue cinematic horror's longstanding ties to periods of social unrest and political strife—gunslingers walk out of hell to once again besiege dusty towns; Native Americans rise from the grave to right ancient wrongs; vampires, mummies, and zombies ensure that human sins are, in fact, deadly; and ghostly cowboys guide the living from atop fire-breathing steeds—confronting twenty-first-century fears with traditional frontier justice. Often, they all collide within the most controversial of Western locales, the saloon.

The saloon

From the swinging doors, to the dust-covered bottles of bourbon lining the shelves behind its paneled bar, the saloon stands as a quintessential icon of the Old West. Situated in the heart of every Western town, but morally on its margins, the saloon served as a site of refuge and release. It was a gambling den, a meetinghouse, and the place where a man could drink in the company of men; where social convention and morality were loosened, and both bravado and indifference had their place.

Iconic as it is, the saloon of the Western frontier was a complicated place. While other mainstays of Western towns, like the schoolhouse and the church, were artifacts of a West that had *been* tamed, the saloon was there to witness and aid in the taming. And with its roots in a West that was

FIGURE 16.1 *The quintessential Western saloon, as illustrated in* It Came From the West

still wild, it often needed a little taming itself. Its mention evokes a cast of glittering "painted ladies," boisterous clientele, card sharks, and gunslingers.[9] The saloon served as a port of entry for newcomers and a gathering place for those who had already laid their various claims to the West. It was a place where the conflicts between heroes and villains, laborers and owners, farmers and ranchers, young guns and old dogs, simmered just below the surface—and sometimes bubbled over and spilled out into the streets. Time and again, as Diana Reep illustrates, the saloon serves as a killing ground—the stage on which the finalities of economics, morality, and life are played out—in films such as *Duel in the Sun* (1946), *The Gunfighter* (1950), *The Outlaw Josey Wales* (1976), *Young Guns* (1988), and others.[10]

On the surface, the saloon, with its bright lights, music, and pretty women, appears to be an outpost of civilization, each board and nail testifying to human triumph over the wildness of the frontier.[11] The sounds of laughter and clinking glasses that emanate from within give the illusion of safety, like a child whistling in the dark. But in reality, the saloon can be seen as a container for the same struggle between civilization and barbarity that was taking place on a grand scale just outside its swinging doors. A microcosm of the frontier, the space of the saloon calls the control of civilization into question, mixing the promise of law and order with the risky business of the West. Alcohol and easy women lower inhibitions and erode the veneer of morality suggested by settlement, while drunkenness, illicit sex, gambling, and the fistfights that usually ensue give testimony to the dangers of giving way to man's (and woman's) more basic nature.

This weakening, and potential trampling, of "back East" puritanical morality and social control—the ongoing threat of unbridled lawlessness and barbarity in the midst of an oasis of civilization—made the saloon a kind of liminal space. Neither fish nor fowl, betwixt and between, it afforded chaos roots in the frontier town, just as it provided civilization with a foothold in the midst of frontier wildness. But beyond that, the saloon was a place of encounter. Shady ladies and cowboys, gamblers and miners, outlaws and bounty hunters, writers and adventurers, all stepped through its doors, to work, drink, tell tales, hear news, even scores, and satisfy longings. As the Western collided with other genres, such as horror and science fiction, the saloon also became the stage for encounters of a different kind—between the living and the undead—forcing lawmen and bandits to forge alliances, as traditional Western narratives of good versus evil were replaced by those of the living versus the dead, all played out with the saloon at the center, despite one hero's warning "Never go inside. In there, they can outlast you. Never go inside" (*The Quick and the Undead*).

Cast within this framework, the saloon, as the morally ambiguous space where good and evil meet, assumes a position of even greater significance in undead Westerns. More than just a setting for conflicts between gunfighters, shady ladies, and lawmen, the saloon of undead Westerns is a site for the clash between barbarity and law of a different kind—natural law—with villains (and, sometimes, heroes) who challenge not merely social norms, but the very definition of life. The undead violate temporal and existential norms, along with some of civilization's deepest taboos—flesh-eating, blood-drinking, corpse-mutilating—presenting vicious, repugnant threats to humanity and the moral order. They shamble, lunge, fly, "flit," and sometimes just reach up from beneath the ground to make victims of earthly good and evil alike—often, for all of eternity—forging previously unthinkable alliances between human foes, in defense of humanity at large. One of the best-known examples, considered by some to be a "classic," is Quentin Tarantino's box office hit *From Dusk Till Dawn*. The original, along with its lesser known sequel *Texas Blood Money* (1999) and prequel *The Hangman's Daughter* (1999) all use the saloon as a true "den of iniquity," where far more than the usual Western moral order is at stake. In each, outlaws and innocents all take refuge in a seedy Mexican bar, where sensual excesses abound as the crowd gathers for the night. Seemingly mesmerized, characters shed the bonds of civilization as the crowd descends into an orgy of earthly transgressions—only to realize, far too late, that they, too, are about to be devoured by the all-consuming frenzy.

As the undead continue their assault on the American heartland in the twenty-first century, in films ranging from the early vampire tale *Curse of the Undead*, to the zombie-plagued *It Came From the West* (2007), the saloon provides an ideal setting for the workings-out of these tales. Taking advantage of the betwixt-and-between nature of the saloon—as a civilizer of the frontier, and the least civilized site in the frontier town—undead Westerns grant inhumanity, in the form of zombies, vampires, and others, a foothold, compelling the living beings who enter to defend their existence and champion the natural (and with it, the moral) order. The saloon thus becomes a touchstone uniting past and present, a stage on which the moral panics of the newly expanding nation of the nineteenth century and the newly threatened nation of the twenty-first century—with their respective fears of chaos, victimization, and loss of identity are played out.[12]

The Code of the West

Wild and lawless as it may have seemed, the frontier was governed by a code of its own, an unwritten doctrine that staked out moral guideposts for settlers, wanderers, and gunslingers alike, regarding courage, fair play, loyalty, respect, and honor. The Code of the West, as it came to be known, marked the boundaries of right and wrong, civilized and wild, good and evil, and safeguarded the frontier from chaos and abandon.

First chronicled by Western writer Zane Grey, in his 1934 novel *Code of the West*,[13] the Code has been handed-down and adapted throughout popular culture for over three-quarters of a century, in the codes and creeds of cowboy philosophers and Western heroes alike, such as Gene Autry, Hopalong Cassidy, Roy Rogers, Wild Bill Hickok, and the Texas Rangers. In 1969, cowboy historian Ramon F. Adams elaborated on the Code and its functions for individual and community in *The Cowman and His Code of Ethics*, observing that:

> [t]hough the cowman might break every law of the territory, state and federal government, he took pride in upholding his own unwritten code. His failure to abide by it did not bring formal punishment, but the man who broke it became, more or less, a social outcast ... subject to the punishment of the very code he had broken.[14]

Even though the frontier has vanished, the Code persists as the defining ideology of the American West—with twenty-first-century lawmen, in states such as Wyoming and Montana, lobbying to adopt it as the states' official code of ethics.[15] Its mandates, however, are not limited to the West: they inform a sense of honor found in individuals and institutions across America. Most visibly and significantly, perhaps, they are found in military codes of conduct, shaping—at a deeper level than formal international agreements like the Geneva Conventions—the moral imperatives and rules of engagement that, Americans believe, regulate combat and maintain "humanity" in the midst of the horrors of war. The profound violation of this "code of war" by the events of 9/11 not only shook Americans' understandings of the Code, but called into question the parameters of moral integrity more generally. A constellation of conflict, fear, lust for vengeance, and hope for restoration surrounding the Code is strongly in evidence in undead Westerns, where its mandates are both reinforced and violated by vampires, zombies, and other monstrous beings, as they invade the cinematic frontier.

The rotting flesh and unsettled spirits of the undead are both the products and the embodiments of earthly transgressions; their presence and predations violate the laws of nature, mock the laws of man, and scorn the Code of the West. While an increasingly broad range of scholarly work has focused on undead critiques of consumerism, capitalism, religion, racism, nationalism, and other contemporary ideological concerns, here on the frontier it is the traditional dualism of good and evil and the Cowboy Code—the moral foundation of heartland—that are the focus of the undead villain.[16] Unlike the characters of revisionist Westerns, who simply challenge and interrogate the Code and its assumptions, the horrors wrought by the living dead render them obsolete. Director Scott Stewart explains that, in his use of vampire villains in the film *Priest* (2011), "I didn't think the idea of vampires as a modern stand-in for Indians in an old Western was a fungible idea ... I wanted to find a different metaphor that would allow for vampires that are stranger and more feral ... an enemy we don't understand."[17] There is no fair play, no honorable death in the West of the undead, only cannibalism, evisceration, and mutation. Whether lying in wait, like the denizens of the borderlands bars in *From Dusk Till Dawn* and *Seven Mummies*, or laying siege, like the shambling masses conjured from the dead in *It Came from the West* and *Deadwalkers*, the undead defile the living in intimate, yet impersonal ways. Their presence engenders chaos and moral panic, as lawmen and outlaws alike find the framework of their shared existence rent apart and scattered in the dirt.

At the same time, the relevance of that shared framework is also underscored by the undead, as traditional heroes and villains become unlikely partners in the battle against these entities that defy death. Ranging from the calculating vampire figures in films such as *Curse of the Undead*, *Billy the Kid vs. Dracula* (1966) and *Bloodrayne II: Deliverance* (2007), to the mindless, shambling zombies of *The Quick and the Undead*, *Deadwalkers*, and *Devil's Crossing*, the undead present a horrific, incomprehensible

Otherness that terrifies both the bravest and the boldest. While the hero and his villainous counterpart traditionally make visible the dual nature of the Old West—the rugged wildness and unbridled freedom of the frontier on one hand, and the moral order of civilization on the other—the menace presented by the undead complicates this duality and threatens the very context in which earthly good and evil exist.[18] As Brooks notes, "When the living dead triumph, the world degenerates into utter chaos. All social order evaporates."[19]

All undead in the West are not created equal, however, and while many embody earthly transgressions of the Cowboy Code—delivering grisly messages about the consequences of greed, lust, and injustice—others have an even more direct link to earthly morality. They are not merely symbolic reminders of the Code of the West, they also serve as its tutors. "Seek not the plunder that's buried in the evil earth," the eerie sheriff Drake (Billy Drago) warns six convicts who have just arrived at his ghost town's saloon in search of hidden gold, in *Seven Mummies*. The ghostly cowboy Carter Slade (Sam

FIGURE 16.2 *Billy Drago as the menacing Sheriff Drake in* Seven Mummies

Elliott) serves as a moral compass for stuntman Johnny Blaze (Nicholas Cage) after the headstrong motorcyclist sells his soul to the Devil (Peter Fonda) in *Ghost Rider* (2007), while the deceased-and-awaiting-judgment Wild Bill Hickok (Sam Shepard) upholds the Code on behalf of the wayward Sonny Dillard (Brad Rowe), at the risk of his own eternal damnation, in *Purgatory* (1999). In *Dead Noon*, a fearful and troubled lawman (Scott Phillips) seeks refuge in the local church, after learning that a bloodthirsty outlaw named Frank (Robert Bear) has walked out of hell in search of him. As his unseen nemesis appears in the pew behind him, he struggles over a course of action, and the undead gunslinger literally plays "devil's advocate." He could run, long and far, he reckons:

> Frank: Is that what a hero does?
> Sheriff: I'm no hero.
> Frank: Are you a man? How do you think you're going to feel a year from now? Ten years from now? Will you be proud of that decision—that you abandoned this town, your destiny? You chose to be sheriff of this town. You took an oath to protect these people … A man honors his word.

Similarly, in the animated *Rango* (2011), the golf-cart riding Spirit of the West, a serape-draped parody/homage to Clint Eastwood's iconic "Man With No Name," sagely advises the tenderfoot chameleon "It doesn't matter what they call you. It's the deeds make the man."

In each of these instances, we see a twenty-first-century return to the moral code of a Golden Age, portrayed as a time when honor and action went hand-in-hand. As the post-9/11 world grapples with real-world monsters—terrorism, contagion, seemingly-random violence, and economic crises—it seeks to answer a question asked by H. G. Wells in the mid-1930s: "Whither humanity?" The heroes of the American West offered a response at the time, as champions of heartland American values, identity, and community. And here, in undead Westerns of the twenty-first century, the Code of the West offers that down-home reassurance once again. Regardless of the fate of the flesh, the Spirit of the West has been upheld—faith, honor, and civilization have been championed—and the moral force of the Cowboy Code lives on, and the living dead are put to rest. In each of these cases, the undead actively engage with the living in ways that reinforce the Code—cautioning and converting the weak and wayward—acting as complex figures that frequently work to practically or symbolically emphasize the very moral order their presence seeks to undermine.

Retaliation and redemption

Those who, in life, lose sight of their moral compass and willfully flout the Code encounter the undead not as guides but as avengers, ready to inflict sudden death (or worse) for their transgressions. The casual brutality of white settlers toward the Indians is, in films such as *It Came From the*

FIGURE 16.3 *The zombie lawman from* Undead or Alive—*leading citizen in a community made up entirely of the undead*

West, *Deadwalkers*, and *Undead or Alive* (2007), inflicted upon them in turn by hordes of zombies created by Indian magic. The undead in such films, devouring the just and unjust alike, are a shambling extension of the indiscriminate and (nearly) unstoppable forces of Nature itself.[20] The role of the undead in maintaining the Code, however, is not always mindlessly chaotic. They also appear as discriminating agents of retribution; as violators themselves, struggling for redemption; and as catalysts for the redemption of others. This complexity and seeming contradiction mark a unique evolution of the undead in the twenty-first century—a drastic shift wherein, as Sara Sutler-Cohen observes, the undead have become social actors—reflecting popular awareness that, in a post-apocalyptic world, the binary opposition of the living and the dead might not be as clear as it once seemed, the boundary between the two not as impermeable as we assumed.[21] Vampires, ghosts, and even the repugnant zombie have become sympathetic characters that demonstrate more commonality with the living than the dead.

The title character of Clint Eastwood's *Pale Rider* (1985) is, seemingly, just another "Man With No Name": laconic, unshaven, and lethal. Like his unnamed counterpart in *High Plains Drifter* (1974), however, he is implied to be something more: an emissary from beyond the grave.[22] His back bears the scars of multiple, seemingly fatal bullet wounds; he resembles a man known to be dead; and there are subtle signs that he is capable of dematerializing at will. His first appearance is juxtaposed with a girl's prayer for deliverance and his arrival outside her family's home with her reading the Book of Revelations: "And behold a pale horse, and his name that sat on him was death. And Hell followed with him." When he confronts the corrupt marshal and hired thugs who threaten to drive the girl's family and their neighbors off their land, he metes out punishment with the implacable grace of a warrior-angel.

The escaped convicts in *Seven Mummies*, enacting a well-worn narrative by fleeing the law-bound West for the safety of lawless Mexico,[23] are drawn by their greed toward a swifter and more brutal reckoning than the one they fled. Diverted by a lone Indian's tales of a legendary treasure assembled and hidden by the *conquistadors*, they fall victim to the mummies of the title—undead Jesuit priests sworn to guard the gold—and their zombie minions: a town full of earlier gold-seekers slaughtered by the mummies. Given a choice between freedom and riches by the Indian, who tells them that the border and the gold lie in opposite directions, the convicts declare their greed (and seal their fate) by choosing the latter. Having entered the town of the undead they are trapped both by its zombie residents and by their own unwillingness to leave without the gold. Their undead tormentors, however, are as much prisoners as they are: the townspeople shackled to their half-life by the mummies' curse, and the mummies bound by a pledge to keep the gold for masters who will never return to claim it. Among the convicts, only Travis (Billy Wirth)—who disdains the gold and describes his crimes as "mistakes"—is able to escape the twilight world of the undead.

Travis is mortal, but the prospect of redemption extends, in other films, to the undead themselves. In *Purgatory*, which blends the conventions of the Western with those of the 1940s "film blanc,"[24] Wild Bill Hickok and three other recently dead gunfighters live under assumed names in a town that straddles the border between the worlds of the living and the dead. Neither wholly righteous nor irredeemably corrupt, they and the other residents wait for God to pass final judgment on their souls, aware that any miss-step will send them to hell rather than heaven. Jesse James (John David Souther), now keeper of the general store, encourages Sonny Dillard to read "the classics" instead of violent dime novels, and Hickok warns both Sonny and his own deputy, Billy the Kid (Donnie Wahlberg), against swearing and threats of violence. When Doc Holliday (Randy Quaid) counsels a newcomer to avoid the saloon, saying "one drink, and it's all over," it is a warning not about drunkenness, but about losing any hope of redemption for all eternity. All four of the undead gunfighters—James, Hickock, Holliday, and the Kid—knowingly risk just such a fate when, embracing the violent pasts they had tried to bury with their mortal bodies, they arm themselves for a showdown with an outlaw gang that threatens the townsfolk.

The undead heroes of *Purgatory* find, to their surprise and relief, that their intention to protect the weak—even at the cost of their own damnation—has not only justified but ennobled their violence,[25] and so redeemed their souls. God may be a hard master, they are told as they ride away to heaven, "but He ain't blind." Carter Slade, of *Ghost Rider*, also sees the Code of the West as a recipe for his own redemption. A former Texas Ranger who fell from grace in the 1850s, when he broke the law and was hanged for his crimes, he spends a century-and-a-half as the Devil's undead messenger, collecting the souls of those who, like his protégé Johnny, were foolish enough to sign them away. Slade consistently strives, however, to atone for his sins—even, in an act redolent of Western legend,[26] defying the Devil himself—in the hope of earning God's mercy.

Redemption in undead Westerns is neither limited to the undead themselves nor restricted to the immortal soul. Virgil, the sensitive young man at the center of *It Came from the West,* is bullied by his brutish saloonkeeper-father and mocked as a "weak pisser" by the cowboys who frequent the saloon. When zombies overrun the town and invade the saloon, however, Virgil displays courage and a capacity for righteous violence that mark him as a true man of the West and—combined with his quick wits—vanquish the zombies. Virgil's battle with the zombies saves the town, but also redeems him in the eyes of the townspeople, revealing him to be a classic Western hero, fully capable of mastering the unruly frontier.[27] The elderly heroes of *Bubba Ho-tep*, robbed of their masculinity by the effects of aging and the rhythms of life in their Texas nursing home, similarly redeem it in combat with the undead. Their defense of the nursing home and its residents against a marauding mummy dressed in boots, spurs, and Stetson—no less than the undead gunfighters' defense of the town in *Purgatory* or Virgil's of the saloon—brings about a personalized form of the "regeneration through violence" that, Richard Slotkin has argued, is the defining myth of the American frontier.[28]

Conclusion

The central myths of the frontier are myths of transformation: the weak become strong; the defiant are conquered; the wild is tamed. Fueled by tenets of honor, morality, and virtue—the Code of the West—these myths are the stuff of song and story, and the building blocks of closely-held notions of rugged American individualism and national identity.

The intrusion of the undead onto the Western frontier challenges the core ideas of the Code, blurring the once sharp lines separating the wild from the civilized, the righteous from the wicked. It brings the crimes of the past to light and gives human form to their dark legacy, and confronts lawmen and gunslingers alike with forces beyond their comprehension: guardians and guides who bring an otherworldly wisdom to the realm of the living, and enemies who know no honor, defy order and reason, and relentlessly pursue the destruction of all in their path. Unlike the historical subduing of the frontier, when the forces representing the "civilized" moral order moved westward, conquering "savage" lands, animals, and peoples as they progressed, battles against the undead, like the attacks of 9/11, remind us that terror is inescapable. As Sutler-Cohen observes: "Unlike other monsters we are charged with hunting down and killing, [the undead] come and find us."[29] Undead advisors to the living reinforce the centrality of the Code as forcefully as the mute, ravenous undead hordes transgress it. Both, however, exist to articulate its importance and—by their example—remind the living that the cost of violating the Code may be higher than they had ever imagined.

On a larger scale, the presence of the undead in the West simultaneously complicates and reinforces the myth that the taming of the West is inevitable. Their appearance brings chaos—moral as well as physical—that threatens to sweep away the still-tenuous order that the living have painstakingly imposed on the once-wild land. Their insatiable appetites mock the decorum of the church, school, and café, and make the wildness of the saloon seem tame. Their numbers and inhuman resilience make them, collectively, a match for the quickest-drawing, straightest-shooting gunfighters. The triumphs of civilization over wildness, and the righteousness of those triumphs, are articles of faith in traditional Westerns, only recently (and, even then, only rarely) interrogated. With the arrival of the undead, those comforting certainties are up for grabs, reminding audiences that in a West (both national and global) long-since civilized, predatory "others"—the "enemy we don't understand," as Stewart suggested—can come and find them.

Ultimately, however, the cinematic West's struggle against the undead ends as struggles for control of the frontier have always ended on screen: with peace restored, the Code of the West intact, and the townsfolk filtering cautiously back onto the dusty street to carry on their orderly, civilized lives.

Notes

1 Frederick Jackson Turner, *The Frontier in American History* (New York: Henry Holt and Company, 1921), 199.

2 Turner, *The Frontier*, 199.

3 Robert J. Higgs and Ralph L. Turner, *The Cowboy Way: The Western Leader in Film, 1945–1995* (Santa Barbara, CA: Praeger, 1999), xix.

4 Jack Nachbar, *Focus on the Western* (Englewood Cliffs, NJ: Prentice Hall, 1974).

5 Peter Stanfield, *Horse Opera: The Strange History of the 1930s Singing Cowboy* (Urbana and Chicago: University of Illinois Press, 2002).

6 M. Elise Marubbio, *Killing the Indian Maiden: Images of Native American Women in Film* (Lexington: University Press of Kentucky, 2006), 113; C. Sharrett, "The Western Rides Again," *USA Today* 120, July 1991, 91.

7 Kyle Bishop, *American Zombie Gothic: The Rise and Fall (and Rise) of the Walking Dead in Popular Culture* (Jefferson, NC: McFarland & Company, 2010), 199.

8 Brendan Wayne, personal communication with Cynthia J. Miller, September 12, 2011.

9 Anne M. Butler, *Daughters of Joy, Sisters of Misery: Prostitutes in the American West, 1865–90* (Champaign, IL: University of Illinois Press, 1987), ix.

10 Diana C. Reep, "See What the Boys in the Back Room Will Have: The Saloon in Western Films," in *Beyond the Stars: Locales in American Popular Film*, eds Paul Loukides and Linda K. Fuller (Bowling Green, KY: Bowling Green State University Popular Press, 1993), 204–20.

11 Reep, "See What the Boys in the Back Room Will Have", 205–6.

12 Rhetorics of manifest destiny and moral superiority infuse popular press and commentary post-9/11, further linking ideologies of the frontier with the present day. See, for example, http://www.mercatornet.com/articles/view/time_for_a_new_destiny/

13 Zane Grey, *The Code of the West* (New York: Grossett and Dunlap, 1934).

14 Ramon Adams, *The Cowman & His Code of Ethics* (Austin: Encino Press, 1969), 13.

15 David S. Lewis, "The Code of the West: Some Things Never Go Out of Style," *The Montana Pioneer,* March, 2011. http://www.mtpioneer.com/2011-Mar-cover-code-west.html/

16 See Bishop, *American Zombie Gothic*; Mary Y. Hallab, *Vampire God: The Allure of the Undead in Western Culture* (Albany: State University of New York [SUNY] Press, 2009); Sean McIntosh and Marc Leverette, *Zombie Culture: Autopsies of the Living Dead* (Lanham, MD: Scarecrow Press, 2008); and David Flint, *Zombie Holocaust: How the Living Dead Devoured Pop Culture* (London: Plexus, 2009).

17 Scott Stewart, personal communication with Cynthia J. Miller, April 2, 2012.

18 Marubbio, *Killing the Indian Maiden*, 113.

19 Max Brooks, *The Zombie Survival Guide* (New York: Three Rivers Press, 2003), 155.

20 Sean Moreland, "Shambling Toward Mount Improbable to be Born: American Evolutionary Anxiety and the Hopeful Monsters of Matheson's *I Am Legend* and Romero's *Dead* Films," in *Generation Zombie: Essays on the Living Dead in Modern Culture*, eds Stefanie Bolunk and Wylie Lenz (Jefferson, NC: McFarland, 2011), 77–81.

21 Sara Sutler-Cohen, "Plans are Pointless; Staying Alive Is as Good as It Gets," in *Zombies Are Us: Essays on the Humanity of the Walking Dead*, eds Christopher Moreman and Cory James Rushton (Jefferson, NC: McFarland and Company, 2011), 183.

22 David McNaron, "From Dollars to Iron: The Currency of Clint Eastwood's Westerns," in *The Philosophy of the Western*, eds Jennifer L. McMahon and B. Steve McCaskey (Lexington: University Press of Kentucky, 2010), 157–8.

23 Camilla Fojas, *Border Bandits: Hollywood on the Southern Frontier* (Austin: University of Texas Press, 2008), 27–8.

24 Peter Valenti, "The 'Film Blanc': Suggestions for a Variety of Fantasy, 1940–45," *Journal of Popular Film 6*, no. 4 (1978): 294–304.

25 Gregory J. Watkins, *Teaching Religion and Film* (New York: Oxford University Press, 2008), 214–15.

26 Barry Keith Grant, *Shadows of a Doubt: Negotiations of Masculinity in Western Films* (Detroit: Wayne State University Press, 2010), 38.

27 Ibid., 51–3.

28 Richard Slotkin, *Regeneration Through Violence: The Mythology of the American Frontier, 1600–1860* (Norman: University of Oklahoma Press, 2000), 5.

29 Sutler-Cohen, "Plans are Pointless", 192.

17

When matter becomes an active agent:

The incorporeal monstrosity of threat in *Lost*

Enrica Picarelli

A few days after the terrorist attack on the World Trade Center, Mary Gordon wrote in the *New York Times* that the September 11 tragedy was all the more nightmarish because it was perpetrated by an "enemy with no name and therefore no face, or even worse, a name and face that can only be guessed at."[1] Indeed, beyond the shock of the attacks lay the knowledge that the inviolability of the U.S. had been defiled from within by a hand of undetermined origin. Lacking identificatory features, this presence assessed itself through action; the mark it left on the material and cultural landscape of the nation providing the only tangible trace of its elusive singularity. Although it took President Bush a short time to disclose information on the Islamic nature of the attacks, September 11 stands as a paradigmatic moment of unpreparedness in American history: on that occasion, the nation fell prey to the momentum instigated by an event of unprecedented proportions.

Behind the attacks were, as politicians tirelessly reiterated, the machinations of a shady presence which would pound at the gates of fortress America for years to come, with official and unofficial rhetoric resorting to hyperbolic language to stress the vile and aberrant nature of the terrorists. If "a true monster will be remembered for the shock it produces, breaking all chains of association,"[2] it is no surprise that the attacks brought about a proliferation of monstrous tropes not only in the U.S. but in Western culture at large. In the last decade countless movies, television shows, video games, and comic books have incorporated a scenario of alarmism and anxiety, staging the epistemological breakdown that the advent of monsters invariably provokes.

The aim of this chapter is to map the forms of monstrosity appearing in ABC's series *Lost* (2004–10), examining them in the light of the narrative of fear that characterized Bush's presidency. Although this discourse, endorsing neocolonialism and state control into the lives of its citizens, has given way to Barack Obama's more positive grammar of "hope," concerns with security both in the U.S. and abroad continue to address the threat linked to an unpredictable and metamorphic typology of risks. Since *Lost* aired in the hottest years of the War on Terror, from 2004 to 2010, its representation of monstrosity, and the changes it undergoes in its seasonal progression, from material to increasingly incorporeal forms of monstrosity, are useful to examine the emergence of a discourse of global uncertainty that reverberates to this day.

Lost incorporates contemporary feelings of apprehension and terror, associating them to the upsetting ecology of the tropical island on which the characters find themselves in the aftermath of a plane crash. The island is a monstrous realm where biological, cultural and social boundaries collapse and metamorphoses take place. Hallucinations, ghosts, whispers, and a shapeshifting cloud of smoke contribute to stage the categorical instability and ontological ambiguity associated with monstrosity. Coexisting and precipitating these events is the uprooting of linear temporal progression produced by the flashbacks and flashforwards experienced randomly by the protagonists. Beyond the material manifestation of otherworldly presences, *Lost* finds monstrosity at the heart of lives lived without guarantees. Representing the characters' failure to recuperate their memories and anticipate the future, the fictional universe incorporates the anxieties informing post-9/11 obsessions with preemption and absolute control, making them part of a landscape of apprehension that is in itself monstrous.

A bestiary of monsters

"The existence of monsters throws doubt on life's ability to teach us order. … [N]o matter how accustomed we have been to see … like engender like. It is sufficient that this confidence be shaken once by a morphological variation, by a single equivocal appearance, for a radical fear to possess us."[3] With these words, Georges Canguilhem describes monstrosity as pertaining to the realm of ambiguity and perturbation, of material mutation and affective uneasiness. Monstrous is anything that rests on the side of anomaly, proliferating in the uncharted provinces where excess and hybridity turn knowledge and being on their head. Monstrous is similarly what incarnates deviancy and inspires dread. Writing about gendered representations of monsters in horror film, Barbara Creed remarks that the cinematographic contact with the monstrous produces a state of phenomenological turmoil where "alterations in the body" of the spectator occur.[4] As "a form suspended between forms,"[5] the monster inhabits the threshold where opposites meet and unnatural couplings take place between inner and outer realms.

The shocking nature of September 11 spawned a global imaginary of monsters in the West. Reacting to the terror of a seemingly faceless enemy, countless representations appeared which employed traditional motifs of monstrosity, such as deformity and a transgressive sexuality, to attribute a demonic identity to the terrorists.[6] Just like the abominable creatures of countless tales, this discourse, peculiar especially to American media, describes the terrorist as a "diabolical" being and a "shadowy evil."[7] His (very rarely her) shocking manifestation is said to have left a lasting impact on the American psyche since, as Bush declared, on September 11 "night fell on a different world."[8] Indeed, in light of the post-9/11 "culture of fear," monstrosity is best discussed in terms of a symptomatology of negative impressions and affects, more than in the teratological vocabulary of phenomenological anomaly.[9]

The hypertrophic growth of images of the abominable terrorist that took place in the aftermath of the attacks attributes a hyper-visibility to monstrosity. In lieu of the enemy with no face and no name, a recognizable army of devils appears whose beards, robes, and turbaned heads symbolize a wicked morality. Popular culture has contributed to the proliferation of this imaginary. Stacy Takacs investigates the multiplication of science fiction and horror shows that has taken place in the last decade, contending that monstrosity is a prominent presence on twenty-first-century American television.[10] Different shows, like *Heroes* (NBC 2006–10), *Invasion* (ABC 2005), and *Threshold* (CBS 2005-06), incorporate present-day tensions, displaying a "responsive[ness] to the heightened sense of anxiety associated with life in the post-9/11 United States."[11] Existential insecurity also figures in Christine Mueller's reading of the "crisis fetish" in *Lost*.[12] *Lost*'s

... reiterations of the core horrors dominating September 11—utter helplessness, unavoidable mortality, and heroism-at-a-price—effectively fetishized catastrophe by repeatedly foregrounding without resolving the tensions between choice and fate, between incidental survival and inescapable death, without purporting to offer any clear therapeutic value.[13]

Lost's fantasy world is indeed a paradigmatic example of the part that monster narratives played in reworking post-September 11 concerns. Its representation of an island populated by mysterious presences and able to move in space and time foregrounds the conflation of indeterminacy and contingency that characterizes monstrosity. Furthermore, the series engages with the symbols of apprehension that accompany the encounter with an aberrant alterity, effectively staging a spectacle that "moves" the viewer. Prompted by the contact with a horrific entity, apprehension is the affective syndrome of the Bush years. Luciana Parisi and Steve Goodman describe it as the affliction that surfaces in the presence of unexpected phenomena of transformation: the fear of the "future lurking in the present."[14] A similar sensation of apprehension is experienced so often while watching *Lost* that it has become its distinctive trademark, prompting some authors to catalogue the series as a blend of science fiction and horror.[15]

Lost places monsters and the monstrous at the core of its narrative world. A bestiary of monsters populates the narrative scene, ranging from a polar bear whose prodigious appearance in the tropical environment causes the characters to doubt their geographical whereabouts, to a psychotic woman who kidnaps and tortures one of them, a young boy with powers of clairvoyance, and a sentient cloud of smoke that kills human beings. To this list, the series adds the recurring materialization of ghosts and the dead as in "White Rabbit" (1 x 05), where Jack Shephard sees his dead father,[16] and "What Kate Did" (2 x 09) where Kate Austen encounters a black horse that reminds her of an identical one from her past. These revenant presences testify to *Lost*'s fascination with the monstrous. Ghosts and psychic powers are traditional motifs of monstrosity that symbolize doubleness and simultaneity. The convergence of past and present is incorporated into their otherworldly emanation, surviving physical extinction and defying capture. The ghost's appearance is a threat to safety as it makes the domestic alien and therefore monstrous. The prospect of its materialization is itself instrumental to the setting of boundaries, involving as much the realm of actual movement as the immaterial dimension of interpretation. The monstrous "prevents mobility (intellectual, geographical, or sexual), delimiting the social spaces through which private bodies may move. To step outside this official geography is to risk attack by some monstrous border patrol or (worse) to become monstrous oneself."[17]

Forced by the unexpected crash to abandon the bounded confines of their lives as well as their past certainties, *Lost*'s characters step into a realm of excess, where everything is more and other than it appears to be. Beyond unnatural apparitions, life on the island turns some of the characters into monsters who threaten the wellbeing of the community with acts of violence and mischief. In "Confidence Man" (1 x 08), Sayid Jarrah tortures his antagonist Sawyer after the man refuses to hand Shannon the asthma medications he found in the plane's debris. Sayid ties Sawyer to a tree, brutally stabbing him in the arm when he confesses to hide no medications. In "Hearts and Minds" (1 x 13), John Locke drugs Boone after he threatens to reveal to his companions what Locke has been doing in the jungle. Under the effect of the drug, Boone first has horrific visions of being chased and then witnesses his sister's death. Paradoxically, *Lost* represents these acts of inhumanity as a necessary measure to cement a sense of community among the characters who could only survive if they "lived together," as opposed to "dying alone" in alien territory.[18]

The monstrosity of these and other abuses, however, does not just stem from the protagonists' lack of morality. The aberrant imaginary disclosed in *Lost*'s Season 1 seems rather to emanate from the eerie system of relations that the characters establish among themselves and with the island. When Locke drugs Boone, his motivations are that the young man must let go of his sister and devote himself completely to "listening to the island." Similarly, the disquieting discovery that Danielle Rousseau's SOS transmission has gone ignored for decades is explained by means of the island's self-preserving ecology that apparently forestalls communication with the outside world.

Inscrutable threats, inscrutable monsters

The proliferation of *Lost*'s representations of monsters is made even more disquieting by the impression that, beyond the accidental manifestation of horrific figures and behaviors, a monstrous entity lurks in the background. This sensation is seemingly *on and of* the island, at the same time immanent and contingent to it. The aesthetic register of the series greatly contributes to set in place an almost ecological feeling of apprehension. Its look is engineered so that the spectacle accommodates a flow of displacing visuals. Such aberrant visuality perturbs the audience's expectations about the narrative, rendering viewing a material experience where the response to the solicitation of images aims at provoking a bodily reaction of hyperexcitedness in the viewer, much in the same fashion accomplished by horror and thriller movies. This aspect contributes to circulate anxiety on and across the screen, adding a new layer to *Lost*'s exploration of the symptoms of the monstrous by making apprehension infect the domestic sphere of televisual watching.[19]

Interspersed among long takes, tracking shots of characters shown as they explore the island and extreme close-ups that set in place the emotive sphere of the diegesis, are intervals where the scenes seem to adjust to the field of vision of a voyeuristic gaze. Often the narrative events are framed as if a presence hiding in the bush was surveying them. Cameras, arranged behind objects or in the midst of luxurious vegetation, ostentatiously display their position, abandoning the all-seeing perspective of more canonical shooting techniques in favor of an ecological visual span. What would normally be considered disturbing elements (leaves, twigs, patchy shadows, flares, and other uneven optical effects caused by light) are incorporated in the spectacle, while the jerky repositioning of cameras gives restlessness to the cinematographic process. This overlapping of embedded and omniscient points of view marks the image flow as irregular, jamming the cognitive processes by which the audience usually exercises control and builds expectations about the narrative.

In this respect, *Lost*'s editing frustrates the regime of scopic mastery that scholars read into the audiovisual experience.[20] As Jean-Louis Baudry maintains, in American cinematography the spectator's gaze identifies with the camera that operates as a "relay" connecting the human eye with the reality displayed on screen.[21] In the sequences where an embedded point of view is encountered, *Lost*'s ecological and jumpy visuality establishes a perceptual threshold that mediates the apprehension of the spectacle as something that retains an ephemeral quality. Uneasiness grows against the opaqueness of these scenes where the occasional lack of depth of the field of vision, or the oblique close-ups that do not last enough to capture (and thus familiarize with) a character's emotions, impose the timeline of a narrative becoming that forestalls cognitive anticipation.[22] This hybrid aesthetic register communicates an intention to push the show's fascination with monstrosity beyond the limits of diegetic characterization, to imply vision itself in a conspiratorial displacement of the audience's control of the object of vision. The effect is a proliferation of the category of the monstrous whose origins expand beyond an encounter with external bodies to include an intimate experience of apprehension.

What accounts for the monstrous nature of *Lost*'s aesthetic is therefore an impediment to isolate the exact source of disquiet, much less to confine it to the safe realm of television's fantasy world. Beyond the singular manifestations of bodies that become other than themselves, *Lost* is concerned with monstrosity as an ecological factor, something volatile pertaining to the realm of nature, relationality and affect. It is not by chance, then, that *Lost*'s most representative monster is the so-called "Black Smoke." A stable presence throughout the six-season run, this creature appears in a variety of manifestations as an extension of the island's living system. Initially materializing as a dark cloud, the Smoke is an object of unremitting terror for the characters that it attacks and occasionally kills. In "Pilot Part 1" (1 x 01), the Smoke makes its appearance on the night of the crash after the survivors have camped on the beach and lit fires to expedite rescue operations. On this occasion, a vaporous column rises from the jungle, knocking over trees and emitting machine-like sounds of unexplainable origin. The next day the Smoke surprises Jack, Kate, and Charlie as they are reviving the pilot who is trapped inside the airplane. After smashing the man's body against the cockpit, the monster pursues the party into the jungle only to disappear abruptly when the tropical rain stops.

Further manifestations involve the Smoke's encounter with other characters in the 40 days after the crash. In "White Rabbit," Locke walks in on it during a solitary hike in the jungle. Instead of running away, the man faces the black cloud, standing unafraid until the presence subsides without attacking him. Locke later recounts this experience, telling Jack that he has looked into "the eye of the island" and found it beautiful. On another occasion the man declares that the Smoke appeared to him as a bright light ("The Cost of Living" [3 x 05]). Compared to the experiences of Nadine, Mr. Eko, and Montand, who the Smoke kills in, respectively, "This Place is Death" (5 x 05), "The Cost of Living" (3 x 05) and "LAX Part 2" (6 x 02), the monster approaches Locke in a quelled fashion. This behavior shows sentience and a propensity to engage in some sort of relation with the character, suggesting that the Smoke might be an intelligent being of unknown nature, rather than the island's automatic "security system," as Danielle assumes in "Exodus Part 1" (1 x 23).

Visions and tales about the Black Smoke recur in *Lost*, with characters providing multiple interpretations of it. This creates a heterogeneous apparatus of knowledge, which variously describes the monster as "evil incarnate" ("Sundown" [6 x 06]), "that thing" ("The Package" [6 x 10]) and, most disquietingly, "brother." A map of the blast door drawn by DARMA agents also alludes to it as "Cerberus" and a tentative path of the underground tunnels through which it is thought to swarm is added to the scientists' chart in "Lockdown" (2 x 17). The hypothesis of the underground origins of the Smoke is sustained by Benjamin Linus, whose house is built on the opening to an underground passage that he uses to summon the creature. Such variety of designations and names attests to the grip that the Black Smoke retains on the characters, as well as to its metamorphic nature. Appearing either as a dark cloud or a "bright light," it also materializes in Season 6 as an actual human being, the so-called "man in black," whereas in "Exposé" (3 x 14) it is shown mutating into spiders. Finally, the characters also come to associate it with the disembodied voices and whispers they occasionally hear in the jungle.

Passing from gaseous to solid actualizations, biomorphing to mimic human and animal appearances, the Smoke possesses the inscrutable monstrosity of the shapeshifter. Not only does its metamorphosis defy a sure identification, it summons powers of prediction and makes a mockery of them. As none of the survivors knows what the next incarnation will look like, anticipation itself becomes a monstrous endeavor played against the anarchic exuberance of the forces of nature. In this context, monstrosity becomes attached to the hyper-fertility of the environment. Happening in an emergent fashion, events relating to the Smoke's apparition belong to the anti-cosmology of a primordial evolution where life is experimental and deterritorialized.[23] As Matthew and Wendy Cory observe, the island is "a celibate machine, intricate and complexly involved, but only with itself, coupling with nothing outside itself."[24] This description imagines the island as a zone of intensity where "difference-driven morphogenesis comes into its own, and ... matter becomes an active agent, one which does not need form to come and impose itself from the outside."[25]

As the island reinvents itself through the Smoke's multiple actualizations, it reveals itself to be a prodigal world: a field of origination where form (mineral, animal, human) gives into form through a process of incessant transformation. This eccentric behavior engenders insecurity and fear. Questions about the nature, look, and life of animals, plants, and objects are incessantly voiced by *Lost*'s protagonists, whose ignorance of the environment quickly mutates into a terror of the undisclosed and of the undefined.

"Pushing the future off the table": The monstrosity of the time warp

In "Monstrosity and the Monstrous," Canguilhem reflects on the origins of the aberrant imaginary that since immemorial time has generated fantasies of worlds where life is excessive and eccentric: "is it the fact that life might be inscribed, in the geometric sense of the word, in the curve of a poetic élan whose imaginary number is revealed to be infinite?"[26] The anti-logic governing *Lost*'s ecology gestures in the direction of the infinitely multipliable life force that Canguilhem calls élan, stirring up new geometries of exception. The series envisions the latter as new syntheses of the mineral, the human and the animal that, in its destratification of categories, the island seems to create continuously, delivering a recombinant phylum of living matter. In the process, time also comes into play as the island's movement dislodges the causal succession of events, creating a chaotic feedback loop where present, past, and future commingle.

One of the Black Smoke's horrific powers is to present people with images of their past and prescient visions of the future whose effects alter the course of events. This happens in "23rd Psalm" (2 x 10) when the Smoke shows Eko memories of his life as a drug smuggler in Africa, and in "Further Instructions" (3 x 03) when it apparently manipulates Locke's mind to dream about Boone's imminent death. On these occasions, events that belong to another time are made present again, in their turn tripping the emergence of unpredictable occurrences. Similarly, when a water shortage threatens the life of the survivors early in Season 1, the revelation that a waterfall might be nearby comes to Jack as he is staring into a bonfire, going through the events of the past weeks when he flew to Australia to retrieve the dead body of his alcoholic father ("White Rabbit"). The subsequent clip, where the man finds water in a cave-in, is introduced by the sound of ice cubes tinkling in a glass. This acoustic cue, which works as a transitional device, occupies an ambivalent position in the episode. It is hard to divine if the sound is actually perceived by Jack, or if the ping is an extradiegetic signal that only the audience is meant to hear.

As often happens in *Lost*, formal elements (sounds, light, camera angles) operate as ambiguous presences that multiply and jumble the spatio-temporal perceptions of events with their timely apparition. This is more than a narrative trick: the confusion encountered by the characters is reflected in the audience's strained cognitive grip on the spectacle. Commenting on this aspect, Erika Johnson-Lewis observes that "[t]ime is central not only within the space of the narrative but also in its consumption."[27] Yet, in the sequence kick-started by the ice cube sound, *Lost* is demanding more than a resolutive effort from its fans. The clip imposes a profession of faith in the island's uncanny powers of self-differentiation and in the audience's forced submission to unforeseeable developments. The tinkling is a revenant cue of Jack's past to which the episode devotes various flashbacks. It is the acoustic mark of his father's presence that at some point in the man's life was at one with drinking. Yet, the sound is also a precursor that precipitates the advent of the future. It insinuates not a nostalgic resurfacing of memory, but the chain of events that will secure Jack's position as leader of the survivors. Similarly, in "?" (2 x 21), Eko has a vision of his brother Yemi that instructs him to look for Locke and reach the location known as the question mark. Although Yemi has been dead for a long time, his presence on the island is sensed by more than one character. In the same episode, Locke hallucinates about him although the two men have never met. On both occasions, Yemi's apparition triggers a chain of events and in Eko's case it forces the man to succumb to his murderous past. In "The Cost of Living," Yemi, who had been a priest in Nigeria, summons his brother to repent his sins and when Eko refuses he mutates into smoke form and finally kills him.

These examples suggest that, as much as the adventurous discovery of an unexplored world, *Lost* is also an exploration of memory and possibility, of time lived and time to live as characters cavort by means of flashbacks, flashforwards and alternate presents in a realm of intensive becoming where the rules of free will seem not to apply. In this respect, the island becomes a threshold where corporeality meets immateriality and memory generates ever new and unpredictable occurrences, the disjoined timeline becoming a force of futurity that splits the present at the root and changes history. Representations in Seasons 5 and 6 of time travel and flashsideways further shift *Lost*'s focus away from creating a linear narrative progression. Johnson-Lewis addresses this aspect, questioning the interplay of causality and emergence in the series: "How do events that happened in the future change in light of events that happened in the past? How is the past changed by events that occur in the future? How is a sense of the present maintained in spite of a constant shift between past, present and future?"[28]

These questions stress how, in its closing seasons, *Lost*'s representation of the monstrous is markedly associated with the anxieties stemming from an inability to experience time diachronically. If in Season 1 the characters' most pressing question was "Where are we?", by Season 5 it has become "When are we?" A number of very intricate events ensue from this development, which involves the island's power to move people across different epochs. Desmond Hume's interdimensional travel in "The Constant" (4 x 05) exposes the existence of a time differential between the island and the outside world through the man's voyages from 1996 to 2004. A consistent narrative segment of Season 5 is set on the island as two groups of characters find themselves living in the parallel dimensions of 1977 and the present, whereas another strand involves Daniel Faraday's attempts to lock down temporal variation by theorizing the existence of constants that would prevent human consciousness from spinning indefinitely within the temporal loop.

The most obvious effect of the island's movement is a reframing of temporal evolution. Past and future become caught up with the present. In place of a linear conception of moments, conceived as bypassing each other in a teleological process of accumulation and completion, time on the island reallocates potentialities. Future, especially, transmutes into a void, the dark side of what is happening and what has already happened, something like a residue of potential that could emerge at any moment to catalyze a differentiation of the present state of things. Although *Lost* imposes a rationality on this turbulent universe, having a character profess that "the universe has a way of course correcting" ("Flashes Before Your Eyes" [3 x 08]), its non-diachronic, anarchic temporality is a prominent avatar of monstrosity. Characters are constantly confronted with the possible existence of time paradoxes and with the question of what would happen in the present whether an alternate timeline or a change in the past occurred. When Desmond foresees Charlie's death, he frantically wanders the space–time continuum in an attempt to change the course of events and save the man, setting off a chain of occurrences that spans several time dimensions. Similarly, in "The Variable" (5 x 14) Faraday goes back to 1977 to detonate the bomb left on the island by the American Army in the 1950s and prevent the original flight from crashing, thus trying to defuse the contingencies that had brought the characters there in the first place. The consequences of his act initiate another chaotic string of events.

Lost's ultimate challenge then involves a reformulation of linear spatio-temporality in favor of complexity. Isn't the island just a space of possible states where random individuals converge to participate in the unraveling of a complex universe? Tackling issues of fate and becoming, *Lost*'s finale has the survivors meet in a church where they are informed that what happened on the island is only one of a multiplicity of experiences that they might have had in their lives. Most tellingly, in refusing to offer a rational explanation of the events, *Lost* elects to culminate with an open ending where issues of emergence and potential become distinctive of the narrative as a whole. This vision of anarchic temporality incorporates the vitalistic element underlying Canguilhem's notion of the generative élan and tinges it with terror. In *Lost*'s closing installments the monstrous is completely dematerialized and depersonalized: it has become imminent to the island's transformative powers, at one with its recombinant energy. Once the place shows its ability to dislodge linear progression, the unfolding of time becomes a succession of random sequences abstracted from different epochs and jammed without a causal relation of reciprocity in a vortical time warp.

The monstrosity of the island is that it is alive, its power manifested in a turbulent emergence of events and life forms that the characters cannot control. In the grip of the island, the latter have limited free will, forced, as they are, to continuously readjust their expectations and knowledge of the present and of themselves. This alienation from oneself is represented as the island's ultimate motif of monstrosity. On the island, a spiraling flux of change hits 1977, 2005, and the future, living and dead, human, animal and mineral, generating a monstrous splitting of time linearity that the protagonists can neither anticipate nor control. Indeed, as Faraday tells Juliet in "The Constant," the head pain that time-traveling causes him "is not amnesia." Rather than the impossibility to collect the traces of one's past, the monstrousness of the time warp relates to the impossibility of foreseeing and therefore bracing for the future.

Echoes of extradiegetic concerns can be heard in this imaginary of monstrous futurity. Apprehension for a future that cannot be envisioned defined Bush's culture of fear, inspiring the doctrine of preemptive action that lives on in Obama's times. The transformative nature of contemporary threats has spawned discourses about a hyper-generative monstrosity (be it linked to terrorism, natural catastrophes, or the exhaustion of economic cycles of expenditure) spanning macro- and microrealms and endowing them with a markedly emergent and unpredictable character. As Parisi and Goodman maintain, "[f]ear marks the openness of the body to the virtual, the very large and the very small, and therefore explains the response of 'dread' to the infinity of the 'unspecified enemy' and its tendency to exceed classification."[29] This argument has by now become a truism of global security policy that is increasingly being recalibrated against a generalized notion of risk, interpreted as the effect of multifaceted processes of destabilization. Falling under the radar of security operations are not just circumscribed actors which could jeopardize the safety of nations. The object of security is rather constituted by how to implement surveillance and control measures in the face of a redundant typology of danger. In a speech given in 2002, former Secretary of Defense Donald Rumsfeld sums up this argument, discussing a new security strategy directed at "how we might be threatened and what we need to do to deter and defend against such threats."[30] Posing as the main goal the need to "defend our [sic] nation against the unknown, the uncertain and ... the unexpected,"[31] inscrutability becomes the preeminent quality of an abstract and unidentifiable monstrosity. This vision makes the threat's presence, scope, and virulence remain vague, assessable only in the magnitude of their serendipitous incarnations and in the span of the viral spreading of apprehension.

At the time of *Lost*'s broadcasting, which ended in May 2010, a few months after Obama's election purportedly set out to dismantle the post-9/11 climate of paranoia and endless warfare, monsters are therefore envisioned less in individual terms, as the identifiable enemies threatening the American nuclear family (or body politic), as would be with the U.S.S.R. in Cold War times. They have become incorporeal and, indeed, nameless. Through *Lost*'s six seasons, monstrosity evolves from being something visible, to becoming an immaterial presence of "unknown," "uncertain," and "unexpected" nature. If, as politicians declare, America is "faced with urgent near-term require-ments that create pressure to push the future off the table,"[32] it is because the monstrous operates, now more than ever, without guarantees, emerging in the nick of time to aberrantly upturn the course of events. In this light, the monsters without a face that populated Americas's post-9/11 nightmares becomes something even more frightening, as its metamorphic nature allows it to take up a thousand different faces that lurk in the darkness even in the hopeful times of Obama's presidency.

Notes

1 Quoted in Karen Engle, "The Face of a Terrorist," *Cultural Studies—Critical Methodologies* 7, no. 4 (2007): 397.

2 Allen S. Weiss, "Ten Theses on Monsters and Monstrosity," *The Drama Review* 48, no. 1 (2004): 124.

3 Georges Canguilhem, "Monstrosity and the Monstrous," trans. T. Jaeger, *Diogenes* no. 10 (1962): 27

4 Barbara Creed, "Horror and the Monstrous Feminine: An Imaginary of Abjection," *Screen* 27, no.1 (1986): 45.

5 Jeffrey Jerome Cohen, "Monster Culture (Seven Theses)," in *Monster Theory*, (ed.) Jeffrey Jerome Cohen (Minneapolis and London: University of Minnesota Press, 1996), 6.

6 In the aftermath of September 11, hundreds of photoshopped images circulated on the web which associated terrorists with sexual deviancy, homoeroticism, and effeminization. In a revisionist reading of the myth of Medusa, the terrorist organization was also described as a double-headed monster at whose extremities lay Al Qaeda and the Taliban. See Jasbir Paur and Amit Rai, "Monster, Terrorist, Fag," *Social Text* 72 20, no. 3 (2002): 118–40.

7 Ibid., 118.

8 George W. Bush, "Address Before a Joint Session of the Congress on the State of the Union," *The American Presidency Project*, http://www.presidency.ucsb.edu/ws/index.php?pid=29644#axzz1drCzfN9u/

9 Teratology is the science that studies malformations and physical abnormalities. Its etymology, from the Greek *teras* and *logos*, means discourse/knowledge on the monstrous.

10 Stacy Takacs, "Monsters, Monsters Everywhere: Spooky TV and the Politics of Fear in Post-9/11 America," *Science Fiction Studies* 107, no. 36, part 1 (2009), http://www.depauw.edu/sfs/backissues/107/takacs107.htm/

11 Ibid.

12 Christine Muller, "Enduring Impact: The Crisis Fetish in Post-September 11 American Television," *Reconstruction* 11, no. 2 (2011), http://reconstruction.eserver.org/112/Muller_Christine.shtml/

13 Ibid.

14 Luciana Parisi and Steve Goodman, "The Affect of Nanoterror," *Culture Machine* 7 (2005), http://www.culturemachine.net/index.php/cm/article/viewArticle/29/36/

15 See, for example, David Lavery, "The Island's Greatest Mystery: Is *Lost* Science Fiction?," in *The Essential Science Fiction Television Reader*, (ed.) J.P. Telotte (Lexington: The University Press of Kentucky, 2008), 283–298.

16 Christian appears to other characters, becoming a recurring nightmare to some of them. For a comprehensive list of episodes featuring his ghost see http://lostpedia.wikia.com/wiki/Christian_Shephard/

17 Cohen, "Monster Culture", 12.

18 "Live Together, Die Alone" is also the title of Season 2's finale (2 x 23).

19 The same has been argued about other T.V. series. For a discussion of the post-9/11 aesthetics of anxiety in science fiction television see for example Enrica Picarelli, "Beyond Allegory and Seduction: Perceptual Modulation in *Battlestar Galactica*," *Scope: An Online Journal of Film & TV Studies* 22, no.1 (2012). http://www.scope.nottingham.ac.uk/February_2012/issue.php/

20 See on this point, Kaja Silverman, *The Threshold of the Visible World* (London: Routledge, 1996).

21 "The spectator identifies less with what is represented, the spectacle itself, than with what stages the spectacle makes it seen, obliging him to see what it sees; this is exactly the function taken over by the camera as a sort of relay." Jean-Louis Baudry, "Ideological Effects of the Basic Cinematographic Apparatus," in *Movies and Methods*, Vol. II, (ed.) Bill Nichols (Berkeley: University of California Press, 1982), 540.

22 The same is true for diegetic and characteriological evolution as *Lost*'s success is also due to its ability to displace audience's predictions about the plot's unfolding.

23 Matthew O. Cory and Wendy C. Cory, "Is the Island a Body Without Organs?," *Lost Studies* 1, no. 2 (2006), http://www.loststudies.com/1.2/Body_wo_organs.html/

24 Ibid.

25 Manuel de Landa, "Space: Extensive and Intensive, Actual and Virtual," in *Deleuze and Space*, eds Ian Buchanan and Gregg Lamber (Edinburgh: Edinburgh University Press, 2005), 82.

26 Canguilhem, "Monstrosity and the Monstrous," 30.

27 Erika Johnson-Lewis, "'We Have to Go Back': Temporal and Spatial Narrative Strategies," in *Looking for Lost: Critical Essays on the Enigmatic Series*, ed. Randy Laist (Jefferson, NC: McFarland & Company, 2011), 11.

28 Ibid., 13.

29 Parisi and Goodman "The Affect of Nanoterror".

30 Donald Rumsfeld, "Secretary Rumsfeld Speaks on '21st Century Transformation' of U.S. Armed Forces," http://www.defense.gov/speeches/speech.aspx?speechid=183/

31 Ibid.

32 Ibid.

18

Monstrous capital:

Frankenstein derivatives, financial wizards, and the spectral economy

Ryan Gillespie

... and thee knows, father, that fortunes are made nobody knows exactly how, in a new country.

Ruth, in *The Gilded Age*[1]

The freezing of credit markets, subprime mortgages, the collapse of behemoth financial firms, and debt problems in the Eurozone mark the global financial crisis of the late 2000s.[2] But what caused this crisis? Answers to such a question are of course complicated, but financial instruments called derivatives seem to be part and parcel of the crisis. Broadly speaking, derivatives are ostensibly instruments for spreading risk, deriving their value from the underlying asset; they are, essentially, bets on bets. The calculations of some derivatives use mathematics rooted in rocket science, which provides an element of precision and quantification that economics, as the dismal science, seemingly desires. But the potent mixture of scientific innovation and unintended consequences has resulted in them being called *Frankenstein derivatives*.

An unregulated practice, over-the-counter (OTC) derivative trading hit a notional value as high as $684 trillion in 2008,[3] and, given the OTC factor, they exist in a seemingly secondary economy beyond that of nation-states, often called the *shadow economy*. Though financial and speculative capitalism was solidified in the nineteenth century and the trend of neoliberal political economic policies dates from the 1970s, it was major U.S. legislation at the turn of the last century that catapulted the process. It is in the repeal of the Glass–Steagall Act in 1999 (removing the separation between investment and commercial banks), and the modernization of the Commodity Exchange Act in 2000 (which allowed for, inter alia, OTC derivatives), combined with the global collapse of communism as a viable political economic alternative, that one can see a new world take shape.[4] That is, given that the "government had effectively tamed the traditional banking business," writes one economic journalist, "Wall Street expanded to more adventurous terrain ..."[5] This terrain was not a physical space but rather a sort of spectral non-space; and, to borrow from the epigraph at the top of this chapter, fortunes in this (non-) country are *mysteriously made*. The global crisis has created a moment of reflection on financial economic practices, and one story circulating about it in the public sphere is in monstrous and supernatural terms. This seems to articulate the mysterious element of capital.

That is, the mysterious element of capital, a part of scholastic inquiry since at least Marx,[6] is the key trope of this chapter. The mystery of big fortunes and how they are made is a major theme in the story of modern capitalism. When capitalism moves beyond trade and exchange, however, and the act of specu- lation itself becomes what grows wealth, the picture of financial capitalism as a gambling-like process comes into focus. What makes financial capitalism fascinating—and mysterious—is that it combines the rational processes of calculation with the irrationality of sheer luck. Many think of successful gamblers as lucky, but a gambler will insist that she "has a system." Make the system quantifications and formulas made by physics and mathematics PhDs, put it on a global market scale, and we see the language move not from chance and luck to gambling and patterns, but rather to sorcerers and wizards, *financial wizards*, who can systematically control the supernatural realm.

My question is *why* is this monstrous and supernatural language used to characterize financial capitalism and its supposedly mysterious elements?[7] In the rhetorical tradition of language being the expression of thought and emotion, even revealing "the inner man,"[8] I ask why this trope is a part of the contemporary economic story, and what do supernatural and monster tropes reveal about economic work? George Akerlof and Robert Shiller write, "To understand how economies work and how we can manage them and prosper, we must pay attention to thought patterns ... we will never really understand important economic events unless we confront the fact that their causes are largely mental in nature."[9] I posit that monstrous and supernatural language is used to characterize that which is powerful and that which we do not fully understand. Not a resort to metaphorical language,[10] the other-worldly tropes themselves are part of the actual thinking on the subject;[11] they are not mere adornment nor obfuscations, but part of economic thought in the current moment.

In this chapter, I briefly unpack the usage of supernatural and monster metaphors—specifically financial wizards, Frankenstein derivatives, shadow banking, and the spectral economy—and explicate their meaning in relation to material economic practice; argue that, when taken together, the terms represent a general monster trope of financial capitalism that reveals contemporary ambivalence about the ethics of financial capital in its enactment and consequences; and turn back to metaphorical language and highlight the use of monster and supernatural tropes amidst a global financial crisis as suggestive of a contemporary socio-economic imaginary *haunted by the specter of uncertainty.*

The language of monstrous capital is meant to connote a monster in Richard Kearney's sense, being both "fascinating and forbidding."[12] This is because financial capitalism runs on a tension between the rational, ordered, and calculated on the one hand, and chance, fortune, and mystery on the other, and the interplay between the two is both powerful and not well-understood by those both outside and within high finance. Monster and supernatural tropes are especially prevalent given that econometrics and neoclassical rational calculation, especially as derivatives and securitization, failed to adequately exorcise the specter of uncertainty from current economic practices. [13] By analyzing why these tropes are used and the material practices they evoke, we are in a position to better understand the contemporary social imaginary and make the necessary changes to economic thought, speech, and action.

Financial wizards and Frankenstein derivatives

Financial innovators are called wizards precisely because of the complicated nature of derivatives. Derivatives are a financial instrument, typically a contractual specification of details that can be thought of as bets on bets.[14] As an OTC market, credit derivatives operate beyond the control of a specific nation-state, thereby being representative of *global* capitalism. To give a quick picture of how some of this works, let's take collateralized debt obligations (CDOs). A structured asset-back security (the asset often being mortgages), CDOs are sliced up according to tranches, in which three tranches correspond to three levels of risk, with an equity tranche being the riskiest and therefore most profitable, a senior tranche being the least profitable but least risky, and a mezzanine tranche. This slicing creates a way for varying levels of involvement (i.e. exposure and risk). Furthermore, these CDOs can be combined, in which the riskier and less risky portions could be merged in various combinations. The point of such combinations is that it is a way of repackaging and diluting risk so as to take, say, BBB ratings and whirl them into AAA ratings. The re-formations could be done a number of times, making CDOs of CDOs of CDOs (CDO^3), etc., and with not three but perhaps a hundred tranches, thereby aiming to transform "toxic waste into gold-plated security."[15]

The highly complicated nature, and the strikingly innovative element, of derivatives has resulted in their inventors being called financial wizards, for they seemed, through some form of magic or conjuring, to turn trash to treasure. And like wizards, most are astounded as to how they manage to do so. In *The Gilded Age*, Twain and Warner write this about Colonel Sellers, that archetype of speculative capitalism: "The Colonel's tongue was a magician's wand that turned dried apples into figs and water into wine as easily as it could change a hovel into a palace and present poverty into imminent future riches."[16] But unlike Col. Sellers, the wands of the financial wizards of the recent era were not (just) their tongues but their *calculations*; that is, it is through complex mathematics that the magic, so to speak, was worked, and then pitched, broadcast, and sold through stories in financial and general publics. In this way, then, there is a strange dualism to the financial wizard metaphor, in which the agent is both rational and magical.

But the wizard trope also has negative implications; that is, wizardry can be dangerous. Joseph Stiglitz, one of the most prominent public intellectual economists, writes that "The financial wizards invented highly risky products that gave about normal returns for awhile—with the downside not apparent for years ... But the financial wizards got carried away in their own euphoria ..."[17] Like Goethe's *The Sorcerer's Apprentice* (or picture Mickey Mouse in *Fantasia* and that unforgettable music by Paul Dukas), unable to control the spirit he has created (or harnessed), the image of the financial wizard also works as an uncontrollable force with destructive consequences.

The financial wizards were not dealing in magic but rather in incredibly sophisticated mathematical modeling. This, then, is a tension: the innovators are somehow wizards *and* scientists. The image of them as scientist is further evidenced in the invocation of Frankenstein. Stiglitz himself changes to that metaphor, writing, "in the Frankenstein laboratories of Wall Street, banks created new risk products ... without mechanisms to manage the monster they had created."[18] Here the financial innovators are scientists—mad scientists, like Dr. Frankenstein—who have not thought through the ramifications and consequences of their creations.

As evidence of this claim, consider this admission, uncovered in evidence during the S.E.C.'s 2010 fraud suit against Goldman Sachs. In an email to his girlfriend, Fabrice Tourre, a Goldman Vice President and the only individual named in the suit, discusses his involvement in the creation of derivatives:

> When I think that I had some input into the creation of this product (which by the way is a product of pure intellectual masturbation, the type of thing which you invent telling yourself: "Well, what if we created a 'thing,' which has no purpose, which is absolutely conceptual and highly ... theoretical and which nobody knows how to price?") it sickens the heart to see it shot down in mid-flight ... It's a little like Frankenstein turning against his own inventor ...[19]

Misuse of the metaphor aside—Frankenstein was the scientist, not the monster—here we see not just critics using mad-scientist/monster imagery. Rather, financial insiders, indeed a Vice President of arguably the largest and most important financial firm, are not entirely sure what was created or being used – nor what it was capable of doing. One of the complaints against Tourre comes in precisely monstrous terms, saying he was "standing in the middle of all these complex, highly leveraged, exotic trades he created without necessarily understanding all of the implications of those monstrosities!!!"[20]

The invocation of Frankenstein draws to mind the connection of science and nature and the unintended consequences and by-products of innovation from Mary Shelley's novel. But in addition to unchecked scientific innovation, or science without ethics, recall that the subtitle of Shelley's book is "The Modern Prometheus." Today we see the continuation of the supernatural theme of Prometheus stealing fire from the gods. That is, the innovators are not just dealing in the material here and now; they are somehow in touch with realms beyond humanity. And that the monster would then turn against its creators, as Tourre noted, moves agency away from the innovators and to the objects, to the financial instruments, in which, like The Creature from the novel, derivatives seemed to "vow *eternal hatred* and vengeance to *all mankind*."[21] But unlike Dr. Frankenstein, who, upon creation, said that "the beauty of the dream vanished, and breathless horror and disgust filled [my] heart,"[22] Tourre is sickened because his creation is not coming to full fruition (but was "shot down in mid-flight").[23]

The interplay of the natural and supernatural surrounding innovation and potential consequences, then, thrives in economics as it does in science or art. Furthermore, we see the usage of wizards and monsters helps to categorize and try to make sense of complicated, even mysterious, practices.

The shadow banking system and the spectral economy

Moving from discussion of wizards and monsters, as individuals, companies, or objects, let me now discuss the wider economic system. Note that the financial wizards do not, as was mentioned earlier, work in the traditional economy but in a new non-country that is largely unregulated; the system is "something beyond banks and something beyond regulation."[24] This is essentially the domain of financial firms that operate by the nickname *the shadow banking system*. While much work has focused on the geographies of global capitalism and the local–national–transnational dialectic of shadow banking,[25] there is less that focuses on how the shadowy monster trope underscores the geographical invocation.

The purpose of these "banks," economically, is to provide a place for large pools of money (e.g. a hefty pension fund) to be saved. The point, for depositors, is to have the cash protected, and to earn interest. Depositors choose these institutions as opposed to simply putting the pool into regulated banks because the latter have deposit insurances limited by the federal government. So, the money goes outside of the regulated banking system. The assurances of monetary safety, rather than being provided for by the government, are given through bond-ratings. An AAA-rated bond is issued as collateral for a deposit. The deposit, bond, and rating thereby form "another banking system" that has expanded under global capitalism in the last 30 years.[26] Like regular banks, shadow banks then take that cash deposit and attempt to monetize it further. There is an added wrinkle, however, as the depositor is *also* able to take the AAA bond and use it elsewhere as well, initiating a selling process.

The shadowy element is that these transactions are nontransparent and that the financial firms are not subject to the same capital or liquidity requirements as commercial banks. This thereby allows, if not promotes, the opportunity for greater leveraging of assets. In Paul Krugman's words, they were not official banks but were "none the less engaged in banking activities and created bank-type risks."[27] That this type of activity, given its downfalls as a practice as evidenced in the global financial crisis, would become scrutinized seems relatively uncontroversial, and the Dodd-Frank Act, signed into law by President Obama in 2010, means to address as much.[28]

Continuing to unpack the shadow metaphor, shadows are things that require something *real* in order to exist; they are parasitical and not self-subsisting. That is, a shadow is a "causal concept;" it is something that results from a material object blocking a light source.[29] Thus they have a liminal quality; without a material object, they cannot exist. Given this, one can see how the term *spectral economy* is given to this entire domain: it is much like the regulated economy in operation and transaction except that, by being OTC, it is not subject to the same oversight and constraints, it does not exist in any single nation-state space, and yet it has significant physical effects.[30]

The spectral economy seems to haunt the regulated economy: it stalks, it annoys, it scares, reminding what is possible, and what could be *if only*. The further and further one gets from the root sources of an economy in the form of money, or labor, moving up the chain of abstraction to credit, bond, leverage, CDO, CDO^2, CDO^3, etc., at some point the link back to reality, so to speak, is tenuous; it seems to operate almost in its own sphere, with its own laws and rules, with its own language and culture, and the seeming impenetrability of this world and its rules and language is both part of its allure and part of its power. But while its culture and language and its rules and its power are indeed real and different, the metaphor with ghosts and the spectral realm breaks down in so far as the spectral economy is still subject to labor and the traditional economy. The caster of the shadow matters.

But this is not simply to point out economic haunting or trying to weave together a metaphorical story of the spectral economy run by financial wizards and the creation of zombie banks along the way;[31] it is to show the material practices that the terms are describing. That is, in one semi-simplistic explanation, the tie of exotic financial instruments and securitization of home mortgages worked, and worked well, as long as one truism remained: home prices always go up. As they plummeted, so the financial system plummeted; that is, the housing market crash "triggered the collapse of the shadow banking system."[32]The key here is that the housing market crash creates a financial crisis due to the interconnectedness of markets and capital via derivatives and securitization packages; that is, the shadow economy and regulated economy are as entwined as shadows and casters.

The collapse of the shadow banking system, then, pulled some of the spectral economy into purview.[33] Four U.S. Senate Hearings on the financial crisis[34] and a bi-partisan Financial Crisis Inquiry Commission[35] culminated in the aforementioned, unfinalized Dodd-Frank Bill.[36] Despite these hearings and given the still-unfinalized law, the overarching question thus remains: "how ... will we reform global capitalism?"[37]

That said, given the possibility for such fantastic market fluctuations, in which the exact cause of the fluctuation, and the ability to control or correct as much, is not understood despite exotic and complicated calculations and now significant inquiry into the matter, it makes sense that in this moment we are talking about, and in turn actors think about, matters of political economy not in terms of rational actors but rather as monsters whose actions are not foreseeable nor fully understood. And furthermore, usage is not of ordered markets but of spectral economies. The monstrous and supernatural language, similar to that of the mad scientist trope, reveals contemporary ambivalence about the ethical practices of financial capitalism as currently hegemonic over global capitalism writ large.

Mysterious capital, monstrous capital

What is seen in the trope of monstrous capital, then, is material power and hegemonic influence combined with the mysterious nature of capital, as a fusing of *rational* with *irrational*, the orders of prediction and calculation enjoined with the peculiar forces of chance and uncertainty. The idea, then, of a science of gambling represents the sort of philosopher's stone for financial economics, the goal being wealth without risk; full exorcism of uncertainty through sophisticated logics of probability. But as the crisis shows, and continued derailment as seen in the M. F. Global and J. P. Morgan debacles, such an exorcism is unsuccessful.

That Fortuna spins her wheel, that luck and uncertainty are always involved in financial capitalism, is seen in the touchstone economic distinction between *risk* and *uncertainty* as noted by Frank Knight in 1921. The view is that *risk*, which is a calculable, probable outcome, is distinguished from *uncertainty*, where the outcome is not calculable at all.[38] This makes those able to both calculate risk and overcome uncertainty seem like they are operating with supernatural powers—at least temporarily.

There is, then, an irony in calling something so mathematically sophisticated as financial capitalism (i.e. something so ordered and rational), magical and mysterious. But this is the inherent tension in speculative economics: the gambling spirit is harnessed by and filtered through rational calculation, as the precision of quantification and social and economic ordering is designed to delimit, if not erase, the chance element, the unknown; and yet if it ever fully succeeded in doing so—if it ever actually eliminated risk—the possibility of profit would be greatly diminished (because everyone *could* and *would* do it). The system needs secrets and mystery.[39] So, without a spin of Fortuna's Wheel, one cannot win *big*, but of course with it there is no science precise enough to guarantee even *not losing*, let alone winning.

The tension of speculative capitalism, then, is that agents have, on the one hand, a belief in science and mathematics so strong that they can tame and control chance,[40] to exorcize uncertainty, while, on the other hand, they know full well that uncertainty cannot be overcome, and yet, like a gambler, they continue to act. The language of monsters, wizards, shadows, and specters captures this tension, as evidenced by critics and practitioners both within and outside of financial economics, in which that which is rational, ordered, and calculated runs up against chance, fortune, and mystery. The global financial crisis and ensuing monster and supernatural tropes suggest a contemporary social imaginary haunted by the specter of uncertainty. Thus we have a way of understanding why monstrous language is used to describe and think about financial capitalism in the current moment. The monster capital tropes, taken collectively, are meant as both derision and admiration, as they strike the right mixture of fear and fascination between that which is knowable and that which isn't, the role of human creation in the process of economics in particular and science more generally, and the anxiety induced by the impossibility of exorcising the unknown—economic or otherwise.

Furthermore, in addition to the great gains, there have been great losses through current speculative capitalistic practices, now for the so-called First World as well as the Third World, and monstrous capital and the monster tropes about financial capitalism speak to a contemporary ambivalence about the ethical consequences of financial innovation. Like Dr. Frankenstein, the financial wizards were exploring and creating, and also like Dr. Frankenstein, the innovations and practices had significant unintended consequences. The consequences—global institutional banking collapses, U.S. domestic income inequality rising, U.K. double-dip recession, Eurozone woes, people's pensions and 401ks halved, home values halved, etc.—partly resulted from using risky and misunderstood and/or not-understood financial instruments and practices, and from a significant lack of individual and social virtue.[41]

In conclusion, one can see in speculative financial capitalism the promise, or the allure, of the massive returns of gambling combined with the precision of scientific economics, if only the right formula or spell could be invoked, if only uncertainty could be exorcized. This gives speculative capitalism its mysterious aura; and when it turns dark, mysterious capital quickly becomes monstrous capital. The gambling spirit and its move from outsider vice to the heart of economic enterprise has indeed conditioned existence in novel ways in the last decade or so.[42] Moments of crisis, while prone to hyperbole and figurative-monstrous language, are not just epideictic moments but deliberative ones; as Roubini and Mihm put it, the financial crisis "would be a terrible—indeed, a tragic—thing to waste."[43]

What I have shown in the preceding pages are some of the material practices that the monster and supernatural terms are describing, and I have also offered an answer to why monster-terms are used when, of course, many different words could have been chosen: monster and supernatural language in economics is used to describe that which is powerful and that which we do not fully under-stand. I also suggested that, to extend rather than to analyze the trope, the economic human imaginary, especially as econometrics and neoclassical rational modeling, is haunted by uncertainty. We know the magnitude of global financial capitalism is *huge*: we've seen as much with the gains and now the losses. Given that magnitude, it makes sense, I have argued, that we do not talk about these instruments and practices as math nor even as market-making but as nothing less than otherworldly: monsters capable of success and tragedy alike, whose actions are not fully predictable, let alone fully understood, by mere mortals.

It is important, however, that the usage of monster tropes and supernatural talk ought not be invoked as an evasion of responsibility in matters of morals and markets; there is a sense in which the labeling of economic concepts and practices as such makes the matter so otherworldly as to remove our agency. In matters of political economy, in terms of starting, stopping, and modifying practices, we are assuredly not powerless.

Notes

1 Mark Twain and Charles Dudley Warner, *The Gilded Age* (New York: Library of Congress), 109.

2 How to date the crisis is contested. Some mark it with the bursting of the housing bubble in 2007, while others mark it with the global banking sector and credit freezing in 2008, which is when President Obama marked it in his 2012 State of the Union address ("In 2008, the house of cards collapsed"). The U.S. recession, technically speaking, was from 2007 to 2009, but of course most do not consider 2010–11 to be stellar economic years in the U.S., and, looking globally, U.K. and Eurozone economic woes are contemporaneous with this writing in 2012. Furthermore, the U.S. Federal Reserve plans to keep short-term investment rates near zero through 2013 and probably 2014, thereby "pushing out its easy-monetary policy even further." See Barak Obama, "Remarks by the President in State of the Union Address," January 24, 2012: http://www.whitehouse.gov/the-press-office/2012/01/24/remarks-president-state-union-address/; Don Lee, "Fed Says Key Rate Likely to Stay Near Zero Through Late 2014," *Los Angeles Times*, January 25, 2012: http://www.latimes.com/

3 To put that figure in perspective, it is "more than ten times the Gross Domestic Product of all nations." Phil Angelides, "Opening Remarks of Phil Angelides Chairman of the Financial Crisis Inquiry Commission at the Hearing on 'The Role of Derivatives in the Financial Crisis'," http://www.fcic.gov/hearings/pdfs/2010-0630-Angelides.pdf/

4 For extended analysis of this as a discursive cultural formation beginning in the nineteenth century, see Ryan Gillespie, "Gilders and Gamblers: The

Culture of Speculative Capitalism in the United States," *Communication, Culture & Critique* 5, no. 3 (2012): 352–71.

5 Peter S. Goodman, "Rule No. 1: Make Money by Avoiding Rules," *The New York Times*, May 22, 2010: http://www.nytimes.com/

6 Marx writes about the "secret" and "mysterious character" of the commodity form, and also the mystery of surplus value. David Harvey adds that the financial capital system "is shrouded in mystery born out of sheer complexity." Jean and John Comaroff note how "finance capital has always had its spectral enchantments, its modes of speculation based on less than rational connections between means and ends." See Marx, *Capital*, vol. 1, trans. Ben Fowkes (New York: Penguin, 1976), 161, 162, and esp. 258–69; Harvey, *The Limits of Capital: New and Fully Updated Version* (London, Verso, 2006), 316; Comaroff's "Millennial Capitalism: First Thoughts on a Second Coming," *Public Culture* 12, no. 2 (2000): 310.

7 To be more clear, this chapter is only about speculative financial capitalism and not capitalism writ large, nor global capitalism. This makes a vulgar Marxist analysis inadequate, even though Marx's description of the capitalistic process—of gaining surplus value through the exploitation of labor—is easily understood in vampiric terms: capitalists suck productive labor in the expansive and never-ending accumulation of wealth for its own sake. Even putting aside the confusing "for its own sake" formulation, this is too obtuse an explanation for speculative capitalism in the twenty-first century; how do leveraging, securitization, and derivatives fit into such a picture? Media, especially the Internet and the social life of information in the global–local dialectic? One place to go here would be the debates surrounding deconstructive approaches to Marxism, but contemporary Marxism and hauntological politics typically come up short either in economic understanding of financial capitalism or metaphysics of meaning beyond free-play of signifiers. See, e.g., the essays collected in *Ghostly Demarcations: A Symposium on Jacques Derrida's Spectres of Marx*, (ed.) Michael Sprinker (New York: Verso, 2008).

8 This view characterizes, at least, Aristotle, Isocrates, Longinus, Cicero, and Quintilian, and most Renaissance rhetoricians. The quote is from a good explication of the connection between tropes, thought, and psychology: Brian Vickers, *In Defense of Rhetoric* (New York and Oxford: Clarendon, 1989), 301.

9 George A. Akerlof and Robert J. Shiller, *Animal Spirits: How Human Psychology Drives the Economy, and Why It Matters for Global Capitalism* (Princeton: Princeton University Press, 2009), 1.

10 The idea is that metaphor is a way of producing insight and not just dressing up simple thoughts, and that economics, like literature and other fields, is full of them: e.g. demand curves, game theory, cycles, function, human capital, etc. Donald McCloskey, *Rhetoric of Economics* (Madison: University of Wisconsin Press, 1985), esp. 74–7.

11 See, e.g. the work of Antonio Damasio, Mark Johnson, and George Lakoff, as explicated in communication terms in Manuel Castells, *Communication*

Power (New York: Oxford University Press, 2006), esp. 137–92. Explicitly adding the work of metaphors to the communicative process as frame power, see Ryan Gillespie, "From Circulation to Asymmetrical Flow: On Metaphors and Global Capitalism," *Journal of Cultural Economy* (forthcoming; preview DOI: 10.1080/17530350.2012.686887).

12 Richard Kearney, *Strangers, Gods and Monsters* (New York: Routledge, 2003), 121.

13 In addition to tropes in the classical sense, Derrida's discussion of Marx attempting to dispel Stirner's specter talk provides some precedent for this reflexivity in a psychological–diagnostic sense. Marx castigates Stirner's specter and ghost metaphors, and yet he continues to use such language as well: "Marx could go on forever launching barbs at the wounded dead. He could never leave his victim … [because] Marx scares himself … [he is] … obsessed, haunted, possessed *like/as* Stirner … [and] Stirner talked about all of this before he did [and hence he] poached the spectres of Marx." Jacques Derrida, *Spectres of Marx*, trans. Peggy Kampf (New York: Routledge, 1994), 139–40.

14 Derivatives are notoriously complicated to explain. James Carville wrote an op-ed piece in the *Financial Times* saying that one of the cornerstones of presidencies is the ability to explain complicated matters in simple, plain language—like the way a parent would explain it to an inquisitive child. Carville's point is that President Obama has had trouble explaining the financial crisis to the public because there is no way to distill and simplify what a derivative is. James Carville, "Daddy, Tell Me, What Exactly is a Derivative?" *Financial Times.com*, March 25, 2009: http://www.ft.com/

15 Nouriel Roubini and Stephen Mihm, *Crisis Economics: A Crash Course in the Future of Finance* (New York: Penguin, 2010), 67. NB: my description is culled from theirs.

16 Twain and Warner, *The Gilded Age*, 63.

17 Joseph E. Stiglitz, *Freefall: America, Free Markets, and the Sinking of the World Economy* (New York: Norton, 2010), 13–14.

18 Ibid., 14.

19 Steve Eder and Karey Wutkowski, "Goldman's 'Fabulous Fab's' Conflicted Love Letters," *Reuters.com*, April 25, 2010: http://www.reuters.com/article/idUSTRE63O26E20100425/

20 Ibid.

21 Mary Shelley, *Frankenstein: or, The Modern Prometheus* (New York: Penguin, 2003), 143.

22 Ibid., 58.

23 Furthermore, Frankenstein, as an image, has bearing beyond just an individual or single object. Steven M. Davidoff feared, in September 2008, just after the collapse of Lehman Brothers and on the heels of the bailouts for Fannie Mae, Freddie Mac, and American International Group (AIG), that Henry Paulson, U.S. Treasury Secretary, was "creating Frankenstein" by reanimating dying companies and even expanding them. See "Henry

Paulson's Frankenstein," *Dealbook: The New York Times*, September 17, 2008.

24 Nelson D. Schwartz and Julie Creswell, "Searching for the Cause of the Crisis on Wall Street," *The New York Times*, March 24, 2008: http://www.nytimes.com/

25 The geographies of global capitalism and finance are an entire area of study, but two key works here are David Harvey, *A Brief History of Neoliberalism* (New York: Oxford University Press, 2007) and Edward LiPuma and Benjamin Lee, *Financial Derivatives and the Globalization of Risk* (Durham, NC: Duke University Press, 2004).

26 Gary Gorton, "Banking Panics: Déjà Vu All Over Again," *Dealbook: The New York Times.com*, October 5, 2009: http://www.nytimes.com/

27 Paul Krugman, "Wall Street Whitewash," *The New York Times*, December 16, 2010: http://www.nytimes.com/

28 Some critics, however, see the (re-)regulation as providing more, not less, of an opportunity for *shadowy* activities, as strictures on what investment and commercial banks can and cannot do creates, if not forces, money to flow through opaque and unregulated firms. See Ben Protess, "Shadow Banking Makes a Comeback," *Dealbook: The New York Times*, May 27, 2011: http://www.nytimes.com/

29 In Roy Sorensen's words, *shadow* "is a causal concept; a shadow is a shadow in the light created by an object that blocks the light. No blocker, no shadow. You cannot tell whether something is a shadow by looking at it alone. You also need to consider the caster of the shadow." The metaphysics of shadows, as applied to the shadow economy, would make for a fascinating study. See Sorensen, *Seeing Dark Things* (New York: Oxford University Press, 2008), 192.

30 Some writers continue the figurative language and call one the real economy and the other the spectral. I find this dubious, given that both are just as *real*, and that the effects of the spectral are, in many ways, more damaging and therefore even more *real*. Most strictly, the distinction would be between the regulated and the unregulated economy, but given that my focus is on language and trope, the usage of spectral remains.

31 The invocation of zombie banks is most prevalent in the Eurozone, coming mostly on concerns of the diminishing euro. That the more stable and powerful economies would not go for devaluation as an option seems obvious, and precisely this struggle is at work in the E.U. right now, with decisions of redenomination and breaking up of the euro—once the "unthinkable"—being a live option. The period in-between, however, can produce something that is called a zombie bank, in which depositors empty accounts and refuse to redeposit, but the banks continue to function, being propped up by national or other bailout funds. The banks are, from a profit perspective, dead; but the structure, the body, so to speak, remains, and functions. See Tyler Cowen, "Euro v. Invasion of the Zombie Banks," *The New York Times*, April 16, 2011: http://www.nytimes.com/; Martin Wolf, "Thinking Through the Unthinkable," *Financial Times*, November 8, 2011: http://www.ft.com/

32 Paul Krugman, *The Return of Depression Economics and the Crisis of 2008* (New York: Norton, 2009), 169–70. Though the details are not essential to this chapter, it is worth quickly showing how this was accomplished. Basically, when highly leveraged firms (e.g. Lehman Brothers, Bear Stearns) lost, they went underwater. But these were not localized effects, and for two reasons. The first is that many of their risks were insured (e.g. by AIG) and so losses amounted to a sort of run on not just one, but multiple, "banks," who, given the revocation of the Glass-Steagall, were also operating as commercial banks, and hence the "too big to fail" problem. Second, these losses resulted in these shadow banks being now unable to provide the billions of dollars of credit into the system that they had been.

33 The figurative language here can get very confusing, even when trying to make the matter clearer. Consider Mark Taylor writing about the spectral and the real economy: "As the economy evolves from [abstract] level to level, it becomes increasingly spectral until it is virtually nothing but the play of floating signifiers endlessly recycling in recursive loops that are unmoored from what once was called the 'real' economy. The real, however, does not simply disappear but is temporarily repressed and eventually returns to disrupt what had seemed to replace it. The spectral economy continues to be haunted by the real economy, which hides but does not vanish. When the repressed finally returns, collateral damage is difficult to contain." Writing in 2004, Taylor seems to be discussing the house-of-cards nature of the spectral economy, and the collateral damage, as seen in the global financial crisis, is indeed sprawling and painful. But aside from the contrast of spectral with *real*, notice that he also has the most abstract financial innovations as "virtually" free-floating signifiers. But what does it mean to be virtually free-floating? If it is free-floating, then it would have no effects, which, as seen, is untrue; and if it is not free-floating, then what does the invocation of it do? Perhaps the point is that it is so abstract ("intellectual masturbation," recall, were Tourre's words) as *almost* to be meaningless. Perhaps. But as the financial crisis fall-out shows, that is not a small *almost*. Furthermore, he speaks of the real economy as repressed but that, while repressed, it somehow is the one that *haunts* the spectral economy. So the real economy haunts the ghostly one? While the underlying referents in the story seem to be relatively accurate, the layers of metaphor seem to darken rather than illuminate. Mark Taylor, *Confidence Games: Money and Markets in a World Without Redemption* (Chicago: University of Chicago Press, 2004), 180.

34 The four U.S. Senate Hearings by the Subcommittee on Investigations called "Wall Street and the Financial Crisis—The Role of High Risk Home Loans, The Role of Bank Regulators, The Role of Credit Rating Agencies, and the Role of Investment Banks," are available from: http://hsgac.senate.gov/public/index.cfm?FuseAction=Subcommittees.Investigations/

35 Financial Crisis Inquiry Commission documents are available from http://www.fcic.gov/

36 The Bill/Public Law, entitled the "Dodd-Frank Wall Street Reform and Consumer Protection Act," has as its mission: "To promote the financial stability of the United States by improving accountability and transparency in the financial system, to end 'too big to fail', to protect the American taxpayer by ending bailouts, to protect consumers from abusive financial services practices, and for other purposes." Available from: http://www.sec.gov/about/laws/wallstreetreform-cpa.pdf/

37 Roubini and Mihm, *Crisis Economics*, 11.

38 Frank Knight, *Risk, Uncertainty, and Profit* (Boston: Houghton Mifflin, 1921). Roubini and Mihm give a succinct example of the difference: playing Russian roulette, a player has a one in six chance of shooting himself. That calculation is one of risk. Uncertainty, on the other hand, is being handed a gun, and asked to shoot; there isn't even enough information to assess the level of risk. Roubini and Mihm, *Crisis Economics*, 94. However, in that last example, there is some data to work with, like the weight of the gun, so maybe another example might be in order: one might think of counting cards in single-deck Blackjack as assessing risk, whereas lightning striking at the moment the dealer flips over the card is uncertainty.

39 In *The Confidence-Man*, from 1857, the mysterious and secretive matter is dramatized to great effect: "'But, but,' in a kind of vertigo, 'what do—do you do—do with people's money? Ugh, ugh! How is the gain made?'

'To tell that would ruin me. That known, everyone would be going into the business, and it would be overdone. A secret, a mystery—all I have to do with you is to receive your confidence, and all you have to do with me is, in due time, to receive it back, thrice paid in trebling profits.' Herman Melville, *The Confidence-Man* (New York: Oxford, 1989), 97.

40 Ian Hacking, *The Taming of Chance* (Cambridge: Cambridge University Press, 1990).

41 From a chastising perspective, we might see not economic instruments and practices as monstrous but rather that the instruments and practices *bring out* vices in humans, turning them into monsters: as a French maxim goes, "adversity makes men, prosperity [makes] monsters." As a temper, Deirdre McCloskey's lively Smithean defense of bourgeois capitalism as consistent with and promoting virtue is particularly relevant here, as the onus is, rightly, put not solely on abstract systems of organization but on the individual characters of those working within, and partly formed by, bourgeois capitalism. Though she seems to underestimate the power of economic systems in shaping the character of participants in a collective global (and not local) way, that I fault speculative capitalism for harnessing vices and not rewarding virtues here seems consistent with her analysis, and there is much to endorse in a virtue-ethics approach to and understanding of capitalism. See *The Bourgeois Virtues: Ethics for an Age of Commerce* (Chicago: University of Chicago Press, 2006); for the maxim, Robert Christy, *Proverbs Maxims and Phrases, of All Ages* (New York: G. P. Putnam, 1887), 8.

42 From another perspective: "Put these things together—the explosion of popular gambling, its legitimate incorporation [in]to the fiscal heart of the nation-state, the global expansion of highly speculative market 'investment,' and changes in the moral vectors of the wager—and what has happened? 'The world,' answers a reflective Fidel Castro, has 'become a huge casino.'" Comaroff and Comaroff, *Millennial Capitalism*, 297.

43 Roubini and Mihm, *Crisis Economics*, 301.

19

Domesticating the monstrous in a globalizing world

Carolyn Harford

I am the vampire for these times.

The Vampire Lestat[1]

The *Twilight* series of novels and films have achieved enormous international popularity since the publication of *Twilight* (Stephenie Meyer) in 2005. *Twilight* and its companion novel and films draw on three significant sources. The first source is English Romantic novels such as *Pride and Prejudice* (1813), *Jane Eyre* (1847), and *Wuthering Heights* (1847). In addition, *Twilight* draws on the genre of European and American vampire novels and films, whose prototype is Bram Stoker's *Dracula*; and, third, on the genre of European fairy tales, later popularized in the United States, whose most relevant examples are *Bluebeard* and *Beauty and the Beast*. These sources provide the narrative structure which has helped *Twilight* take root in the popular imagination. These three genres converge in *Twilight* in which the figure of the vampire takes on the role of the suitor in the mismatched pair of *Beauty and the Beast*, one of whom must change to enable the plot to be successfully resolved. However, *Twilight* is more than a reinscription of these sources in contemporary attire. It also inverts them. First, the vampire is no longer a monster to be defeated and killed, but a highly attractive and mysterious suitor, now on the side of good, that is, on the side of humanity. Second, the resolution of the impasse relies not on the monster turning into a handsome prince but on the heroine becoming a vampire herself, the narrative equivalent of Beauty turning into a Beast in order to marry him. This chapter suggests that the traditional plotline, in which the monstrous suitor must change to become like the heroine in order to enter her world as her husband, reflects a still widely held point of view in which people are expected to marry and socialize within their groups, while defining outsiders as the Other, and, at the furthest extreme, monstrous. The inversion of this plotline seen in *Twilight* reflects another viewpoint that has gained ground as an outcome of globalization in the twentieth and twenty-first centuries, according to which marriage outside traditional ethnic, religious, and racial groups is more acceptable and difference is seen as alluring rather than terrifying.

Twilight's popularity with the public has also been mirrored in academic interest[2] and much commentary in the media and on the Internet.[3] Apart from the skill in constructing the novels and films, the *Twilight* series undoubtedly draws a large measure of its appeal from the power of the genres of which it is a recent representative. At the same time, it innovates on these genres in a way that reflects its contemporary cultural context in Western culture, particularly the increased multicultural awareness that is part of the phenomenon of globalization. It does not detract from its originality and power to evoke response in its readers and viewers to examine its antecedents as a way of accounting for the fertile cultural and psychological soil in which its popularity has flourished.

It is possible to describe the plot of *Twilight* from a variety of perspectives, which is an indication of the extent to which it symbolically reinscribes archetypal and mythic content, capable of providing expression for a wide range of local and individual concerns.[4] This chapter focuses on how *Twilight* reworks the figure of the vampire, from monster to Byronic hero to (almost) boy next door, reflecting, in the process, contemporary concerns about mutual understanding and de-demonizing the Other at the stage of globalization reached in the twentieth/twenty-first centuries.

At a basic level, the *Twilight* narrative concerns a love relationship between two teenagers, a human girl and a vampire boy.[5] The girl (Bella Swan) is introverted and self-deprecating, whereas the boy (Edward Cullen) is mysterious and charismatic, with a secret that the heroine must discover on her own. The plots of the novels and films revolve around the dangers and conflicts posed to the human girl by her association with vampires and how she must surmount the problems that arise in order to remain united with her beloved. A significant subplot involves a secondary relationship between the girl and another boy, who turns out to be a werewolf, deadly enemies of vampires.

The most popular reading of *Twilight* situates it within the teenage romance genre. This reading is strongly suggested by its first-person female protagonist and the theme of dangerous love whose demands transcend all worldly concerns, characteristics which link it to adult romance novels, such as those targeted at women from Harlequin/Mills and Boon and Silhouette Books.[6] These plot elements have inspired immediate recognition of *Twilight*'s literary and cultural antecedents. Within English literature, *Twilight* has been compared to Jane Austen's *Pride and Prejudice*,[7] a novel whose plot revolves around the misunderstandings between two lovers who eventually overcome their own differences and the opposition of others to unite themselves in marriage.[8] Emily Brontë's *Wuthering Heights*[9] has also been cited, with its narrative of passionate love that transcends conventional boundaries, whose Byronic hero, Heathcliff, is considered to be one of the models for Edward Cullen.[10] However, more attention has been focused on the parallels between *Twilight* and Charlotte Brontë's *Jane Eyre*,[11] a work cited by *Twilight*'s author, Stephenie Meyer, as being among her primary influences in writing the series.[12]

Parallels between *Twilight* and *Jane Eyre* have been analyzed in detail by Elizabeth Hardy.[13] Hardy points out the many similarities between Bella/Jane and Edward/Rochester, including the inwardness, intellectual accomplishments, and nurturing nature of the heroines, juxtaposed with the mysteriousness, mesmerizing good looks and wealth of the heroes, who continually brood over the problematic situations in which they find themselves, both rewritings of the Romantic Byronic hero.[14] However, the most significant parallelism lies in the plot structure: each Byronic hero has a secret that threatens his relationship with the heroine. Each one knows in advance that he should spare her from the consequences of this secret. Neither restrains himself, and both must cope with the disasters that follow the secret's revelation. When it is revealed, each heroine is faced with the problem of having fallen passionately in love with a man with whom she cannot have the normal relationship she was expecting. This is the essential tension that drives the plot: the hero has something to hide; the heroine finds out what it is and struggles to bring about a resolution. In other words, "the tale of the lover of the other that is not what it seems," to quote Larry DeVries's description of *Beauty and the Beast*[15] (to which I return shortly).

When *Twilight* and *Jane Eyre* are stripped down to these plot elements, it becomes apparent that they reinscribe a basic plotline that also appears in fairy tales.[16] *Jane Eyre*, in particular, can be traced back to *Bluebeard*, 425a,b,c in Aarne and Thompson's classification of fairy tales.[17] itself a rewriting of the myth of Cupid and Psyche. The tale of *Bluebeard* involves a young wife and her mysterious older husband who forbids her to enter a particular room while he is away. Driven by curiosity, she enters the room and discovers the bloody corpses of her husband's previous wives. Upon discovering this transgression, Bluebeard, enraged by her disobedience, is about to murder her, when her brothers intervene and kill him instead. The key element here, again, is the man's secret, which threatens the woman's desire for a normal relationship (and, in this case, completely destroys it). Rochester's madwoman in the attic[18] is *Jane Eyre*'s equivalent of Bluebeard's bloodied wives in the forbidden room. Narratives such as *Jane Eyre*, *Twilight*, and other literary descendants of *Bluebeard* rewrite and expand this tale[19] to include the possibility of salvaging the situation, reflecting the desires of many women in problematic relationships.

Edward Cullen has been cast as a Bluebeard figure by bloggers who see him as a stalker and a domineering, controlling man.[20] In this reading, it is less important that Edward has a secret that Bella, like Bluebeard's wife, must uncover, than that he chauvinistically manages every detail of Bella's life. Some are also revolted by Bella's changing into a vampire, seeing it as a sacrifice of true human life to enter a horrific undead existence (ironically, this is exactly what Edward and his vampire sister Rosalie think), symbolic of the unreasonable sacrifices made by women in real-life relationships.[21] One conclusion drawn from this reading is that Bella is a poor role model for young women.[22] Still, Edward genuinely loves Bella, and his mistreatment of her is a misguided effort to protect her, overbearing in Bella's contemporary context but virtuous in Edward's imaginary history as a Victorian gentleman.[23]

However, *Twilight* has also been compared to *Beauty and the Beast*,[24] classified as 425c by Aarne and Thompson.[25] The classic version of *Beauty and the Beast* by de Beaumont was published in 1756, while its best known contemporary reinscription is the 1991 Disney animated film with the same title.[26] In *Beauty and the Beast*, a handsome prince is changed into a beast (as punishment for an act of cold indifference in the film version). In order to regain his original form, he must fall in love with a woman and win her love in return. In the process of carrying through this quest, his initially cruel persona gives way to one capable of giving and receiving love. Beauty's love breaks the spell and restores his original form. In this tale, although, like *Bluebeard*, the Beast has secrets forbidden to Beauty (in some versions), the plot element most relevant to *Twilight* is the Beast's Otherness, the fact that he is a beast and not a human being, and that the resolution of the plot hinges on his change.

Here, to me, the comparison with *Twilight* is more revealing. In *Beauty and the Beast*, the Beast is not unredeemably villainous, like Bluebeard. The problem is his hideousness.[27] In traditional readings of the tale, this hideousness is a barrier to the union of Beauty with the Beast. The resolution of the plot lies in breaking the spell that binds the Beast, turning him back into the handsome prince he once was. This transformation removes the obstacle to his union with Beauty, an outcome that may have delivered great satisfaction in eighteenth-century France. However, in the contemporary context in which *Twilight* is situated, and in which it is read and viewed as fiction, there is a twinge of disquiet: if Beauty loves him as a Beast, why are we being positioned to think that it would be better if he were a handsome prince?[28] What's so terrible about a Beast, if you love him and he loves you back? This twinge provides the key to the essential plot twist of *Twilight*. Edward Cullen is definitely not hideous, quite the opposite, as befits a Byronic hero.[29] He is, however, monstrous, a prince in a body that is beastly, albeit gorgeous, because it is a vampire's body. The monstrosity of vampires comes from the vampire legends and narratives that form part of Bella's backdrop to her relationship with Edward, and our backdrop to the story of Bella. These legends and narratives are part of the lore of popular culture derived from a genre of European and American vampire novels and films, in which the vampire, like the nearly universal vampire of folklore, is a figure of horror. According to this lore, vampires do not turn back into handsome princes, i.e. they don't become human again.[30] In this *Beauty and the Beast* situation, in which the plot is resolved by one partner changing to become like the other, there is only one option: Bella must change into a vampire to become like Edward. In this respect, *Twilight* represents an inversion of the plotline of *Beauty and the Beast*.[31]

How can the inversion of this traditional archetypal plotline be interpreted? In the original, the transformation of the Beast represents his redemption by love.[32] I suggest that, in *Twilight* as well, Bella's change into a vampire also represents redemption of the monstrous. How do these transformations, of the original Beast and of Bella/Beauty, come to play the same role in their respective narratives? The common factor lies in the reconciliation of the monstrous outsider with society. In *Beauty and the Beast*, this reconciliation is effected by changing the monster to conform to society's norms, i.e. by bringing the monster back inside society's boundaries. In *Twilight*, the monster cannot change, so society's boundaries are expanded to include him. This expansion of social boundaries constitutes the inversion. The boundary expansion is effected by Bella's solitary but significant step of redefinition, brought about by her voluntary change to vampirism, a challenge to the Cullen family ethos in which no one becomes a vampire unless death is the only alternative.[33] This redefinition actuates the vampire identity that the Cullens have been living all along: vampires are not condemned to be monsters (from the perspective of humans) but can regulate their actions to help, not harm, the human communities of which they were once part. They may therefore coexist with humans within the same communities. If vampires such as James and Victoria kill humans and live outside of human society, it is because they have chosen this path. This redefinition is made possible by Bella's love. In spite of Edward's objections, Bella does not see herself as becoming a monster, and never regards Edward and his family as monsters. Rather, the construction that Bella puts on this situation, from the moment she understands that Edward is a vampire, is that he is not a monster, because she cannot reconcile Edward's beauty and goodness with monstrousness. Furthermore, she believes that he has a soul, contrary to the idea that vampires are soulless.[34]

Bella's change amounts to redefinition because it enacts a common *human* action. If we factor out the monstrous element in the union between Edward and Bella, the situation emerges as a familiar one within the Western cultural tradition of *Twilight*: a woman, upon marriage, joins her husband's group. This, I believe, is the key significance of Bella's change. By enacting this human tradition with Carlisle Cullen's vampire clan, Bella stretches the boundaries of human society to include them. From this perspective, Bella may be compared to the biblical Ruth, who leaves her people to join the people of her husband with profound consequences for those people.[35] The consequence for Bella's new vampire group is the establishment of a link, however covert, with human society, and, more significantly, the affirmation of their attempt to establish a new vampire culture.[36] Bella's act enables a further rapprochement in *Breaking Dawn*, between the vampires and the werewolves, when Jacob imprints on Edward and Bella's daughter Renesmee, thus establishing a future genetic link between the two clans.[37] In this way, Bella plays one of the roles of Bonnie Honig's foreigner: as an outsider, she valorizes the ethos of the group in a way that no insider can.

As indicated by the comparison to Ruth,[38] group intermarriage and mutual attraction has a long history in human society. However, I suggest that the precise way in which domestication and rehabilitation of the figure of the vampire in *Twilight* is constructed would not have been possible before the latest era of globalization, that of the twentieth and twenty-first centuries. In particular, during this period, the Other has been, and continues to be, the focus of unprecedented scrutiny and empathy, in part as a contribution and response to social movements such as the American Civil Rights Movement, gay liberation, and second-wave feminism. In *Twilight*, produced in the early twenty-first century, vampires are constructed as members of a minority group living with discrimination and prejudice. One way in which this is accomplished is through the presentation of traditional vampire attributes as part of a negative stereotype.[39] For example, vampires require blood for sustenance and their craving for human blood can be uncontrollable. They are immortal and ageless, they have pale, stone-like bodies, piercing eyes, and superhuman strength, and possess added abilities, like mind reading or seeing the future, all characteristics which demonstrate a clear continuity between *Twilight* and the genre of European and American vampire narratives.

However, what is also important is that, although the Cullens possess these particular attributes of traditional vampires, other well-known characteristics, such as living in dark castles, sleeping in coffins, not being able to come out during daylight, are laughed off as myths. Other vampire novels and films, such as *Dracula*, are referenced intertextually in familiar vampire traits, which are here revealed to be untrue, hence implicitly unfair, components of the stereotype. For example, Bella, trying to find out what Edward is really like, asks him how he can come out during the day and whether he is burned by the sun: "Myth," he responds.[40] Later, her visit to the Cullen's home produces a surprise: no "Dracula's castle," the vampiric equivalent of the Gothic pile which is a staple of Gothic novels,[41] but an open, airy, modern home, such as real (rich) people might live in (says Edward: "No coffins, no piled skulls in the corners ... what a disappointment this must be for you").[42] Later still, Bella reacts stiffly to Jacob Black's reference to "fangs," informing him that Edward doesn't have any. There is also an assault on the assumption that vampires are supernatural creatures.[43] Edward talks about how vampires could have evolved side-by-side with humans, removing vampires from the realm of the horrific supernatural and returning them to the natural world, where they might have been encountered by Charles Darwin on the *Beagle*.[44] By retaining some traditional vampire traits while discarding others, *Twilight* is positioned as a true story within the context of all this previous fiction.[45] The selection of a subset of vampire traits as a kind of "reality" which has been distorted by non-vampires suggests that "real" vampires, as a group, have been the target of unfair stereotyping by outsiders out of ignorance and fear. This in turn is reminiscent of real-world stereotyping of groups such as women, homosexuals, Muslims, and others which constitute minorities in particular societies, as part of the process by which certain groups construct outsiders as Other.[46]

In addition, a second way in which vampires are portrayed as members of a twentieth-/twenty-first-century minority group stems from the representation of the Cullens themselves as suffering from a sense of stigma[47] due to the vampire attribute of killing human beings, a striking departure from the attitudes of traditional vampires, including the "bad" vampires in *Twilight*, who regard themselves as superior to humans because of their immortality and enhanced abilities. The Cullen family principle, alluded to earlier, that no human can be changed into a vampire except to avoid imminent death, is part of this package of negative self-esteem. Edward himself is adamant, since the beginning of his relationship with Bella, that he is a monster, damned, unredeemable, and dangerous[48] ("What if I'm the bad guy?" he asks in the film).

In line with this interpretation, other components of the Cullen family ethos are outcomes of their attempts to repair this spoiled identity. The Cullens, led by Carlisle Cullen, are driven by the desire to help humans and avoid harming them. They are "vegetarian" vampires, i.e. they feed only on animals, not on humans. Carlisle has trained himself to resist the craving for human blood, to the point where he can work as a doctor, surrounded by temptation all day, and he manages his vampire family to live the same way. (One almost expects to hear about Vampires Anonymous and a 12-step program.) His determination to devote his unending existence to the welfare of humans, simply because he used to be one of them, casts him as a kind of vampire bodhisattva. At the same time, this Cullen family commitment makes clear that they conceive of themselves as belonging to a human-like group, defined in part, like all human groups, by its relationship to other groups.[49] Without this sense of belonging, no sense of spoiled identity would be possible.

The vampiric craving for blood is thus portrayed as something that can be controlled and managed, like any other bad habit, rather than as the inescapable ascriptive attribute of the traditional vampire. In terms of social identity theory,[50] control of this craving then becomes a marker of the ingroup of "good" vampires, the Cullens and the clan living in Denari, Alaska, as opposed to the outgroup of "bad" vampires, Victoria, James, Laurent, the Volturi, and Victoria's vampire army.[51] The Cullens' search for positive distinctiveness and self-esteem repositions their relation to humans as well, by acknowledging a debt to human origins and ties in a way unique to this genre of vampire narratives. In so doing, they lay claim, implicitly, to democratic inclusion,[52] a challenge taken up by Bella.

The Cullens are good vampires (perhaps, persons living with vampirism), and, in terms of the story, they are also sympathetic vampires, because they are sympathetic characters, in that we identify with them and care about their fate. Even the bad vampires benefit by association with them, becoming merely bad guys rather than monsters. Vampires become figures of horror when they are constructed as completely Other,[53] as they are in works such as Polidori's *The Vampyre*,[54] Le Fanu's *Carmilla*,[55] Kostova's *The Historian*,[56] and, of course, *Dracula*.[57] However, it is also possible to construct a bad vampire as a sympathetic character. When vampires are protagonists, such as the Vampire Lestat in Anne Rice's *The Vampire Chronicles* and others, the horror fades, replaced by existential fascination, even though we still know that vampires kill people.

I now return to an idea proposed at the beginning of this chapter, that the appeal of Edward and Bella's romance owes something to the production and reception of *Twilight* within the period of twentieth-/twenty-first-century globalization. Globalization in the twentieth and twenty-first centuries is the continuation of processes that have been in place since the beginning of human history.[58] One of the major effects of globalization is greater communication and contact among an increasing number of people and groups internationally. However, in terms of multicultural awareness, respect, and tolerance, globalization can have mixed effects.[59] For example, the knowledge and experience enhanced by globalization can increase negative stereotypes, or ameliorate them, depending on the circumstances. One outcome of globalization that is relevant to the popular reception of *Twilight* has been the sharp increase in recent years of international marriages.[60] International marriages are themselves a mirror of globalization in general: there are positive and negative aspects. The negative aspects include the possibility of human trafficking and other abuse of younger brides from poorer countries.[61] On the other hand, there appear to be genuinely positive aspects: people marrying people from other countries for good reasons with reasonable outcomes.[62]

These observations provide a different perspective on the traditional plotline, in which the monstrous suitor must change to join the group of the protagonist heroine in order to enter her world as her husband. This plotline may be seen as reflecting a worldview, one more common a century ago[63] but still prominent, in which people are expected to marry and socialize within their own groups, while defining outsiders as the Other and, at the furthest extreme, monstrous. The inversion of this plotline in *Twilight* may be seen as reflecting changes long underway that have been gradually transforming the globalizing world, in which it is becoming more common to marry outside traditional ethnic, religious, and racial groups. The de-Othering of vampires resonates with international social trends towards de-Othering human groups by debunking damaging stereotypes and promoting mutual understanding.[64] It is now more likely for the Other to be valorized, domesticated, and regarded as (almost) normal, with more and more people all over the world dating and marrying outside of traditional group boundaries. The Other is now an acceptable mate and, furthermore, more desirable for being different. This desirability of difference, the allure of the Other, can be traced back at least as far as the Byronic hero[65] in Western culture, continuing to the genre of Gothic novels[66] and, to a certain extent, the contemporary genre of women's romance fiction. In earlier Gothic novels, the attraction of the virtuous heroine to her potential ravisher[67] was implicit and it could not redeem the villain. Acknowledging this attraction would put the heroine on the wrong side of the line in the chaste/unchaste woman division.[68] Now, however, because of the difference in attitudes between earlier periods, such as the Victorian, and the present, readers and viewers respond more positively to narratives in which the heroine not only follows through on her attraction to the potentially villainous Other, but may also identify with him, to the point of changing into a being formerly regarded as entirely monstrous. Such a scenario may be seen as reflecting greater freedom of choice for women in choosing men, but, from another perspective, may also be seen as reflecting the ways in which women give up too much for them. Such variation in interpretation, in turn, is an indication of the psychological significance of the traditional and literary narratives of which *Twilight* is a recent inscription.

This chapter has analyzed the enormously popular *Twilight* series in terms of its literary and cultural antecedents. These antecedents range from traditional European fairy tales, with numerous counterparts in non-European cultures, to English Romantic novels. They share a basic plot structure involving a mysterious hero who must change in order to unite with the heroine in marriage. *Twilight*, like other contemporary texts, inverts this structure, casting the heroine as the one who changes. In *Twilight*, this change is represented by Bella Swan becoming a vampire in order to join Edward and the Cullens as part of their family. The chapter has suggested that this inversion of traditional plot elements reflects a social change in attitudes toward group outsiders at a time when contact among groups who have previously lived relatively isolated lives is increasing due to the changes brought about by increasing globalization. This social change may also be correlated with a process in European and American culture whereby the monstrous/villainous Other in folklore and narrative has become increasingly an alluring romantic figure who is now a more acceptable and potentially domestic partner.

Notes

I would like to thank Marina Levina and Diem-My Bui for incisive comments on an earlier draft of this chapter that have improved it greatly. Any errors are my own. I am also grateful to the University of Swaziland for providing the facilitating environment and resources that have made this chapter possible.

1 Anne Rice, "The Vampire Lestat" [1985], *The Vampire Chronicles Collection*, vol. 1 (New York: Ballantyne Books, 2002), 200.

2 Nancy Ruth Reagin (ed.), *Twilight and History* (Hoboken: John Wiley and Sons, 2010); John Granger, *Spotlight: A Close-Up Look at the Artistry and Meaning of Stephenie Meyer's Twilight Saga* (Cheshire, CT: Zossima Press, 2010); Rebecca Housel and J. Jeremy Wisnewski (eds), *Twilight and Philosophy, Vampires, Vegetarians, and the Pursuit of Immortality* (Hoboken: John Wiley & Sons, 2009); E. David Klonsky and Alexis Black (eds), *The Psychology of Twilight* (Dallas: Smart Pop, BenBella Books, 2011); Maggie Parke and Natalie Wilson (eds), *Theorizing Twilight: Critical Essays on What's*

at *Stake in a Post-Vampire World* (Jefferson: McFarland & Company, 2011); Natalie Wilson, *Seduced by Twilight: The Allure and Contradictory Messages of the Popular Saga* (Jefferson: McFarland & Company, 2011), among others.

3 See, among others, Angela Aleiss, "Mormon Influence, Imagery Run Deep Through 'Twilight'" (Huff Post Religion, 2010, www.huffingtonpost. com/2010/06/24/mormon-influence-imagery_n_623487.html/ (accessed January 31, 2012); Gail Collins, "A Virginal Goth Girl", *Opinion*, July 12, 2008 (The New York Times); Liesl Schillinger, "Children's Books/Young Adult", *Sunday Book Review*, August 12, 2007 (The New York Times); and other references in this chapter.

4 Carolyn Harford, "Violation and the Inscription of Opposites in the *Homeric Hymn to Demeter* and Bram Stoker's *Dracula*", *Journal for Studies in Humanities and Social Sciences* 1, No. 2, 2012: 49–56.

5 Another popular series of teenage vampire romance novels, with an accompanying television series, is L. J. Smith's *Vampire Diaries*. L. J. Smith, *The Awakening and The Struggle* and *The Fury and The Reunion* (London: Hodder Children's Books, Hachette Children's Books, 2001 [1991]).

6 The popularity of this reading is suggested by descriptions of *Twilight*'s fans, who have been characterized as "exclusively female and post-pubescent" (Sarah Seltzer, "'Twilight': Sexual Longing in an Abstinence-Only World," (Huff Post Entertainment, August 9, 2008, www.huffingtonpost.com/sarah-seltzer/twilight-sexual-longing-i_b_117927.html/ (accessed January 26, 2012)), a claim belied by the number of adult academics and bloggers who are also fascinated with it.

7 Jane Austen, *Pride and Prejudice*, (New York: Bantam Dell, Random House, 2003 [1813]); Kate Cochran, "Your Basic Human-Vampire-Werewolf/ Shape-shifter Triangle, Bella, Edward, and Jacob," in Reagin, *Twilight and History*.

8 Christopher Brooke, "Pride and Prejudice," in *Bloom's Modern Critical Interpretations: Pride and Prejudice*, update Edn, (ed.) Harold Bloom (New York: Infobase Publishing, 2007).

9 Emily Brontë, *Wuthering Heights* (New York: Bantam Dell, Random House, 2003 [1847]).

10 Denise Covey, "Byronic Hero Series, Part 4 – Heathcliff from Wuthering Heights compared to Edward Cullen and Twilight", April 26, 2011, laussieswritingblog.blogspot.com/2011/04/Byronic-hero-series-part-4-heathcliff.html/ (accessed August 2, 2012).

11 Charlotte Brontë, *Jane Eyre*, Signet Classics edn (New York: New American Library, Putnam Penguin, 1997 [1847]); Cochran, "Your Basic ...".

12 Karen Valby, "Stephenie Meyer: 12 of My 'Twilight' Inspirations" (EW.Com, Entertainment Weekly, www.ew.com/ew/gallery/0,,20308569_20308554_20 533693,00.html/ (accessed January 31, 2012).

13 Elizabeth Baird Hardy, "Jane Eyre 4: Edward (Cullen) Rochester, I Presume? *Twilight*'s *Jane Eyre* Roots," Hogwarts Professor Thoughts for Serious Readers, January 7, 2011, www.hogwartsprofessor.com/

jane-eyre-4-edward-cullen-rochester-i-presume-twilight's-jane-eyre-roots/ (accessed January 24, 2012).

14 Peter L. Thorslev, *The Byronic Hero: Types and Prototypes* (Minneapolis: University of Minnesota Press, 1962).

15 Larry DeVries, "Literary Beauties and Folk Beasts: Folktale Issues in *Beauty and the Beast*," Appendix 1 in Betsy Hearne, *"Beauty and the Beast": Visions and Revisions of an Old Tale* (Chicago: University of Chicago Press, 1989).

16 Fairy tales themselves have been described as encoding archetypal content (Marie-Louise von Franz, *An Introduction to the Psychology of Fairy Tales* (Irving: Spring, 1973); Steven F. Walker, *Jung and the Jungians on Myth* (New York: Routledge, 2002)), and this observation provides an indication of why the narratives of *Twilight* and *Jane Eyre* have proved to be so compelling.

17 Antti Aarne and Stith Thompson, *The Types of the Folktale*, FF Communications No. 184 (Helsinki, Academia Scientarium Fennica, 1961); Heta Pyrhönen, *Bluebeard Gothic:* Jane Eyre *and its progeny* (Toronto: University of Toronto Press, 2010).

18 Sandra Gilbert and Susan Gubar, *The Madwoman in the Attic* (New Haven: Yale University Press, 1979).

19 Pyrhönen, *Bluebeard Gothic*; Maria Tatar, *Secrets Beyond the Door* (Princeton: Princeton University Press, 2004).

20 Owen Gleiberman, "Edward Cullen, Stalker? Yes, but so is the Hero of 'The Graduate'," Inside Movies, EW.com, November 30, 2009, insider movies. ew.com/2009/11/30/Edward-cullen-stalker/ (accessed February 4, 2012).

21 Amy, "The Twilight Saga: Beauty and the Beast Redux", *Oracles and Archetypes*, July 20, 2010, yourdaily oracle.blogspot.com/2010/07/twilight-saga-beauty-and-beast-redux_20.html/ (accessed February 2, 2012).

22 Krystal Clark, "Twilight's Bella Swan is a Feminist's Nightmare," November 11, 2009, ScreenCrave, screencrave.com/2009-11-11/twilights-bella-swan-is-a-feminist-nightmare/ (accessed February 8, 2012); Seltzer, "Twilight."

23 Cochran, "Your Basic ...".

24 Amy, "The Twilight Saga"; Elizabeth Baird Hardy, "Jane Eyre 1: 'Once Upon a Time in Thornfield ...' Reading Bronte's 'Jane Eyre' as a Fairy Tale," Hogwarts Professor Thoughts for Serious Readers, December 23, 2010, www.hogwartsprofessor.com/jane-eyre-1-once-upon-a-time-in-thornfield... jane-eyre-as-fairy-tale/ (accessed January 24, 2012).

25 Aarne and Thompson, *The Types of the Folktale*.

26 Jerry Griswold, *The meanings of "Beauty and the Beast": A Handbook* (Peterborough: Broadview Press Ltd., 2004); Hearne, *Beauty and the Beast*.

27 Jean Marie LePrince de Beaumont, *La Belle et la Bête* (Paris: Gallimard Jeunesse, Éditions Gallimard, 2002 [1757]); *Beauty and the Beast* (Walt Disney Feature Animation, The Walt Disney Company, 1991). The Disney film version also emphasizes the Beast's anger and destructive behavior, less prominent in the de Beaumont version.

28 In one redaction of this fairy tale, the Disney animated film of *Beauty and the Beast* has Beauty/Belle hesitate before accepting the handsome prince, to make sure he is really the same Beast she fell in love with.

29 For the vampire as Byronic hero, see James B. Twitchell, *The Living Dead: A Study of the Vampire in Romantic Literature* (Durham: Duke University Press, 1981); Atara Stein, *The Byronic hero in Film, Fiction and Television* (Carbondale: SIU Press, 2009), Atara Stein, "Immortals and Vampires and Ghosts, Oh My!" Romanticism and Contemporary Culture, Romantic Circles Praxis Series, April 21, 2011, http://www.rc.umd.edu/praxis/contemporary/stein/stein.html/ (accessed January 28, 2012).

30 Some may not want to see Edward stripped of his superhuman powers, which enable him to be Bella's knight in shining armour in Port Angeles.

31 *Twilight* is not the only narrative whose plot line makes this inversion. Other examples from popular culture are listed by Shmoop Editorial Team, including *The Lord of the Rings* and *X-Men*, Shmoop Editorial Team, "Twilight," Shmoop University, Inc., November 11, 2008, http://www.shmoop.com/twilight/ending.html/ (accessed February 3, 2012). One particularly close parallel is the Disney animated film *Brother Bear* (Walt Disney Feature Animation, Disney Enterprises, Inc., 2003). Also, in the Disney animated film *The Princess and the Frog* (Walt Disney Feature Animation, Disney Enterprises, Inc., 2009), the heroine temporarily becomes a frog, like her frog prince, and is prepared to remain with him in that condition.

32 Sarah Sawyer, "Beauty and the Beast: Themes (Part Two of Four)", September 6, 2010, www.sarahsawyer.com/2010/09/beauty-and-the-beast-themes-part-two-of-four/ (accessed August 3, 2012).

33 Ultimately, both Bella and Edward get their way in the debate about whether Bella should become a vampire. Edward agrees that she may be changed without the threat of imminent death but, in the end, it is in precisely that circumstance that Bella is changed.

34 Meyer, *Breaking Dawn*, 24.

35 Bonnie Honig, *Democracy and the Foreigner* (Princeton: Princeton University Press, 2001).

36 The link between humans and vampires established by Bella's marriage is not the same as the links between vampires and humans established before vampirization. There is a difference between connections established between humans, one or both of which later become vampires, and connections established between humans and individuals who are already vampires.

37 Aleiss, "Mormon Influence."

38 Pointed out to me by Diem-My T. Bui.

39 Walter Lippman, *Public Opinion* (New York: Harcourt, Brace, 1922); Henri Tajfel, "Social psychology of intergroup relations," *Annual Review of Psychology* 33: 1–39; Henri Tajfel, *Human Groups and Social Categories* (Cambridge: Cambridge University Press, 1991).

40 Meyer, *Twilight*, 161–2.

41 Norman N. Holland and Leona F. Sherman, "Gothic Possibilities," *New Literary History* 8, no. 2, 1977: 279–93.

42 Meyer, *Twilight*, 280–1. In *New Moon* (142), the Cullen house takes on an additional symbolic dimension when its emptiness and impending dereliction symbolize the disaster that has overtaken Bella in her relationship with Edward, similar to the role played by Manderley in Daphne du Maurier's *Rebecca* (New York: Avon Books, HarperCollins Publishers, 1971 [1938]) and Rochester's house in *Jane Eyre*.

43 In the main subplot of the Twilight series, Jacob the werewolf must also debunk stereotypes: "You don't need a full moon? ... Hollywood's version doesn't get much right" (*New Moon*, 274).

44 Meyer, *Twilight*, 269.

45 In this respect, it resembles the film ET: The Extraterrestrial, in which the fictional story of extraterrestrial contact positions itself against the backdrop of Star Wars and Star Trek, which are regarded as fictional within this narrative ("Why can't he just beam up?" "This is reality, Greg!" (Melissa Mathison, 1982, "E.T.," www.imsdb.com/scripts/E. T..html/ (accessed February 3, 2012)).

46 Susan T. Fiske, "What We Know Now About Bias and Intergroup Conflict, the Problem of the Century," Current Directions in Psychological Science (Thousand Oaks: Sage Publications, 2002).

47 Erving Goffman, *Stigma Notes on the Management of Spoiled Identity* (New York: Simon & Schuster Inc., 1963); Gerhard Falk, *Stigma: How We Treat Outsiders* (Amherst: Prometheus Books, 2001).

48 As befitting a Byronic hero, he could describe himself as "mad, bad and dangerous to know."

49 Fredrik Barth, "Introduction," in *Ethnic Groups and Boundaries*, ed. Fredrik Barth (Universitetsforlaget, Oslo, 1969); Ulf Hannerz, "Fluxos, fronteiras, híbridos: palavras-chave da antropologia transnacional," *Mana* 3, no. 1, 1997: 7–39, translation, "Flows, Boundaries and Hybrids: Keywords in Transnational Anthropology," http://www.transcomm.ox.ac.uk/working papers/hannerz.pdf/ (accessed October 21, 2011).

50 Henri Tajfel and John Turner, "An Integrative Theory of Group Conflict," in *The Social Psychology of Intergroup Relations*, eds W. G. Austin and S. Worchel (Monterey: Brooks/Cole Publishing Co., 1979), 33–53.

51 Bree Tanner is changed into a vampire in *Eclipse* and, presumably, could have been reformed by the Cullens if she had not been murdered by the Volturi; Stephenie Meyer, *The Short Second Life of Bree Tanner* (New York: Little, Brown and Company, Hachette Book Group, 2010 [2009]).

52 Honig, *Democracy*.

53 Edward Said, *Orientalism* (New York: Vintage Books, Random House, 1979 [1978]).

54 John William Polidori, "The Vampyre," republished in Robert Morrison and Chris Baldick (eds), *The Vampyre and Other Tales of the Macabre* (Oxford: Oxford University Press, 1998 [1819]).

55 Sheridan Le Fanu, *Carmilla: A Tragic Love Story* (New York: Cosimo Classics, 2008 [1872]).

56 Elizabeth Kostova, *The Historian* (London: Sphere, Little, Brown and Company, 2005).

57 Bram Stoker, *Dracula* (Oxford: Oxford University Press, 1996 [1897]).

58 Anthony Giddens, *Sociology*, 6th edn (Cambridge and Malden: Polity Press, 2009).

59 Jan Nederveen Pieterse, "Emancipitory Cosmopolitanism: Towards an Agenda," *Development and Change* 37, no. 6, 2006: 1247–57.

60 "Herr and Madame, Señor and Mrs", *The Economist*, November 12, 2011, http://www.economist.com/node/21538103/print/ (accessed June 30, 2012).

61 Ibid.

62 Ibid.

63 Ibid.

64 The relationship between Bella and the Cullens exemplifies the de-Othering of vampires by a human. Another significant example of de-Othering in *Twilight* occurs in *Breaking Dawn*, in which the vampires and werewolves, who may be seen as competing minority groups, reach a better understanding and rapprochement with each other.

65 Stein, *The Byronic hero*.

66 Holland and Sherman, "Gothic possibilities."

67 Ibid.

68 Leila S. May, "Foul Things of the Night: Dread in the Victorian Body," *The Modern Language Review* 93, no.1, 1998: 16–22.

Index

79547591R00191

Made in the USA
Lexington, KY
23 January 2018